ARCHITECTURAL
DETAILING

DRAWINGS
BY
JOSEPH IANO
EDWARD ALLEN

ARCHITECTURAL DETAILING

FUNCTION
CONSTRUCTIBILITY
AESTHETICS

EDWARD ALLEN

JOHN WILEY & SONS, INC.

NEW YORK ╱ CHICHESTER ╱ BRISBANE ╱ TORONTO ╱ SINGAPORE

Library of Congress Cataloging in Publication Data:

Allen, Edward, 1938–
    Architectural detailing / Edward Allen : drawings by Joseph Iano
and Edward Allen.
        p.   cm.
    Includes index.
    ISBN 0-471-54792-1
    1. Architectural drawing—Detailing.   I. Title.
NA2718.A44   1992
720′.28′4—dc20   92-19378

Printed in the United States of America

10 9

ACKNOWLEDGMENTS

M Y longtime colleague Joseph Iano, who prepared many of the drawings for this book, also reviewed the entire manuscript and most of the illustrations. His comments and ideas have strengthened the book in many important ways. At John Wiley & Sons, Inc., Everett Smethurst, senior editor, guided all phases of the preparation and publication of this book with wisdom, patience, and good humor; Karin Kincheloe applied her limitless talent and resourcefulness to its design and production. The production of the book was managed with style by the unflappable Diana Cisek. Lu Wendel Lyndon, Maynard Hale Lyndon, and Mary M. Allen were my informal advisors throughout the writing and illustrating of the book. To all these friends and co-workers, I extend my sincere thanks. I would like to express my gratitude also to my many students in detailing classes at the Massachusetts Institute of Technology and Yale University, who helped sharpen the focus of this book.

A number of the drawings in this book are based on illustrations in my previous book, *Fundamentals of Building Construction: Materials and Methods* (2nd ed.), 1990. They have been adapted for this volume with the permission of the publisher, John Wiley & Sons, Inc.

E. Allen
South Natick, MA
April 1992

DISCLAIMER

T H E drawings, tables, and descriptions in this book are presented in good faith, but the author, illustrator, and publisher, while they have made every reasonable effort to make this book accurate and authoritative, do not warrant, and assume no liability for, its accuracy or completeness or its fitness for any particular purpose. It is the responsibility of users to apply their professional knowledge to the use of information contained in this book, to consult original sources for additional information when appropriate, and to seek expert advice when appropriate.

CONTENTS

INTRODUCTION

A S a way of guiding the transition from architectural idea to built reality, an architect designs and draws for each building a set of details that show how it will be put together.

How does the architect know if these details will achieve the desired result? Will the building that they represent go together easily and economically? Will it shed water? Will it be easy to heat and cool? Will the details look good with one another and with the overall form and space of the building? Will the building grow old gracefully, and will it last for the requisite period of time? There are many more questions of similar importance.

The experienced architect does not leave the answers to chance. Each detail, no matter how special or unprecedented, is designed in conformance with universal, timeless patterns that, given competent execution on the construction site, virtually guarantee satisfactory building performance. These *detail patterns* are the subject of this book.

Detail patterns are elemental fragments that are present in all successful building details. They represent an accumulation of centuries of wisdom about what works in building construction and what doesn't. Many of the patterns are firmly grounded in scientific fact. Others are based just as solidly on common sense and the realities of human performance. The experienced architect employs all these patterns automatically, as if by instinct, when designing details.

The architect also uses the detail patterns as a reliable means of analyzing and understanding existing details. They are helpful in reviewing one's own work, in checking the work of other detailers in the office, in judging the quality of manufactured building components, and in diagnosing problems in existing buildings. The absence of a particular detail pattern, or the presence of a feature that contradicts a pattern, usually indicates a problem or a potential problem that should be corrected.

The detail patterns are straightforward and easy to learn. There are fewer than a hundred of them. Each is irreducibly simple. The first section of this book introduces each of the patterns in turn, explains it, and illustrates several instances of its use. Each pattern is given a simple descriptive name and a graphical icon to assist in its memorization.

The patterns are arranged in three main groups: *Function*, *Constructibility*, and *Aesthetics*, corresponding to the three major concerns of the detailer. Under each of these groupings, the patterns are further categorized by similarity of intent. The first category of patterns under *Function*, for example, is *Controlling Water Leakage*, comprising eleven detail patterns that offer a complete strategy for accomplishing this important task.

The second section of the book demonstrates the use of the detail patterns during the process of designing the details of three different buildings: one in wood, one in architectural concrete, and one in brick veneer over a reinforced concrete frame.

The book closes with an annotated listing of publications recommended for the detailer's own reference shelf.

It is assumed that the reader has a general background in the materials and methods of building construction, and is familiar with the conventions of architectural drawing. In the detail drawings throughout the book, outdoors is always to the left or the top 'of the drawing.

DETAIL PATTERNS

DETAIL PATTERNS:
FUNCTION

▽

DETAIL PATTERNS:
CONSTRUCTIBILITY

▽

DETAIL PATTERNS:
AESTHETICS

FUNCTION:
CONTROLLING WATER LEAKAGE

I N order for water to penetrate through a building assembly, three conditions must all occur at the same time:

1. There must be an opening through the assembly.

2. There must be water present at the opening.

3. There must be a force to move the water through the opening.

If any one of these three conditions is not met, water will not penetrate the assembly.

In designing any exterior detail, therefore, we can pursue one or more of three strategies:

1. We can try to eliminate all the openings in the assembly.

2. We can try to keep water away from any openings.

3. We can try to neutralize all the forces that can move water through openings.

Complete success in any one of these three strategies will result in the complete elimination of water leaks. But sometimes in detailing we pursue two of these strategies or even all three of them at the same time, because this gives added security in case one of them fails due to poor workmanship or building deterioration. Let us consider each of these strategies briefly, and list the detail patterns that relate to each.

1. ELIMINATING OPENINGS IN BUILDING ASSEMBLIES

Every building is full of openings. A shingled roof has an opening under each shingle. A wall has cracks around windows and doors, and joints between the units of material from which the wall is made. Additional cracks and holes may form as the building ages and deteriorates.

We can attempt to eliminate all these openings by using preformed gaskets and sealants. As a sole strategy this is unreliable. Gaskets may not seal securely if they are the wrong size or resiliency, or if the surfaces they touch are rough or unclean. Sealants may fail to adhere properly if the materials to which they are applied are not scrupulously clean and properly primed, or if the installer does not compress the sealant fully into the seam. Both sealants and gaskets can deteriorate from weathering and from the flexing and stretching they may undergo as the building ages. A building skin that relies on sealants and gaskets alone for watertightness will leak sooner or later. Furthermore, even a small defect in a sealant or gasket that is exposed to the weather can leak very large amounts of water, just as a small hole in a bathtub can create a very large puddle. Small defects in devices for keeping water away from openings or neutralizing the forces that can move the water are seldom as catastrophic.

Sealants and preformed gaskets are extremely useful, however, as components of an overall strategy for making a building skin watertight. Therefore, it is important to know how to detail sealant joints and gasket joints correctly, and how to incorporate them into more complex schemes for controlling water penetration. The detail pattern that relates to eliminating openings in building assemblies is

Sealant Joints and Gaskets (page 31)

2. KEEPING WATER AWAY FROM OPENINGS

There are a number of effective ways to keep water away from openings. Often it is useful just to be able to keep most water away from an opening—to reduce the volume of water that must be dealt with at the opening itself. In many cases we can easily and securely keep *all* water away from an opening.

The detail patterns that relate to keeping water away from openings in building assemblies are

Wash (page 7)

Overlap (page 12)

Overhang and Drip (page 14)

Drain and Weep (page 17)

Cold Roof (page 19)

Foundation Drainage (page 21)

3. NEUTRALIZING THE FORCES THAT CAN MOVE WATER THROUGH OPENINGS IN BUILDING ASSEMBLIES

There are five forces that can move water through an opening in a wall or a roof: (1) gravity, (2) surface tension, (3) capillary action, (4) momentum, and (5) air pressure differentials. In most cases, it is surprisingly easy to detail a building assembly so that all five of these forces are neutralized, and the most secure strategies for keeping water out of a building are based on this approach.

We have already encountered the detail patterns for neutralizing two of these forces, because these same patterns are useful in keeping water away from openings in buildings. The force of gravity is neutralized by

Wash (page 7)

Overlap (page 12)

Surface tension, a force that causes water to cling to the underside of a surface where it can run through into an opening, is neutralized by

Overhang and Drip (page 14)

The patterns for neutralizing the other three forces are

Capillary Break (page 22)

Labyrinth (page 24)

Rainscreen Assembly (page 25)

Upstand (page 29)

The capillary break neutralizes capillary action. The labyrinth neutralizes momentum, and the rainscreen assembly and the upstand neutralize air pressure differentials. By combining these seven patterns in each exterior joint of a building, we can make a building entirely waterproof.

WASH

A wash is a slope given to a horizontal surface to drain water away from vulnerable areas of a building. In general, every external horizontal surface of a building should have a wash.

1.   A window or door sill, whether made of stone, concrete, wood, or metal, always has a wash to keep water from accumulating next to the door or sash. A minimum slope for this type of wash is about 1:10 or 1:12 (1″ per foot). A steeper slope drains water faster and is more secure, because the more quickly water is removed from a surface, the less time it has to leak through. It is also more difficult for wind to drive water up a steeper slope.

2.   The wash on this concrete chimney cap keeps water away from the vulnerable crack between the clay flue tile and the concrete. The slope should be at least 1:12. The outer edge of the cap should have a thickness of at least 3″ (75 mm) to discourage cracking of the concrete, not the feather edge that is commonly used (see *Clean Edge*, page 154). The cricket on the upslope side of the chimney consists of two washes that divert water around the shaft of the chimney.   ▷

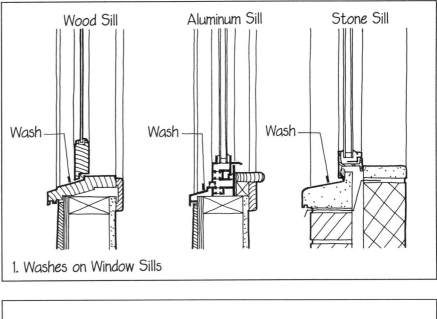

1. Washes on Window Sills

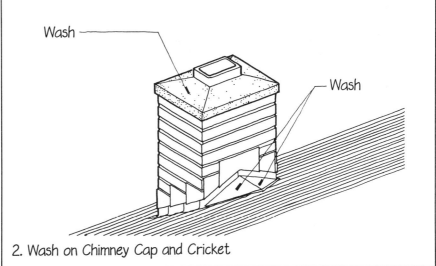

2. Wash on Chimney Cap and Cricket

3. The coping on a building parapet has a wash to keep standing water away from the seams in the parapet. Usually the wash drains toward the roof, to minimize water staining of the face of the building.

4. The bottom surface in a horizontal joint between wall panels should have a wash to drain water to the outside. Even if the joint will be closed at the outside face with sealant, the wash should be provided to discourage leaking if the sealant should fail.

5. The sloping roof is a special case of the wash. A shingled roof will not shed water unless it has a considerable slope. If the slope were too shallow, water would linger on the roof and would flow around and under the shingles and penetrate the gaps beneath. Each type of shingle material has its own recommended minimum slope. A slope steeper than the minimum is advisable on exposed sites where rain is often driven against the building by wind. A good rule of thumb is to avoid roof slopes less than 4:12. Wood shakes and shingles and asphalt shingles can go as flat as 3:12 with a special underlayment (consult the appropriate literature from trade associations or manufacturers for more information).

6. So-called flat roofs are seldom really flat but are given a positive slope toward points at which water is removed by roof drains or scuppers, because standing water on a roof can cause deterioration of the roof membrane and even structural collapse. The correct name for "flat" roofs, in fact, is "low-slope" roofs. Drains in a low-slope roof should be located either at points of maximum structural deflection (usually the midspan of a beam or joist) or at low points purposely created by sloping the structure that supports the roof.

Tapered insulation or roof fill should be used if necessary to create additional slope that will cause water to drain properly from a roof. If a drain is located at a point of maximum structural deflection, the minimum recommended slope is ⅛″ per foot (1:100),

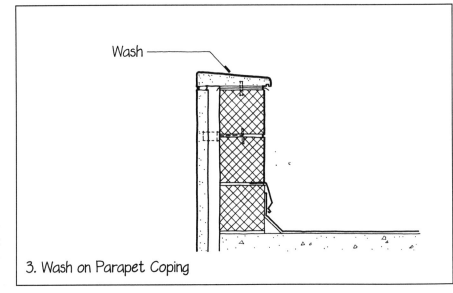

3. Wash on Parapet Coping

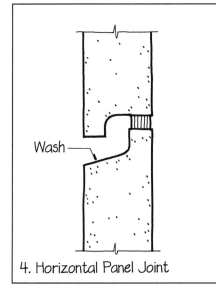

4. Horizontal Panel Joint

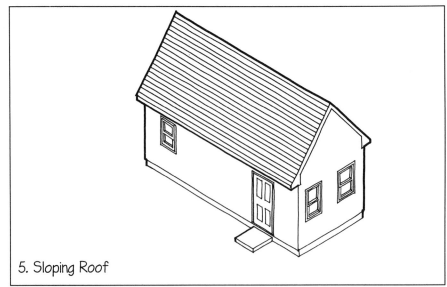

5. Sloping Roof

and more slope than this is desirable. If a drain is located at a low point created by sloping a beam, the overall rise along the length of the beam should be at least twice the expected maximum deflection in the beam, plus another ⅛″ per foot (1:100) of the length of the beam, to be sure water cannot be trapped by the curvature of the beam. The detailer should work closely with the structural engineer to design a system of roof drainage that complies with these guidelines. This is especially important if the roof is composed of cambered elements such as precast concrete planks or beams.

It is desirable (and mandatory under some building codes) to provide a complete, independent set of auxiliary roof drains or scuppers to take over in case the primary drains become clogged with debris. The auxiliary drains or scuppers are usually located 2″ (50 mm) higher in elevation than the primary drains and must be served by their own network of piping.

7. A rooftop plaza is usually drained through open joints between its dead-level paving stones or tiles. The water drops through the joints and is funneled to a system of roof drains by the low-slope roof membrane below. The same recommended slopes apply to this membrane as to any low-slope roof. The plaza paving is held level by small, adjustable-height pedestals that stand on the roof membrane and support the paving units at each intersection. These pedestals are marketed in several proprietary designs and are usually made of plastic.   ▷

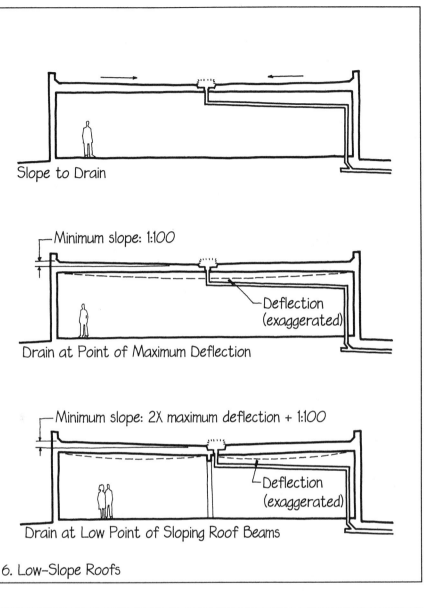

Slope to Drain

Minimum slope: 1:100

Deflection (exaggerated)

Drain at Point of Maximum Deflection

Minimum slope: 2X maximum deflection + 1:100

Deflection (exaggerated)

Drain at Low Point of Sloping Roof Beams

6. Low–Slope Roofs

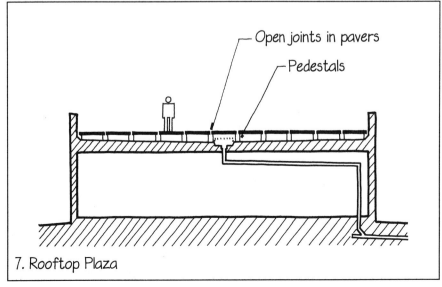

Open joints in pavers

Pedestals

7. Rooftop Plaza

8.   Another special case of the wash is indicated on architectural drawings by the note "pitch to drain." The rain gutter at the eave of a roof is usually pitched (sloped) to drain water toward the nearest downspout. Common slopes used for gutters are ⅛″ or ¼″ per foot (1:100 or 1:50). A steeper slope gives a greater capacity to handle water in a heavy rainstorm.

9.   An industrial or basement floor slab is often pitched toward floor drains to eliminate puddles of standing water. A rule-of-thumb pitch for slab drainage is 1:50 (¼″ per foot), but to prevent puddles this should be increased for surfaces that are not very flat, and can be decreased for very smooth surfaces. In the case of a floor or paving, however, pitches should not become too steep or they will be awkward for pedestrians and vehicles to navigate.

10.   If there is no interior floor drain, a residential garage floor is usually pitched so water dripping off a car will run under the garage door and out. Minimum pitch recommendations are the same as for industrial and basement slabs.

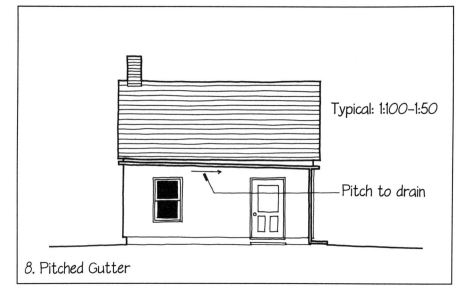

8. Pitched Gutter

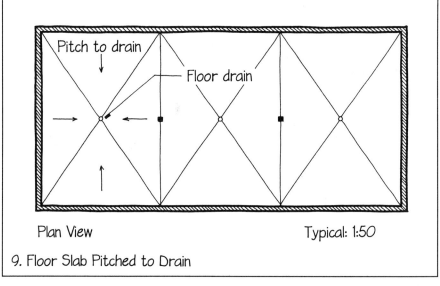

9. Floor Slab Pitched to Drain

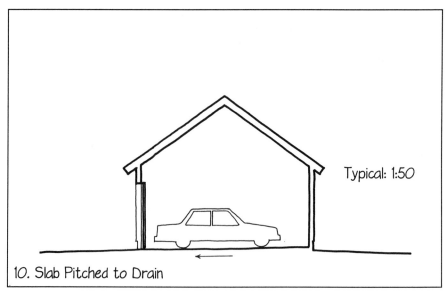

10. Slab Pitched to Drain

11. Roads, driveways, and walks are usually crowned to shed water in both directions and to avoid puddling. The slope on each side of the crown should be at least 0.5%. Parking lots should slope at least 1% to shed water, but not more than 5%.

12. The ground surrounding a building should slope away from the building at a rate of at least 2%. This helps keep water from puddling against the foundation and leaking into basements and crawl spaces.

A wash assures that gravity will act to keep water away from an opening, but its action can be overcome by strong wind currents. Thus a wash that is contained within a joint is often combined with an air barrier and a pressure equalization chamber to form a rainscreen joint (page 25). ■

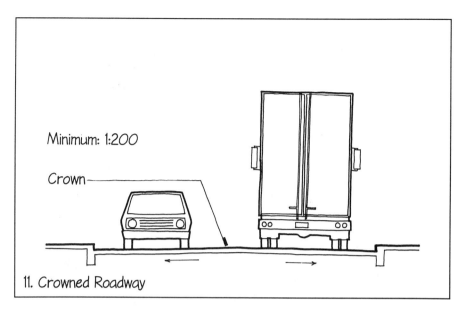

Minimum: 1:200

Crown

11. Crowned Roadway

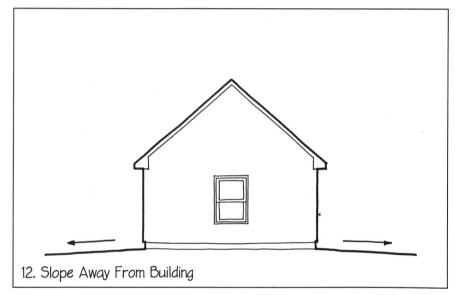

12. Slope Away From Building

OVERLAP

In an overlap, a higher surface is extended over a lower surface so water moved by the force of gravity cannot run behind or beneath them. In order for an overlap to work, the surfaces must be sloping or vertical.

1.   Roof shingles and tiles keep water out by overlapping in such a way that there is no direct path through or between them. Each unit covers a joint between units in the course below. The overlap only works, however, if the roof surface slopes steeply enough so that water runs off before it can find its way around the backs of the shingles or tiles to the open cracks beneath.

2.   Wood bevel siding sheds water by overlapping each board over the one below. The weak spots in wood siding are the end joints, which should be caulked and flashed to prevent water penetration.

3.   Flashings keep water out by overlapping. This simple Z-flashing of sheet metal or thin plastic keeps water from coming through the crack above a window or a door frame.

4.   This lintel flashing in a brick cavity wall is another example of overlapping. Any water that penetrates the outer brick facing is caught by the metal or plastic flashing sheet and is conducted through weep holes to the outdoors. Notice the overhang and drip on the outside edge of the flashing. These keep water out of the crack between the flashing and the steel angle lintel (see *Overhang and Drip*, page 14).

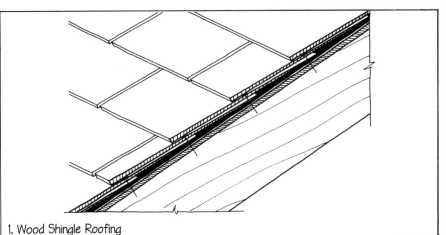

1. Wood Shingle Roofing

2. Wood Bevel Siding

3. Z-Flashing Over Door

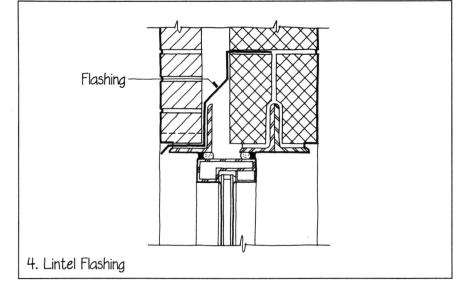

4. Lintel Flashing

5.   A reglet (also called a raggle) is an upward-sloping slot in a vertical surface into which a flashing or the edge of a roof membrane may be inserted. The slope (wash) acts to prevent water from being forced into the vulnerable joint by gravity, and the overlap of the upper lip of the reglet over the flashing keeps water from reaching the joint between the two components. The reglet shown in this drawing is a traditional type that is largely obsolete; it is molded into glazed terra-cotta tiles that are built into a parapet wall by masons. Shims and/or a sealant bead must be inserted into the reglet to hold the flashing or membrane in place.

6.   This contemporary type of reglet is created in a concrete wall or spandrel beam by using a preformed strip of metal or plastic that is nailed lightly to the formwork before the concrete is poured. The opening in the reglet is usually closed temporarily with an adhesive tape or a strip of plastic foam to prevent its being accidentally clogged with concrete. There are many patented profiles for this type of reglet that are intended to interlock securely with a folded edge on the top of the flashing. Diligent inspection is needed just prior to concrete pouring to be sure that the reglet is installed right side up.

   If a reglet is wetted, water may find its way through by capillary action. A continuous bead of sealant between the flashing and the reglet can be helpful in preventing this.

7.   There are also a number of patented designs of surface-mounted reglets made of plastic or metal. A bead of sealant is intended to keep water from behind the reglet. This is somewhat risky, because the success of the detail is entirely dependent on perfect workmanship in installing the sealant and perfect adhesion of the sealant to the wall.

   An overlap is generally very effective in preventing entry of water driven by the force of gravity. If wind is allowed to blow through an overlap, however, it may carry water with it. An overlap is useless against standing water, so it cannot be used on a level surface. ■

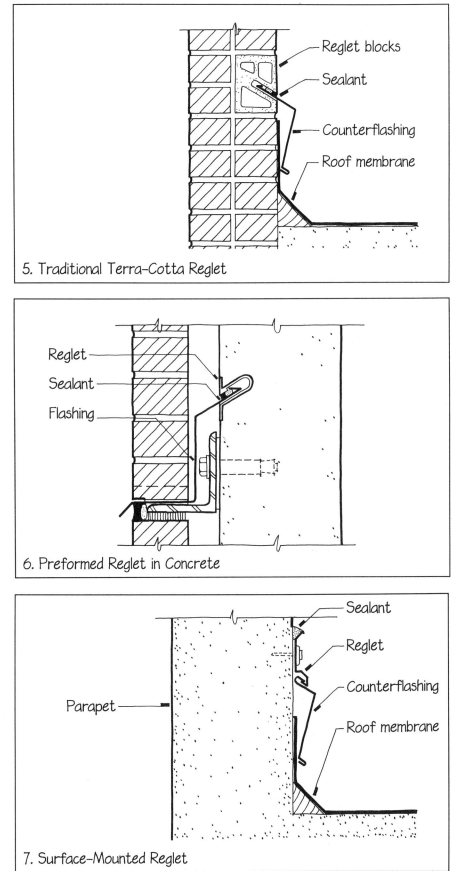

5. Traditional Terra-Cotta Reglet

6. Preformed Reglet in Concrete

7. Surface-Mounted Reglet

OVERHANG AND DRIP

Adhering drops or streams of water running down the wall of a building can be kept away from an opening in the wall by a twofold strategy: (1) creating a projecting profile (an overhang) just above the opening and (2) creating a continuous groove or ridge in the underside of the projection (a drip) so that gravity will pull the adhering water free of the overhang.

1, 2.   These are two versions of a door sill detail: one executed entirely in wood and the other in a combination of wood and aluminum components. There are two openings that must be protected in either case: the crack between the door and the sill, and the joint between the sill and the wall of the building. The door cannot fit tightly to the sill because a generous clearance is required to allow free operation of the door. We would certainly weatherstrip this crack, but weatherstrip is intended only as a barrier to the passage of air and cannot be relied upon to prevent water from passing. We would want the installer to bed the sill in sealant, but the sealant work might be imperfect and it would deteriorate over time. The overhang and drip is a simple, economical, but very effective detailing element that shows up in many kinds of details. In these two drawings we see it being used to protect the two openings beneath a door. In the lower part of both these details, the sill overhangs the wall below. In the wood sill detail (1), the drip is simply a groove milled into the bottom of the wooden sill. The groove must be wide enough and deep enough so that a drop of water cannot bridge across it: Usually a width of ¼″ (6 mm) and a depth of ⅛″ (3 mm) are about right. In the aluminum sill detail (2), the drip is formed by the downturned outer edge of the extrusion. In either case, adher-

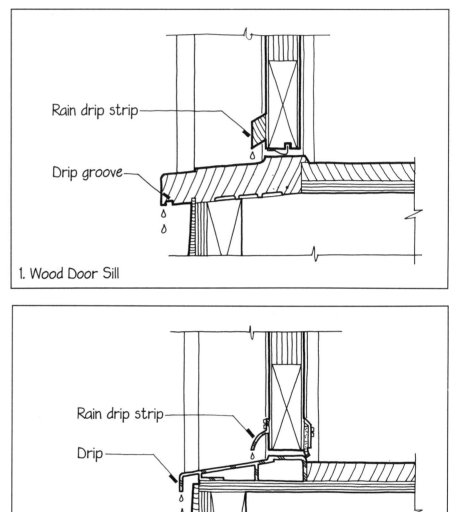

1. Wood Door Sill

2. Aluminum Door Sill

ing drops of water cannot move across the drip, because, in order to do so, they would have to move uphill, against the force of gravity. Therefore, they collect at the outer edge of the drip and fall free. Notice in both cases that the sill has a *wash* to drain water away from the door.

On the bottom of the door in both details is a second type of overhang and drip that protects the crack between the door and the sill. The overhang is provided by a wooden or aluminum drip strip that is screwed tightly to the door. The underside of the drip strip is configured so that water must drip free at the outer edge, well clear of the crack between the door and the sill. The top of the drip strip, of course, has a steep *wash* in each case.

3. Standard exterior details of wood frame houses contain several examples of the overhang and drip principle. The roof shingles overhang the fascia board and slope upward beneath so that water will drip clear of the joint between the fascia and the shingles. The lower edge of the fascia projects below the horizontal soffit so that water running down the fascia will drip free of the crack between the fascia and the soffit. The whole eave, of course, is a large overhang and drip that keeps water off the vulnerable upper edge of the wall and also gives some protection to window and door openings. At the base of the wall, a traditional water table detail consists of an overhang and drip designed to keep water out of the crack between the wood wall and the foundation. Whether or not a water table is used, the bottom edge of the siding should be spaced away from the foundation wall to create another overhang and drip.

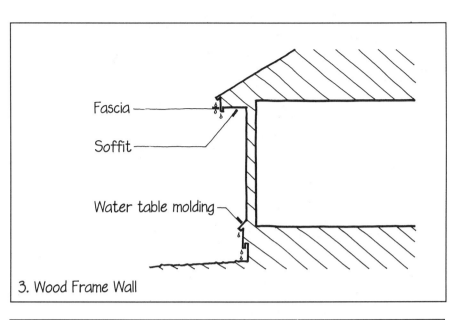

Fascia
Soffit
Water table molding

3. Wood Frame Wall

4. The stone or concrete coping atop a masonry parapet wall is sloped toward the inside of the building to help prevent staining and leaking of the outer surface of the wall. A generous overhang and drip are provided to keep water out of the mortar joint immediately beneath the coping. Additionally, the metal flashing in this mortar joint projects outward and downward to provide another overhang and drip.

The seam between the metal counterflashing and roof membrane where the roof joins the parapet wall is potentially troublesome. The counterflashing and roof membrane often fit closely enough that water entering the seam would be pulled into it by capillary action. The overhang and drip in the counterflashing profile keep the seam dry. As a backup precaution, the coun-

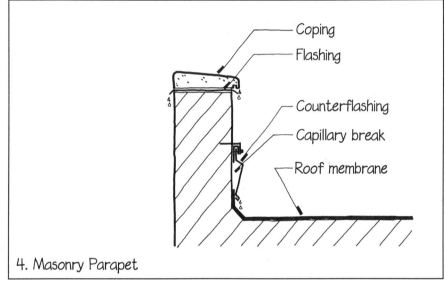

Coping
Flashing
Counterflashing
Capillary break
Roof membrane

4. Masonry Parapet

terflashing is also folded out to create a *Capillary Break* (page 22). For ease of installation, the counterflashing is often made in two pieces as shown. The first piece is embedded in the wall by the masons, and the second piece is inserted into the first and screwed to it by the roofing installers.   ▷

5.   A drip should always be provided under the outer edge of an overhanging story of a building. In a wooden building, the bottom edge of the siding can usually be projected below the soffit to provide a drip. In a concrete or stone building, a drip groove around the outer edge of the soffit will prevent leakage and staining of the soffit area.

6.   Internal flashings in masonry veneers sometimes catch and divert relatively large volumes of water as the mortar joints in the veneer above age and deteriorate. Each flashing should project completely through the outer face of the masonry by roughly ¾″ (20 mm) and turn down at 45° to keep the draining water from wetting the mortarless horizontal joint beneath the flashing. The detailer should resist the urge to recess the outer edge of the flashing into the mortar joint. This might look better than a projecting flashing, but it can lead to serious leakage and deterioration problems beneath the flashing.

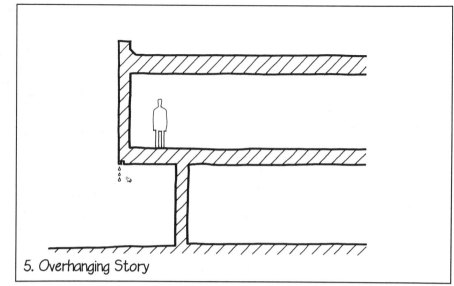

5. Overhanging Story

7.   A larger scale overhang and drip in the form of a porch roof or marquee offers the building user the opportunity to leave a door or a window open for ventilation or access even during moderately severe rainstorms.

The problems in making the cracks around exterior doors waterproof are such that it is not a bad idea to provide a small protecting roof above every exterior door in a building. ∎

Sheet metal flashing

45°

3/4" (20 mm)

6. Flashing Drip Detail

7. Roof Over Door

DRAIN AND WEEP

It's often wise to include provisions for collecting and conducting away any water that may leak through the outer layer of a building cladding system. This internal drainage system is a frank and useful acknowledgement that things can go wrong in sealants, glazing compounds, gaskets, mortar joints, and metal connections, whether caused by faulty materials, inadequate workmanship, building movement, or deterioration of materials over time. It is also inexpensive insurance against the damage that can be caused by uncontrolled leakage and the expense of rebuilding a wall of flawed design. An internal drainage system is comprised of spaces or channels that conduct water by gravity to weep holes or other openings that direct the water back to the outdoors.

1. The rafter detail of a traditional redwood-framed greenhouse is extremely simple. The sheets of glass that bear on the rafter are bedded in glazing compound and fastened down with a strip of redwood held on with screws. This is not a rainscreen detail; any defect in the glazing compound will result in water leakage between the glass and the rafter. Because of surface tension, water that has leaked through will cling to the rafter and run down its sides. This detail furnishes a small drainage gutter milled into the rafter on either side to catch this water and conduct it to the bottom of the rafter, where it is wept to the outdoors.

2. The outer wythe of a masonry cavity wall is expected to leak water, especially as the mortar joints age and deteriorate. The leakage drains down the cavity until it encounters an interruption of the cavity such as a window or door lintel or the base of the wall. At each of these points, a continuous flashing collects the water and drains it through weep holes that are provided at horizontal intervals of from 2 to 4 feet (0.6 to 1.2 m).   ▷

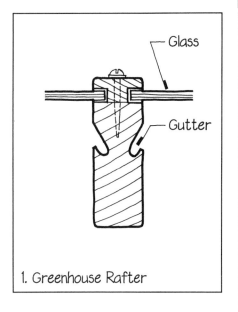

1. Greenhouse Rafter

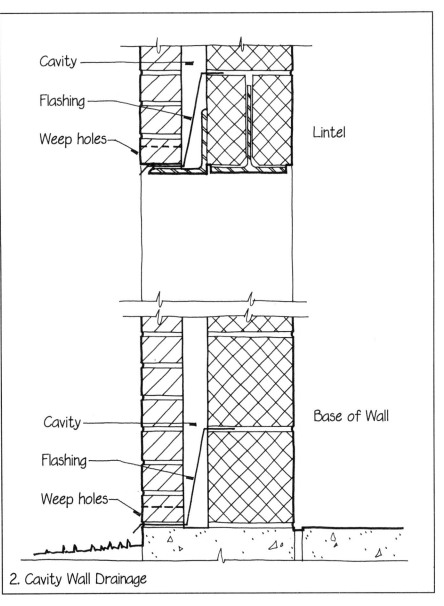

2. Cavity Wall Drainage

3. The horizontal mullion of an aluminum curtain wall acts as a gutter to accumulate leakage if the seal between the glass and the glazing gasket is imperfect. Weep holes discharge this leakage back to the outdoors. A window of average width might have three weep holes distributed across its sill.

Wind can drive water back through a weep hole if there is not an adequate air barrier between the weep hole and the interior of the building. This possibility can be minimized by locating the weep hole in a sheltered location that is not likely to become wet and by inserting a baffle behind the weep hole. The baffle is made of a nondecaying, noncorroding open-celled material that allows water to filter out by gravity but that slows entering air currents enough so that they are unlikely to be able to move water through the opening. A typical baffle material is a nonwoven mat composed of stiff plastic filaments.

4. In detailing a rainscreen panel system, it is important to design a three-dimensional system for draining the open joints. Especially crucial is the design of the intersections of the horizontal and vertical joints, which need to be detailed carefully for ease of assembly and for raintightness. Any cavity between the rainscreen panels and the air barrier wall must also be drained, using much the same detail as for a masonry cavity wall (detail 2, preceding). ∎

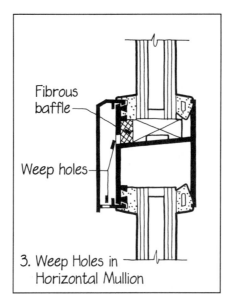

3. Weep Holes in Horizontal Mullion

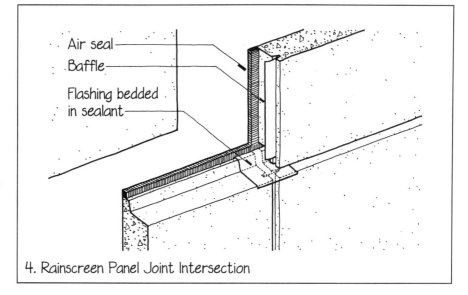

4. Rainscreen Panel Joint Intersection

COLD ROOF

The outer surface of a roof in a snowy climate should be kept cold in winter to prevent snow from melting. Roof drainage systems often become clogged with snow and ice during cold winter weather. When melt water that runs down the roof reaches ice-clogged gutters, drains, or eaves, pools can form that are deep enough to back up around shingles and flashings and leak into the building. By ventilating the underside of the roof deck with outdoor air, the roof can be kept cold enough so that the snow will not melt except in above-freezing outdoor temperatures that will also melt the snow and ice in the drainage system.

1.   Most building codes require a prescribed minimum amount of ventilation area at eave and ridge in a sloping roof—commonly 1/300 of the area of the ceiling. A building with a ceiling area of 3,000 square feet, for example, would require a total of at least 10 square feet of ventilation opening. Half this amount should be distributed along the ridge or high in the gable ends, and the other half should be distributed along the eaves. These high and low ventilation openings allow convection to work efficiently to remove heat from the roof space or attic. Appropriate ventilation louvers for this purpose are available from a number of manufacturers.

2.   It is important to detail the roof so that all ventilation takes place above the thermal insulation in the roof. In any situation in which there is a chance that the insulation might accidentally block the ventilating cavities beneath the roof sheathing, vent spacer channels made of foam plastic or paperboard should be used to maintain open air passages.

Roof ventilation also serves to carry away any water vapor that may escape through defects in the vapor retarder or through ceiling penetrations such as light fixtures and attic hatches. ▷

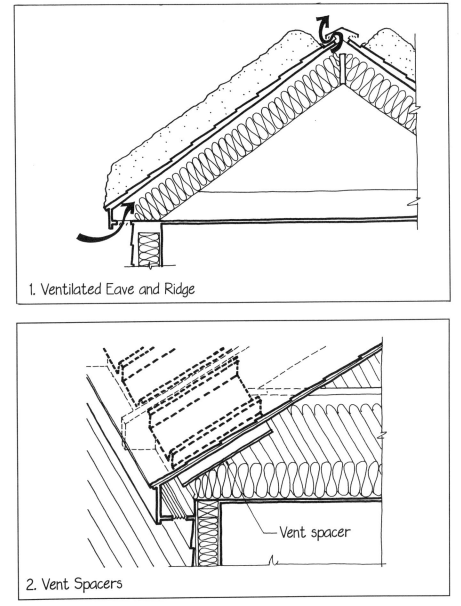

1. Ventilated Eave and Ridge

2. Vent Spacers

Vent spacer

3. Some buildings with low-slope roofs in very snowy environments are furnished with a strong horizontal lattice construction several feet above the roof that catches and holds snow, keeping the roof membrane below free of snow and ice. When the weather is warm enough to melt the snow, the water drips through the lattice and is carried away by the membrane and roof drains. The space between the roof membrane and the lattice is open to the air and is tall enough for inspection and maintenance as well as free air flow. ■

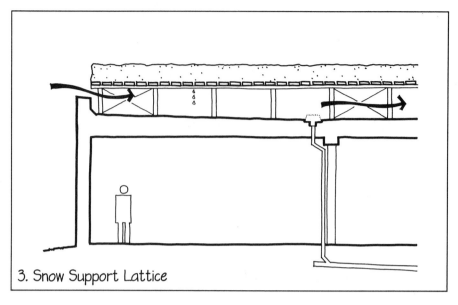

3. Snow Support Lattice

FOUNDATION DRAINAGE

Basements tend to leak. Water is almost always present in the surrounding soil. There are always openings in basement walls: Concrete and masonry foundation walls are full of cracks and pores, and the joint between a basement floor slab and a foundation wall is difficult to make waterproof. There are also strong forces to move the water through the openings, especially hydrostatic pressure. Removing water from the soil around a basement by means of foundation drainage is the surest way to keep the basement from leaking. Foundation drainage has the added benefit of reducing or eliminating the water pressure that tends to collapse the basement walls.

1. Slopes and swales are a first line of defense against water around a basement. They provide a simple system of sloping surfaces (washes) of earth or paving that encourage surface water to drain away from the basement rather than toward it. Gradients of 2% to 10% are recommended.

Also part of the first line of defense are roof drainage systems, either perimeter gutters or internal roof drains, which keep roof water away from the basement.

2. The second line of defense against water around a basement consists of open drainage pipes that are laid in porous material at the base of the basement wall. Sometimes on very wet sites drainage pipes are laid under the floor slab as well. The porous material may be either crushed stone (of uniform particle size, for maximum porosity) or a thick panel or mat of synthetic material that contains large internal passages for water. When water moves through the ground toward the basement wall, it first reaches the porous layer, where gravity pulls it rapidly downward. As the water accumulates at the base of the wall, it enters the open drainage pipe and flows by gravity either to an outlet down the slope from

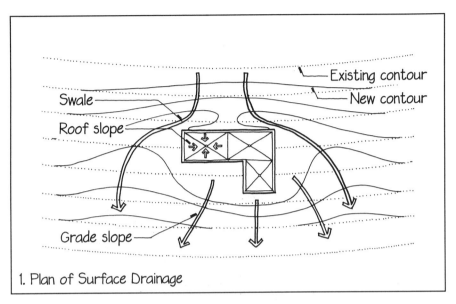

1. Plan of Surface Drainage

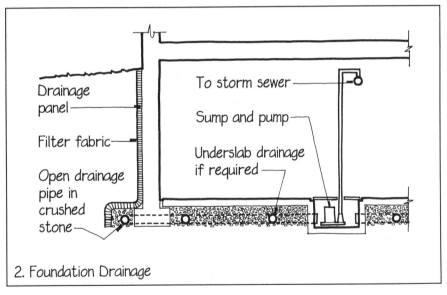

2. Foundation Drainage

the building or to a sump in the basement floor from which it is ejected by an automatic pump.

The drainage pipe has a line of holes or slots in it to allow water to enter. The function of the pipe is to provide an unobstructed lateral passage for water through the crushed stone. Provided the pipe is placed lower than the slab of the basement it is protecting, it makes no difference whether the holes face up, down, or sideways, except that downward-facing holes allow water to

enter the pipe at a lower elevation than the other orientations.

Fine soil particles can be carried into the drainage layer by water percolating through the soil. Eventually, these particles may clog the pores of the drainage material. To prevent this, it is good practice to provide a synthetic filter fabric between the drainage material and the soil. The fabric allows water to pass freely while straining out the soil particles. ■

CAPILLARY BREAK

Water can pull itself by capillary action through a narrow crack, but not a wide one. To prevent capillary entry of water, we create a capillary break by enlarging a crack internally to a dimension large enough so that a drop of water cannot bridge across it, at least ¼″ (6 mm).

1. This drawing shows a vertical edge between two exterior cladding panels that we want to fit only ⅛″ (3 mm) apart. If this edge is wetted, water will be drawn into the narrow opening by capillary action. When the water reaches the capillary break, however, it will be unable to bridge across it, and it will not pass farther toward the interior of the building unless pushed by wind forces.

2. In this horizontal joint between wall panels, a capillary break is created by enlarging the clear dimension of the labyrinth joint in the center of the panels.

3. Traditional detailing of the sill of a wood window shows a capillary break created by milling a groove in the under edge of the sash.

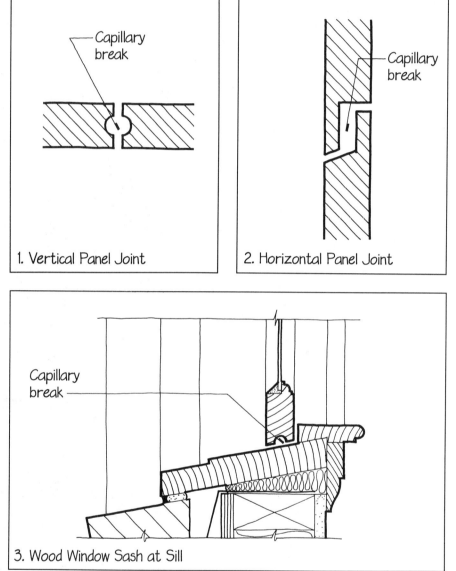

1. Vertical Panel Joint

2. Horizontal Panel Joint

3. Wood Window Sash at Sill

4. There are two capillary breaks in this detail of an aluminum window: one between the sash and the frame, and another between the aluminum frame and the stone sill.

5. A parapet counterflashing can pull water by capillary action through the narrow crack between itself and the upturned edge of the roofing membrane underneath. This possibility can be avoided by bending the flashing so that it creates a capillary break.

A capillary break serves only to neutralize capillary action as a force that can move water through a building assembly. It is a reliable and useful component of an overall strategy for making an assembly watertight, but it is not capable of resisting water penetration caused by gravity, momentum, or wind. ■

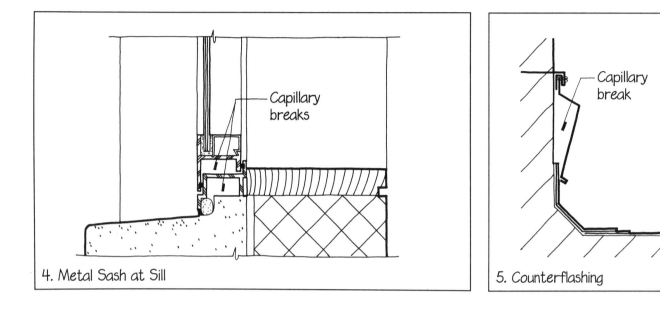

4. Metal Sash at Sill

5. Counterflashing

LABYRINTH

If a joint is designed so that no straight line may be constructed through it without passing through solid material, a raindrop or a snowflake cannot pass through the joint by its own momentum.

1. A windblown raindrop or snowflake possesses momentum that can move it through an opening in a building wall. A raindrop striking this open horizontal joint between two stone or precast concrete wall panels, for example, will splatter water through the joint toward the interior of the building unless the joint is configured as a simple labyrinth.

2. This is a labyrinth design for the vertical joints in the same stone or concrete panels.

3. A labyrinth can also be executed in aluminum or other metal.

4. This rigid metal or plastic baffle is another approach to designing a vertical labyrinth joint. It is intended only to block water driven by momentum, so it fits loosely in the grooves. In this type of joint the panel edges are not so fragile as in some of the other kinds of labyrinth joints, and there are no left-hand and right-hand panel edges to keep track of—both vertical edges of every panel are the same.

5. The astragal is a traditional labyrinth design that is used to keep water drops from being blown through the vertical crack between a pair of swinging doors.

A labyrinth is a very useful part of an overall strategy for preventing water penetration into a building, but it is not sufficient in itself to prevent the passage of windblown water or snow; it must be combined with an air barrier and a pressure equalization chamber (see pages 25–28). ∎

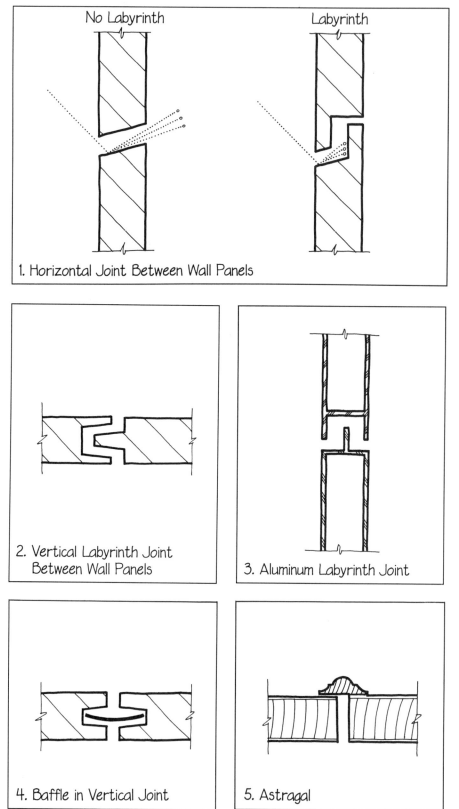

1. Horizontal Joint Between Wall Panels

2. Vertical Labyrinth Joint Between Wall Panels

3. Aluminum Labyrinth Joint

4. Baffle in Vertical Joint

5. Astragal

RAINSCREEN ASSEMBLY

A detail that blocks air currents from passing through a joint will prevent water from being pushed through the joint by air pressure differentials.

1. By using a combination of *Wash*, *Labyrinth*, *Capillary Break*, and *Overhang and Drip*, we can design a sealant-free wall or window joint that will resist the entry of water driven by the forces of gravity, momentum, capillary action, and surface tension. If this joint is wetted, however, and if a current of air is passing through from outside to inside, the air current can blow or "pump" water through the joint. To look at it another way, the passage of the air current indicates that the air pressure outside the joint is higher than the air pressure inside. This difference in pressure represents potential energy that can move water from outside to inside. Such differences in pressure exist on every building exposed to wind, which is why most building leaks occur in windy, rainy weather.

2. This is the same pair of details as in the previous drawing, with the addition of a bead of sealant along the interior edge of the joint. We will assume for the moment that the sealant is perfectly airtight. Now air can pass in and out of the joint, but it can no longer pass *through* it. If a sudden gust of wind raises the pressure on the outside of the wall, air will be forced into the open interior of the joint by the increased external pressure. After only a very small amount of air has moved into the joint, however, the air pressure inside the joint will equal the air pressure outside, and air movement will cease. Because the two air pressures are equal, there is no energy available to pump water, and the interior of the joint will remain dry. The

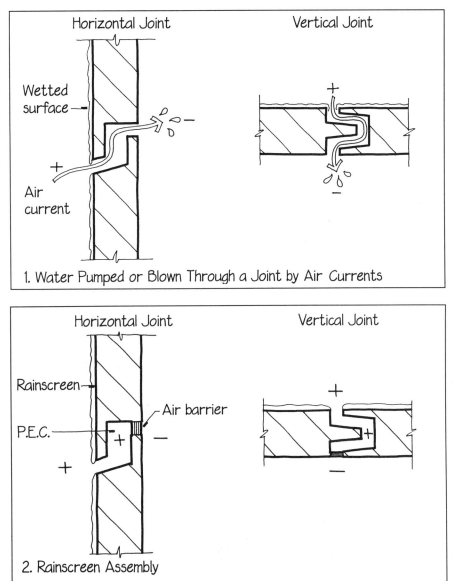

sealant joint in this detail never becomes wet; it serves only as an air barrier. The large capillary break inside the joint has now taken on a second function: It works also as a pressure equalization chamber (abbreviated P.E.C.), a small container of air that is maintained at the same pressure as the air outside the wall by tiny movements of air in and out of the joint. The wall panels themselves are referred to as a rainscreen, meaning that they act to screen out rainwater except at the joints. The entire assembly of rainscreen, air barrier, and P.E.C. is known as a rainscreen assembly, and the principle by which it works is known as the rainscreen principle.

▷

3. Let us look one more time at the same joint, but this time let us assume that there is a defect in the sealant. Perhaps the sealant never adhered properly to one of the panels, or perhaps it has grown old and cracked, creating a small opening through which air or water can pass. Unless the sealant falls completely out of the joint, however, it will prevent *most* air from passing, and the small amount of air that does pass will not be sufficient to disrupt seriously the automatic pressure-equalizing action that prevents pumping of water through the joint. (As a rule of thumb, if the total area of leaks in the air barrier is no larger than a tenth of the total area of the openings that the air barrier protects, leakage is unlikely.)

Contrast this with a defective sealant installation on the *outside* of the same joint instead of on the *inside*. The sealant will be bathed with water during a rainstorm, and water will be forced through the defect by even small differences in air pressure between inside and outside. This demonstrates that the outside of a joint is not the place to install an air barrier, because in this position the air barrier only works if it is perfect. The proper location for an air barrier is on the *inside* of the joint, where it is always dry and where small holes, cracks, or other defects will not impair its action.

4. This is the sill of an ordinary wood window. The detail to the left incorporates all the principles we have identified so far for keeping water from penetrating: There is a **Wash** on the sill to prevent water entry by gravity, and an **Overhang and Drip** beneath it to prevent water entry by surface tension. The L-shaped crack between the sash and the sill is a **Labyrinth** that eliminates momentum as a force that can move water through the window unit. The groove in the bottom of the sash is a

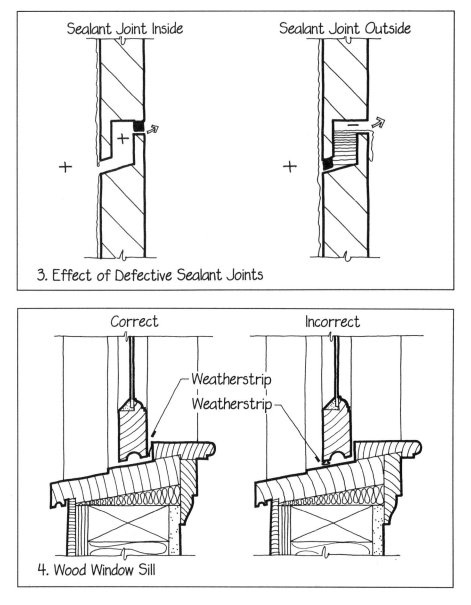

3. Effect of Defective Sealant Joints

4. Wood Window Sill

Capillary Break. With the addition of a reasonably airtight weatherstrip at the inside end of the crack, the groove becomes also a pressure equalization chamber (P.E.C.), and wind forces are neutralized. This detail represents a complete strategy for keeping water out—a true rainscreen detail.

The detail to the right differs from the one to the left only in the location of the weatherstrip. If the weatherstrip

in this example has even a small leak, water can be forced through it during wind-driven rainstorms and can easily be pumped up onto the window stool inside.

5. To the left is a door sill that represents a complete rainscreen strategy for preventing water penetration. The P.E.C. is the space under the aluminum drip strip. The air barrier is a weatherstrip on the inside face of the door (it could also be inside the crack). The rainscreen is the door itself.

The sill detail to the right shows an available type of drip strip that incorporates a synthetic rubber weatherstrip. The weatherstrip is placed just to the inside of the P.E.C. and will remain dry and effective in this location. If it were placed, instead, at the outside edge of the drip strip, the entire detail would be unreliable.

6. The left-hand detail represents a horizontal joint between two metal panels of a curtain wall system. It includes a *Wash*, a *Labyrinth*, and an internal *Drip*. An air barrier is provided by two synthetic rubber gaskets that are inserted into a narrow aluminum channel just behind the metal panel. This is a rainscreen detail. Even if the gasket does not seal perfectly, this detail will not leak. (Rainscreen wall designs are often referred to in manufacturers' literature as pressure-equalized wall designs.)

The right-hand detail is not a rainscreen detail. It relies completely on the integrity of the sealant joint. It is much simpler and less expensive to manufacture and install, but it is unreliable, because any defect in the sealant will cause a water leak.

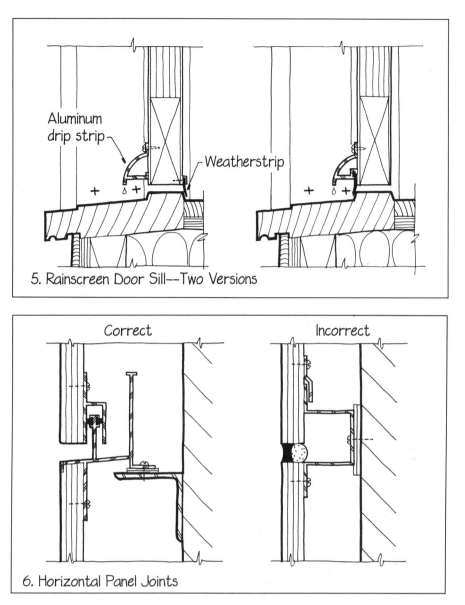

5. Rainscreen Door Sill—Two Versions

6. Horizontal Panel Joints

7. This is a sill detail from an aluminum-and-glass curtain wall system. It has a synthetic rubber gasket that is located on the outside of the glass. If the gasket is slightly defective, water will move past it and into the interior aluminum channel beneath the glass. The manufacturer of the wall system has anticipated this possibility, however, and has provided weep holes that will allow the leakage to drain back to the outdoors. Furthermore, there is also a gasket on the inside face of the glass that acts as an air barrier, preventing the water from being pumped farther toward the inside of the building. In other words, if the external gasket leaks, this detail functions as a rainscreen detail. In a detail like this the external gasket is called a deterrent seal because its role is only to deter the passage of as much water as possible, not to act as a perfect seal against all water penetration. The internal gasket is called an air seal to indicate that it functions as an air barrier in a rainscreen detail. ▷

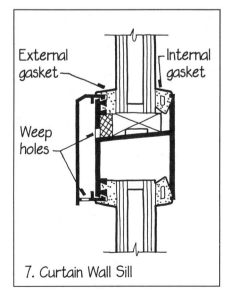

7. Curtain Wall Sill

8. The traditional masonry cavity wall is a rainscreen design. The outer wythe of masonry is the rainscreen. The cavity is the pressure equalization chamber. The inner wythe of masonry is the air barrier, and the weep holes provide not only for drainage but also for the passage of air to equalize air pressure between the cavity and the outdoors.

9. This drawing represents an adaptation of the cavity wall rainscreen design to a building faced with story-high panels of cut stone. The air barrier wall is composed of steel studs and gypsum sheathing, covered with a rubberized asphalt mastic coating to make it airtight and water resistant.

In looking at these last two rainscreen designs with their large P.E.C.s, we can make three observations that are very important for the detailer to keep in mind.

First, the air barrier, whether it is a backup wall, a gasket, or a bead of sealant, supports all the wind load on its proportion of the face of the building. *Every air barrier must be engineered to support full wind load.* In a masonry cavity wall, the backup wall, not the facing, supports the wind load. In the stone wall shown here, regardless of the stiffness of the stone panels, the metal studs must be engineered to withstand the full wind load. At a door sill, the weatherstrip must be sufficiently stiff to resist the force of wind upon it. Fortunately the area of the weatherstrip is small so the total wind force on it is similarly small, but the backup wall is large in area and must absorb a large load.

Second, wind pressure varies considerably across the face of a building. In a tall building especially, pressures are much higher at higher stories of the building than at lower stories, and pressures near the edges of a facade are much different from those in the middle; often some areas of a wall are even subject to suctions rather than pressures because of the aerodynamics of a building. Because of this, it is important to divide a very large P.E.C. into compartments not larger than two

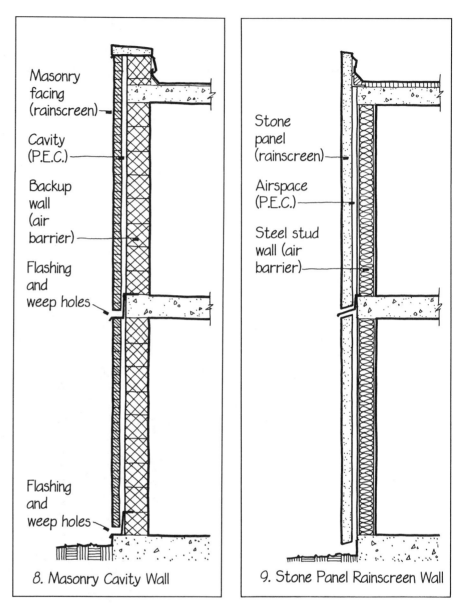

8. Masonry Cavity Wall

Masonry facing (rainscreen)

Cavity (P.E.C.)

Backup wall (air barrier)

Flashing and weep holes

Flashing and weep holes

9. Stone Panel Rainscreen Wall

Stone panel (rainscreen)

Airspace (P.E.C.)

Steel stud wall (air barrier)

stories high and a bay or two in width. If this is not done, air can rush from one part of the building facade to another within the P.E.C. and cause localized pressure differentials that may result in water leakage. The divisions between the compartments need not be absolutely airtight, but they should be designed to choke off most airflow. The dividers can be made of masonry, sheet metal, or any other material appropriate to the wall construction system.

Third, every pressure equalization chamber, whether small or large, must be drained and wept to the outdoors to dispose harmlessly of any water that

may enter (see **Drain and Weep**, page 17).

The rainscreen approach cannot be applied to solid walls because a solid wall, by definition, cannot contain a pressure equalization chamber. Solid masonry or concrete exterior walls are thought of as "barrier walls," meaning that they are so thick and so well constructed that they are unlikely to leak. The barrier wall approach is far from foolproof, however, because a single crack can allow water to enter the building. ∎

UPSTAND

An upstand is simply a dam. The principle of the upstand is that wind pressure can drive water uphill only to a height such that the hydrostatic pressure of the standing water retained by the dam is equal to the pressure exerted by the wind. We use an upstand in detailing when it is impractical to provide a reliable air barrier to prevent water from being driven through a horizontal crack by air pressure differentials. This can happen in situations where installation access to the proper location for an air barrier is blocked by a spandrel beam or a column. It can happen at the sill of a door or a window as a gasket or weatherstrip ages, wears, and begins to leak large volumes of air. Sometimes we just want to be double sure that a detail won't leak. In any of these cases, a simple upstand can serve to prevent wind pressure from pushing water through a horizontal joint, even if the joint is totally unsealed against air leakage. The required height of an upstand is determined by the maximum expected wind pressure. To find the wind pressure, find the design wind speed in the appropriate building code. Then determine the necessary height of upstand according to the accompanying table, interpolating as necessary.

1. A manufacturer of sliding glass doors recognizes that if the interior weatherstrip becomes sufficiently worn with years of use, the rainscreen action of the sill detail may become inoperative. A 2″ (50 mm) upstand at the interior side of the door offers a degree of back-up protection by preventing leakage up to a maximum wind pressure of 10 psf (480 Pa), equivalent to a 60 mph wind (100 km/hr). A taller upstand would offer even more protection against leakage, but this advantage must be weighed against the increased tripping hazard of a taller sill.   ▷

REQUIRED HEIGHTS OF UPSTANDS

Approximate Wind Speed	Wind Pressure	Upstand Height
45 mph (70 km/hr)	5 psf (240 Pa)	1″ (25 mm)
60 mph (100 km/hr)	10 psf (480 Pa)	2″ (50 mm)
90 mph (145 km/hr)	20 psf (960 Pa)	4″ (100 mm)
110 mph (175 km/hr)	30 psf (1,440 Pa)	6″ (150 mm)
125 mph (200 km/hr)	40 psf (1,920 Pa)	8″ (200 mm)
140 mph (225 km/hr)	50 psf (2,400 Pa)	10″ (250 mm)

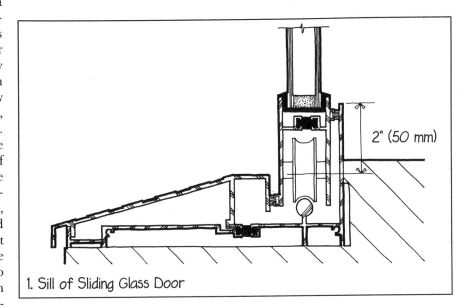

2″ (50 mm)

1. Sill of Sliding Glass Door

2. This horizontal joint between metal curtain wall panels has a 3″ (75 mm) upstand, giving protection against water penetration at wind pressures as high as 15 psf (720 Pa), even if the gasket should be inadvertently omitted during installation.

3. To be absolutely safe against water being pumped back through a weep hole by wind pressure, the hole can be drained through a vertical weep tube that exits the wall a distance below the point that is being drained. If there is a vertical distance of 10″ (250 mm) between the inlet and outlet of a weep tube, for example, it would take a wind of approximately 140 mph (225 km/hr) to pump water up and into the building through the tube. This is the principle of the upstand applied in a slightly different disguise, using the same table to equate heights of water to pressures of air.

When detailing an upstand, remember that its ends must be dammed carefully at vertical joints or the water will simply drain out of the ends to become unwanted leakage. In aluminum cladding details, end dams are often plugs molded of synthetic rubber. ■

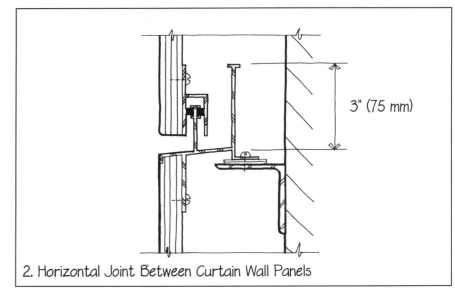

2. Horizontal Joint Between Curtain Wall Panels

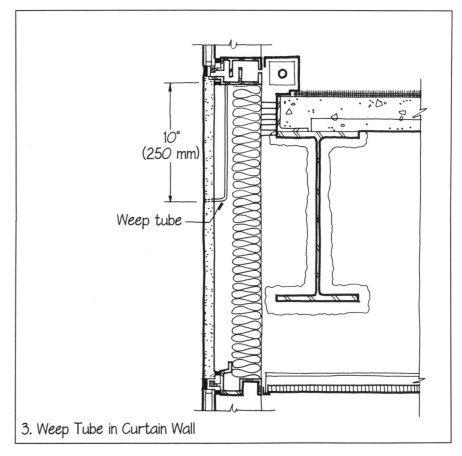

3. Weep Tube in Curtain Wall

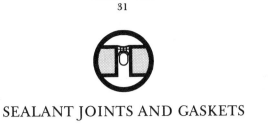

SEALANT JOINTS AND GASKETS

Sealants and gaskets are elastic materials that can be placed in a joint to block the passage of air and/or water while allowing for relative movement between the two sides of the joint. A gasket is a strip of synthetic rubber that is compressed into the joint. Most sealants are mastic materials that are injected into the joint and then cure to a rubberlike state. A gasket seals against a surface by being compressed tightly against it. A sealant seals by adhering tightly to the surface.

1. The width and depth of a sealant joint must never be left to chance; they should be determined in accordance with the procedure shown on pages 35 and 36. The foam plastic backer rod is a very important part of every sealant joint: It limits the depth of the sealant to the predetermined dimension, provides a firm surface against which to tool the sealant, and imparts to the sealant bead the narrow-waisted shape that helps minimize stresses.

2. If the sealant joint is too narrow, normal amounts of movement between the adjoining components can overstretch the sealant and tear it.

3. If the sealant bead is too deep, stresses in the bead will be excessive and tearing is likely.

4. Tooling forces the sealant material to fill the joint, assume the desired profile, and adhere to the adjoining components.   ▷

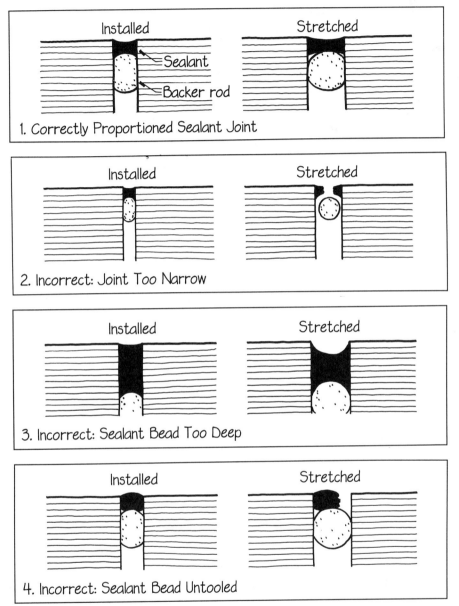

1. Correctly Proportioned Sealant Joint

2. Incorrect: Joint Too Narrow

3. Incorrect: Sealant Bead Too Deep

4. Incorrect: Sealant Bead Untooled

5, 6. In a three-sided sealant joint, a bond breaker should be inserted against the back of the joint to allow for full extension of the sealant bead when the joint opens.

7. If a sealant joint is too narrow, the sealant may become overcompressed, squeezing it out of the joint and tearing it.

8. Sealant should be applied at an air temperature that is neither too hot nor too cold. If application at very hot or very cold temperatures is anticipated, the initial joint width should be adjusted to compensate for the seasonal overstressing that might otherwise occur.

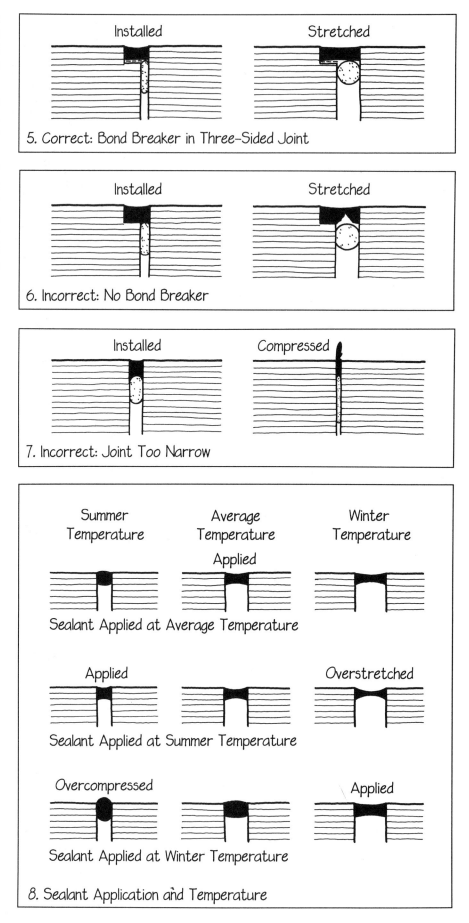

9. A sealant lap joint may be dimensioned using the same procedures as for a butt joint.

10. There are many types of glazing details that include wet (gunnable) sealants. In general, these incorporate synthetic rubber spacers that regulate the depth and thickness of the sealant according to the principles laid out earlier. In the detail to the left in the drawing, the glass is set on synthetic rubber blocks and centered in the metal frame with the aid of compressible spacer strips that also serve as backer rods. This detail minimizes the number of different components needed to install the glass by eliminating any gaskets. The detail to the right uses a preformed synthetic rubber gasket on the interior side for easy installation and a neat appearance. The outside is sealed with a gunnable sealant for maximum security against leakage. Glazing details are usually developed by manufacturers of cladding and glazing systems rather than by detailers in architectural offices.

11. This is an example of a preformed synthetic rubber gasket used to close a movement joint in a high-traffic horizontal surface, such as a roadway or a parking garage. The gasket is slightly wider than the joint and must be compressed during installation.   ▷

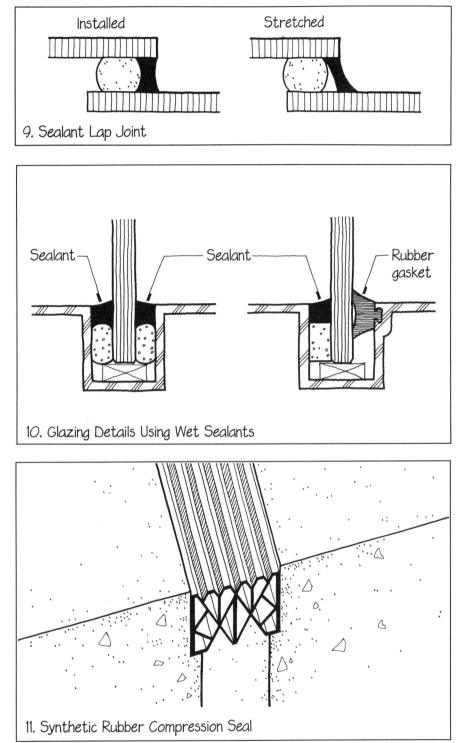

9. Sealant Lap Joint

10. Glazing Details Using Wet Sealants

11. Synthetic Rubber Compression Seal

12. Preformed gaskets are widely used to seal between window glass and metal framing. In this example, a closed-cell sponge gasket is inserted first; then the glass is inserted. Finally, a dense gasket in a roll-in wedge profile is forced between the inside face of the glass and the frame, compressing the sponge gasket and holding the entire assembly together. For additional security against water penetration, a bead of gunnable sealant is sometimes placed over the outside gasket. This is called a cap sealant.

13. There are many types of synthetic rubber lockstrip gaskets that are useful in glazing. This example incorporates a pine tree spline that is inserted into a slot in a concrete sill or jamb. The glass is installed in the gasket, and then the synthetic rubber lockstrip is inserted with a special tool to make the gasket rigid and lock the glass in place.

14. Preshimmed tape sealants are made to be compressed between components of nonworking joints. The tape is thick and very sticky. The semirigid shim rod in the center of the tape controls the thickness of the joint and limits the tendency of the surrounding mastic to squeeze out.

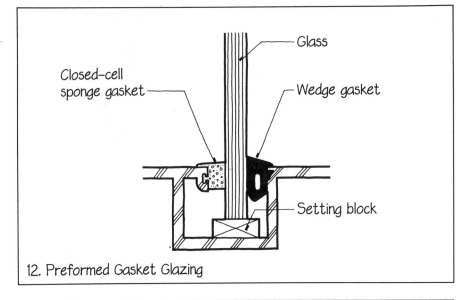

12. Preformed Gasket Glazing

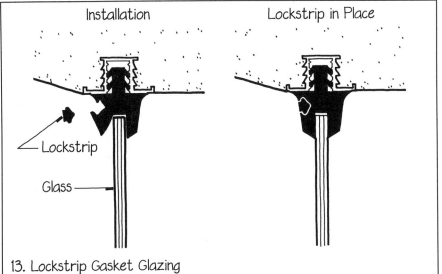

13. Lockstrip Gasket Glazing

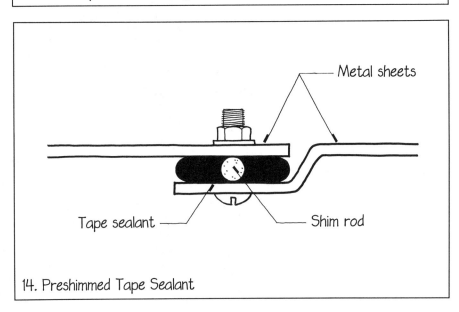

14. Preshimmed Tape Sealant

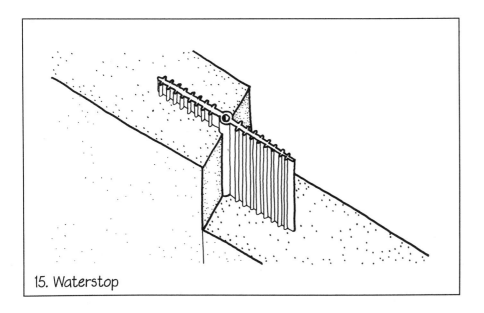

15. Waterstop

15. The waterstop is a preformed synthetic rubber gasket used to seal pour joints and movement joints in concrete foundation walls. The example shown here features a center tube that allows the waterstop to stretch or compress considerably in response to movement in the concrete walls. Many other shapes of synthetic rubber waterstops are also manufactured, along with alternative designs made of rigid plastic, metal, mastic, even bentonite clay, which expands and seals when wetted.

PROPORTIONING SEALANT JOINTS

Sealant joints should be provided at frequent enough intervals in a surface so that the expected overall movement in the surface is divided into an acceptably small amount of movement in each joint. Usually sealant joint spacing is determined by the desired sizes of the panels or sheet materials that make up a wall.

Generally, a sealant joint should not be narrower than ¼″ (6 mm). A joint narrower than this is difficult to make and has little ability to absorb movement. Joints can be as wide as 1–2″ (25–50 mm), depending on the ability of the sealant not to sag out of the joint before it has cured. The depth of sealant in a joint should be equal to half

the width of the joint, but not less than ¼″ (6 mm) or more than ½″ (13 mm). Thus, a ¼″ wide joint should be ¼″ deep (6 mm × 6 mm), a ¾″ wide joint should be ⅜″ deep (19 mm × 9 mm), and a 1¼″ wide joint should be ½″ deep (32 mm × 13 mm).

DETERMINING WIDTHS OF SEALANT JOINTS

The width of a sealant joint should be determined by the designer of the building, the detailer, the specifications writer, the suppliers of the components or materials on either side of the joint, and the structural engineer, working together and using all available information on temperature extremes at the building site, the time of year when the sealant will be installed, the properties of the materials on either side of the joint, the properties of the sealant itself, and the structural characteristics of the frame and skin of the building. For preliminary purposes, the following equation may be used to determine the width of any sealant joint:

$$W = \frac{100}{X}\,(\varepsilon L \Delta T + M_o) + t$$

where

W = required width of sealant joint

X = plus or minus movement capability of sealant, expressed as a whole number

ε = coefficient of expansion of skin material

L = length of building skin between joints

ΔT = annual range between extreme high and low temperatures. If specific temperature data are lacking, assume that ΔT is 130°.

M_o = anticipated movement due to such nonthermal factors as structural deflections, creep, or moisture expansion and contraction

t = construction tolerance

This formula may be used with either conventional or SI units. Following are three examples of its use.

SEALANT JOINT WIDTH CALCULATION EXAMPLE NO. 1

Calculate the required width of a horizontal sealant joint for an all-aluminum curtain wall panel, dark gray in color, that is 6′8″ (80″) high. The temperature ranges annually between −40° and +100°. The building is framed with steel. A sealant with a movement capability of ±25% is recommended by the wall panel manufacturer.

The annual range of air temperature is 100° − (−40°) = 140°, but the sun will heat the dark-colored panel to well above the temperature of the air. As an estimate, we will add 40° to the air temperature to account for this phenomenon, making a total temperature range of 180°.

The structural engineer estimates that deflections of the spandrel beams and columns under live and wind loadings can total as much as 0.04″ per panel.

The construction tolerance, the accuracy of the aluminum panels as installed on the building, is estimated by the curtain wall contractor to be ±⅛″. ▷

From the accompanying table, we determine that the coefficient of thermal expansion of aluminum is 0.0000128 in/in/°F.

Starting with the given equation

$$W = \frac{100}{X}(\varepsilon L \Delta T + M_o) + t$$

and substituting,

$$W = [100/25][(0.0000128''/''/°F)(80'') (180°F) + 0.04''] + 0.125''$$

we have $W = 1.02''$; use a 1″ wide sealant joint or 1⅛″, if we wish to be conservative. The depth should be ½″ (page 35).
This example may be worked in SI (metric) units using the same formula and procedure, so long as all the units are consistent.

SEALANT JOINT WIDTH CALCULATION EXAMPLE NO. 2

Calculate the required width of a sealant joint between white granite wall panels that are 4′7″ (55″) in maximum dimension. The annual range of air temperature is from −10° to 110°. The building structure will be of reinforced concrete, and the structural engineer estimates that creep in the frame will eventually reach about 0.03″ per panel but that structural deflections will be insignificant. The sealant will have a movement capability of ±25%. The supplier and installer of the granite panels expect to work to an accuracy of ±³⁄₁₆″.

From the table below, we find a coefficient of thermal expansion for granite of 0.0000047 in/in/°F. Starting with the given equation

$$W = \frac{100}{X}(\varepsilon L \Delta T + M_o) + t$$

and substituting,

$$W = [100/25][(0.0000047''/''/°F)(55'') (120°F) + 0.03''] + 3/16''$$

we have $W = 0.43''$; use a ½″ joint. A depth of ¼″ is suitable (page 35).

SEALANT JOINT WIDTH CALCULATION EXAMPLE NO. 3

Calculate the required width of a vertical sealant joint in a brick wall with a joint spacing of 6.5 meters. The air temperature range is 60°C. The contractor would like to use a sealant that has a movement capability of ±12.5%. According to Technical Note No. 18 of the Brick Institute of America, the brickwork will expand over time by about 2/100 of 1% due to moisture absorption. A construction tolerance of ±6 mm is expected.

According to the table to the left, the coefficient of thermal expansion of brick masonry is about 0.0000065 mm/mm/°C. Starting with the given equation

$$W = \frac{100}{X}(\varepsilon L \Delta T + M_o) + t$$

and substituting,

$$W = [100/12.5][(0.0000065 \text{ mm/mm/°C})(6500 \text{ mm})(60°C) + (6500 \text{ mm})(0.0002)] + 6 \text{ mm}$$

we have

$$W = 36.7 \text{ mm}$$

This is very wide—nearly 1½″—which would make sealant installation difficult. If a sealant with a ±25% movement capability were used instead, the joint would only need to be 22 mm wide, which could be rounded up to 25 mm. ∎

COEFFICIENTS OF EXPANSION OF COMMON BUILDING MATERIALS

		in/in/°F	mm/mm/°C
Wood (seasoned)			
Douglas fir	Parallel to grain	0.0000021	0.0000038
	Perpendicular to grain	0.000032	0.000058
Pine	Parallel to grain	0.0000030	0.0000054
	Perpendicular to grain	0.000019	0.000034
Oak	Parallel to grain	0.0000027	0.0000049
	Perpendicular to grain	0.000030	0.000054
Masonry			
Limestone		0.0000044	0.0000079
Granite		0.0000047	0.0000085
Marble		0.0000073	0.0000131
Brick (average)		0.0000036	0.0000065
Concrete masonry units		0.0000052	0.0000094
Concrete			
Normal weight concrete		0.0000055	0.0000099
Metals			
Steel		0.0000065	0.0000117
Stainless steel, 18–8		0.0000099	0.0000178
Aluminum		0.0000128	0.0000231
Copper		0.0000093	0.0000168
Finish Materials			
Gypsum board		0.000009	0.0000162
Gypsum plaster, sand		0.000007	0.0000126
Glass		0.0000050	0.0000090
Acrylic glazing sheet		0.0000410	0.0000742
Polycarbonate glazing sheet		0.0000440	0.0000796
Polyethylene		0.000085	0.000153
Polyvinyl chloride (PVC, vinyl)		0.000040	0.000072

FUNCTION:
CONTROLLING AIR LEAKAGE

L E A K I N G air can cause uncomfortable drafts. It wastes heated and cooled air that represent lost energy. It can cause condensate or frost to form in winter where warmer, more humid indoor air leaks out into cold building cavities. Air leaks are also sound leaks that can destroy the acoustical effectiveness of building enclosures. Air leaks can transmit a fire's heat and smoke from one part of a building to another. Air leaks can bring dust and insects into a building. And leaking air can transport rainwater through a wall, window, or door.

The principle behind airtight detailing is similar to that for watertight detailing: In order for air to penetrate through a building assembly, three conditions must all occur at the same time:

1. There must be an opening through the assembly.
2. There must be air present at the opening.
3. There must be a force to move the air through the opening.

If any one of these three conditions is not met, air will not penetrate the assembly.

Despite the similarity in principle, however, the detailing strategy for controlling air leakage is rather different from that for controlling water leakage. We are submerged in air, so we can't keep it away from openings. Of the forces that move air through openings, convection and wind pressure are largely beyond the control of the building designer. Pressure differentials caused by heating, cooling, and ventilating equipment within the building are consciously regulated in some large buildings to minimize the loss of conditioned air to the outdoors, but not in most buildings. Therefore, airflow through a building assembly must be controlled primarily by closing openings in the building assembly to the best of our ability. The detail patterns that relate to this are the following:

Air Barrier Surface (page 38)
Weatherstripped Crack (page 40)

In addition to these two patterns, we have already considered another pattern that is useful in controlling air leakage:

Sealant Joints and Gaskets (page 31)

It is important to recognize that air barrier surfaces, weatherstrips, sealant joints, and gaskets are all elements that must withstand wind forces. Therefore, they must be designed with sufficient structural strength and stiffness for this task.

AIR BARRIER SURFACE

A building should be wrapped in an airtight surface in order to reduce air leakage through the many different types of small openings that are commonly present in the exterior walls and roof.

1. The exterior surfaces of a building of wood light frame construction are riddled with openings, primarily the cracks between sheathing panels and the cracks around window and door units. These allow air to filter through electrical boxes, baseboards, and door and window casings into or out of a building. The air leakage along these paths can be reduced greatly by covering the sheathing, just beneath the siding or roofing, with an airtight sheet material. A traditional and fairly effective form of air barrier surface consists of asphalt-saturated paper. Because the paper (usually referred to as "felt," "building paper," or "tar paper") is furnished in rolls only 36″ (900 mm) wide, it is easy to install, but the resulting air barrier has numerous seams that can leak air unless they are laboriously sealed with asphalt mastic. A contemporary alternative is an air barrier sheet made of nonwoven polypropylene fibers. This sheet, sometimes referred to as "house wrap," is manufactured in such a way that water vapor can pass through but air and liquid water cannot. It is so thin and light in weight that it is usually furnished in rolls that are 9′ (2.7 m) wide, allowing each story of a simple residential-scale building to be wrapped in a single horizontal band. This greatly reduces the number of seams. The structural resistance to wind loading is furnished not by the air barrier sheet itself, but by the materials between which it is sandwiched—for example, the wall sheathing on one side and the siding on the other.

2. In masonry-faced buildings of cavity wall construction, the air barrier is

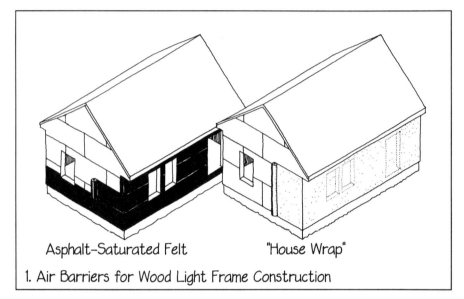

Asphalt-Saturated Felt   "House Wrap"

1. Air Barriers for Wood Light Frame Construction

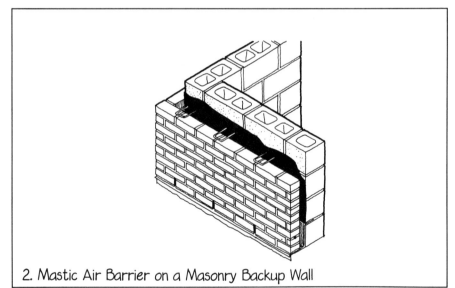

2. Mastic Air Barrier on a Masonry Backup Wall

generally placed on the outside of the inner, structural layer of the wall. If the inner layer is a wythe of concrete masonry, it is sometimes parged with a layer of portland cement plaster on the side facing the continuous wall cavity to reduce air leakage. Preferably, this surface should be coated with a heavy asphaltic mastic or with horizontal strips of a manufactured membrane that are cemented to the wall and to one another at the seams. In any of these cases, it is very important to maintain the integrity of the air barrier by sealing carefully around the edges of the backup wall where it joins columns, spandrel beams, slabs, window openings, and roof edges.

If air leakage requirements are not stringent, as in some mild climates, the concrete masonry alone will serve as a slightly porous air barrier. The edges of the backup wall must still be sealed.

3. If the masonry facing is backed up by a wall of steel studs and gypsum sheathing, the minimum air barrier that should be detailed is a layer of asphalt-saturated felt applied to the outside of the sheathing before the masonry ties are attached. For greater security against air and water leaks, the sheathing can be coated instead with a fiber-containing asphaltic mastic or strips of manufactured membrane. These transform the sheathing into a highly effective air barrier, and provide protection against water for the materials in the backup wall. The fibers in the mastic help it bridge cracks and holes in the sheathing and adjust to small amounts of movement in the sheathing. ■

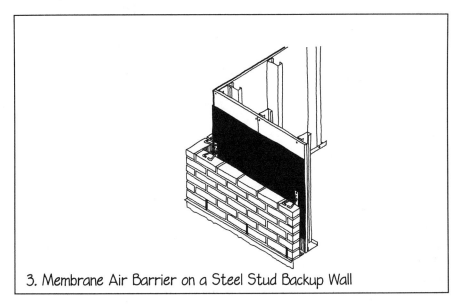

3. Membrane Air Barrier on a Steel Stud Backup Wall

WEATHERSTRIPPED CRACK

Cracks around doors and window sashes need to be wide enough to allow an operating clearance. To keep air from blowing through, various kinds of weatherstrip are installed in the cracks.

1. One of the oldest and simplest kinds of weatherstrip is spring weatherstrip of bronze or plastic that adjusts automatically to the width and contour of a crack.

2. The interlocking weatherstrip is more effective and much more laborious to install than spring weatherstrip. It is made of thin strips of spring bronze.

3. Interlocking weatherstrip details have been updated with the use of rigid components of extruded aluminum. With the addition of a synthetic rubber tubular compression gasket, a high degree of airtightness can be achieved.

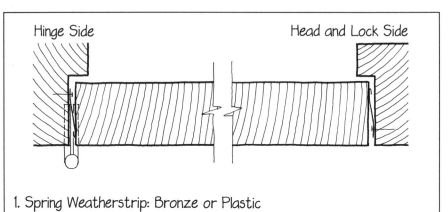

Hinge Side   Head and Lock Side

1. Spring Weatherstrip: Bronze or Plastic

Hinge Side   Head and Lock Side

2. Spring Bronze Interlocking Weatherstrip

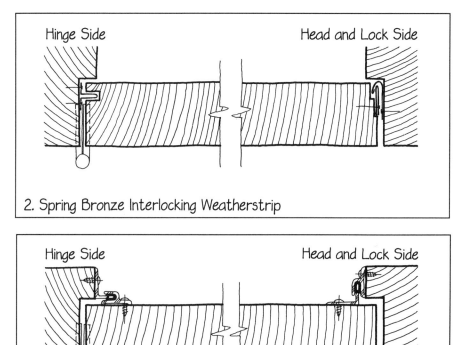

Hinge Side   Head and Lock Side

3. Rigid Aluminum Interlocking Weatherstrip

4. Compression gaskets of synthetic rubber have many uses in weatherstripping. They can be designed to seal very large cracks or very small ones, and adaptations are available for every conceivable type of door, including overhead garage doors and airplane hangar doors. Two types are shown here: a tubular gasket of solid rubber and a solid gasket of sponge rubber.

5. Pile weatherstrip resembles a small, continuous brush with very dense, fine bristles. The pile is usually made from a synthetic fiber with excellent wear characteristics, but eventually it will require replacement due to abrasion or compression of the fibers. Pile weatherstrip, because of its low friction, is one of the few types that works well in joints of sliding windows and doors. The pile is generally very short and cannot tolerate much dimensional variation in the crack when compared with spring bronze or synthetic rubber weatherstripping.

6. Door bottom weatherstrip may be of any of the types already shown. In addition to the three examples shown here, aluminum thresholds that interlock with weatherstrip on the door bottom are also available. In particularly demanding applications, an automatic door bottom may be used. This is a mechanism that lifts the weatherstrip above the sill when the door is opened and presses it down against the sill just as the door is closed, reducing friction and wear and assuring a very tight seal. It is actuated by a small plunger that bears against the jamb when the door is closed.

Weatherstripping devices are manufactured in a wide range of materials and configurations, often using combinations of the types shown here to meet particular demands for differing door and window types and for sealing against wind, smoke, or sound. Manufacturers' catalogs are the best source of up-to-date information. ∎

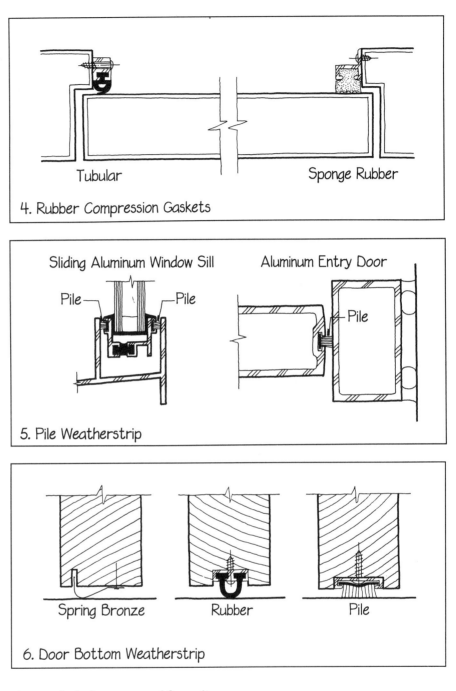

4. Rubber Compression Gaskets

Tubular   Sponge Rubber

5. Pile Weatherstrip

Sliding Aluminum Window Sill   Aluminum Entry Door

Pile — — Pile   Pile

6. Door Bottom Weatherstrip

Spring Bronze   Rubber   Pile

FUNCTION:
CONTROLLING HEAT FLOW

E X C E S S I V E heat flow through building assemblies results in wasted energy, unnecessarily high investment in oversized heating and cooling equipment, water damage in winter from condensation and frost on interior surfaces, and discomfort for the occupants of the building. In detailing a building, there are three basic ways of minimizing heat transmission and maximizing thermal comfort:

1. Control the conduction of heat through the building envelope.

2. Control the radiation of heat onto and through the building envelope.

3. Utilize thermal mass to regulate the flow of heat through the building envelope.

Each of these ways generates its own detail patterns.

1. CONTROLLING THE CONDUCTION OF HEAT

Most building materials are dense and conduct heat rapidly. In assembling layers of material to make a wall, roof, floor, foundation, window, or door, we almost always include one or more low-density materials with low thermal conductivities.

Detailing patterns that relate to controlling conduction of heat include

Thermal Insulation (page 44)

Thermal Break (page 45)

Multiple Glazing (page 49)

2. CONTROLLING THE RADIATION OF HEAT

There are two very different sources of radiated heat that we must control in a building: One is the sun; the other is warm surfaces and objects within and around the building.

Radiant heat from the sun strikes the building from a single direction at any given moment, but that direction changes constantly with time of day and time of year in a pattern that we can predict with great accuracy. Solar radiation is transmitted across a broad spectrum of wavelengths. Most of its energy lies within the visible spectrum and the shorter infrared wavelengths. These wavelengths can be reflected efficiently by both white surfaces and bright metallic surfaces. Solar radiation can also be blocked effectively with simple shading devices.

The detail patterns that relate to controlling the radiation of solar heat include

White and Bright Surfaces (page 50)

Reflective Glazing (page 51)

Warm surfaces and objects in and around buildings radiate heat in all directions, primarily in the longer infrared wavelengths. These wavelengths are reflected efficiently only by bright metallic surfaces. The detail pattern that relates to controlling radiation from warm building surfaces and objects is

Reflective Surface and Airspace (page 52)

3. UTILIZING THERMAL MASS

When exposed to warm air or solar radiation, large masses of such dense materials as soil, masonry, concrete, and water absorb and store considerable quantities of heat. They do so over a period of time that depends on the thickness of the material and its thermal properties; in a building, this period typically can be as much as 12 hours. In hot climates with large temperature differences between day and night, we can turn this delay to our advantage. We detail the building in such a way that its thermal mass absorbs heat during the day and gives it off again at night, acting to maintain a comfortable temperature range inside the building while the outside air temperature fluctuates over a much wider range. Thermal mass can also be useful in allowing a building to receive large amounts of solar radiation or heat from machinery during the day without overheating and then giving this heat back to the building at night when the building would otherwise tend to become too cool. The detail pattern that relates to utilizing thermal mass is

Outside-Insulated Thermal Mass (page 54)

THERMAL INSULATION

We use thermal insulating materials as components of the walls, ceilings, and floors of a building in order to reduce energy consumption and to maintain interior surfaces at comfortable temperatures.

1. Insulating materials are very low in density. This makes them fragile and easily damaged. Except for carpets, draperies, tapestries, upholstery, and clothing, insulating materials are also unattractive to the eye. Foam plastic insulations are combustible and must be covered with fire-resistant materials. Foam plastics also degrade rapidly when exposed to light. For these reasons, we nearly always detail building assemblies so that the insulating materials are sandwiched in the middle, protected and hidden from view by exterior and interior finish layers.

2. Insulating materials vary in their efficiencies: An inch of phenolic foam has a much higher resistance to heat flow than an inch of lightweight concrete. The accompanying table lists the thermal resistances of common insulating materials. The detailer's task includes selecting insulating materials that can furnish the required thermal resistance in the amount of space available within the building assembly that is being detailed.

3. The least expensive insulating materials, measured in terms of units of thermal resistance per dollar of installed cost, are generally those made of glass fibers. These can be used only in dry locations, because they lose their insulating value when they become wet. Glass fiber batts should not be compressed, because their effectiveness depends on their thickness and fluffiness.

4. Insulation is often required in wet locations, such as on the outside of a foundation wall, inside a masonry cavity wall, or in a protected membrane roof assembly. Closed-cell polystyrene foam is the one material that retains most of its insulating value when wetted over very long periods of time.

5. In climates with cool or cold winters, thermal insulation should *always* be installed with a vapor retarder on its interior side. See *Warm-side Vapor Retarder* (page 60), where the concept of a vapor retarder is explained and several examples of thermal insulation are shown.

∎

THERMAL RESISTANCE OF COMMON INSULATING MATERIALS

	$hr\text{-}ft^2\text{-}°F/BTU\text{-}in$	$m\text{-}°K/W$
Cellulose fibers, loose fill	3.2	23
Cellulose fibers, sprayed	3.5	24
Concrete, insulating, 30 lb/ft³	1.1	7.7
Glass fibers, normal batts	3.2	23
Glass fibers, high-density batts	4.3	29
Glass fibers, boards	4.0–4.7	27–32
Glass fibers, loose fill	2.2	15
Glass foam board	2.8	20
Perlite, loose fill	2.7	19
Phenolic foam	8.3	58
Polystyrene foam, extruded	5.0	35
Polystyrene foam, expanded bead board	4.0	28
Polyurethane or polyisocyanurate board	5.6	39
Polyurethane, sprayed	5.0–6.0	35–42

THERMAL BREAK

A thermal break is a strip of insulating material that is inserted into a building assembly to prevent rapid heat conduction through dense, highly conductive materials such as metal and masonry.

1. The spaces between steel studs and steel rafters can be insulated effectively and economically with glass fiber batts, but the steel framing members themselves will continue to conduct heat through the wall or roof at a very high rate. The framing members in this case are referred to as thermal bridges, meaning that they furnish a way for heat to flow easily through an otherwise well-insulated assembly, much as a road bridge furnishes a way for traffic to flow readily across an otherwise impassable obstacle. In detailing, we block a potential thermal bridge with a thermal break, which is made of a material with a low thermal conductivity. In the example shown here, the thermal bridges are steel studs in a wall, and the thermal breaks consist of strips of plastic foam that are placed between the exterior cladding material and the studs. Although one of these thermal breaks may not insulate the framing member to the same thermal resistance value as the insulated space between the members, it greatly reduces the flow of heat through it, and it raises the temperature of the indoor side of the member enough so that moisture will not condense on it. The steel screws that pass through the thermal break constitute another set of thermal bridges, but they are so small in cross section that little heat flows through them. ▷

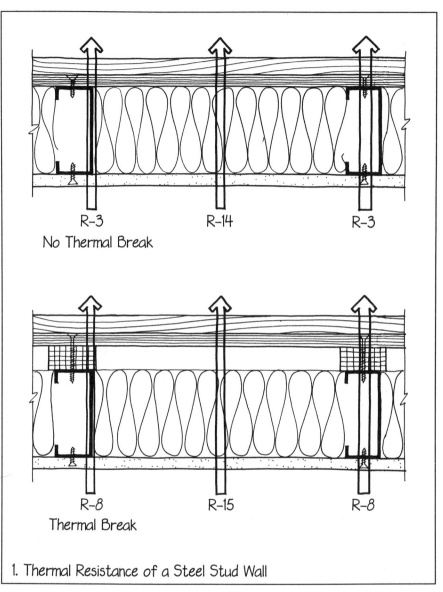

No Thermal Break

Thermal Break

1. Thermal Resistance of a Steel Stud Wall

2. Aluminum conducts heat even more readily than steel. This can be a problem in aluminum window frames, door frames, and cladding components in cold climates. Where aluminum passes continuously from outdoors to indoors in these components, large quantities of water and frost often condense on the cold inner surface in winter. To prevent this from happening, several types of thermal breaks have been developed for use in aluminum members. In the example shown here, a hard plastic is cast into a groove in the aluminum member during manufacture. Then the groove is "debridged" (the thermal bridge is removed) by milling away the aluminum at the bottom of the groove. This leaves only the low-conductivity plastic thermal break to connect the indoor side of the member to the outdoor side.

3. A second type of thermal break for an aluminum cladding assembly is a simple plastic or rubber strip that is inserted between the outer and inner layers of a mullion during assembly. The aluminum screws remain as thermal bridges, but they are too small in area to conduct much heat. A third type of thermal break for an aluminum assembly is the use of small, intermittent plastic clips that mount the interior cover components to the mullion.

4. Although wood is not highly conductive of heat as compared to metals, wood studs and rafters do conduct heat much more rapidly than the insulated cavities between them. In some highly energy efficient buildings, plastic foam insulation is added across either the outside or the inside of the framing members as a thermal break. This may be done either as a continuous layer, as shown here, or as narrow strips of foam applied to the edges of the framing members only.

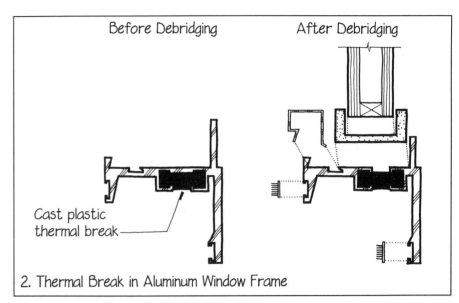

2. Thermal Break in Aluminum Window Frame

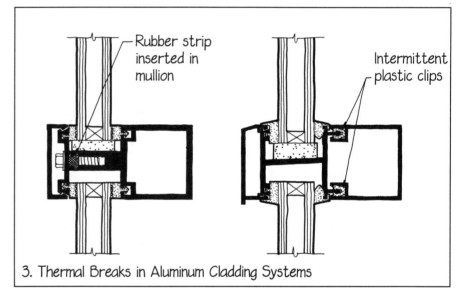

3. Thermal Breaks in Aluminum Cladding Systems

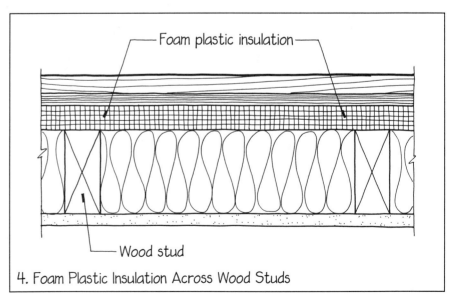

4. Foam Plastic Insulation Across Wood Studs

5. There are also other ways to insulate the studs in wood light frame construction. One is to apply horizontal furring strips and a second layer of insulating batts across the outside or inside face of the studs. Another is to construct another stud wall just outside the first, leaving an inch or so of airspace between the studs to act as a thermal break.

6. Hollow concrete masonry units can be insulated by filling their cores with either a granular fill insulation or plastic foam inserts, but the webs of the units act as thermal bridges. Many different schemes have been invented to break these bridges. Several kinds of proprietary masonry units have been designed with webs that are as small in cross section as is structurally feasible, to reduce the thermal bridging effect.

7. A generic approach to the thermal bridging problem in concrete masonry is to furr the masonry wall on the inside and to insulate between the furring strips. ▷

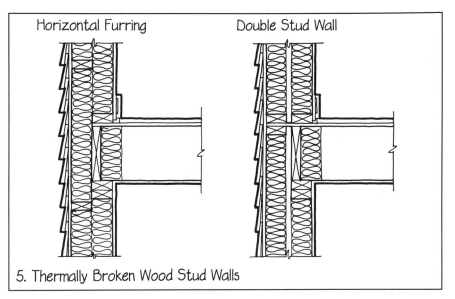

Horizontal Furring   Double Stud Wall

5. Thermally Broken Wood Stud Walls

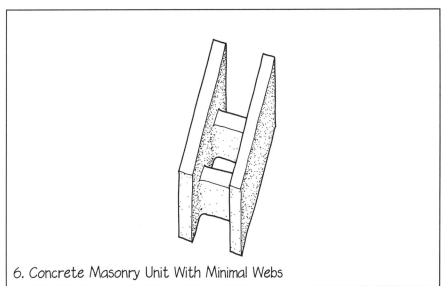

6. Concrete Masonry Unit With Minimal Webs

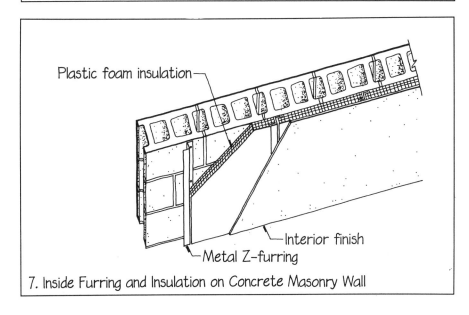

Plastic foam insulation

Interior finish

Metal Z-furring

7. Inside Furring and Insulation on Concrete Masonry Wall

8. Another generic approach is to clad the outside of the wall with an exterior insulation and finish system (EIFS) consisting of a continuous layer of plastic foam board insulation adhered to the outside of the masonry wall and coated with a synthetic stucco finish.

9. In a masonry cavity wall construction, a continuous layer of foam insulation can be placed inside the cavity to break the thermal bridges in the concrete masonry units (see page 237). ■

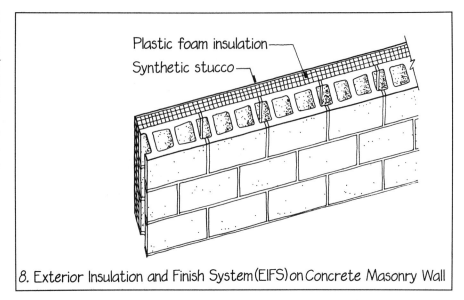

Plastic foam insulation
Synthetic stucco

8. Exterior Insulation and Finish System (EIFS) on Concrete Masonry Wall

MULTIPLE GLAZING

Glass is a poor thermal insulator. For more thermally efficient windows, two or more layers of glass can be assembled with spaces between.

1. A single sheet of glass conducts heat about 20 times as rapidly as a well-insulated wall. If a second sheet of glass is added with an airspace between the two sheets (double glazing), this rapid heat flow is cut in half. If a third sheet of glass and a second airspace are added (triple glazing), the overall flow is about a third of what it was for a single sheet of glass. The thickness of the airspace, provided it is at least ⅜″ (9 mm), makes relatively little difference in its insulating ability. Multiple glazing can be created by adding a removable sheet of glass on the outside (a storm window) or inside of the window. In most cases, however, it is more satisfactory to use double or triple glazing units that have been assembled at the factory. These units have a hermetic seal around the edge, a fill of dry air between the panes of glass, and an insert of silica gel crystals in the edge seal to remove any stray moisture from the trapped air. This avoids problems of dust and condensation between the panes, as well as the need to wash the interior surfaces.

2. The major problem with conventional multiple glazing units is that they are still highly conductive of heat when compared with a well-insulated wall. More sheets of glass and more airspaces may be added, but the glazing unit becomes thick and heavy, and each successive layer that is added to the assembly does less than the one before to contribute to its insulating qualities. Therefore, several other paths are often followed to increase the thermal resistance of multiple glazing

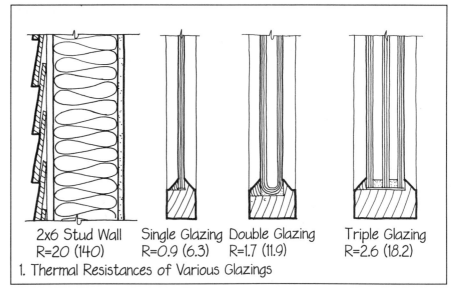

2x6 Stud Wall R=20 (140) Single Glazing R=0.9 (6.3) Double Glazing R=1.7 (11.9) Triple Glazing R=2.6 (18.2)

1. Thermal Resistances of Various Glazings

units. Many manufacturers of glass and windows utilize one or more of the following.

a. Interior glazing sheets of very thin, durable, highly transparent plastic film. These add airspaces while adding little thickness and almost no weight.

b. Low-conductivity gas fills instead of dry air between the panes, using gases such as argon or sulfur hexafluoride.

c. Low-emissivity (Low-E) coatings on inside surfaces of glass. These coatings are usually formulated for use in cold climates, to be highly transparent to solar wavelengths of light and heat, but to reflect the longer infrared wavelengths that are characteristic of heat radiated from the interior of a building. For use in climates and buildings where summer cooling is the primary problem, other formulas are used to produce coatings that reflect most solar heat.

d. Edge spacer details between the sheets of glass that are less conductive of heat than the conventional metal spline.

At this writing, the most thermally efficient multiple glazing units, by utilizing a combination of these devices, achieve an insulating value of R-8 (56)—about 40% as good as that of a well-insulated wall. For more information on the thermal resistance of various types of glazing, see manufacturers' literature for windows and glazing. When we are evaluating alternative types of windows for their thermal resistances, it is important that we compare test values for entire window units, rather than for center of glazing. Window unit values include the effects of the glass, edge seal, and frame, while center-of-glazing values relate only to the glass itself. ∎

WHITE AND BRIGHT SURFACES

Bright metallic surfaces and bright white surfaces are very effective in reflecting the heat of the sun from the exterior of a building.

1. The accompanying table indicates the ability of various surfaces to reflect solar heat. A whitewashed or white-painted building will remain substantially cooler in summer than a dark-colored building. A roof covering that is bright white or bright metal will be very helpful in keeping the sun's heat out of a building, especially when compared with a black or dark-colored roof. A curtain wall that has a white or bright metallic finish will not be subject to as great a range of temperatures as a darker one, making it less subject to extremes of expansion and contraction. Very light colors are somewhat effective in reflecting solar heat. Medium to dark colors tend to absorb solar heat rather than reflect it. White or metallic surfaces that have oxidized, chalked, or grown dirty become absorptive rather than reflective, so regular cleaning and recoating are important.

APPROXIMATE PERCENTAGE OF SOLAR RADIATION REFLECTED BY VARIOUS SURFACES

Surface	Percentage
Bright Aluminum	80%
Bright copper or brass	70%
White paint	70%
White Concrete	60%
White marble	55%
Aluminum paint	50%
Steel, galvanized, new	45%
Steel, galvanized, weathered	30%
Concrete, natural gray	35%
Red clay tiles	30%
Brown, red, green paint	30%
Black paint	10%

REFLECTIVE GLAZING

Windows that are reflective can turn away most solar heat before it enters a building.

1. Clear glass transmits most of the sunlight that shines upon it, and most of the solar heat as well. Clear glass windows that are poorly oriented and unshaded can be major sources of summertime discomfort and high cooling costs in buildings. Tinted glass can reduce the solar heat transmission of a window by a quarter to a half. Reflective glass, which has a metallic coating on one surface, can reflect solar heat before it enters the building and is extremely effective in maintaining comfortable interior temperatures at low cooling cost.

2. When choosing glass, use the "shading coefficient" figures from manufacturers' catalogs to evaluate the relative abilities of various types of glass to reduce solar heat gain. A shading coefficient of 0.35, for example, means that the glass will admit only 35% as much solar heat as double-strength clear glass and half as much heat as glass that has a shading coefficient of 0.70. The shading coefficient of reflective glazing depends mostly on the density of its metallic coating.

3. The detailer should keep in mind some potential problems that are often associated with reflective glazing: It can reflect the sun into the eyes of pedestrians and motorists. It can cause solar overheating problems in adjacent buildings and outdoor spaces by reflecting sunlight onto surfaces that would not otherwise receive it. And, while reflective glass gives complete privacy to the interior of the building during the day, at night it appears from the outside as dark but transparent glass, and the interior of the building is fully visible to passersby if the lights are on. ∎

REFLECTIVE SURFACE AND AIRSPACE

A bright metal sheet or foil is an excellent reflector of radiant heat energy at any wavelength and can be used within a roof or wall assembly as an insulating material. To be effective, however, it must face a clear airspace that is at least ½″ (13 mm) thick.

1. A bright aluminum foil in a wall or roof construction with a 1″ (25 mm) airspace on one side has an insulating value of approximately R-2 in conventional units, which is R-14 in SI units. If the foil is bright on both faces and has airspaces on both sides, its insulating value is approximately twice as great.

2. A bright metal foil sandwiched tightly between two pieces of building material has no insulating value. A reflective foil used as a facing on an insulating batt has no insulating value if it is installed tightly against the back of the interior wall finish material. If the wall finish is furred out to provide an airspace, however, the foil facing adds considerably to the thermal resistance of the insulating batt. Similarly, foil-backed gypsum wallboard gains no insulating value from the foil if the board is installed tightly against batts of insulation. If the board is spaced away from the insulation on furring strips, or if there is space behind the board between the wall studs, the foil becomes effective.

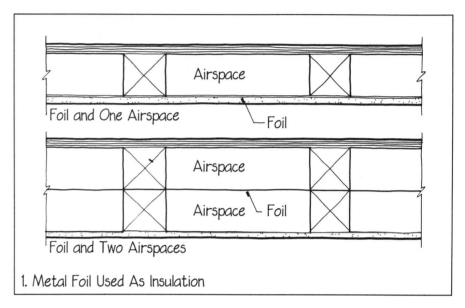

Foil and One Airspace — Foil

Foil and Two Airspaces — Foil

1. Metal Foil Used As Insulation

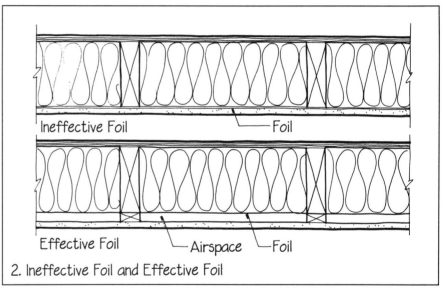

Ineffective Foil — Foil

Effective Foil — Airspace — Foil

2. Ineffective Foil and Effective Foil

3. A bright foil surface makes an excellent radiant heat barrier between rafters in a roof. Several products of this type are commercially available. The one shown here is a bright aluminum foil laminated to a cardboard backing, configured so that it forms an air passage just beneath the roof sheathing of a wood light frame building. This is particularly effective in keeping solar heat from being transmitted from the roof into the rooms below, blocking as much as 40% of summer heat gain. The airspace between the foil and the sheathing serves both as a clear space into which one side of the foil can reflect and as a ventilated airspace to carry away solar heat. In winter, the foil acts as additional insulation to retard the heat flow out of the building into the cold outside air. It does this, not only because foil is a poor absorber (that is, a good reflector) of radiant energy but also because it is a poor emitter, meaning that it does not radiate heat effectively into space. In fact, its rate of absorbance and its rate of emittance are exactly the same, meaning that it doesn't make any difference

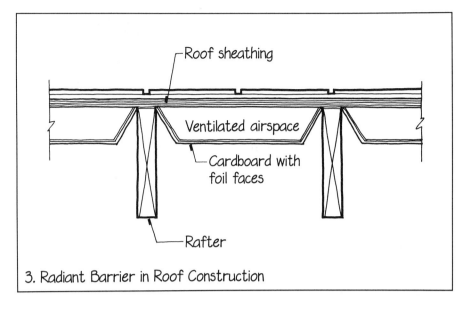

3. Radiant Barrier in Roof Construction

which way heat is trying to flow through a foil that faces an airspace; the foil will be equally effective in blocking heat flow in either direction.

4. The reflective qualities of a bright metal surface diminish rapidly as the surface becomes dusty or tarnished. A foil in a dead, dry airspace will generally stay cleaner and retain its thermal effectiveness better than one in a circulating stream of air.

5. Metal foils are excellent vapor retarders and should be installed on the warm side of a wall or roof assembly (see *Warm-side Vapor Retarder*, page 60). If a foil must be used on the cold side, it should be perforated to allow water vapor to pass freely. ∎

OUTSIDE-INSULATED THERMAL MASS

The ability of such massive materials as concrete, masonry, and earth to store large quantities of heat can be harnessed to create buildings that are easy to heat and cool.

1. The thick walls and heavy roof of an uninsulated adobe building in a desert climate absorb large quantities of heat during the day, both from the sun and from the hot outdoor air. This heat warms the adobe material layer by layer, starting from the outside and working its way slowly toward the inside. After the sun sets, however, the outside air quickly cools off, the night sky becomes an absorber of heat, and the outside of the adobe structure begins to radiate and convect its stored heat back to the outdoors. If the wall or roof is thick enough, this happens before the heat of the day has traveled all the way through the adobe to the interior of the building. Much of the stored heat that is advancing through the walls and roof does a slow U-turn and dissipates to the outdoors during the cold night. The interior of the building stays within a relatively narrow and comfortable range of air temperatures. The adobe functions as thermal

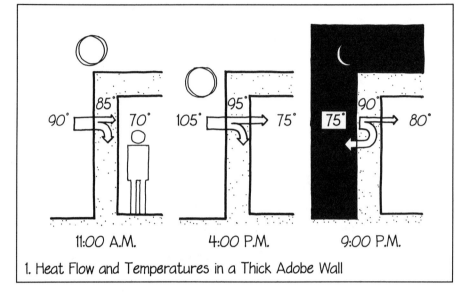

1. Heat Flow and Temperatures in a Thick Adobe Wall

mass, a large volume of heat-absorbing material that can be used to moderate interior temperatures.

2. In a hot, humid climate the outdoor air does not cool off very much at night and uninsulated thermal mass is of little use. Uninsulated thermal mass is also useless in a winter climate that is cold both day and night. It is only effective in a climate that features warm days and cool nights year-round.

3. If a layer of thermal insulation is added to the outside of a massive building such as an ordinary masonry or concrete structure, the mass becomes effective in almost any climate because it becomes a thermal "flywheel" that stabilizes the interior temperature of the building despite short-term inputs of heat. A building with outside-insulated thermal mass can receive large amounts of solar heat through windows during a winter day and still maintain comfortable indoor air temperatures, because the concrete and masonry absorb and store much of the heat. When the interior air cools down at night, the mass slowly gives back this stored solar heat to stabilize the indoor temperature. Heat-producing machinery that runs for only part of the day can be operated without overheating the building; much of the excess heat is saved in the thermal mass of the structure for use when the building needs it. The outside layer of insulation also has the advantage of stabilizing the thermal movements in the frame and surfaces of the building, eliminating most of the expansion and contraction that are characteristic of building structures exposed to outdoor air. One common example of outside-insulated thermal mass is a reinforced concrete frame building that is completely enclosed by well-insulated curtain wall panels. Another is a masonry bearing wall building that is clad with exterior insulation and finish system (EIFS). A third example is a wood frame house with large masonry fireplaces or heavy ceramic tile floors.

4. Thermal mass will not control interior air temperature as closely as a thermostat and a mechanical heating and cooling system, but during the spring and the fall it can maintain a daily temperature swing of only a few degrees in either direction from an optimum temperature, and it will help the building's comfort control system maintain comfortable temperatures during the rest of the year.

5. A building with outside-insulated thermal mass should be designed in close collaboration with the designer of the building's heating and cooling system. A thermally massive design may be inappropriate for a building that is heated or cooled intermittently, such as a house of worship that is only heated on Sundays, or a weekend ski cottage, because the thermal mass makes the building very slow to warm up.

6. In order to be fully effective, thermal mass must be exposed directly to the indoor air. Carpets, suspended ceilings, and furred walls all reduce the effectiveness of a massive building. ■

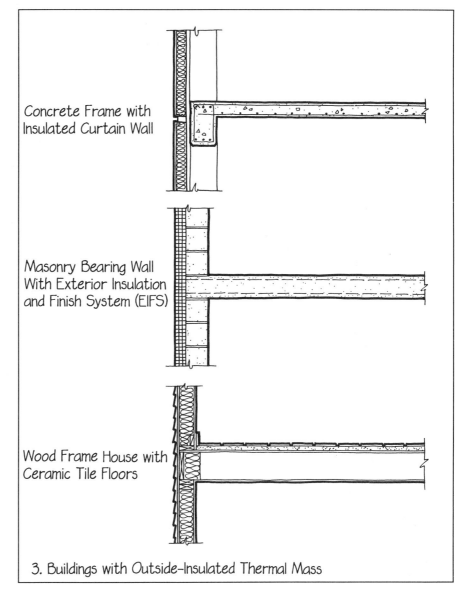

Concrete Frame with Insulated Curtain Wall

Masonry Bearing Wall With Exterior Insulation and Finish System (EIFS)

Wood Frame House with Ceramic Tile Floors

3. Buildings with Outside-Insulated Thermal Mass

FUNCTION:
CONTROLLING WATER VAPOR

W A T E R vapor is a colorless, odorless gas that is always present in the air. Water vapor is of interest to the detailer because of the problems that it can create if it condenses on or within a component of a building. Condensation occurs when moist air is cooled below its dew point temperature, either by mixing with colder air or by contacting cold surfaces. Condensation can cause fogging or frosting of the surfaces of glass and metal cladding components. It can saturate insulating materials in walls and roofs and render them ineffective. It can create drips, puddles, water stains, and fungus growth inside a building. It can blister and rupture paint coatings and roof membranes on the outside of a building.

Water vapor inside a building is produced mainly by cooking, bathing, washing, industrial processes, and human metabolic activity. In a new building, water vapor may also come from wood, concrete, plaster, and masonry work that are still giving off excess moisture. A building's mechanical system is often designed to reduce the amount of water vapor inside a building by ventilation, by dehumidifying the air with an air conditioning system, or both. But whether or not such mechanical systems are installed, there are four precautions we take in detailing to avoid water vapor problems in a building:

1. We use thermal insulation, multiple glazing, and thermal breaks to keep interior surfaces at temperatures above the dew point of the air.

2. We use a warm-side vapor retarder to keep air and water vapor from reaching surfaces and spaces that are cool enough to cause condensation to occur.

3. In every building assembly, we ventilate the portion that lies on the cold side of a vapor retarder to be sure that no moisture is trapped there.

4. Where condensation is likely to occur despite any such precautions, we provide a gravity-driven system to catch and remove condensate before it can create problems.

These actions translate into four detail patterns:

Warm Interior Surfaces (page 58)

Warm-side Vapor Retarder (page 60)

Vapor Ventilation (page 63)

Condensate Drainage (page 66)

WARM INTERIOR SURFACES

To prevent condensation, surfaces inside a building should be detailed so that their temperatures will always remain above the dew point temperature of the air.

1. When interior air humidity is high, moisture condenses on the outside of a cold water pipe and drips onto whatever is below. To prevent this, we wrap the pipe with thermal insulation. The outside of the thermal insulation is at a temperature that is very close to room temperature, so condensation does not occur. However, it is very important to cover the outside of the pipe insulation with a vapor retarder, such as plastic sheeting or metal foil, to prevent water vapor from moving through the insulation to condense on the cold surface of the pipe. Without the vapor retarder, the insulation would soon become saturated with water and the dripping would begin again (see *Warm-side Vapor Retarder*, page 60).

2. In a similar fashion, the tank or cistern on the back of a water closet becomes cold because of the temperature of the water that it contains, and drips condensate onto the floor under humid conditions. This is messy and can cause decay of the floor structure. There are two ways of tackling this problem: One is to install a mixing valve on the pipe that supplies water to the water closet. The mixing valve adds enough hot water to keep the temperature of the outside of the tank above the dew point of the air. The other approach is not so wasteful of energy: We simply add an insulating liner of plastic foam to the inside of the tank. This isolates the cold water from the wall of the tank so that the wall stays at a temperature above the dew point of the air. The tank wall is made of porcelain or plastic, neither of which is permeable to water vapor. Thus, the tank itself serves as a vapor retarder.

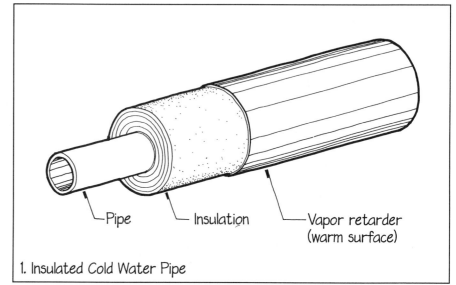

Pipe Insulation Vapor retarder (warm surface)

1. Insulated Cold Water Pipe

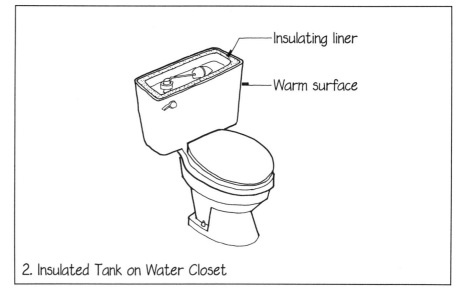

Insulating liner

Warm surface

2. Insulated Tank on Water Closet

3. Air-conditioning ducts that pass through nonconditioned space often have surface temperatures below the dew point of the surrounding air. They must be wrapped with insulation and an outside vapor retarder to prevent condensation. Ducts that run within the conditioned space carry air that is only slightly cooler than the room air, so condensation does not occur and insulation is not required.

4. A basement wall of concrete or masonry stays cool in the summer because of the vast thermal mass of the soil outside. Even a basement that is in dry soil will often become damp and musty because of water condensing on the cool interior side of the walls. The best answer to this problem is to use plastic foam to insulate the basement wall on the outside, between the wall and the soil. This allows the interior

surface of the wall to stay near the interior air temperature so condensation will not occur.

Often, however, it is necessary to insulate a basement wall on the inside, especially when retrofit or remodeling work is being done. This is usually done by furring the wall and adding thermal insulation between the furring strips. A vapor retarder should be installed just beneath the interior wall finish to keep out moist air. Unfortunately this leaves a potential problem unsolved: Basements also tend to leak water from the soil outside, and any leakage will be trapped behind the vapor retarder and insulation where it can cause decay, rust, and mildew. There is no good answer to this problem. We can only dampproof and drain the foundation carefully on the outside (see *Foundation Drainage*, page 21), and hope for the best.

5. Exterior walls, roofs, window frames, and glass can become cold enough in winter to condense moisture on their interior surfaces. Three detailing patterns in the preceding section of this book, *Thermal Insulation* (page 44), *Thermal Break* (page 45), and *Multiple Glazing* (page 49), are often used to keep these interior surfaces warm enough to prevent condensation. There are standard calculation procedures for finding the temperature at which condensation is likely to occur in a building and for determining the amount of thermal resistance necessary in a wall, window, or roof to maintain its interior surface above this temperature. While relatively simple, these procedures are beyond the scope of this book. They are presented in any standard reference book on the heating and cooling of buildings. The detailer may perform these procedures directly or consult with the engineer who is designing the mechanical systems for the building. ■

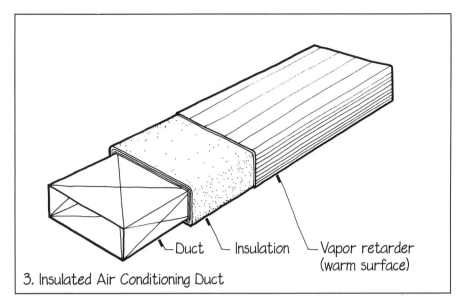

Duct · Insulation · Vapor retarder (warm surface)

3. Insulated Air Conditioning Duct

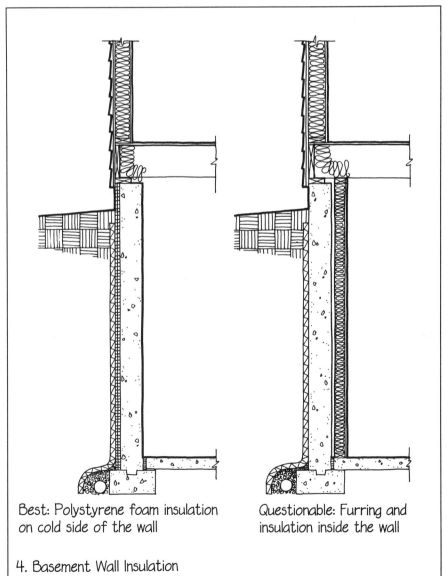

Best: Polystyrene foam insulation on cold side of the wall

Questionable: Furring and insulation inside the wall

4. Basement Wall Insulation

WARM-SIDE VAPOR RETARDER

A vapor retarder sheet should always be installed on the warm side of any insulating material used in a building.

1. Because warm air generally contains more water vapor than cool air, water vapor almost always enters a layer of thermal insulation from the warm side. Somewhere within the layer of insulation, this vapor is likely to condense if there is a large difference in temperature between the indoors and the outdoors. To prevent thermal insulation from becoming saturated with condensate, a vapor retarder sheet /such as polyethylene plastic or aluminum foil should be installed on the warm side of the insulation. This keeps water vapor from entering the insulation. In the previous detail pattern, *Warm Interior Surfaces* (page 58, 59), we saw the use of a warm-side vapor retarder on the outside of pipe insulation, air conditioning ductwork insulation, and toilet tank insulation. In walls, floors, and roofs of buildings in climatic areas with cold and moderately cold winters, the warm side is the interior side of the insulation. In extremely humid tropical and subtropical climates, the warm side is the outside of the insulation if the building is artificially cooled. In some very mild climates, condensation is unlikely at any time of year under normal climatic conditions and no vapor retarder is needed, but except for warm, damp southern climates, the safe thing to do in North America is always to provide a vapor retarder on the *interior* side of any thermal insulation in the shell of a building.

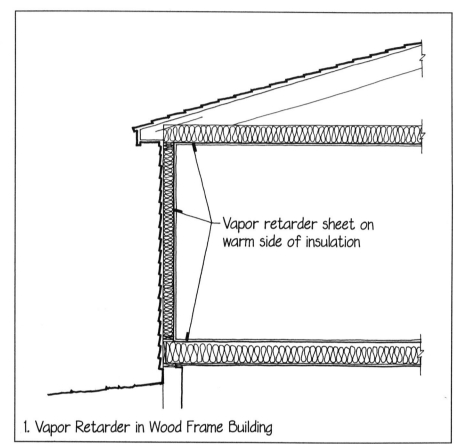

Vapor retarder sheet on warm side of insulation

1. Vapor Retarder in Wood Frame Building

It is important to avoid leaks in the vapor retarder. Although many types of insulating batts are furnished with a vapor retarder sheet already attached to the interior side, the seams between the batts furnish paths for major leakage of air and water vapor. In most cases, it is preferable to use unfaced batts and to detail a seamless vapor retarder sheet between the insulation and the interior finish layer.

2. A low-slope roof is made waterproof by an impervious membrane made of synthetic rubber, plastic, or asphalt laminated with felt. This membrane is also an effective vapor retarder. If insulation is installed below it in a cool or cold climate, two precautions should be taken: A vapor retarder should be installed on the underside (warm side) of the insulation, and a ventilated space should be

provided between the insulation and the roofing membrane. This drawing shows how this can be done for insulation below the roof deck.

3. In the most conventional type of low-slope roof construction, rigid board insulation is installed above the deck and beneath the waterproof membrane. In cool and cold climates, condensation of moisture is likely to occur in this type of roof, because a vapor retarder (the waterproof membrane) is placed on the cold side of the insulation, which is directly contrary to the logic of this detail pattern. If this type of detail must be used, a vapor retarder should be installed as close as possible to the warm side of the insulation. Additionally, the roofing manufacturers' literature should be consulted with regard to installing topside roof vents and a ventilating base sheet over the insulation to release any trapped moisture. (The ventilating base sheet is generally a sheet of asphalt-saturated felt that has been embossed in such a way that it provides tiny open channels along which water vapor can move in both directions.) If these precautions are not taken, vapor pressure can blister and rupture the roof membrane, and trapped moisture can destroy the insulation board and roof deck.

See *Vapor Ventilation* (pp. 63–65) for further information on ventilating insulated roof assemblies.

4. A preferable detail for a low-slope roof in a cool or cold climate is the inverted roof assembly, in which polystyrene foam insulation is installed on top of the roof membrane, allowing the membrane to serve both as waterproofing membrane and warm-side vapor retarder. The polystyrene foam absorbs very little water, so it retains its insulating effectiveness even when it is fully immersed.   ▷

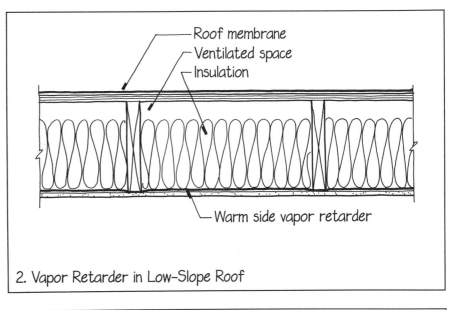

2. Vapor Retarder in Low-Slope Roof

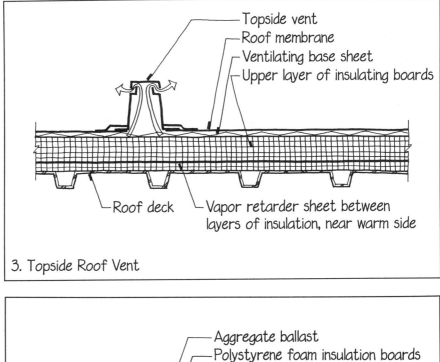

3. Topside Roof Vent

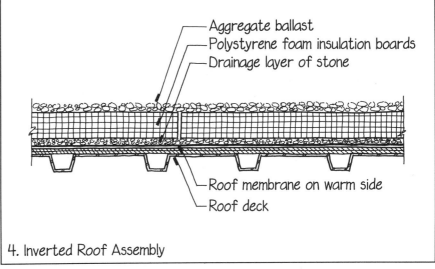

4. Inverted Roof Assembly

5. Spandrel glass for a curtain wall is often furnished by the manufacturer with insulation and vapor retarder already in place. It is especially important in this application that the vapor retarder be free of holes and well sealed around the edges, because the spandrel glass is vaportight and will not allow any trapped moisture to escape from the insulation.

6. Water vapor enters a wall or ceiling construction by two different means. One is air leakage through cracks and openings from the interior of the building into the wall or ceiling. The other is vapor diffusion, in which water vapor is forced through porous building materials by the difference in vapor pressure between the indoor air and the outdoor air. In most cases air leakage transports far more water vapor than vapor diffusion. Working under this assumption, some builders and designers of houses do not install vapor retarders in their buildings. Instead they take extreme care to seal all potential air leaks in and around the interior finish layer of construction. Sealants and gaskets are installed behind all the edges of the gypsum wallboard on ex-

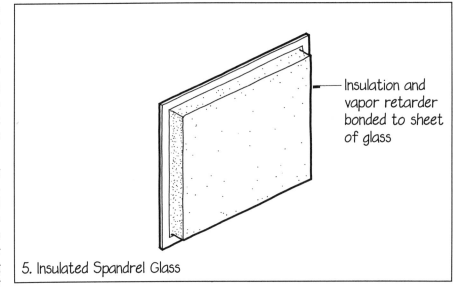

Insulation and vapor retarder bonded to sheet of glass

5. Insulated Spandrel Glass

terior walls. Electrical boxes are carefully sealed to prevent air leakage. This strategy is called the airtight drywall approach (ADA).

7. Vinyl wallcoverings are fairly effective vapor retarders. Because they are installed on interior surfaces of buildings, they cause no problems in cold climates, but in air-conditioned buildings in humid, warm climates they can become cold-side vapor retarders, causing moisture to condense on their exterior surfaces. This can result in mildew growth, unpleasant odors, and wall deterioration. Special vapor-permeable vinyl wallcoverings with integral mildewcides are available and should be specified for projects in southern climates.   ■

VAPOR VENTILATION

Water vapor must be given an easy escape route from the cold side of any vapor retarder. Try not to place vapor-impermeable materials on the cold side of insulation. This avoids trapping any small amounts of moisture that may get through the vapor retarder. It also allows stray moisture to be baked out of the insulation during periods of warm weather.

1. In the detail pattern *Warm-side Vapor Retarder* (pages 60–62) we have seen two common examples of vapor-impermeable materials being placed on the cold side of insulation. In one of these, a conventionally insulated low-slope roof, topside roof vents and a ventilating base sheet are used to release trapped moisture. In the other example, insulated spandrel glass, defect-free fabrication and installation of the glass units is required to avoid condensation problems, because no provision can be made for vapor ventilation through the glass to the outdoors. These are both less than optimal solutions.

2. In ordinary wood light frame construction, an air barrier sheet is used on the cold side of the wall to reduce air infiltration (see *Air Barrier Surface*, page 38). It is important that this air barrier sheet be permeable to water vapor so that it will not trap stray moisture in the wall, but will allow it to diffuse to the outdoors in warm weather. Asphalt-saturated felt and polypropyl-

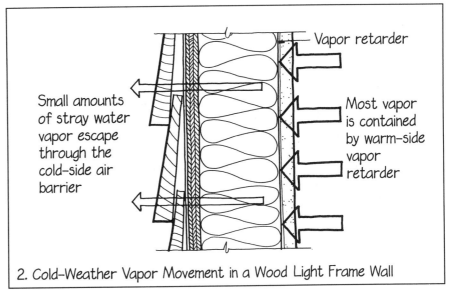

2. Cold-Weather Vapor Movement in a Wood Light Frame Wall

ene fabric air barrier sheets are effective barriers to the passage of air and liquid water but are permeable to the passage of water vapor. These qualities make them suitable for use on the cold side of a wall. Polyethylene sheeting and metal foil are impermeable to water vapor and should never be used on the outside of a wall in a cold climate.

3. There is controversy about the use of plywood sheathing on the outside of a wood frame wall. Because of its continuous internal surfaces of glue, plywood is not very permeable to water vapor and, in theory, can trap moisture in the wall cavities and insulation. Some detailers call for holes to be drilled a few inches apart in both directions all across the sheathing to ventilate moisture. Others space the sheathing away from the insulation and provide screened ventilation openings to the outdoor air at the top and bottom of each wall cavity. Investigations of thousands of houses have failed to turn up very many examples of moisture trapped inside plywood-sheathed walls, however, especially when a warm-side vapor retarder has been carefully installed, so most detailers feel safe in continuing to use plywood sheathing in the conventional way.   ▷

4. In attics and roofs, unlike walls, cold-side ventilation is very important for several reasons. One is to prevent ice dams (see *Cold Roof*, page 19). Another is to reduce summertime overheating of the building. A third is to remove water vapor. The vapor problem can be much more acute in attics and roofs than in walls, because convection transports moist air from indoors into the roof structure through such openings as lighting fixtures, ventilation fans, and attic hatchways. Attics are relatively easy to ventilate, using soffit vents and either a ridge vent or gable vents. Building codes generally require both high and low ventilation openings in an attic, and specify the required area of the openings (see *Cold Roof*, p. 19).

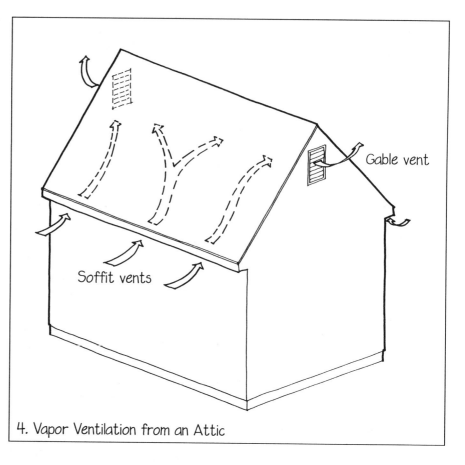

Gable vent

Soffit vents

4. Vapor Ventilation from an Attic

5. Insulated rafters with the ceiling surface directly attached to their undersides ("cathedral ceilings") can present a more difficult detailing problem than attics in creating the necessary vents and air passages for code-mandated ventilation. A 2″ deep air passage beneath the sheathing is often required and can be created easily and economically by using preformed vent spacer channels made of plastic foam or paper fiber. This usually leaves insufficient space for the code-mandated amount of thermal insulation, however. Sometimes this problem can be overcome merely by using deeper rafters than are structurally required, perhaps increasing their spacing from 16″ to 24″ (from 400 to 600 mm) for greater economy of material. More often this also leaves insufficient space for insulation, and the designer must replace some or all of the thickness of glass fiber batts with high-efficiency plastic foam insulation or else furr above the rafters and add a second layer of roof sheathing to provide the required ventilation.

6. Several manufacturers market proprietary vented roof insulation assemblies that include thermal insulation, cold-side ventilation passages, and a nail-base top sheet to accept shingles. These are especially useful where the rafters themselves are to be exposed in the room below, as in heavy-timber framing. The assemblies are quite thick and are attached to the roof with special long nails that are driven through the insulation assembly into the roof decking. ■

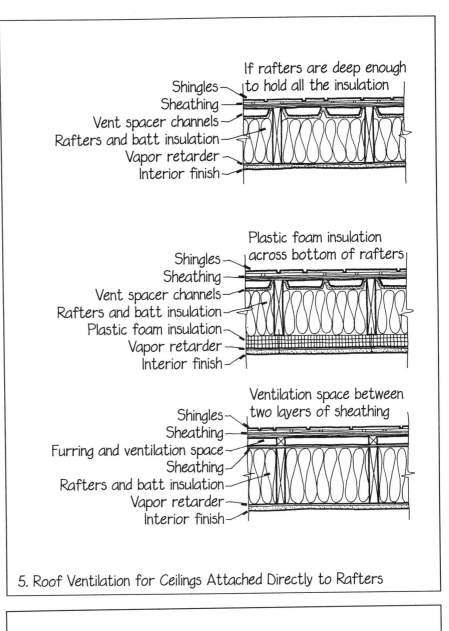

5. Roof Ventilation for Ceilings Attached Directly to Rafters

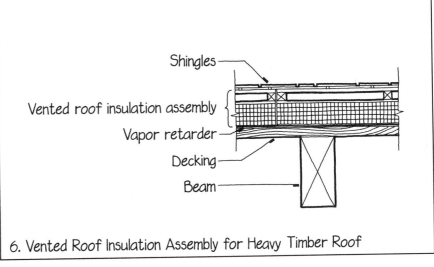

6. Vented Roof Insulation Assembly for Heavy Timber Roof

CONDENSATE DRAINAGE

Where condensation may occur within a building, provide channels and weep holes that allow gravity to remove the moisture without damage to the building.

1. Many proprietary designs for slope glazing systems and skylights are designed to catch and drain condensate that may run off the interior surface of the glass in cold weather. If this is not done, the condensate will drip into the room below. In this slope glazing purlin, condensate gutters are built into the lower flanges of the aluminum structural member. The gutter on the uphill side will catch moisture that runs off the glass above it. (The gutter on the downhill side is of no use, but having gutters on both sides makes it impossible for careless workers to install the purlin upside down). Each purlin is supported at each end by an aluminum rafter. The rafter has a similar cross section to the purlin but is deeper. The connection between the two is made in such a way that water draining from the end of the purlin is caught in the gutter at the bottom of the rafter. Here it drains rapidly by gravity to the bottom of the rafter slope, where it escapes to the outside through weep holes.

2. Though condensation problems are generally much less severe in wall assemblies than in slope glazing systems, most proprietary metal curtain wall systems include channels, weep holes, and sometimes weep tubes to drain condensate and leakage from internal cavities (see also **Drain and Weep**, p. 17). ■

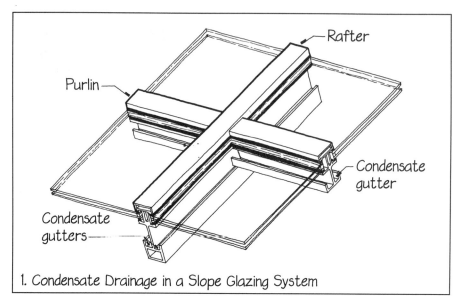

1. Condensate Drainage in a Slope Glazing System

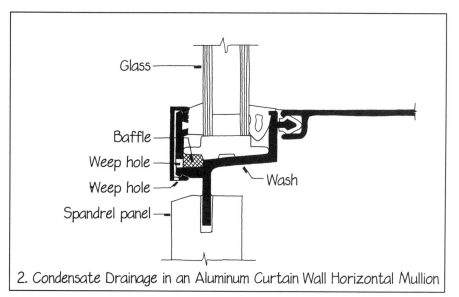

2. Condensate Drainage in an Aluminum Curtain Wall Horizontal Mullion

FUNCTION:
CONTROLLING SOUND

N O I S E reduction, acoustic privacy, and good hearing conditions are qualities we seek in almost every building. The details of a building contribute in important ways to achieving these qualities. To reduce noise inside a building we detail the exterior walls to exclude outdoor noise. We detail potentially noisy components of a building in such a way that they remain quiet. We use sound-absorbing materials within rooms to reduce noise levels from conversations and machinery. To achieve acoustic privacy, we detail interior doors, partitions, floors, and ductwork to reduce sound transmission between rooms to a minimum. For good hearing conditions, we reduce noise and provide an optimum combination and configuration of absorbing and reflecting surfaces within a room. Often it is advisable to work with a specialized consultant to achieve good acoustical qualities in a building, but many ordinary problems of noise, hearing, and privacy can be solved by means of four detail patterns:

Airtight, Heavy, Limp Partition (page 68)

Cushioned Floor (page 71)

Quiet Attachments (page 73)

Sound-absorbing Surfaces (page 74)

AIRTIGHT, HEAVY, LIMP PARTITION

The ideal soundproof partition is airtight, heavy, and limp. A thick, hanging sheet of soft lead that is sealed around the edges fulfills all these requirements. It is expensive and unattractive, however, so we detail partitions of a combination of standard materials in such a way that we incorporate the necessary qualities of airtightness, heaviness, and limpness.

1. The degree of resistance of a partition to the transmission of sound is measured in units of decibels and is called its sound transmission class (STC). For a variety of partition construction details, STCs are tabulated in references such as the Gypsum Association's *Fire Resistance Manual* and the National Concrete Masonry Association's *Tek Notes*. The accompanying table gives recommended minimum STCs for residential partitions in a variety of situations; higher values than these are desirable. Because background noise masks the intelligibility of sounds, partitions of lesser acoustical quality are considered acceptable in noisier neighborhoods.

2. This sampling of partition details illustrates the fundamentals of detailing a framed partition for acoustical privacy. The STCs of these partitions may be related to the preceding table. All of these constructions utilize readily available, inexpensive materials: gypsum wallboard and wood stud framing. (Similar details have been developed for steel stud framing.) Each partition is made airtight by using acoustical sealant around the edges, by avoiding electrical outlets that pierce the wall, and by using heavy, tightly gasketed doors. The lowest-rated partition (far left) uses gypsum board attached directly to the studs. In the next detail to the right, limpness is created by mounting the gypsum board

SELECTED SOUND ISOLATION CRITERIA FOR RESIDENTIAL WALLS

	Very Quiet Neighborhood	Average Neighborhood	Very Noisy Neighborhood
	Minimum STC	Minimum STC	Minimum STC
Between Dwelling Units			
Bedroom to bedroom	55	52	48
Living room to living room	55	52	48
Bathroom to bedroom	59	56	52
Kitchen, dining, or family room to bedroom	58	55	52
Within Dwelling Units			
Bedroom to bedroom	48	44	40
Living room to bedroom	50	46	42
Bathroom to bedroom or living room	52	48	45
Kitchen to bedroom	52	48	45

Adapted from Federal Housing Administration "Guide to Airborne, Impact, and Structure Borne Noise Control in Multifamily Dwellings."

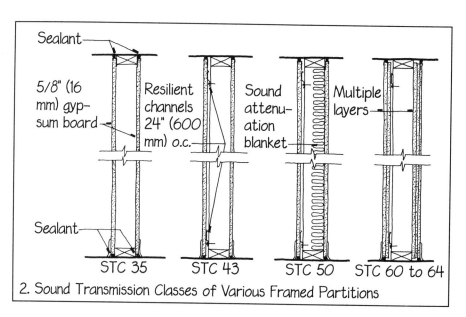

2. Sound Transmission Classes of Various Framed Partitions

on one side of the partition on resilient sheet metal channels that absorb vibrations. This results in an 8-decibel improvement in performance. A sound attenuation blanket of mineral fiber adds a further 7 decibels (second from right). The best partition (far right) is made heavy by applying additional layers of gypsum board and by making the two sides of the partition unequal in mass so that they will not vibrate at the same frequencies. The channels, sealants, and batts are all items that are available from stock.

3. Masonry partitions generally have fairly high STCs. Masonry is a heavy material. Some types of concrete masonry are fairly porous but can be made airtight with paint or plaster. Limpness is a difficult quality to achieve in masonry itself but can be added by mounting resilient channels to a masonry wall and attaching a gypsum board finish layer to the channels.

4. An opening in or around a door—a keyhole or ventilation grill, an under-cut bottom edge, or a crack between the door and frame—can make an otherwise effective partition almost transparent to sound. Doors in privacy partitions should be avoided where possible. If a door is necessary, it should be solid-core wood or composite steel designed and tested for acoustic isolation. These are typical acoustical gasketing details, using commercially available components, to seal the cracks around a door. (See also *Weatherstripped Crack*, p. 40).   ▷

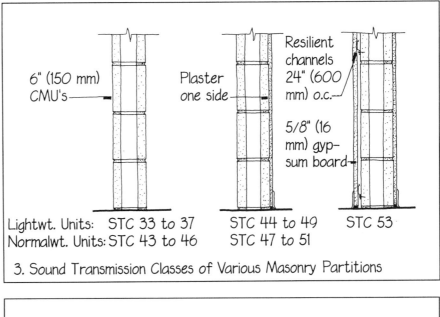

6" (150 mm) CMU's

Plaster one side

Resilient channels 24" (600 mm) o.c.

5/8" (16 mm) gypsum board

Lightwt. Units: STC 33 to 37   STC 44 to 49   STC 53
Normalwt. Units: STC 43 to 46   STC 47 to 51

3. Sound Transmission Classes of Various Masonry Partitions

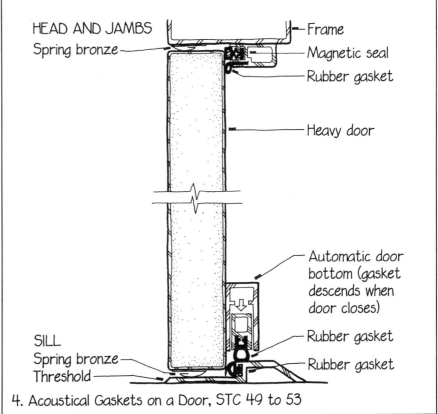

HEAD AND JAMBS
Spring bronze

Frame
Magnetic seal
Rubber gasket

Heavy door

Automatic door bottom (gasket descends when door closes)

Rubber gasket

SILL
Spring bronze
Threshold

Rubber gasket

4. Acoustical Gaskets on a Door, STC 49 to 53

5. Ductwork should be laid out so that it does not furnish a path for sound to travel between one room and the next, rendering even the best of partitions acoustically worthless. If such ductwork is inevitable, it should be lined with sound-absorbing material to prevent sound waves from propagating.

6. Windows in buildings near airports, highways, and heavy industries often need to be as soundproof as possible. A single sheet of ordinary glass has an STC of only 28 to 36. Two layers of glass with an airspace between, sealed carefully around the edges, provide a moderate amount of mass, airtightness, and some resiliency to achieve an STC in the range of 32 to 40. The same range of STCs can be accomplished with a single sheet of laminated glass, which consists of two layers of glass tightly sandwiching a soft plastic interlayer that imparts resiliency. In each of these examples, the lower STCs correspond to a glass thickness of ¼″ (6.5 mm), and the upper STCs to a glass thickness of ½″ or ¾″ (13 to 19 mm). Operable windows should be avoided in high-noise environments, because they are difficult to make airtight.   ■

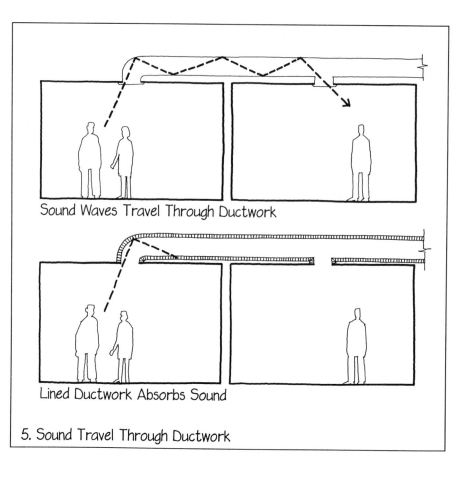

Sound Waves Travel Through Ductwork

Lined Ductwork Absorbs Sound

5. Sound Travel Through Ductwork

CUSHIONED FLOOR

The control of sound transmission through floors is often critical, especially in apartments, hotels, and dormitories, where people live above one another. In addition to blocking airborne sound, floors must also impede impact and vibration noises from heels and machinery. The criteria of airtightness, heaviness, and limpness that apply to partitions are joined in designing floors by a fourth criterion, cushioning.

1. The resistance to sound transmission of a floor assembly is measured in two ways. Resistance to the transmission of airborne sound is expressed in decibels as a sound transmission class (STC), the same as for partitions. Resistance to the transmission of impact noise is expressed in decibels as the impact insulation class (IIC). Both of these quantities need to be controlled through detailing to achieve the desired acoustical performance. The accom-

panying table gives recommended minimum STC and IIC values for residential floors in a variety of situations; higher values than these are desirable. Because background noise masks the intelligibility of sounds, floor/ceiling constructions of lesser acoustical quality are considered acceptable in noisier neighborhoods. ▷

SELECTED SOUND ISOLATION CRITERIA FOR FLOOR/CEILING
CONSTRUCTIONS BETWEEN DWELLING UNITS

	Very Quiet Neighborhood		Average Neighborhood		Very Noisy Neighborhood	
	Minimum STC	*Minimum IIC*	*Minimum STC*	*Minimum IIC*	*Minimum STC*	*Minimum IIC*
Bedroom above bedroom	55	55	52	52	48	48
Living room above bedroom	57	60	54	57	50	53
Kitchen above bedroom	58	65	55	62	52	58
Bedroom above living room	57	55	54	52	50	48
Living room above living room	55	55	52	52	48	48
Kitchen above living room	55	60	52	57	48	53
Bath above bath	52	52	50	50	48	48

Adapted from Federal Housing Administration "Guide to Airborne, Impact, and Structure Borne Noise Control in Multifamily Dwellings."

2. Airtightness is easily achieved in a concrete or concrete-topped steel floor structure if openings for pipes, wires, and ducts are carefully sealed. Wood floor structures may be made airtight by adding a topping of poured concrete or gypsum, or by careful plaster or gypsum board work on the ceiling below. A concrete, steel, or wood floor is sufficiently heavy for acoustical purposes. Limpness or resiliency can be achieved in several ways. The most effective way in most situations is to install a heavy carpet and pad on top of the slab. This provides resiliency and also cushions heel impacts. Notice in the accompanying examples, however, that the carpet and pad do little to improve the STC of a floor. In the wood floor illustrated here, the increase in STC is achieved by mounting the gypsum board ceiling on resilient channels.

3. Hard floor finishes such as ceramic tile, vinyl tile, sheet vinyl, or wood flooring are ordinarily very good generators and transmitters of impact noise. Sound-deadening board, resilient matting, or floating floor isolators installed between the top of the structural floor and the bottom of the finish floor can cushion these floors effectively. ∎

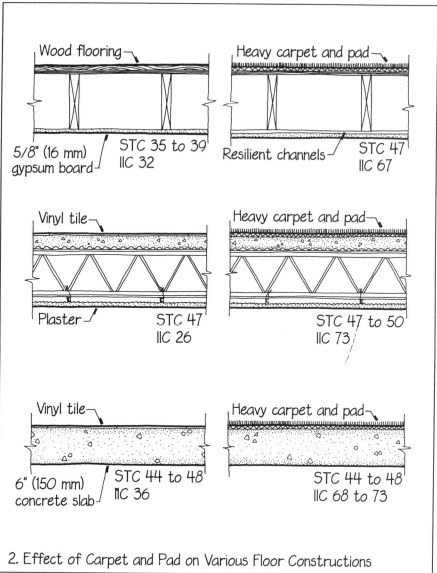

2. Effect of Carpet and Pad on Various Floor Constructions

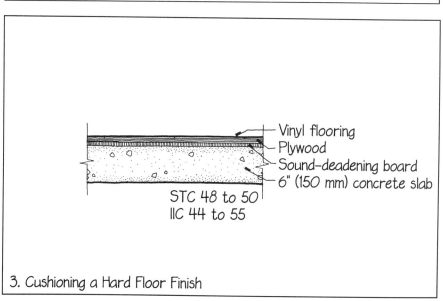

3. Cushioning a Hard Floor Finish

QUIET ATTACHMENTS

Squeaks, bangs, rumbles, and other structural and mechanical noises in buildings can be reduced or prevented by careful detailing.

1. A wood subfloor that is glued to the supporting joists as well as nailed is much less likely to loosen and squeak over time than a subfloor that is merely nailed. Screws or ring-shank nails are much less likely to loosen and squeak in a subfloor than common nails.

2. A prefabricated wood stair with housed stringers uses wedges and glue to create a tight unit that is highly resistant to loosening and creaking underfoot.

3. Doorstops, frame pads, and door closers reduce dramatically the amount of noise that a door can generate as it opens and closes.

4. Motors, pumps, fans, and other machinery should be isolated acoustically from the structure of the building to reduce the transmission of structure-borne noise. Many types of resilient equipment mounts that use metal springs or rubber pads are available. Flexible duct connectors should be used to join ductwork to fans.

5. Hot water pipes and hydronic heating pipes expand and contract longitudinally when they heat and cool. This causes them to rub against their mounting brackets. A smooth plastic mounting bracket reduces friction against the pipe and virtually eliminates the ticking and scraping noises that a metal bracket would generate. ■

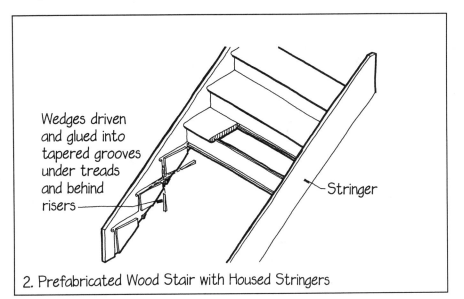

Wedges driven and glued into tapered grooves under treads and behind risers

Stringer

2. Prefabricated Wood Stair with Housed Stringers

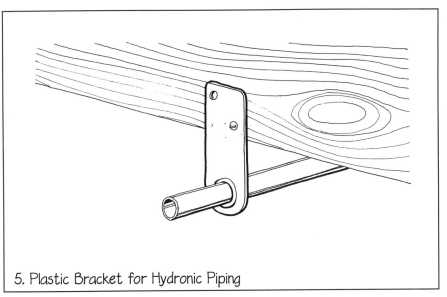

5. Plastic Bracket for Hydronic Piping

SOUND ABSORBING SURFACES

Soft, porous, thick finish materials absorb most sound and reflect little. This makes them useful in achieving quiet conditions inside a building.

1. A carpet and pad, upholstered furniture, and window draperies all absorb sound and are effective in reducing sound levels within a room. Unpadded carpet and thin upholstery and curtains absorb only very high frequencies of sound, however, leaving noise at middle and low frequencies as a continuing problem.

2. The capability of a finish material to absorb sound is measured and expressed as its noise reduction coefficient (NRC). A material with an NRC of 0.80 absorbs 80% of the noise incident upon it, measured across a broad range of frequencies.

3. Ceiling-mounted acoustical tiles and acoustical panels are manufactured in a wide range of noise reduction coefficients. Full ceilings of highly absorbent panels or tiles are useful in quieting noisy office or retail spaces. The ability of an acoustical ceiling to absorb lower frequencies of sound can

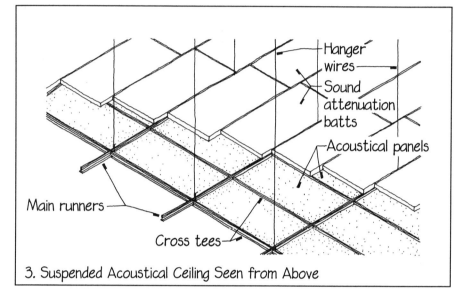

3. Suspended Acoustical Ceiling Seen from Above

be enhanced by suspending it or furring it down from the structure above, and by installing sound attenuation batts on top of it. Acoustic plaster, even if properly installed, is an effective absorber only at higher frequencies.

4. Hard, acoustically reflective ceilings of wood, plaster, gypsum board, or prefabricated panels are appro-priate in many types of spaces designed for good hearing of speech or music. Such spaces should be designed in collaboration with an acoustical consultant. ∎

FUNCTION:
ACCOMMODATING MOVEMENT

A B U I L D I N G is never at rest. Its movements, though seemingly small, are extremely powerful and can cause irreparable damage unless the building is detailed to accommodate them. There are a number of sources of movement in buildings that the detailer must keep in mind:

Temperature movement is caused by the expansion and contraction of building materials with rising and falling temperatures.

Moisture movement occurs in porous materials such as wood, plaster, masonry, and concrete. These materials swell as they absorb moisture from water or humid air and shrink as they dry.

Phase change movement accompanies a change in the physical state of a material. The phase change movement that is of primary interest to the detailer is the expansion of water as it freezes.

Chemical change movement takes place in certain construction materials as they cure or age. Gypsum plaster expands slightly as it changes from a slurry to a solid. Solvent-release coatings and sealants shrink as they cure. Reinforcing bars that rust expand and can crack the masonry or concrete in which they are embedded.

Structural deflections always accompany changes in the loads on a building. Beams, slabs, trusses, and arches sag more as they are loaded more heavily, and less as their loads are reduced. Columns grow shorter as loads are applied to them. Wind and seismic loads flex and rack exterior wall components, and move buildings laterally by substantial amounts.

Structural creep is characteristic of wood and concrete, both of which sag permanently by a small amount during the first several years of a building's life and then stabilize.

Foundation settlement occurs when the soil beneath a building deflects or creeps under loading. All foundations settle; if the settlement is small and is uniform across the entire building, little movement occurs within the components of the building itself. If settlement is nonuniform from one wall or column to another, considerable movement must be accommodated.

We can predict, often with impressive accuracy, the magnitude of movement that will occur from each of these sources: Temperature movement can be quantified rather precisely using the expected range of temperature difference and the coefficient of thermal expansion of the material (page 36). Moisture movement cannot be quantified with such precision, but we can predict it accurately enough to prevent it from causing damage to a building (pp. 77, 78). Phase change and chemical change movements can be estimated with varying degrees of accuracy. Structural deflections are computed very closely using standard engineering techniques, and structural creep can be quantified to within manageable limits. A geotechnical or foundation engineer can provide enough data on expected levels of foundation movement to guide the detailer.

In detailing a building, we concede that most movements are unpreventable and are caused by forces so large that we cannot restrain them. Instead we provide movement joints between building components at such intervals and in such configurations that the movements can be absorbed without harm in these joints. If we did not provide movement joints, the forces that cause movement in a building would create their own joints by cracking and crushing components until the building's internal stresses were relieved. At best, the result would be unsightly; at worst, the result would be a leaky, unstable, unsafe building.

The detail patterns that relate to accommodating movement in buildings are associated with several simple strategies. The first of these is to manufacture and configure building materials in ways that minimize their tendency to move in undesirable ways. Its associated patterns are:

> *Seasoning and Curing (page 76)*
>
> *Vertical-grain Lumber (page 78)*
>
> *Equalizing Cross Grain (page 80)*
>
> *Relieved Back (page 82)*
>
> *Foundation Below Frost Line (page 83)*

A second strategy is to separate building elements that are likely to move at different rates and in different ways. Its patterns are:

> *Structure/Enclosure Joint (page 84)*
>
> *Abutment Joint (page 86)*

A third strategy is to divide large building surfaces that are likely to crack, crush, or buckle into smaller units of such a size that the likelihood of such failures is greatly reduced. This leads to the following patterns:

> *Expansion Joint (page 87)*
>
> *Control Joint (page 89)*
>
> *Sliding Joint (page 92)*

A fourth and final strategy is to divide a large building, especially one with a complex geometry, into two or more geometrically simple buildings, each of a size and compactness such that we can reasonably expect it to move as a unit in response to such large forces as foundation settlement and seismic accelerations. This leads to the pattern

> *Building Separation Joint (page 93)*

SEASONING AND CURING

Many porous construction materials should be seasoned or cured for a period of time following their manufacture, before they are incorporated into a building. This allows them to reach an equilibrium moisture content and to stabilize dimensionally before their movement is restrained by adjoining components of a building.

1. Wood is the building material that is by far the most subject to dimensional change from changes in moisture content. At the time it is cut, it is fully saturated with water. As it dries, it becomes stronger and stiffer. It also shrinks by very large amounts until it reaches a moisture content at which it no longer gives off moisture to the air. Wood is seasoned commercially either by stacking it in loose arrays for a period of many months to allow it to dry in the air or by drying it in a kiln over a period of a few days. Kiln drying generally produces a more stable product. Throughout its lifetime, however, a piece of wood seasoned by either method will absorb moisture and expand during humid periods, and give off moisture and shrink during dry periods. Wood shrinkage and expansion in 11 common species of softwoods can be quantified using the Western Wood Products Association's *Dimensional Stability of Western Lumber Products* (see the bibliographic reference on page 272 for ordering information). A shrinkage graph for a typical softwood is shown on page 78.

2. Unseasoned ("green") lumber is often used in construction, especially for framing. Special care should be taken in detailing the finish components of buildings framed with unseasoned lumber, because framing components will shrink by large amounts in the perpendicular-to-grain direction, which will apply severe stresses to finish components that are rigidly fixed to the frame. Unseasoned lumber should never be used for interior finish components; in fact, finish lumber should be the most carefully seasoned of all, dried to a moisture content that is in equilibrium with the air, usually about 11% by weight.

3. Concrete masonry units are available in two types: Type II units, which may be relatively high in water content, and Type I units, whose moisture content has been controlled at the plant to reduce drying shrinkage after the units have been laid. Clay bricks, on the other hand, are devoid of moisture when they come from the kiln and expand very slightly over a period of weeks and months as they absorb small amounts of moisture from the air. It is wise to allow bricks to season for a time before using them in a wall; this has usually occurred before the bricks are purchased by the contractor.

4. Concrete contains far more water than is needed for curing at the time that it is poured. This excess evaporates later from the concrete, causing it to shrink slightly. In most concrete walls and slabs on grade it is possible to provide control joints to absorb the cracking that will be caused by this shrinkage (page 89). When pouring structural slabs that are very large in area and cannot have control joints, minimize shrinkage distress by pouring each story of the building in smaller sections, separated by open shrinkage strips. After these sections have cured and dried long enough so that most shrinkage has occurred, the shrinkage strips are poured to complete the floor. Reinforcing bars should be spliced within the shrinkage strips so the separate areas of the floor can move independently while the strips are open. The concrete in the strips should be keyed mechanically to the slabs on either side. Supporting formwork must be left in place until the concrete in the shrinkage strips has cured. The locations of the shrinkage strips must be determined by the structural engineer.

5. Moisture movement of cementitious materials and masonry can be approximated using the accompanying table.

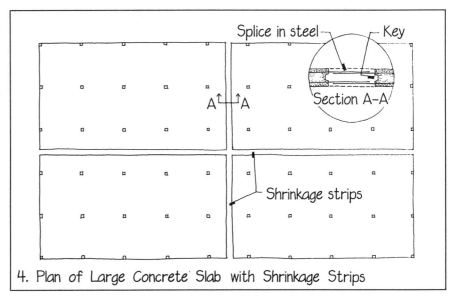

4. Plan of Large Concrete Slab with Shrinkage Strips

MOISTURE MOVEMENT OF CEMENTITIOUS MATERIALS AND MASONRY

Curing and drying shrinkage of concrete	0.0005 in/in (mm/mm)
Curing and drying shrinkage of concrete masonry units	0.0001–0.0010 in/in (mm)
Moisture expansion of brick masonry	0.0002 in/in (mm/mm)
Moisture expansion of gypsum wallboard	0.0004 in/in (mm/mm)

Example No. 1: About how much will a concrete slab 210′ long shrink during curing and drying?

(210 ft)(12 in/ft) = 2,520 in

(2,520 in)(0.0005 in/in) = *1.26 in*

Example No. 2: Approximately how much moisture expansion should be anticipated in a new brick wall 175′ long?

(175 ft)(12 in/ft) = 2,100 in

(2,100 in)(0.0002 in/in) = *0.42 in*

■

VERTICAL-GRAIN LUMBER

Lumber used for flat finish components of a building should be sawn from the log in such a way that the growth rings of the wood run approximately perpendicular to the surface of the board.

1. When a log is seasoned, it shrinks very little along its length. It shrinks considerably in its radial direction (perpendicular to the growth rings), and it shrinks most of all in its tangential direction (along the growth rings). The amounts of shrinkage are very large, as can be read from the accompanying graph.

2. The larger shrinkage in the tangential direction causes a log to check (split along radial lines). It also causes pieces of lumber cut from different parts of the cross section of the log to distort during seasoning in a variety of ways.

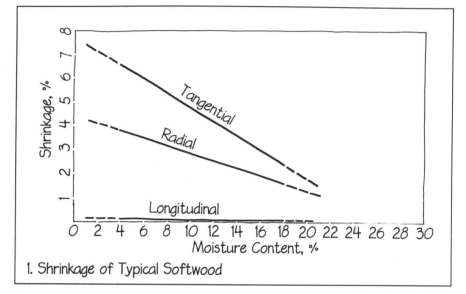

1. Shrinkage of Typical Softwood

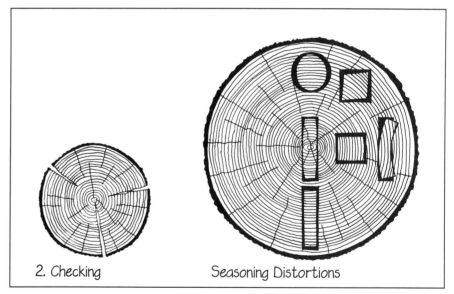

2. Checking   Seasoning Distortions

3. To avoid seasoning distortions as much as possible, lumber can be cut from the log in such a way that the face of each board is approximately perpendicular to the annual rings in the wood. This is referred to as rift sawing or quartersawing, and lumber cut in this way is often called vertical-grain lumber. Vertical-grain lumber is best for flooring and for finish lumber that must remain flat—baseboards, window and door casings, and tabletops, for example. Vertical-grain lumber also wears better in furniture and flooring because the harder summerwood bands occur very close together at the surface of each piece, protecting the soft springwood between from abrasion. Vertical-grain lumber takes longer to saw than plainsawed lumber, however, and it is more wasteful of the log, so it costs more. For most uses, especially ordinary framing, plainsawed lumber is a satisfactory and economical choice, despite its tendency to distort.

4. Most outdoor decks are made of plainsawed decking. If the boards are laid with their "bark side" up, they will cup in a way that traps water during rainstorms. The proper way to lay decking is bark side down.　■

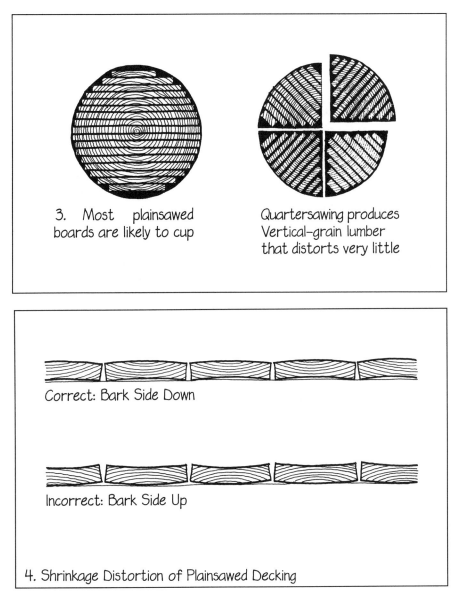

3. Most plainsawed boards are likely to cup

Quartersawing produces Vertical-grain lumber that distorts very little

Correct: Bark Side Down

Incorrect: Bark Side Up

4. Shrinkage Distortion of Plainsawed Decking

EQUALIZING CROSS GRAIN

As its moisture content changes, wood shrinks and swells a great deal across its grain, but very little along its grain. For purposes of detailing ordinary wood buildings, we assume that the longitudinal shrinkage and expansion is essentially zero. Movement in the cross grain direction is large in magnitude and is difficult to quantify, because tangential movement (movement along the growth rings) is substantially larger than radial movement (movement perpendicular to the growth rings). In the plainsawed lumber that we use for framing, we can't be sure whether cross grain shrinkage in a joist or a plate will take place at the radial rate, the tangential rate, or something between the two. The best we can do is to assume that the rate will be something between the two.

1. In platform framing, which is the most common way of structuring a house, each level of floor framing interrupts the vertical studs that form the walls and that support the upper floor and roof. The studs will shrink very little in the vertical direction of the building, but the floor framing, even if it consists of seasoned lumber, will shrink by a substantial amount, often ¼″ to ⅜″ per floor (6 to 9 mm). When detailing wood platform framing, it is important to provide equal amounts of cross grain wood at each level so that shrinkage will not cause tipping of floors or distress in interior finish materials. It is good practice to leave a space of about ½″ (12 mm) in the sheathing panels at each floor platform, because the platform will shrink considerably and the panels will not.

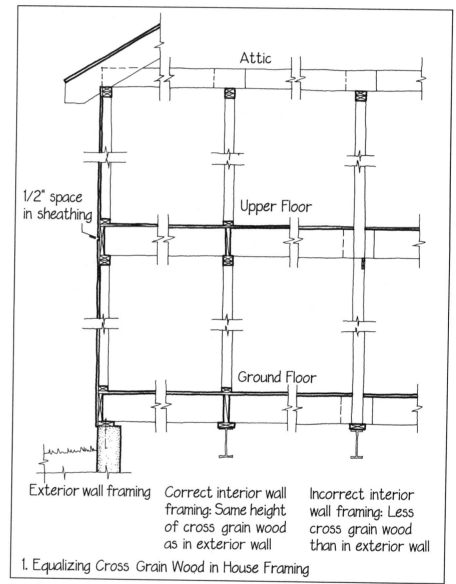

1. Equalizing Cross Grain Wood in House Framing

2. Masonry components of a wooden building, such as chimneys and exterior facings, do not shrink appreciably when compared with the wooden frame. Details of structural attachments and flashings that connect the wood and masonry must be designed to accommodate the differential movement. A sliding masonry tie will allow the frame to shrink without stressing the brick facing.

3.The flashings and counterflashings around a masonry chimney slip freely to allow the roof to drop a fraction of an inch in relation to the brickwork. ■

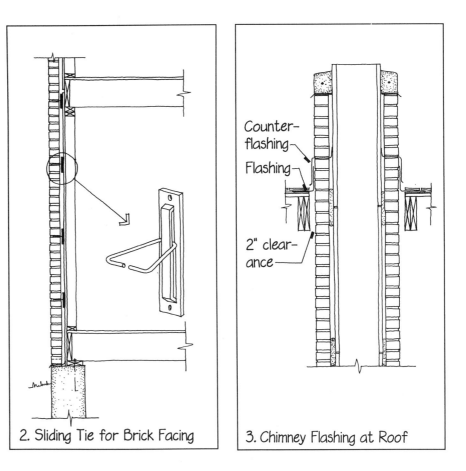

2. Sliding Tie for Brick Facing

Counter-flashing

Flashing

2" clearance

3. Chimney Flashing at Roof

RELIEVED BACK

Problems caused by cupping distortions in flat finish pieces of wood can be minimized by using a profile with a relieved back and by back priming each piece.

1. Cupping distortion of a wood board is caused by a difference in the amount of shrinkage experienced by the opposite sides of the board. The thinner the board is, the less the force that can be exerted on it by this difference in shrinkage. It is common practice to relieve the backs of flat pieces of wood millwork by cutting one or more grooves, thus effectively reducing the thickness of the pieces and diminishing their tendency to cup. If a single, wide groove is cut, it also makes the piece easier to attach to a flat surface, because only the two edges need to touch.

In factory-produced millwork the grooves are usually cut by shaping machinery. On the jobsite, it is usually more practical to cut multiple grooves on a portable table saw.

2. Back priming, the application of a coat of primer paint to the back side of a board, is also helpful in preventing cupping distortion of flat pieces of wood that will be painted. Siding boards, corner boards, exterior trim pieces, casings, and baseboards can all benefit from back priming. The effect of back priming is to cause both the front and back surfaces of the board to react to moisture at roughly the same rate. The back priming needs to be done at least a day in advance of installation to give the primer time to dry. It should be

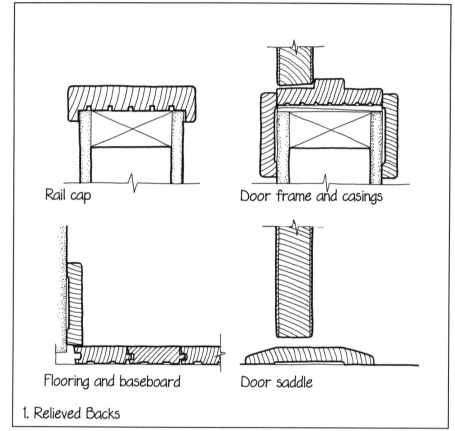

Rail cap

Door frame and casings

Flooring and baseboard

Door saddle

1. Relieved Backs

noted in the millwork section of the specifications for the building and specified in detail under the painting section.

3. Closely related in principle to back priming is the practice of back facing a door or shelf that is surfaced with plastic laminate. The back facing prevents warping caused by unequal absorption of moisture by the two sides of the panel. Where it will not show, the back facing is usually made of a plain, low-cost laminate. Although it is virtually a necessity on shelves and doors, back facing is usually not required on surfaces that are tightly connected together box-fashion, such as countertops and cabinet frames, because the bracing action of the box prevents severe warping. ∎

FOUNDATION BELOW FROST LINE

One type of building movement that we can prevent is frost heaving. Frost heaving is caused by water freezing in the soil beneath a building's foundations. Phase change expansion of the water can cause the soil to expand, lifting the building slightly. Larger amounts of lifting can occur due to the growth of long vertical crystals of ice under the foundation under certain conditions of temperature and moisture.

1. Building codes generally require that the bottom of a foundation be placed at a level below the deepest level to which the ground freezes during a severe winter; consult the applicable building code to find out how deep this is.

2. Isolated pier foundations are economical and effective for decks, porches, and small wooden structures. A post hole digger is used to excavate for each pier. The concrete should not be cast directly against the rough sides of the hole, however, because frost can heave upward against the rough sides of the pier. A smooth fiber tube form should be used to cast piers whose sides are smooth above the frost line. Similarly, a foundation wall should be cast in smooth forms, not directly against the walls of the trench.

3. Though most building codes in North America do not allow it at this time, many buildings in cold European climates are built on foundations that are quite shallow. An exterior layer of plastic foam insulation allows interior heat that escapes from the building to warm the soil beneath the foundation and keep it from freezing. This detail should not be used for an unheated building, such as a barn or storage building.

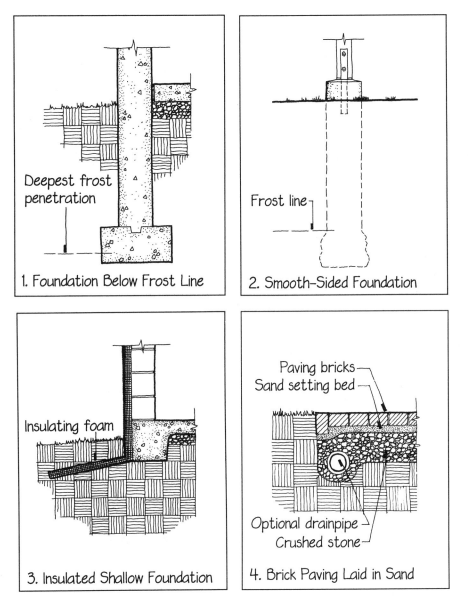

1. Foundation Below Frost Line

2. Smooth-Sided Foundation

3. Insulated Shallow Foundation

4. Brick Paving Laid in Sand

4. It is not practical to support outdoor pavings, such as roads, patios, and walks, on foundations that go below the frost line; they must be supported at a much shallower level. Most frost heaving can be prevented, however, by placing the paving (concrete, asphalt, brick, or stone) on a thick, well-drained layer of crushed stone that is graded (sorted) so that it has no fine particles. The spaces between the stones drain water away from the underside of the paving and also furnish expansion space for water that freezes in the soil below. For brick and stone pavings, a sand setting bed above the crushed stone gives the mason a precise means of regulating the height of the masonry units. ■

STRUCTURE/ENCLOSURE JOINT

The structural frame of a building and its infill components move in different ways and have different structural capabilities. They must be joined in ways that recognize these differences.

1. Interior partitions in buildings with steel or concrete frames are not strong enough to support the floors above and are not intended to do so. If a partition fits tightly against the underside of a floor slab, any deflection whatever of the floor slab will apply a load to the top of the partition. This may cause the building structure to behave in unanticipated and possibly dangerous ways, and it may cause the partition to buckle. To keep the partition from supporting a load, its structure should stop short of the underside of the floor slab. The size of the gap should be determined in collaboration with the structural engineer. The gap should be closed with an acoustical sealant or a soft rubber gasket, either of which will compress readily if the slab should deflect. In the steel stud partition illustrated here, the studs are cut short and are merely inserted into the upper runner track without fasteners, creating a slip joint to allow for floor movement.

2. A basement wall usually supports a portion of the weight of the building above. A basement floor slab does not. If the slab were rigidly connected to the wall, any slight settlement in the wall foundation would bend the slab and cause it to crack near the connection. A simple movement joint between the two isolates the slab from any movement in the structural wall. A similar joint should be detailed around interior columns where they intersect the floor slab. This type of joint is often called an isolation joint.

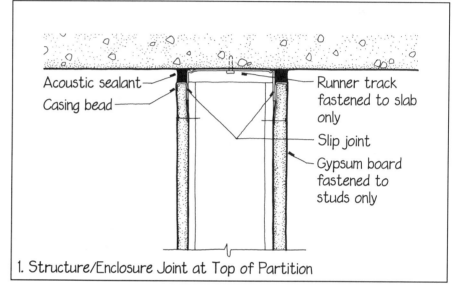

Acoustic sealant
Casing bead
Runner track fastened to slab only
Slip joint
Gypsum board fastened to studs only

1. Structure/Enclosure Joint at Top of Partition

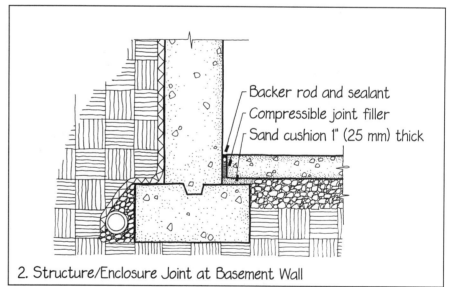

Backer rod and sealant
Compressible joint filler
Sand cushion 1" (25 mm) thick

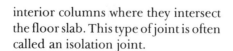

2. Structure/Enclosure Joint at Basement Wall

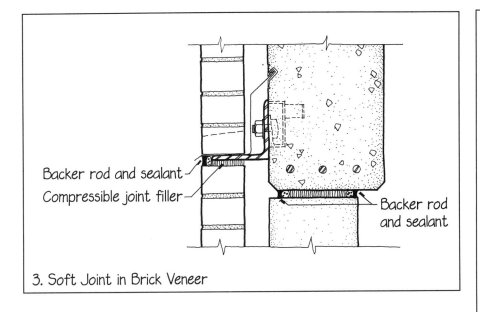

3. Soft Joint in Brick Veneer

Backer rod and sealant
Compressible joint filler
Backer rod and sealant

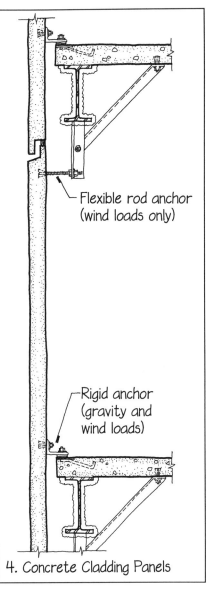

Flexible rod anchor (wind loads only)

Rigid anchor (gravity and wind loads)

4. Concrete Cladding Panels

3. A brick veneer curtain wall stands on a concealed steel shelf angle that is supported by the frame of the building at each story. The veneer is too slender to support any load except its own weight. If an ordinary mortar joint were used below the shelf angle, a slight deflection or creep in the structural frame could cause the veneer to carry the weight of the building instead of the frame. This would be disastrous: The thin brick veneer would buckle and virtually explode off the building. To keep this from happening, a "soft joint" of sealant is provided under each shelf angle. A similar "soft joint" is installed between the backup wall and the spandrel beam.

4. Story-high stone or precast concrete cladding panels are generally supported on the frame of the building near their lower edge. If a similarly rigid attachment were made to the frame near the upper edge, any deflection or creep in the frame would transfer the weight of the building to the cladding panel. A flexible rod anchor supports the panel against wind loads near its upper edge but does not permit the transfer of gravity loads between the frame and the panel. An alternative to the flexible rod anchor would be an angle clip with a vertically slotted bolt hole to allow free vertical motion in the anchor. Horizontal and vertical sealant joints isolate the panels from one another.

5. Bay-width spandrel panels should be supported at the column lines only; otherwise they may be subjected to bending forces when the spandrel beam deflects under normal loadings.

The connections between frame and cladding are critical ones. Shelf angles and panel connections should always be designed in consultation with the building's structural engineer (see *Small Structures*, p. 95). ∎

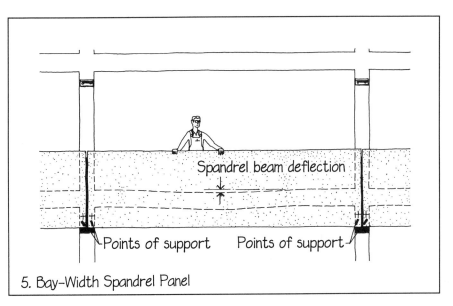

Spandrel beam deflection

Points of support   Points of support

5. Bay-Width Spandrel Panel

ABUTMENT JOINT

Abutment joints allow for movement between dissimilar materials, or between old and new construction. Dissimilar materials tend to move at different rates and in different patterns. Old construction has already undergone foundation settlement, long-term structural movements, and initial moisture movements, while new construction has not. In either case, an abutment joint should be provided to allow for differential movement between the two parts of the construction.

1. This drawing shows an abutment joint between a masonry wall and a wood-frame wall. A sealant joint of generous width allows for differential movement.

2. New and old masonry should not be interleaved but should be separated cleanly and connected by a flexible abutment joint. This is easier for masons to lay and avoids the cracking that might be caused by the shrinkage of the new mortar. ■

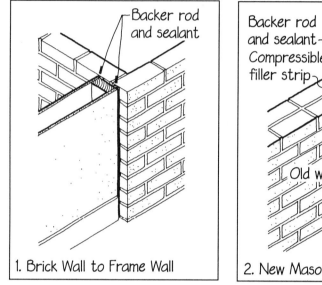

1. Brick Wall to Frame Wall

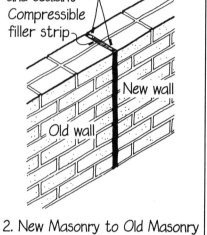

2. New Masonry to Old Masonry

EXPANSION JOINT

Large surfaces of materials that tend to expand after installation should be divided into smaller surfaces by a regular pattern of expansion joints.

1. This expansion joint accessory for plaster allows for the slight expansion in the curing plaster, as well as for subsequent moisture movement and movement in the underlying structure of the wall. The metal lath must be discontinuous along the line of the joint to allow for free movement. The expansion joint accessory is a simple metal or plastic bellows shape. At the time it is installed, it is closed with a plastic tape that prevents it from becoming clogged with plaster, which would be unsightly and would destroy its function. After the plaster has been applied, the tape is stripped away, creating a straight, clean, dark shadow line in the plaster surface. As with any joint, the pattern created by the expansion joints should be worked out and described to the builder in elevation view.

2. Long walls of brick masonry are subject to expansion as the bricks absorb moisture and require periodic expansion joints to relieve the pressure that this otherwise would cause. Any reinforcing in the brickwork should be discontinued across the joint. In masonry expansion joints, it is often important that a spline or tongue-and-groove feature be provided that will maintain the alignment of the wall while allowing for the necessary in-plane movement.

3. Expansion joints in any material should be located at lines of structural weakness in the surface, where cracking or crushing would tend to occur if no joints were provided. ▷

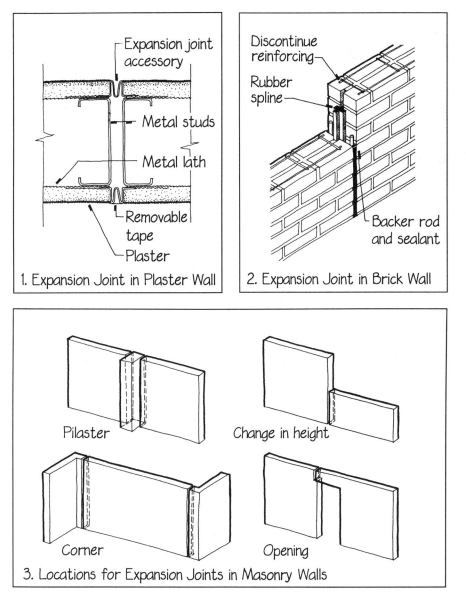

1. Expansion Joint in Plaster Wall

2. Expansion Joint in Brick Wall

3. Locations for Expansion Joints in Masonry Walls

4. Aluminum cladding components are subject to large amounts of expansion and contraction caused by daily and seasonal differences in air temperatures and by direct solar heating of the metal. Both horizontal and vertical expansion joints must be provided at appropriate intervals. Each joint must be designed to maintain the alignment of the components and to keep out weather while allowing for movement. In this example, vertical movement is accommodated by a sliding mullion connection at every other floor of the building and by the movement of the spandrel glass into and out of a deep recess in the horizontal mullions.

5. In aluminum cladding systems, horizontal movement may be taken up by vertical mullions that are split or that have a bellows action. It can also be accommodated by sliding connections where each horizontal mullion piece joins the verticals, and by glass movement in and out of the vertical mullions.

6. Suggested maximum expansion joint spacings are 30′ (9 m) for gypsum and gypsum/lime plaster, and 200′ (60 m) for brick masonry. Expected moisture movement of these materials can be quantified by using the procedure shown on page 77. Expected amounts of total movement in each joint can be calculated by following the procedure outlined on pages 35 and 36. ∎

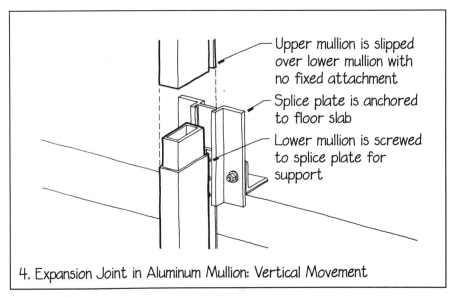

Upper mullion is slipped over lower mullion with no fixed attachment
Splice plate is anchored to floor slab
Lower mullion is screwed to splice plate for support

4. Expansion Joint in Aluminum Mullion: Vertical Movement

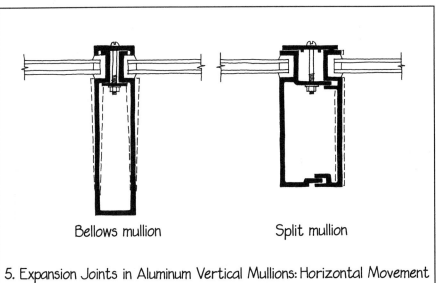

Bellows mullion   Split mullion

5. Expansion Joints in Aluminum Vertical Mullions: Horizontal Movement

CONTROL JOINT

A control joint is an intentional line of weakness that is created in the surface of a brittle material that tends to shrink. Its role is to encourage any shrinkage cracking that would occur within itself, in order to avoid random cracking of the surface around it.

1. A sidewalk crack is a control joint that is formed by tooling a deep crack into the wet concrete. When the sidewalk shrinks, cracking is channeled to the tooled crack. The sidewalk remains as a group of large, stable rectangular units, rather than as a weak array of irregular concrete fragments.

2. A concrete slab floor on grade should be divided by control joints into smaller rectangles that can be expected to stay crack-free. The joints can be created by tooling the wet concrete or by sawing it during the early stages of its curing. With either method, the depth of the joint should be at least 25% of the depth of the slab. Any reinforcing in the slab should be discontinued across the line of the joint. If it is important to maintain a level surface across the joint, smooth, greased steel rod dowels can be inserted. These allow for in-plane movement while preventing out-of-plane movement.

3. As seen in this plan view, slabs should be divided in a way that avoids odd-shaped panels that are prone to cracking. A rectangular panel whose length is greater than 1.5 times its width is likely to crack across its middle. Control joints around columns and pilasters should be cut on a diagonal, as shown, to avoid inside corners that foster cracks. ▷

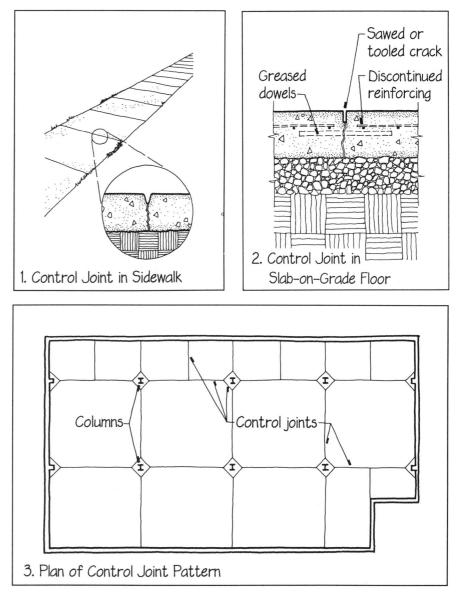

1. Control Joint in Sidewalk

2. Control Joint in Slab-on-Grade Floor

3. Plan of Control Joint Pattern

4. Poured concrete walls are also subject to shrinkage cracking. Control joints are usually created by inserting strips into the formwork to create linear slots along which cracking will occur. The slots should reduce the wall thickness by at least 25%. Every second reinforcing bar should be discontinued to encourage cracking forces to concentrate at the line of the joint.

5. Concrete masonry walls tend to shrink and crack, the more so if non-moisture-controlled (Type II) units are used. Walls that are made of either Type I or Type II units need control joints, of which two examples are shown here. Both of these details interlock in a way that allows in-plane but not out-of-plane movement.

6. Control joints in masonry or concrete walls should be located at points of structural weakness, as seen in drawing 3 on page 87.

7. Stucco control joints are formed with an accessory that is similar to the expansion joint used in gypsum plaster walls. The lath should be cut completely along the line of the control joint to create a line of weakness.

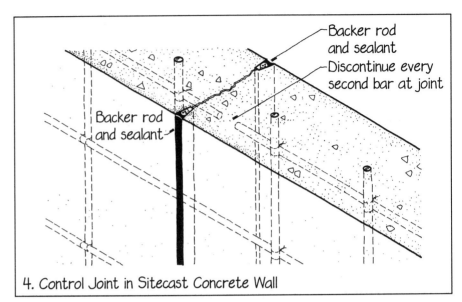

4. Control Joint in Sitecast Concrete Wall

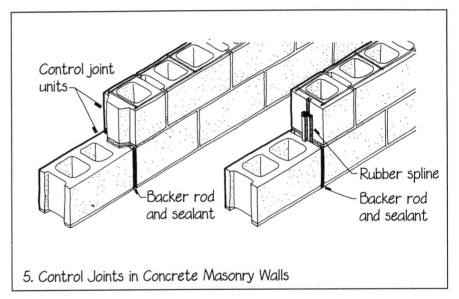

5. Control Joints in Concrete Masonry Walls

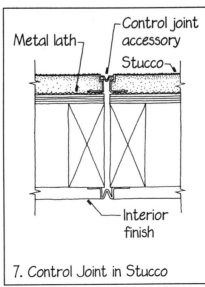

7. Control Joint in Stucco

8. Recommended control joint spacings for various materials are as follows:

Material	Control Joint Spacing
Concrete slabs on grade	24 times slab thickness
Concrete exterior walls	20' (6 m)

Concrete masonry walls, unreinforced:

Type I units	40' (12 m) or twice the height of the wall, whichever is less
Type II units	20' (6 m) or twice the height of the wall, whichever is less

Concrete masonry walls, joint reinforcing every second course:

Type I units	50' (16 m) or three times the height of the wall, whichever is less
Type II units	25' (8 m) or three times the height of the wall, whichever is less
Stucco walls	10' (3 m)

■

SLIDING JOINT

Several traditional wood details rely on joints that allow components to slide past one another as they expand and contract with changing moisture content.

1. Wood siding is subject to relatively large amounts of moisture movement because it is exposed to rain and snow, as well as to the drying effects of sunlight and wind. Overlapping horizontal siding should be nailed to the building in the pattern shown here, which allows each piece to slide beneath the piece above as it moves, thus relieving potential stresses.

2. Board-and-batten siding should be nailed in the pattern shown here in plan view, to provide sliding joints for moisture movement.

3. The entire width of a simple Z-brace door lies across the grain of its boards. The door is subject to so much moisture movement across its width that it is difficult to keep it fitted to its opening during both the dry and humid seasons of the year. The traditional panel door responds to this problem by minimizing the amount of cross grain shrinkage across the width of the door, limiting it to the width of the two stiles, which totals only about 9″ (230 mm). The narrow edges of the panels are recessed loosely into the grooves in the stiles and rails. This allows differences in moisture movement to be relieved within the structure of the door. ■

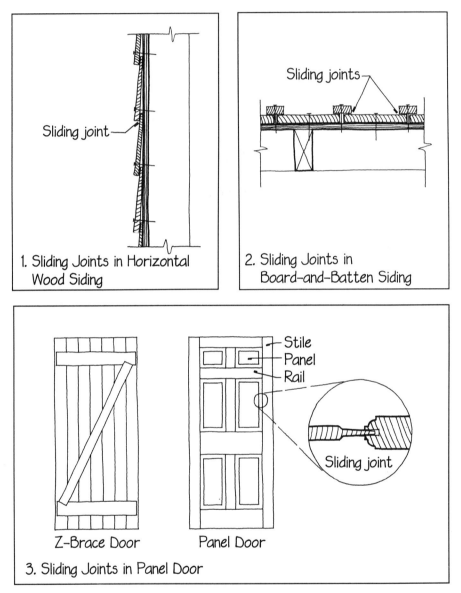

1. Sliding Joints in Horizontal Wood Siding

2. Sliding Joints in Board-and-Batten Siding

3. Sliding Joints in Panel Door

Z-Brace Door

Panel Door

Stile
Panel
Rail

Sliding joint

BUILDING SEPARATION JOINT

Buildings that are large in horizontal extent should be divided into separate structural entities, each of which is compact enough so that it can react as a rigid unit to foundation settlement and other movements, thereby avoiding damage.

1. This drawing shows how building separation joints should be located at points of geometric weakness where cracking would otherwise be likely to occur. Notice how the joints divide the building into compact rectilinear volumes. At each joint plane, the structure of the building is cut completely through, with independent structural support on each side of the joint. Building separation joints are often referred to as "expansion joints," but they are really intended to separate a large building into a set of smaller buildings so that the building can deal effectively with not only thermal expansion but also soil settlement, materials shrinkage, and seismic deflections. The locations, clear spacing between parts of the building, foundations, structural support, and detailing of building separation joints should be designed in consultation with the structural and foundation engineers so that combinations of thermal and moisture movement, foundation settlement, and the relative seismic motions of the adjoining parts of the building can be dealt with adequately. As a general guide, spacings between building separation joints should not exceed 150 to 200 ft (45 to 60 m).

2. Building separation joints must be covered to keep out the weather and to provide continuity to interior surfaces. This is a typical design for a separation joint cover for a low-slope roof. A flexible bellows keeps water and air from

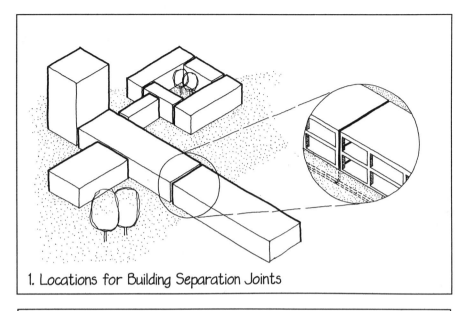

1. Locations for Building Separation Joints

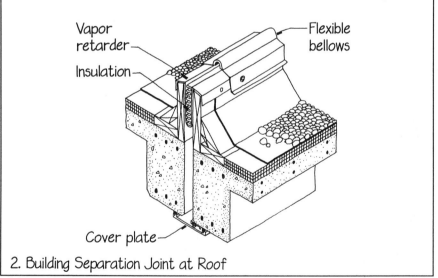

2. Building Separation Joint at Roof

leaking through the joint but adjusts readily to movement between the two sections of the building. A high curb on either side keeps the bellows from being submerged in water. The joint is filled with thermal insulation and a vapor retarder. The ceiling below is provided with a gasketed metal cover plate that can adjust to movement while retaining a reasonably attractive appearance. The bellows and the interior cover plate are common off-the-shelf components, typical of dozens of designs offered by a number of manufacturers.   ▷

3. This building separation joint in a masonry exterior wall is closed with a flexible waterstop and sealant. The waterstop may be made of metal, plastic, or rubber. The interior wall surface is finished with the same cover plate used at the ceiling in drawing 2.

4. At the floor, a building separation joint cover must adjust to differential movements while supporting traffic loads and providing a smooth, non-tripping transition between the floor planes on either side. Manufacturers offer many devices for achieving this. This example is based on two mirror image aluminum extrusions that are cast into the edges of the two floor slabs. When the building is finished, two rubber bellows strips are snapped into the extrusions. Then a metal cover plate is fastened down to steel clips with spring-loaded bolts that hold it firmly in place despite any relative motion of the slabs on either side. ■

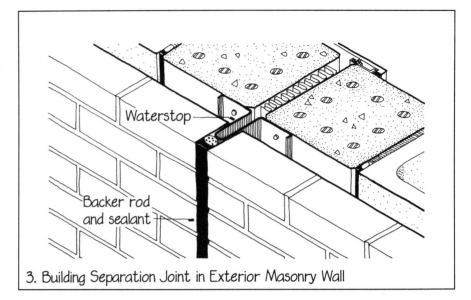

3. Building Separation Joint in Exterior Masonry Wall

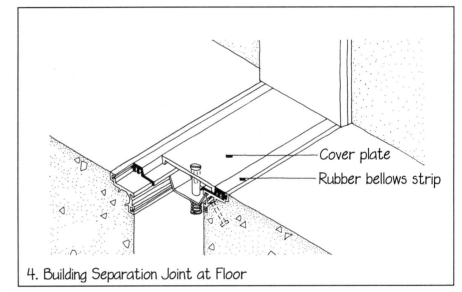

4. Building Separation Joint at Floor

FUNCTION:
PROVIDING STRUCTURAL SUPPORT

SMALL STRUCTURES

It's obviously important that a building have a structural frame that has been carefully laid out, calculated, and detailed so that it is stable and will not deflect excessively. Less obvious is the need to engineer smaller but still very important structures that are component parts of the larger building.

1. There are many small, seemingly trivial structural problems that the detailer must recognize and solve through standard engineering design procedures, working alone or with the help of a structural engineer:

- Rainwater gutters and downspouts and their attachments to the building must be strong enough to resist worst-case snow and ice loadings.

- Fascias and soffits at the eaves of a wood frame building often need special support details. These must provide a solid base for nailing.

- Any component of an exterior rainscreen wall that acts as an air barrier must be designed to resist full wind pressures and suctions, even if it is only a small weatherstrip gasket.

- Masonry ties need to be checked for strength and rigidity to prevent deflection and cracking of the face veneer under wind loads.

- Backup walls of concrete masonry need to be designed to carry wind loads and to transmit them to the building frame; this often requires steel reinforcing and special attachment details for the top of the wall. Steel stud backup walls must be engineered carefully to control lateral deflection so as to prevent cracking of exterior masonry veneers.

- The selection of glass thickness and mullion section requires engineering analysis. The depth of "bite" of the mullion on the glass also needs to be worked out. Too shallow a bite may allow the glass to pop out under wind load; too deep a bite may restrict excessively the wind-induced bending of the glass. Literature from glass and mullion manufacturers usually offers guidance in these matters, provided that you know the magnitudes of the expected wind pressures on the building.

- Projecting sashes need to have sufficiently rigid frames and attachments to resist loads from gusting winds. The larger the sash is, the stiffer its frame must be.

- Flat metal spandrel panels need to be stiff enough so that they will not buckle under wind loads. They also need to be designed to *appear* flat under all conditions. Stone cladding panels must be strong enough so that they will not crack or deflect excessively. Extra panel thickness may be required to counteract the thermal warping potential of thin stone panels that are exposed to sunlight.

- Attachments of cladding systems to the frame of the building—components such as shelf angles, mounting clips, and concrete embedments—must be carefully engineered for both strength and deflection.

- A guardrail at the edge of a balcony, mezzanine, or deck must meet building code requirements for resistance to lateral force. This requires a full-scale engineering analysis that includes meticulous attention to designing attachment details.

- Elaborate suspended plaster ceilings may require stronger support than the standard hanger wires and attachments.

- Large, heavy doors need frames, frame-to-wall attachments, hinges, latchsets, and closers with commensurate structural strength. Sometimes the wall itself must be strengthened around a heavy door.

- An ordinary bookshelf needs careful attention to the stiffness of the shelves. A nominal 1-in (19 mm) board often is not stiff enough. A freestanding bookcase needs attention to lateral stability in both directions.

- Grab bars, towel bars, and stair railings must be sufficiently rigid and must be fastened to the wall with sufficient strength.

- Pipe hangers, conduit hangers, duct hangers, and equipment mounts all need engineering attention.

- Lighting fixtures often require special attachments that are designed to bear their weight safely.

It is frequently left up to the detailer to recognize such smaller-scale structural problems as these and to see that they are fully engineered and detailed. ∎

FUNCTION:
PROVIDING PASSAGES FOR MECHANICAL AND ELECTRICAL SERVICES

E V E R Y building is laced with a three-dimensional web of distribution lines for mechanical and electrical services—ductwork, piping, and wiring for heating, cooling, ventilating, hot and cold water, sewage, fire suppression, electrical energy, illumination, telephones, temperature controls, computer networks, intercommunication systems, antennas, and alarm systems. Almost every existing building has been retrofitted with distribution lines for which it was not originally designed, making it a safe bet that every building that is on the drawing boards today will be called upon in the future to house services that we cannot even imagine. In detailing a building, it is important to work with the designers of the mechanical, plumbing, electrical, and communications systems to furnish passages for the service distribution lines, both present and future, that will run through the building. In most cases, these lines should be comfortably concealed; if they are exposed to view, it should be by design, not by default. Generous spaces should be provided for the lines, with sufficient worker access points and workable interconnections from one plane of distribution to another. This will allow economical installation, maintenance, and future change of the services. It will also avoid having the appearance of the building and its details spoiled by the improvised installation of service systems that its designer and detailer did not anticipate.

To provide a fully three-dimensional network of passages, two detail patterns must be combined:

Vertical Chase (page 98)

Horizontal Plenum (page 101)

At each point of intersection between chase and plenum, the various services must have space to make the transition from vertical to horizontal.

Ductwork, piping, and conduits may be exposed in a building rather than concealed in chases and plenums, but this will not necessarily lead to more economical construction. Vertical and horizontal spaces will still have to be reserved for these services, and money must be allocated for additional design time to lay out neat arrangements of lines, additional installation time to permit a high standard of workmanship, and the cost of painting and finishing the lines.

VERTICAL CHASE

A vertical chase is a concealed passage in which services can run from ground to roof and floor to floor. A hollow wall that serves as a vertical chase can often perform some horizontal distribution functions as well.

1. The hollow vertical spaces between wood or steel studs in a wall or partition furnish convenient passages for small-diameter services, usually without further attention from the detailer. Vertical runs of electrical wiring or water supply piping fit easily into these spaces, provided they can penetrate the bottom and top plates where the wall meets the floor and ceiling. Steel studs with their prepunched holes also make horizontal runs of wiring easy. Horizontal runs of wiring through wood studs require that the studs be drilled, which is easy and acceptable if the holes are not too large. Long horizontal runs of piping are generally difficult to thread through holes in studs. Waste and vent piping, with their larger diameters, often require deeper studs, a double row of studs, or a dedicated chase.

2. In an exterior wall or any wall adjoining unheated space, water piping must be kept on the interior side of all thermal insulation to prevent freezing in cold weather, even if the pipes themselves are jacketed with insulation. It is safest to lay out a building so that all water piping is contained in interior partitions, avoiding exterior walls entirely. If water piping must be installed in an exterior wall, be sure the insula-

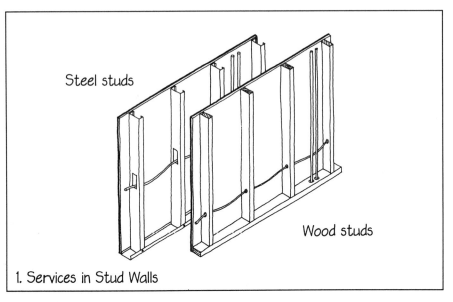

1. Services in Stud Walls

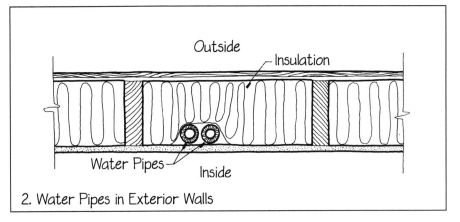

2. Water Pipes in Exterior Walls

tion detail is noted in the section of the specifications relating to thermal insulation. Be sure also to make a note to inspect the wall after it has been insulated and before it is closed up, to be sure the pipes are fully inside the insulation.

3. A masonry wall, even one composed of hollow concrete blocks, does not offer easy routes for piping and wiring. A typical solution for small-diameter service lines is to furr the interior face of the wall with metal or wood strips. The service lines pass through or between the strips and are concealed by a finish layer on the inside. Thermal insulation may also be added between the furring strips. For larger-diameter service lines, the furring may take the form of a stud wall spaced away from the masonry by the required distance.

4. Plumbing waste and vent lines generally will not fit within a standard-thickness stud partition. In some cases larger studs can be used to create a sufficient space for the pipes. In most cases it is preferable to frame a double wall with enough clear space between so that the pipes can run freely in both the horizontal and vertical directions. It is not enough to allow a space a little larger than the diameter of the largest pipe in the wall; there must also be space enough for supply piping to cross in front of the waste and vent risers, and in many cases for smaller-diameter horizontal waste and vent pipes to cross the larger-diameter vertical runs.

5. Certain sizes of flat and oval ducts are designed to fit between wall studs but have limited air-handling capacity. Additional thickness is often required for thermal insulation around the ducts, especially in exterior walls. Even if a duct fits between studs, it may require the removal of so much of the top and bottom plates of the wall that remedial strengthening of these elements is required. Larger ducts often require special framing. ▷

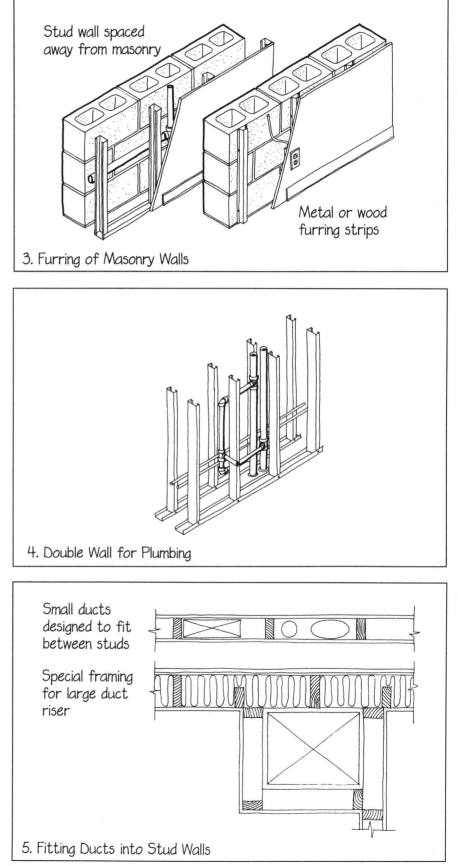

Stud wall spaced away from masonry

Metal or wood furring strips

3. Furring of Masonry Walls

4. Double Wall for Plumbing

Small ducts designed to fit between studs

Special framing for large duct riser

5. Fitting Ducts into Stud Walls

6. Most larger buildings require dedicated chases or shafts for major vertical runs of mechanical and electrical distribution lines. These must be located and sized through extensive consultation with the professionals who design each system. A vertical electrical shaft generally adjoins an electrical closet at each floor where transitions are made to horizontal lines of distribution. A vertical shaft for ductwork sometimes connects to a fan room at each story, but more often it connects directly to the horizontal runs of ductwork at the ceiling or floor. If a ductwork shaft is hemmed in by stair towers, elevator shafts, and plumbing walls, these connections may be difficult or impossible.

7. Vertical pipes and electrical conduits are sometimes housed in interior or exterior column covers. The interior location is usually preferable, both for protection from freezing and for ease of connection at each story. Air ducts, if they are small enough, can also be routed through these passages.

8. There are some general precautions that relate to any type of vertical chase or shaft. These vertical passages must line up accurately from one story to the next, avoiding horizontal zigs and zags that are costly and troublesome. Access panels must be provided at points specified by the designers of the various systems. The passages must be fully enclosed with materials that meet the fire resistance requirements of the applicable building code. In many instances, the spaces where piping, conduits, or ductwork go through each floor must be fire-

stopped, using mineral batt or putty materials that have been designed and tested for this purpose. ■

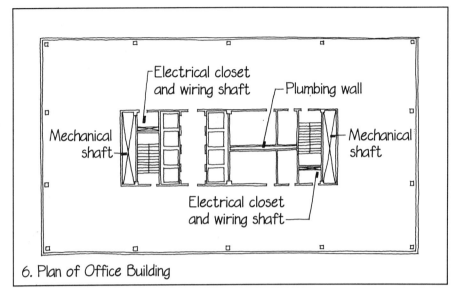

6. Plan of Office Building

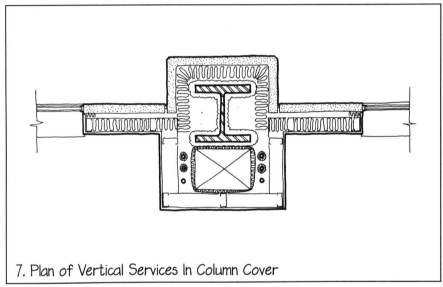

7. Plan of Vertical Services In Column Cover

HORIZONTAL PLENUM

A horizontal plenum is a space that permits each service to be routed to any point on a floor.

1. Most floor/ceiling constructions structured with wood or steel joists afford considerable space for ducts, wires, and pipes. Open-web joists allow easy distribution in both directions, provided that ductwork of the required sizes fits their triangular openings. Holes have to be created in wood or sheet metal joists to allow services to run in a perpendicular direction. The sizes and locations of these holes must be cleared with the structural designer.

2. A furred-down ceiling creates lateral passages for electrical wiring but not enough height for piping or ductwork.

3. A suspended ceiling creates a horizontal plenum within which every type of service can run. The plenum space must be high enough to accommodate all the planned services, but its height should be minimized to avoid excessive overall building height. Horizontal zones must be reserved within the plenum for each of the major services. Generally, the lowest stratum is reserved for lighting fixtures and sprinkler pipes, the next higher stratum for ductwork, and the highest for structure and fireproofing. The height of each of these strata must be agreed upon in advance, and the plenum plan of each bay of the building must be designed so that columns, fire separation walls, air diffusers, lighting fixtures, speakers, and sprinkler heads all have reserved zones in which to descend through the ceiling without encountering other systems. This requires full cooperation among all of the professionals involved in the design of the building. The ceiling surface must provide service access at all required points, either through removable tiles or panels, or through special access doors. ▷

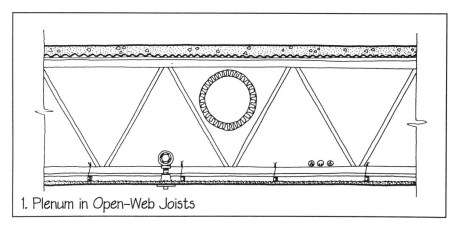

1. Plenum in Open-Web Joists

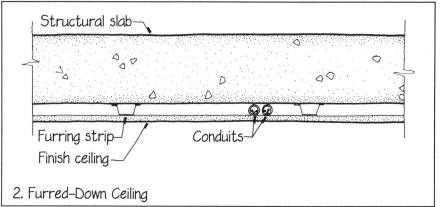

Structural slab

Furring strip
Finish ceiling
Conduits

2. Furred-Down Ceiling

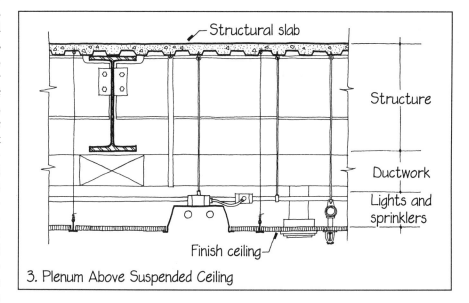

Structural slab

Structure

Ductwork

Lights and sprinklers

Finish ceiling

3. Plenum Above Suspended Ceiling

4. Access doors, air diffusers and grills, sprinkler heads, speakers, fire sensors, and lighting fixtures can create visual chaos in a ceiling. Reflected ceiling plans should be designed cooperatively by the entire design team to create an orderly overhead landscape.

5. An alternative to the suspended ceiling plenum is an underfloor plenum created by an access floor raised a few inches above the structural floor. This permits the floor structure of a building to be left exposed beneath as a finish ceiling. This is a particular advantage in such situations as converting an old building with heavy timber floors to a new use.

6. In some laboratory and hospital buildings that have unusually elaborate services that must be serviced and altered frequently, standing-height plenums called interstitial ceilings are constructed to facilitate maintenance access. These are usually created by means of a thick, heavily reinforced plaster ceiling suspended on steel rods from the floor above. The ceiling is designed to support safely the weight of workers and tools.

7. There are various systems for creating hollow passages for electrical and communications wiring within the structure of a floor. These include cellular steel decking, and cellular raceways that are cast into concrete floor structures. Any such system must be designed in collaboration with the mechanical and electrical designers, the structural designer, and the manufacturer of the raceway components.

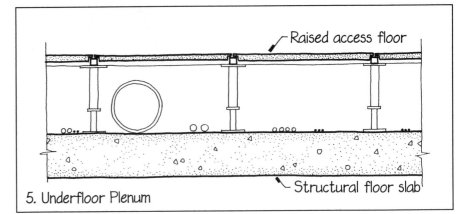

5. Underfloor Plenum

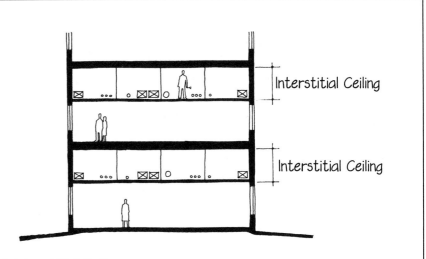

6. Interstitial Ceilings

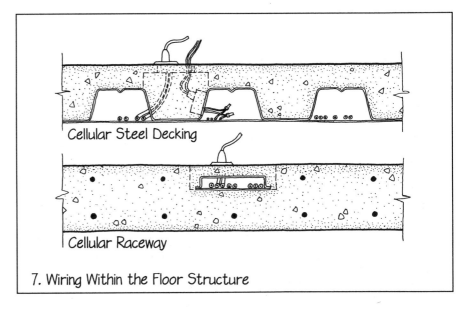

7. Wiring Within the Floor Structure

8. In buildings with relatively modest requirements for mechanical services, horizontal distribution may take place primarily above a central corridor or above a strip of dropped ceiling that runs around the perimeter of the building. This is an economical approach that can work well in hotels, dormitories, apartment buildings, and classroom buildings.

9. In general, any horizontal plenum space must connect generously with the vertical passages that feed it. Where it meets a fire wall or a fire separation wall, the wall must penetrate up through the plenum to close tightly against the structural floor above. Any ducts that cross this fire separation must be provided with fire dampers, and any other penetrations must be sealed with fire-rated construction. Care should be taken to avoid acoustical flanking paths through a plenum space (page 70).

■

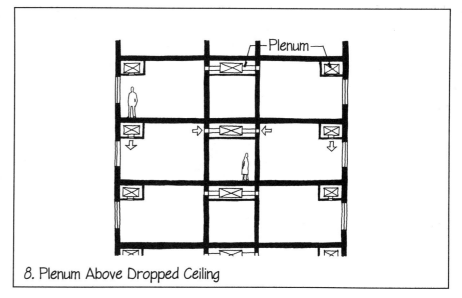

8. Plenum Above Dropped Ceiling

FUNCTION:
HEALTH AND SAFETY

M I L L I O N S of people are injured needlessly each year in unsafe buildings, and millions more become ill because of unhealthy buildings. People trip and fall on unsafe floors and stairs. They cut, scrape, and gouge themselves on rough surfaces, sharp edges, and broken glass. They are poisoned by fumes from various adhesives and plastics, and by smoke from building fires. People who are ill, aged, or otherwise disabled may find themselves unable to reach whole areas of a building because of physical barriers that have been incorporated into the architecture. Most health and safety issues in detailing are regulated by building codes; others are merely based on common sense.

Detail patterns relating to health and safety are the following:

SAFE FOOTING

Tripping and slipping are two occurrences that the detailer must guard against in floor and stair details.

1. Tripping on floors can be caused by floor-mounted doorstops, unusually high thresholds, and abrupt changes in floor level or floor material.

2. Tripping on stairs can be avoided by careful compliance with building code provisions. Proportion treads and risers as the code requires, and take care when inspecting construction that excessive variations do not creep into tread and riser dimensions. Do not design stairs that have only one or two risers; people tend not to see them until they have fallen on them.

Always comply exactly with handrail requirements of the building code.

3. Use abrasive tread inserts to prevent slipping on stairs that are made of polished materials such as marble or metal.

4. Pay particular attention to flooring materials that may become wet. In public entries and lobbies with stone or tile floors, use a slightly rough surface finish rather than a highly polished one. In bathrooms, kitchens, and showers, avoid smoothly glazed floor tiles.

5. Although there are no legal guidelines for the coefficients of friction of floor materials, such coefficients are published by many flooring manufacturers. In general, avoid flooring materials with a coefficient of friction less than 0.5. Use higher values for ramps, and for floors or stairs that may become wet.

6. It is difficult to watch both one's head and one's feet at the same time. A person is likely either to trip or to bump his or her head on stairs with insufficient headroom. Always draw large-scale sections of stairways to be sure that code requirements for headroom are met. Given the general increase in height of the population, it's not a bad idea to provide more than the required headroom wherever possible. ■

FALL PROTECTION

Handrails are required by code to help prevent falling on stairs and ramps, and guardrails are required at open edges of floors, balconies, mezzanines, decks, ramps, stairs, and landings.

1. Building codes and accessibility standards are very explicit in their requirements for detailing handrails and guardrails. Handrails are provided on stairs and ramps to help steady the users and to prevent them from falling. They must be of such size and shape in cross section that a human hand can grip at least three-quarters of the perimeter of the rail. Generally a round piece of metal pipe or wood is best. Rectangular pieces of wood are hard to grip and are illegal under most codes. Every handrail must be set away from the wall by a specified distance and must be mounted a specified distance above the floor or ramp. The wall behind the handrail must be smooth to prevent scraping of knuckles.

2. At the top and bottom of each flight of stairs, a handrail that is mounted on the wall must run out horizontally a code-specified distance beyond the end of the stair, and it must be turned into the wall so that it will not snag clothing. Handrail mountings must be engineered carefully to keep the rail rigid and to hold it tightly to the wall against any expected pull. The center handrail in a switchback stairway must be continuous from one flight to the next. If there is no center wall in a switchback stairway, the center handrail is also a guardrail and must be provided with balusters, as described in the following paragraphs. ▷

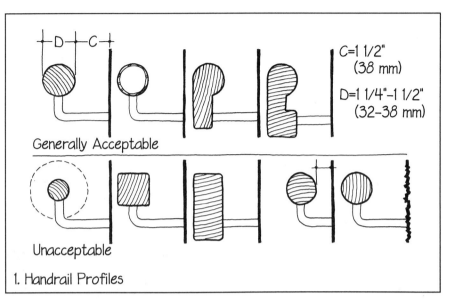

C=1 1/2" (38 mm)

D=1 1/4"–1 1/2" (32–38 mm)

Generally Acceptable

Unacceptable

1. Handrail Profiles

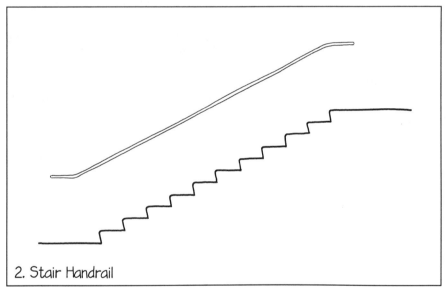

2. Stair Handrail

3. Guardrails must be provided to prevent people from falling over the edge of any abrupt change in floor level. Minimum guardrail heights are specified in the building codes, but it is often desirable to make the guardrail higher to avoid unpleasant psychological feelings of danger. A guardrail around a court or an atrium should be at a height that is comfortable to lean on with the elbows.

The balusters or other infill between the guardrail and the edge of the floor must be spaced closely enough so that an unsupervised small child cannot slip through. Research has shown that the maximum clear opening within a guardrail should be no more than 4″ (100 mm), and many building codes now use this figure. Even if the applicable code allows a larger dimension than this, it would be wise to stick to the 4″ figure, because larger dimensions are demonstrably unsafe. Horizontal balusters are generally legal, but if balusters are vertical, it is very difficult for a child to climb over the guardrail.

Building codes often require that there be a solid kick strip several inches high at the base of a guardrail. Its function is to prevent debris on the floor

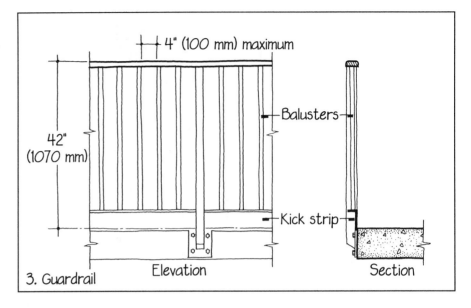

3. Guardrail   Elevation   Section

from accidentally being kicked through the guardrail and onto people below.

4. Building codes specify structural requirements for guardrails to prevent them from collapsing under the forces that people apply to them. This means that the rails, posts, and particularly the attachments of the posts to the floor edges must be engineered with great care to resist large lateral loadings. ■

SAFE EDGES

Although not generally covered by building codes, an important safety concern of the detailer is to provide safe edges and surfaces wherever people come into contact with a building.

1. Avoid splinters from wooden interior components by using vertical-grain wood and chamfering or rounding all corners.

2. Don't place rough surfaces of masonry, plaster, stucco, or concrete along stairs, hallways, and entrance areas where people are likely to brush against them. Avoid sharp edges and corners, especially in handrails, guardrails, and in door and window hardware.

3. Use round concrete columns rather than square ones in corridors and lobbies.

4. Be sure that doorknobs, locks, and handles are set back sufficiently from the frame of the door so that knuckles will not be skinned accidentally.

5. Nonpinching aluminum doors are available for use in entrances to schools and commercial buildings. These are designed so that they are unlikely to injure a child's hand. The hinge stile is cylindrical and is hinged at the centerline of the cylinder so that it cannot draw in and pinch a hand or a finger. The lock stile has a generous clearance between the door and the frame that is closed with a large, soft rubber gasket. ■

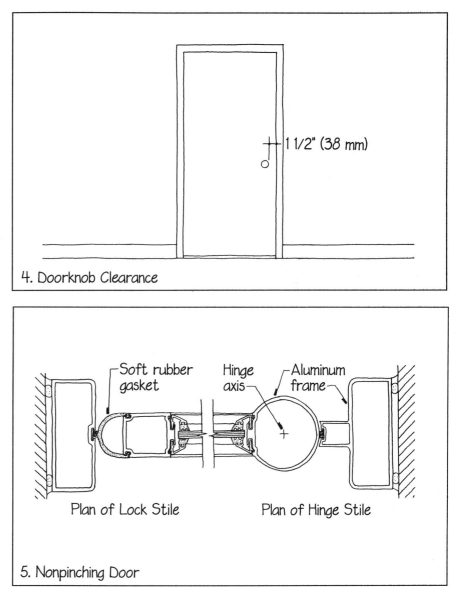

4. Doorknob Clearance

5. Nonpinching Door

SAFE GLAZING

Glass usage in buildings is code regulated to prevent several types of glass-related injury.

1. Avoid using glass in such a way that it doesn't seem to be there. Many early buildings in the modern style featured sheets of glass that ran from floor to ceiling and were purposely detailed to be virtually invisible. People tended to run into these transparent walls, sometimes shattering the glass and injuring themselves badly, even fatally, on the sharp spikes of glass. Building codes now require that any glass in or near doors must be either tempered glass or plastic glazing sheet. The same requirement applies to glass walls and to large areas of glass that come near the floor. The tempered glass or plastic is much stronger than ordinary annealed glass and much less likely to break. If the tempered glass does break, it disintegrates into small, blunt granules rather than large, sharp spears.

2. Tempered glass alone does not solve the safety problem with floor-to-ceiling glass. People can be injured just by the impact of running into a large, invisible, unbreakable sheet of glass. It is wise to install a horizontal mullion or a guardrail at railing height across the glass to warn of its presence.

3. All-glass doors or balcony fronts must be made of tempered glass.

4. Overhead glass can cause injury if it is broken by a windblown or falling object and falls on people below. Building code requirements for the glass in skylights and slope glazing systems are complex, but the most common code-conforming solution is simple: Use laminated glass in any overhead glazing. If broken, the laminated glass with its soft plastic interlayer tends to hang together and to remain in its frame.

■

NONTOXIC MATERIALS

Buildings can make people ill unless great care is taken to select and detail materials so as to avoid toxic effects.

1. The toxicity of materials used in construction is coming under increasing regulation at all levels of government. Specific laws relate to lead paint, asbestos in all its forms, such preservatives as creosote and pentachlorphenol, formaldehyde emissions from insulating foam and wood panel products, and hydrocarbon solvents that evaporate from coatings and adhesives.

Usually, the primary responsibility for avoiding toxic substances in construction rests with the specifier, but the detailer should take care especially to avoid using particle board products that give off formaldehyde in interior applications, unless the board is completely encased in plastic laminate or is painted or varnished on all its surfaces. Some plastics also give off irritating gases that can cause allergic reactions in many people.

2. Certain external elements of buildings need to be kept distant from openable windows and from any area where people might be walking or standing. These include cooling towers, air exhaust louvers, and plumbing vents. Cooling towers harbor several kinds of pathogenic microorganisms that can cause Legionnaire's disease and other respiratory illnesses. Air exhaust louvers discharge stale air from a building, with its moisture, smoke, odors, and bacteria. Plumbing vents (the open top ends of vertical runs of waste and vent plumbing) smell very bad and carry disease organisms. ■

FIRESAFE MATERIALS

Select interior finish materials in buildings to minimize danger from fire.

1. Building codes regulate on the basis of fire safety the finish materials that may be used inside buildings. Several factors are considered: How fast will flame spread across a surface of a given material? How much smoke will the burning material give off? And how much fuel will the material contribute to the blaze? These factors are measured by laboratory tests and are expressed in terms of a Flame Spread Rating, a Smoke Developed Rating, and a Fuel-Contributed Rating for each material.

The detailer should become familiar with the way in which the building code applies these ratings to interior finish materials.

2. Generally, the taller and larger a building is, the less the amount of combustible material that may be used in its construction. A single-family dwelling may be made entirely of combustible materials, but in a very tall or a very large building the structural members must be noncombustible, and combustible finish materials are permitted only in limited quantities.

3. Some building codes also regulate the toxicity of the combustion products that a material may give off. Many building materials produce highly toxic gases when they burn. Among these materials are wood, asphalt, some synthetic carpets and fabrics, and many rubber and plastic materials. Foam plastic insulation inside a building must always be covered with a fire-resistant finish, such as plaster or gypsum wallboard. Carpets, draperies, and upholstery should be chosen to avoid highly combustible materials and toxic combustion products. ∎

FIRE-RESISTANT ASSEMBLIES

A building code limits the designer's choice of structural systems and building components according to the occupancy, height, and floor area of the building that is being designed.

1. Every building code centers on two comprehensive tables: One designates the height and area limitations for buildings of different uses, according to the type of construction that is used; the other defines each construction type in terms of the fire resistance rating required for each of its major components (columns, bearing walls, beams, slabs, corridor and stair enclosures, shaft walls, and exterior walls). Using these two tables, the detailer can quickly establish the range of construction materials and systems from which the building may be built.

2. Additional tables in each building code give required fire resistance ratings for fire walls and fire doors.

3. Fire resistance ratings for available building components and systems are determined through standardized testing procedures carried out by impartial laboratories. These ratings are tabulated both in the publications of those laboratories and in literature that is available from relevant trade associations and individual manufacturers. The detailer should assemble and keep current a collection of these publications for use in selecting appropriately fire-resistant building components. A good start on this collection would be to acquire the Underwriters Laboratory's *Fire Resistance Directory* and the Gypsum Association's *Fire Resistance Design Manual*; see the reference list in the back of this book for information on ordering these publications.

4. Penetrations of fire-rated assemblies such as floors, fire walls, and fire separation walls must be sealed or otherwise protected against the passage of fire by code-approved means. Small holes through floors, such as pipe and conduit penetrations, are usually closed with fire-rated sealant systems marketed by a number of manufacturers. Gaps between exterior cladding and the edges of floors are sealed with safing, which usually consists of high-temperature mineral fiber batts supported by simple metal hooks or clips. Doors and door frames in fire walls and fire separation walls must have fire resistance ratings, as specified by the relevant building code. Glass areas in fire doors and in fire-rated walls are restricted by building codes, and must be wired glass, which holds together even after it has been broken by fire. At the point where a duct passes through a fire-rated wall, it must be fitted with a metal fire damper, a flap that closes automatically by means of a fusible link if the temperature in the duct rises above a set level. Vertical chases and shafts that pass through floors must be enclosed by walls of specified fire resistances. ■

BARRIER-FREE DESIGN

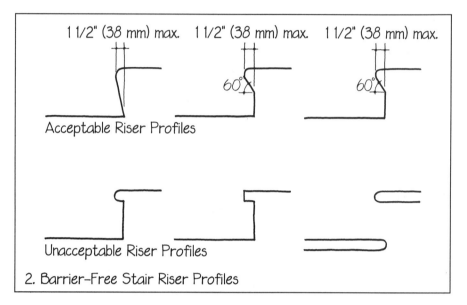

2. Barrier-Free Stair Riser Profiles

Buildings that are open to the public must be planned and detailed in specified ways that make them accessible to all members of the population, including those who are in wheelchairs or on crutches; the aged, blind or deaf; those in ill health or otherwise incapacitated. In multifamily housing projects, a small percentage of the dwelling units must conform to barrier-free standards so that they may be occupied by handicapped people. The legal requirements for barrier-free design of buildings are detailed in the Americans with Disabilities Act (1990), in various building codes and state laws, and in ANSI National Standard A117.1, *Providing Accessibility and Usability for Physically Handicapped People. Architectural Graphic Standards* gives extensive information on barrier-free design. This detail pattern can list only a few of the ways in which provisions of these documents affect the detailing of a building.

1. The most prominently visible result of barrier-free regulations is that there must be accessible routes into and through the building. Outdoors this can involve handicapped parking spaces, curb ramps, and specified types of ground surfaces. Accessible doors and entrances are assured by regulations that relate to clear widths, types of floor surfaces, wheelchair maneuvering clearances, vestibule size and configuration, door hardware, door closers, door opening force, and automatic doors. Ramps, elevators, and/or platform lifts may be required. The dimensions and inclination of ramps, the provision of landings, and the details of ramp handrails are all closely specified, as are elevator dimensions and controls.

2. Stairs must be profiled so that people on crutches can climb them easily. This rules out abruptly projecting nosings that can catch the toes of a person on crutches as they slide up a riser. Open-riser stairs are also prohibited. Instead, a smoothly profiled riser is required.

3. Accessibility regulations furnish minimum dimensions and details for wheelchair maneuverability in interior doorways, vestibules, corridors, and toilet rooms. Specified numbers of wheelchair-accessible toilet compartments and lavatories are required. Grab bars are required in toilet compartments to allow wheelchair occupants to move on and off toilets, and generous compartment dimensions are necessary to allow for wheelchair access. A percentage of the lavatory basins must be designed to allow a wheelchair to move in underneath, and their fittings must be of a type that can be operated by persons with impaired hand and arm dexterity. Showers and bathtubs require grab bars and access dimensions for wheelchairs.

Reception and sales counters must be designed with lower sections for the use of wheelchair users.

4. Drinking fountains must be of specified types that allow a wheelchair occupant access to the stream of water, and the valve must be operable by persons with impaired hand and arm dexterity. Public telephones must meet accessibility requirements.

5. Dwelling units designed for occupancy by handicapped persons generally must feature easy access from ground level, wide doorways and generous vestibules, handicapped toilet and bathing facilities, and kitchen cabinets, appliances, and storage facilities that are designed to be accessible from a wheelchair.

6. Building codes specify minimum numbers of wheelchair spaces in assembly halls, such as athletic arenas, auditoriums, concert halls, opera houses, and theaters. Accessibility and space requirements are spelled out in considerable detail. ∎

FUNCTION:
PROVIDING FOR THE AGING OF THE BUILDING

W H E N we design and build a building we hope that it will last a very long time. Most buildings do. But as the months and years go by, every building changes. Its surfaces wear, weather, and gather dirt. They undergo such chemical changes as fading and corrosion. Components of the building fail and are replaced. The building is remodeled or renovated from time to time. Often a beautiful building grows less so as these changes take place. The same sorts of changes may cause another building to grow more beautiful and take on added character. Some buildings last only a short time; others last for centuries. What accounts for these differences? Many of the reasons have to do with detailing.

Many of the detail patterns throughout this book have a profound effect on the rapidity with which a building ages, but there are three categories of detail patterns that relate specifically to managing the aging of a building. The first is a single pattern that defines an important principle in designing a building that will look good throughout its lifetime:

Surfaces That Age Gracefully (page 116)

The second category relates to the need to maintain a building:

Repairable Surfaces (page 117)
Cleanable Surfaces (page 118)
Maintenance Access (page 119)

The third category includes four patterns that have to do with preventing building deterioration:

Dry Wood (page 120)
Similar Metals (page 121)
Less Absorbent Materials (page 124)
Building Armor (page 125)

SURFACES THAT AGE GRACEFULLY

Some materials take on added visual interest as they age; others look progressively worse with the passing years.

1. Most species of wood deteriorate rapidly outdoors unless they are stained or painted. A few species are naturally resistant to decay, however. If left uncoated, they weather gradually to attractive shades of brown and gray. These species include cypress, redwood, white and red cedars, teak, and various tropical hardwoods. Weather slowly erodes the surfaces of these woods, requiring eventual replacement.

2. Outdoors, bright paint colors fade quickly to unattractive, streaky pastel shades. Clear coatings such as varnish allow sunlight to attack the wood beneath, and they peel off in a year or two. White paint, through an intentional chalking process, renews itself continually and tends to remain attractive. Earth color pigments and soft grays tend to hold their colors longer in sunlight than do brighter hues.

3. Among the metals, ordinary steel rusts away unless it has been painted. Stainless steel, especially in a brushed finish, retains its good looks indefinitely without painting. Aluminum forms a self-protecting oxide coating and does not corrode further, but this coating is thin, easily damaged, and looks splotchy. Through the process of anodizing, aluminum can be manufactured with a thick, durable coating of oxide that contains integral color of the designer's choice, and it will look good for decades. Copper forms a self-protecting oxide coating that is usually an attractive blue-green or black in color, depending on the pollutants in the atmosphere, and is a traditional choice for a metal that ages gracefully outdoors. Lead protects itself with a white oxide coating. A steel alloy is available that forms a tenacious, self-protecting coating of red-brown oxide and needs no painting. Weathering steel, lead, and copper tend to shed some of their oxide coatings, staining surfaces below, so care should be taken in detailing them to catch and drain all rainwater that has flowed over them before it can run onto such stainable surfaces as stone, concrete, wood, and glass.

4. In general, matte surfaces age more gracefully than glossy surfaces, which tend to weather rapidly to a matte finish on most materials. A mirror finish stainless steel panel, for example, soon grows dirty and its luster is obscured, whereas a matte finish stainless steel surface changes relatively little in appearance as it accumulates the same amount of dirt. Glossy paints lose their luster quickly in sunlight, chalking to a matte texture. The exceptions are glass and glazed ceramic tiles. These lose some of their sheen as they grow dirty, but when washed they regain their lustrous surfaces and bright colors.

5. Smooth concrete surfaces—those formed against steel, plastic, or overlaid plywood—have a tendency to feature every small flaw in the concrete. They also change appearance rapidly as they weather, becoming rougher and attracting more grime. The concrete surfaces that are more tolerant of flaws and that weather more gracefully are those formed with heavy textures, such as exposed aggregate, sandblasted, bush hammered, board formed, or ribbed.

6. Indoors, smooth, shiny, plain-colored surfaces age badly. A high-style shiny black plastic end table shows every grain of dust, every scratch, every water spot or ring, whereas an oak end table with a transparent finish calls attention to its grain figure, distracting the eye effectively from dust, scratches, and stains. A pure white polished marble floor would be a maintenance nightmare, while a rough slate floor would absorb lots of dirt and damage before it required attention. A plain-colored sheet vinyl flooring shows each scuff mark and spill, while a patterned flooring conceals them. A white-painted wall in a public school corridor will need to be washed frequently, while a dark, durable, textured wall surface can go months without cleaning. Bright chromium and brass surfaces need constant polishing, while matte-varnished or oil-finished wood and brushed bronze almost never need it, even growing more beautiful with age. ∎

REPAIRABLE SURFACES

It is wise to anticipate the inevitable need to repair the surfaces of a building and to utilize materials that can be repaired easily and inconspicuously.

1. A wall surface of painted gypsum board or gypsum plaster is only moderately resistant to damage, but if it is gouged or scratched, it is easily and invisibly repaired using materials that can be purchased at any hardware store. Surfaces such as varnished wood paneling, marble wainscoting, or wallpaper are far more difficult to repair if damaged, because their inherent pattern cannot be duplicated easily.

2. A surface made up of a large number of small, individually attached units, such as a roof of shingles or slates, does not tend to look bad if one or two units are damaged. It is easily and unobtrusively repaired by replacing the damaged units.

3. If a very large sheet of glass is chipped or cracked, it becomes unattractive and dangerous, and must be replaced. This requires the services of a crew of professional glaziers, a glass truck, and a crane. But if a small light of glass in a many-paned window cracks or chips, it can safely be left in place until it becomes more badly damaged, and its eventual replacement is easy work for a single, semiskilled maintenance worker.

4. A floor or wall of polished stone or ceramic tile, while inherently durable and attractive, can be very difficult to repair if a unit of material is damaged. The individual stone or tile can be troublesome to remove, and replacement materials often do not match the surrounding material in color or pattern. The matching problem can be minimized by using a more variegated pattern in the original installation—a mix of several colors of tiles, for example, or of a highly variegated blend of stone, in which a slight color mismatch created by a later repair will not attract undue attention. ∎

CLEANABLE SURFACES

Detailing decisions often affect the ease and expense of keeping a building clean.

1. Surface finishes need to be matched carefully to the areas in which they are used. Kitchens, bathrooms, shower rooms, laundries, and wet industrial areas should be finished in materials that can be cleaned by washing in place. Water-resistant materials with smooth, dense surfaces are best: stainless steel, plastic laminates, glazed ceramic tiles, glazed concrete masonry, terrazzo, sheet vinyl flooring, and porcelain. The best detailing of these materials features rounded, crack-free junctions, such as integral cove interior corners and bullnose exterior corners.

2. Avoid installations that complicate the cleaning process. A toilet room with wall-mounted fixtures and ceiling-hung partitions can be cleaned much more quickly and satisfactorily than one in which everything is mounted to the floor. Assembly seating and commercial kitchen equipment represent two other areas in which well-chosen equipment can make cleaning easier.

3. Materials that are susceptible to water damage, such as gypsum products and wood, should be avoided in wet areas. At the very least, they should be finished with gloss or semigloss, water-resistant coatings so that they can be washed. It is better to adopt more durable, washable materials, such as smooth-finished portland cement plaster or plastic laminate.

4. Absorbent materials such as carpet and upholstery are totally inappropriate in wet areas. Even "indoor-outdoor" carpet absorbs food spills, soap, and urine and cannot be cleaned adequately. Wood floors, even with polyurethane finishes, are not resistant to water. Cracks open between the pieces of flooring because of normal seasonal changes in the moisture content of the wood, allowing water to penetrate and lift the varnish from beneath, resulting in an unattractive surface that cannot be washed properly.

5. In "dry" areas of a building, a much wider selection of materials is appropriate. Carpeting can be cleaned economically with regular vacuuming and an occasional shampooing. Wood floors can be kept clean and handsome with dust mopping and periodic sanding and refinishing. Gypsum surfaces finished with either paint or wallpaper require only sporadic cleaning and infrequent renewal. Details with cracks and sharp inside corners will not attract and hold unacceptable amounts of dirt in most dry areas of a building. ■

MAINTENANCE ACCESS

Many components need to be detailed to allow for maintenance access throughout the life of the building.

1. Metal and glass curtain wall systems are available in both "internally glazed" and "externally glazed" systems, referring to whether the glass can be replaced by workers standing inside the building, or only by workers on outside scaffolding. In buildings that are more than a story or two in height, there is an obvious maintenance advantage in adopting an internally glazed system.

2. The glass on buildings that are more than three stories tall cannot be washed by workers on ladders. Special provisions must be made for window washer access. This can be in the form of openable windows that bring all exterior glass surfaces within an arm's reach, but they are not always practical in very tall buildings because of high wind velocities at upper levels. A design for a tall building should include provisions for movable window washing scaffolding and safety attachments.

3. Building components that may require adjustment or replacement during the life of the building should be attached with screws or bolts so that they can be removed and replaced, rather than being welded, glued, or nailed permanently in place. This is why we use screws rather than nails to attach hardware to doors, lighting fixtures to walls and ceilings, and drapery hardware to windows.

4. Concealed mechanical and electrical components that require inspection and maintenance should be placed behind snap-off covers, hinged access panels, manholes, handholes, or access ports of appropriate sizes and shapes. Never seal off permanently any component of a building that moves, that connects electrical wires, that may need cleaning, or that may deteriorate or go out of adjustment prematurely. Examples include pipe valves, ductwork dampers, electric motors, pumps,

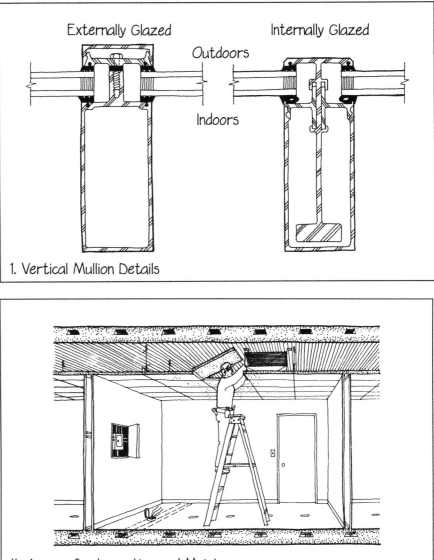

1. Vertical Mullion Details

4. Access for Inspection and Maintenance

plumbing cleanouts, electric junction boxes, lighting ballasts, transformers, heating and cooling coils, and telephone wiring junctions. Work continually with electrical, mechanical, and structural consultants to see that all necessary access devices are provided.

5. Maintenance access requires floor space. A residential oil or gas burner needs a clear space about 3′ (900 mm) square for servicing. A horizontal boiler needs considerable free space for cleaning and replacing tubes. Electrical and communications switchgear need free frontal access and room to remove and replace components. Large boilers, chillers, fans, motors, and pumps that will not fit through normal doors, corridors, and elevators may need to be replaced someday, and require industrial doors or removable access panels for that eventuality. Lay out spaces for mechanical, plumbing, electrical, and communications equipment in close cooperation with engineering consultants to be sure that these concerns are met. ∎

DRY WOOD

Wood must be detailed so that it will stay dry; otherwise, it will decay in only a few years.

1. A covered bridge is covered to keep water off the joints in the wood trusses that support the bridge. Joints between pieces of wood that are exposed to the weather absorb and hold moisture by capillary action. This encourages decay. Uncovered bridges made of ordinary wood seldom last as long as a decade before their joints rot beyond repair. Exposed exterior wood constructions with many joints, such as fences, decks, sunshades, railings, benches, gates, and doors, should be made of decay-resistant wood. It is not enough merely to paint them, because the paint cracks at the joints due to normal seasonal moisture movement in the wood, allowing water to enter.

2. Wood must be kept well away from the ground so that it will remain dry and therefore free from decay. In the sill detail of a wood frame building, all wood is kept at least 6″ (150 mm) above the surface of the soil. As a further precaution, it is wise to use pressure-treated or naturally decay-resistant wood for the sill plate that rests on a concrete or masonry foundation, because moisture may rise from the ground through the porous material of the foundation and wet the underside of the sill. On wet sites or in very damp climates, a continuous flashing should be installed between the sill and the foundation as a barrier against capillary moisture rising from the soil.

3. The microorganisms that cause decay in wood need three things to survive: air, wood for food, and small

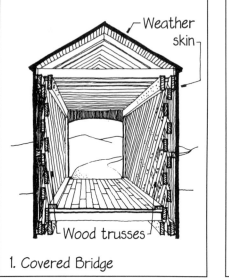

1. Covered Bridge

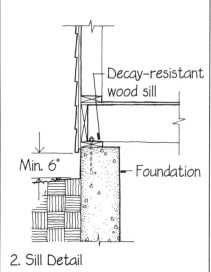

2. Sill Detail

amounts of moisture. Usually we discourage decay either by treating the wood with chemicals that make it unfit for food, by selecting a wood species that is unappetizing to the microorganisms, or by keeping wood completely dry. Paradoxically, wood that is completely and permanently submerged in water will not decay. This is because water does not allow the organisms in the wood access to air. Thus, we sometimes use untreated wood for foundation pilings in soils that are completely saturated with water. This works well as long as the water level in the soil does not drop. In cases where the water level has fallen, piles have rotted off at the level where the saturated soil joins the drier soil above, the one location where air, water, and wood are all available to the decay organisms.

4. All wood-destroying insects require water. Many species can live only in damp wood and are easily discouraged by details that keep wood dry. The most common species of termites can live in dry wood, provided that they have easy access to damp soil. These species are dealt with by keeping wood well above the soil line and by installing a continuous flashing with projecting edges between the sill and the foundation. The tubes that these termites build to make contact with the ground are easily spotted and destroyed where they cross the flashing. Soil poisons are also used against this type of termite, but the safety of these poisons is coming under increasing scrutiny. A few species of termites that thrive only in very warm, damp climates can live in dry wood without soil contact, taking their moisture from the air; these can be dealt with only by poisoning them. ∎

SIMILAR METALS

Avoid exterior details in which two different metals are attached directly to one another.

1. Simple corrosion occurs when air and moisture are present simultaneously on the surface of a metal. Most nonferrous metals (such as aluminum, zinc, brass, bronze, lead, and copper) quickly form stable, self-protecting oxide coatings that prevent further corrosion. Stainless steels and certain "weathering steels" are also self-protecting.

2. Ordinary steel (carbon steel), wrought iron, and cast iron need protective coatings to avoid destruction by oxidation (rusting) if they are used outdoors or in wet interior environments. These may take the form of paint, various factory-applied organic coatings, or metallic coatings.

3. The most common metal used for protective coating of steel is zinc. Zinc coating is known as galvanizing. Galvanizing works because the zinc slowly sacrifices itself through oxidation to protect the underlying steel, even healing small scratches in the coating with its oxide. Eventually, the zinc weathers away, leaving the steel to rust. This can take from 5 to 40 years, depending on the thickness of the coating and the presence of salt and other pollutants in the air. For the longest possible life, use the heaviest available zinc coating. This is usually applied by means of traditional hot-dip galvanizing. There are many other methods of galvanizing, some of which result in only thin coatings that have a short life. It is important to do careful research in order to determine the degree of protection that is required in a given situation and to specify the galvanizing process and thickness of coating that will best satisfy this need.

4. Because of contaminants that are always present, both rainwater and ground water are electrolytes. When rainwater or ground water comes in contact with a building assembly that includes two different metals, a galvanic reaction can occur, generating an electrical current that will corrode one of the metals with astonishing rapidity. The safest approach in detailing is to use the same metal in all of the components of an exterior detail: aluminum nails with aluminum roofing sheet, aluminum screws and bolts in aluminum cladding components, copper nails with copper roofing, and steel bolts in steel structural shapes.

5. It is often necessary, however, to confront such problems as attaching aluminum cladding sheets to a steel frame or an aluminum mast to a copper roof. To solve these problems, we must look more deeply into the nature of the galvanic reaction between dissimilar metals. Metals vary in their chemical activity. When two different metals are brought together and bathed with an electrolyte such as rainwater, an exchange of electrons takes place that protects the less active metal while corroding the more active one. The greater the difference is between the activities of the two metals, the greater the potential for corrosion.

6. In the accompanying table, the common architectural metals are ranked with respect to their relative activities: the most active metals are at the top and the least active are at the bottom. Metals with similar levels of activity are grouped together. In general, it is safe to combine metals that are in the same group.

GALVANIC SERIES OF METALS

Most Active	Magnesium and its alloys
	Zinc
	Galvanized steel and iron
	Aluminum
	Steel
	Wrought iron
	Cast iron
	Active stainless steel*
	Lead-tin solder
	Lead
	Tin
	Brass
	Bronze
	Copper
	Silver solder
	Nickel
	Passive stainless steel*
	Silver
Least Active	Gold

*Whether stainless steel is considered "active" or "passive" depends on its surface finish. Stainless steel normally forms a self-protecting coating of chromium oxide and is considered passive. The electropolished surfaces used on some architectural hardware and trim are also passive. But if the coating of chromium oxide is disturbed by grinding, machining, or wire brushing, the finish becomes active. Most stainless steel fasteners are active. Active stainless steel can be made passive by treatment with acids. The detailer should work closely with the manufacturer of the stainless steel product if these distinctions become important in preparing a detail.

7. If a metal from one group is used with a metal from another group, the potential for galvanic corrosion is roughly proportional to the distance between the two groups. For example, an exterior detail that used zinc nails in copper roofing sheet would combine a metal from the most active group with one from the next-to-least active group; the zinc nails would virtually disappear after only a few rainfalls.   ▷

8. The rate of corrosion is also affected by the relative surface areas of the two metals. If the area of the less active metal is very large in relation to the area of the more active one, corrosion will be very rapid. This would be the case with zinc nails in a copper roof. If copper nails were used in a zinc roof, however, the area of the less active metal would be very small when compared with the area of the more active one, and corrosion would be very slow. One would be foolish to detail a zinc roof with copper nails nevertheless, because of the extreme difference in activity between the two metals. But this area effect is useful in combining metals that lie more closely together on the galvanic series, such as stainless steel screws (which have an "active" finish) in an aluminum window. Aluminum screws in a stainless steel window, on the other hand, would be at great risk because of the very large surface area of the less active metal compared with the more active one.

9. Taking all these factors into account, and relying also upon data from actual installations, the American Architectural Manufacturers Association has developed the accompanying table that suggests the best fasteners to use with different combinations of metals.

FASTENER METALS FOR JOINING VARIOUS METAL COMBINATIONS

(listed in order of preference)

A. *Aluminum to Aluminum*

1. Aluminum
2. Stainless steel
3. Zinc-plated steel
4. Cadmium-plated steel

B. *Aluminum to Stainless Steel or Carbon Steel*

1. Stainless steel
2. Zinc-plated steel
3. Cadmium-plated steel

C. *Copper Alloys to Copper Alloys*

1. Bronze
2. Brass
3. Nickel-silver
4. Stainless steel

D. *Copper Alloys to Aluminum (Note: Joining of these metals is not recommended.)*

1. Stainless steel

E. *Copper Alloys to Stainless Steel*

1. Stainless steel
2. Bronze
3. Brass

F. *Copper Alloys to Carbon Steel*

1. Bronze
2. Brass

G. *Carbon Steel to Carbon Steel*

1. Stainless steel
2. Zinc-plated steel
3. Cadmium-plated steel
4. Nickel-plated steel
5. Chromium-plated steel
6. Carbon steel

H. *Stainless Steel to Stainless Steel*

1. Stainless steel

From the AAMA *Metal Curtain Wall Manual*. Reproduced by permission of the American Architectural Manufacturers Association.

10. In many cases, it is possible to avoid corrosion between dissimilar metals by separating the metals with an electrical insulating material. The insulation might take the form of a plastic or synthetic rubber washer, gasket, shim, sleeve, or bushing that is placed between the materials. It might be a nonconductive coating on one of the materials. It might be a plastic or plastic-headed screw or bolt. Obviously the insulating material should be durable, because if it disintegrates, the metals will come into contact and corrode. Insulating materials would be the best answer to attaching an aluminum mast to a copper roof, because the two metals are too reactive with one another to join in any other way.

11. There are also damaging chemical reactions that can occur between metals and certain nonmetallic materials. Steel will not corrode in concrete, as long as it is completely surrounded by concrete and outside water cannot penetrate. Aluminum, however, is chemically incompatible with concrete, especially when the concrete is fresh, and the two materials should never be used in direct contact. Lead flashings tend to corrode in mortar and are not recommended for use with masonry. Naturally decay-resistant woods contain acids that can react chemically to cause corrosion of some metals, and some chemicals used in pressure treating of wood can cause similar problems. It is best to consult literature from the trade organizations and manufacturers that promote these woods for recommendations on fasteners and flashings.

12. In this detail for anchoring stone facing panels to a building, stainless steel is chosen for the anchor because it will not rust. This avoids staining of the stone and corrosion failure of the anchor. It avoids the spalling of the

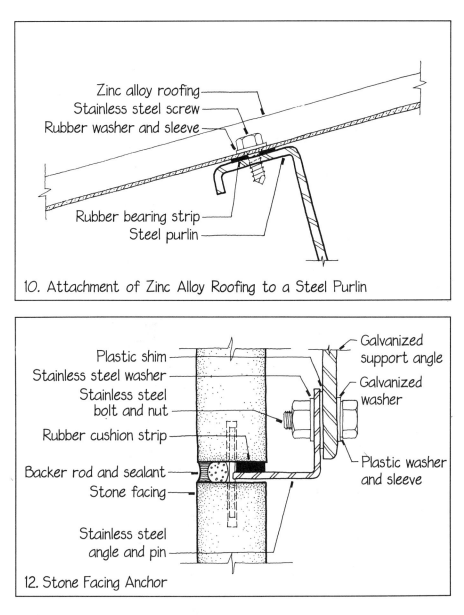

10. Attachment of Zinc Alloy Roofing to a Steel Purlin

12. Stone Facing Anchor

stone that could occur from the expansion of steel as it rusts. Stainless steel is also resistant to the acid chemistry of such stones as granite. The stainless steel anchor is fastened to its support angle with a stainless steel bolt, nut, and washer. A plastic shim and sleeve are used to isolate the stainless steel components from the galvanized steel support angle. A galvanized steel washer is used against the back of the galvanized angle, isolated from the stainless steel bolt head by a plastic washer. The whole detail could be executed in stainless steel, of course, but the support angles would be almost prohibitively expensive in this material. ∎

LESS ABSORBENT MATERIALS

In climates with cold, wet winters, hard materials such as concrete, stone, and brick are subject to spalling and flaking of the surface that is caused by water soaking into the material and then freezing. The expansion of the freezing water exerts pressure from within the material and forces flakes from the surface. This effect can be minimized by using materials that absorb as little water as possible.

1. Concrete that is formulated with a low water–cement ratio has fewer pores created by the escape of excess water and is less susceptible to freeze–thaw damage than more watery concretes. Concrete that will be exposed to cold winter weather should also be formulated with an air-entraining admixture. During the mixing process, this admixture causes the formation of microscopic air bubbles that make up 2% to 8% of the volume of the concrete. The resulting voids in the concrete reduce freeze–thaw damage by acting as expansion chambers for the freezing water.

2. Such denser stones as granite are less water absorptive and hold up better in wet locations in cold climates than more porous stones, such as lime-stone and sandstone. Traditional stone buildings often have granite foundations, and then change over to lime-stone or marble above ground level.

3. Clay bricks for exterior use in cold, wet climates should be Grade SW (ASTM C62), which comprises bricks that do not absorb very much water. Bricks for paving are especially vulnerable to freeze–thaw deterioration; in severe climates, only Class SX clay bricks, as defined by ASTM C902, should be used, and concrete paving bricks should have a water absorption of 5% or less.

4. Mortar joints in masonry are tooled to create a finished profile. But the tooling is more than cosmetic: It also helps the mortar joint shed water, and it compresses the mortar at the face of the joint, making it denser and less absorptive of water, and sealing it more tightly against the masonry units on either side. In climates with cold winters, noncompressed joints such as the flush, raked, stripped, and extruded joints should be avoided, because they are too absorptive. The raked and stripped joints are also undesirable, because they tend to trap water. The concave and vee profiles are the best from the standpoint of weathering. ■

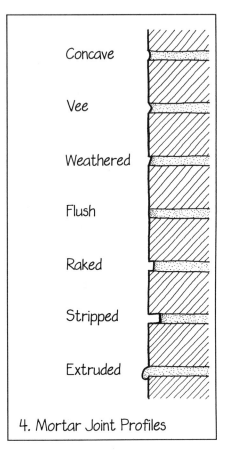

4. Mortar Joint Profiles

BUILDING ARMOR

A building needs to be armored where it is likely to get kicked or scuffed, pushed or punched, bumped into or splashed.

1. A busy door in a public building may need several kinds of armor: An escutcheon plate around the knob and lock where hands and keys rub and scratch; a push plate where people shove against the door to open it; a kick plate across the bottom.

2. An ordinary wall base detail uses a baseboard as armor against scrub mops, vacuum cleaner nozzles, legs of furniture, and flying feet. A traditional dining room adds a wood chair rail molding around the walls at the line where the backs of chairs can gouge the plaster or paneling.   ▷

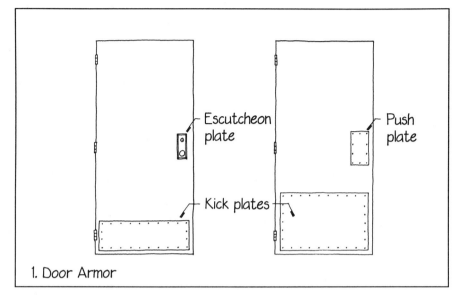

1. Door Armor

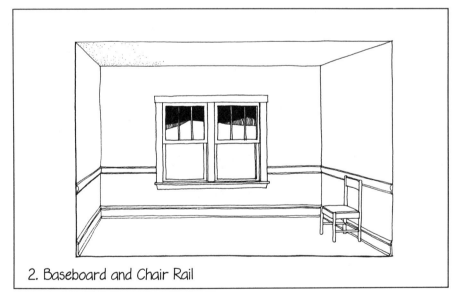

2. Baseboard and Chair Rail

3. Most contemporary wainscoting is a form of armor. It may be made of vinyl wallcovering, tile, concrete masonry, or stone. Often its purpose is to make the wall tough and washable in the zone where it will be rubbed against, poked, kicked, and run into. Sometimes it is intended to make the wall water resistant in wet areas of a building.

4. Hospitals and nursing homes use corner guards and wall guards to armor walls against wheelchairs, gurneys, pushcarts, and cleaning equipment.

5. Outdoor forms of building armor include curbs and bollards to confine vehicles to roads and drives, and corner guards, protective posts, and dock bumpers where vehicles are allowed to come close to the building. ∎

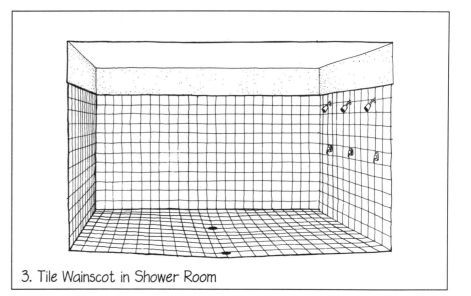

3. Tile Wainscot in Shower Room

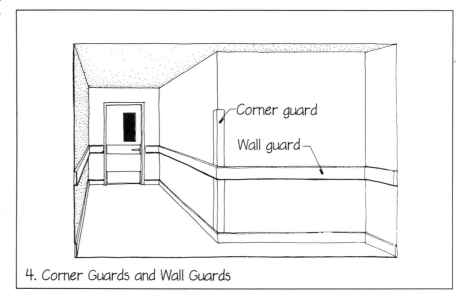

4. Corner Guards and Wall Guards

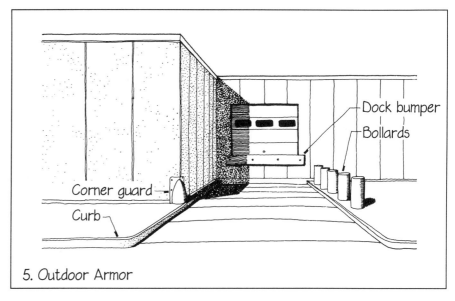

5. Outdoor Armor

CONSTRUCTIBILITY:
INTRODUCTION

A DETAIL may work perfectly with respect to water leakage, air leakage, thermal efficiency, expansion and contraction, and every other functional requirement, but if it is troublesome or unnecessarily expensive to make, it is not a good detail. The owner of a building has a right to expect construction to proceed smoothly, swiftly, and economically. The contractor and workers who construct the building have a right to expect it to go together with no more than the normal degree of difficulty. From the designer's point of view, a smooth construction process generally produces a building with fewer defects and fewer disputes among the participants. Constructible details are essential to a smooth construction process.

As a bonus, the effort to design constructible details can lead the designer into explorations of building craft that may yield substantial aesthetic rewards: Much of what we admire and enjoy most about great buildings can be traced to a deep understanding of craft that is evident in their details. Consider the beauty of Gothic vaulting, whose form sprang from the craft of stone masonry. Think of the interiors of German and Austrian Rococo churches, which owe much of their beauty to their full exposition of the craft of the plasterer, or think of the satisfying forms of Arts and Crafts woodwork, which grew from a thorough understanding of the craft of the joiner. Many contemporary buildings derive visual impact from steel connections or concrete forms and surfaces that make knowledgeable use of the craft vocabularies of these two modern technologies.

Constructibility can be summarized in three general guidelines:

1. A detail should be easy to assemble.

2. A detail should be forgiving of small inaccuracies and minor mistakes.

3. A detail should be based on efficient use of construction facilities, tools, aid labor.

The logic of these three guidelines may be summarized in a single sentence: A building ought to go together easily and efficiently, and it should do so even though many little things can be expected to go wrong during the construction process.

CONSTRUCTIBILITY:
EASE OF ASSEMBLY

E A S E of assembly is important, because a detail that is a struggle to build is likely to be expensive and will often be executed poorly. A detail that goes together in an easy, relaxed manner is economical with regard to labor and will generally be done well. There are seven detail patterns that concern ease of assembly. Their names are almost self-explanatory, because these patterns deal with common sense issues of simplification, reduction of effort, and providing sufficient spaces for workers to do their work.

UNCUT UNITS

In certain materials, it saves time and money to detail in such a way that few if any units of material need to be cut.

1. Brick masonry and concrete masonry should be dimensioned and detailed so that there is little cutting of bricks and blocks. This often involves slight adjustments in the dimensions of the building.

2. Concrete masonry should be dimensioned in multiples of 8″ (200 mm), making small corrections for the thickness of a mortar joint where required. Over its entire length, outside corner to outside corner, a concrete block wall has one fewer mortar joints than it does blocks, so ⅜″ (9 mm) should be deducted from the nominal length of the wall to arrive at the actual dimension.

3. Between an outside corner and an inside corner, a concrete masonry wall has the same number of mortar joints as blocks, so the actual length of the wall is the same as the nominal length. In other words, the length will be an exact multiple of 8″ (200 mm).

4. An opening in a concrete masonry wall has one more mortar joints than it does blocks. Therefore, the nominal dimension must be increased by ⅜″ (9 mm) to find the actual dimension. The same principle applies to an inside dimension between masonry walls.

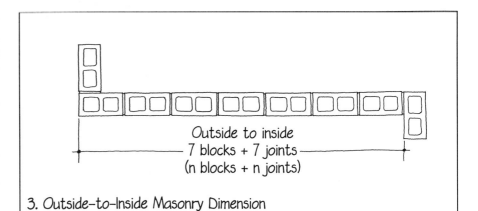

2. Outside-to-Outside Masonry Dimension

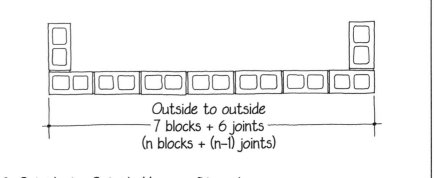

3. Outside-to-Inside Masonry Dimension

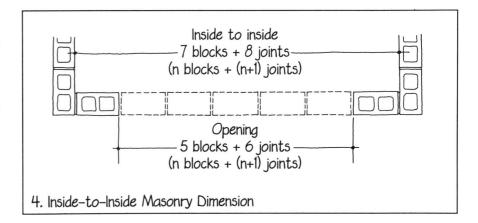

4. Inside-to-Inside Masonry Dimension

5. The general dimensioning principles that have just been described also apply to brickwork, stonework, and other types of masonry. Before preparing a detail, determine what type of masonry units you will be using and what their dimensions are. Decide on the dimension of a standard mortar joint. Then give each dimension two ways on the drawing: as numbers of masonry units, and as feet and inches (millimeters). This makes work easy for the masons.

6. Even for easily cut materials, such as gypsum board, it is economical to work with uncut units as much as possible. An 8′ high wall is easily boarded with two uncut horizontal sheets of gypsum board. An 8′6″ high wall requires the addition of a narrow strip of board that takes time to cut and is not very stiff. Additionally, because of the need to use the tapered edges of the board at all joints, only two 6″ edge strips can be cut from a board, and 75% of the board would have to be thrown away. A 10′ (3 m) high wall can be built without waste and with a minimum of cutting, because a sheet split lengthwise can be fully utilized to make up the extra 2′ (600 mm) of height on two walls.

7. If the floor plan of a wood frame building can be dimensioned in 4′ multiples (1220 mm), few sheets of subflooring will have to be cut, and there will be little waste. This dimensioning scheme also minimizes waste of joist material, which is furnished only in lengths that are multiples of 2′ (610 mm).

8. It is almost impossible to avoid cutting in *all* the different materials used in a building. It's difficult to make the floor of a room come out to even dimensions for ceramic tile units, for example. Tile setters are accustomed to having to cut all the tiles around the edge of a room. The same is true for vinyl composition tile, ceiling tiles, wallpaper, baseboards, and many other interior finish materials. ∎

MINIMUM NUMBER OF PARTS

The fewer the number of different parts a detail requires, the more efficient and trouble-free the construction process is likely to be.

1. A construction worker who is assembling a connection in a building needs to have all the required parts close at hand. The fewer the number of different parts there are, the less time will be spent looking for misplaced items or restocking depleted supplies and, generally, the fewer tools will be required. A framing carpenter needs to have at least three sizes of common nails available at all times, as well as a hammer, a tape rule, a square, and a pencil. All these items are carried in the pouches of a tool belt so that they are always close at hand. This works out reasonably well, because the carpenter does a standardized set of operations and can rely on the tool belt as an organizer. But if a special framing detail requires several sizes of screws as well as nails, the tool belt no longer has sufficient pouches, and the carpenter's efficiency drops off.

2. In an operation such as installing aluminum curtain wall mullions, the installer may need one or more wrenches, one or more screwdrivers, a rubber mallet, a tool for inserting rubber gasketing, a level, a tape measure, and a large variety of parts: mullion sections, connecting angles, shims, bolts, screws, and gasketing. The number of these different parts and tools should be kept to a minimum. It is especially important to avoid parts that differ so little from one another that they can be confused easily, such as 1″ long and 1⅛″ long screws of the same diameter and head style.

3. A masonry wall pattern that requires three different kinds of brick and two colors of mortar would tax a mason's patience. There would not be sufficient space at the mason's workstation to keep the five different types of materials within reach, and such an elaborate pattern would present a maximum number of opportunities for errors to occur—errors that would be difficult and costly to correct. ∎

PARTS THAT ARE EASY TO HANDLE

The detailer should always be conscious of the size and weight of building components, and of what will be required on the jobsite to handle them.

1. A standard brick takes its size, shape, and weight from the dimensions and capabilities of the human hand. A bricklayer works efficiently and comfortably by holding the trowel in one hand while lifting and placing bricks repeatedly with the other. If a substantially larger brick is specified, the bricklayer may fatigue more quickly, have muscular problems, and have difficulty in maintaining proper alignment of bricks in the wall. Many masons' unions have work rules concerning maximum weights of various kinds of bricks and blocks, and these must be taken into account.

2. Very small parts should be avoided, especially where the worksite might be dark, wet, or cold, making it difficult to see and handle the parts. Tweezer-size parts should be avoided altogether. Finger-size parts, such as nails, screws, bolts, and nuts, are easy to handle in warm to moderate temperatures and in adequate light. Hand-size components, such as wood shingles, bricks, and tiles, are ideal for the worker to handle. A concrete block, wood stud, clapboard, or plywood panel requires the use of both hands, which is acceptable but less desirable because it necessitates laying down tools to lift the component. Some components take two persons to handle: a jumbo concrete block, a full-thickness wall panel, a frame for a wall or partition, or a large sheet of glass. This is reasonable in most situations. Components that require three or more workers are awkward and waste time.

3. Hoists and cranes come in many configurations, reaches, lifting capacities, and maneuverabilities. Components requiring the use of a crane

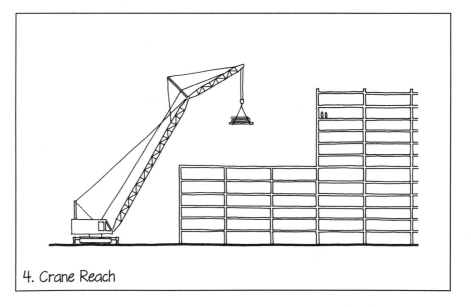

4. Crane Reach

should be avoided, unless there will be a crane on the site to lift many other components as well. Sometimes, of course, it is economical or unavoidable to rent a crane to hoist a single large component into place, but such situations should be studied carefully, because crane time is expensive.

4. Cranes and hoists must be selected and located on the site so that they are able to lift the required components and to place them where they are wanted. This is largely the business of the contractor, but the detailer should be sure that all details that require crane lifts lie within reach of likely crane locations. A typical problem is that of lifting materials over a lower portion of a building to reach a higher portion. Overhead power and telephone lines can also inhibit the work of a crane.

5. Building components must be sized to fit available transportation modes. Highway widths and clearances govern the sizes and weights of trucks, which in turn determine the maximum sizes of most building components. Oversize loads can be trucked in some situations, with accompanying cost

penalties for off-hour deliveries and special police details. Barges or railroad cars can be used to carry oversize components to some waterfront and railside construction sites.

6. Building openings have a lot to do with sizes of components. In an ordinary house, a temporary opening must be left in the exterior wall of each floor to allow a delivery truck to hoist bundles of gypsum board to the interior of the building; this can be a large window or door opening, or it may be necessary to leave a portion of the wall unframed and unsheathed. A standard, one-piece, tub-and-shower unit can be used only if it is installed before the interior framing is completed. Once the partitions are framed and the wallboard is on, the one-piece tub can no longer be brought in, and a three-piece unit must be used instead. Installation of some large-building equipment, such as boilers and fans, can require that wall cladding and partitions be omitted temporarily from certain areas.   ▷

7. Ease of handling includes consideration of the possibility that parts can be inadvertently installed backward or upside down. Wedge anchor inserts that are installed in formwork before concrete is poured are useless and impossible to replace if they are installed upside down. They should be manufactured with prominent "UP" indications, and the detailer should make a note to pass on to the construction supervisor to check the installation of these components very carefully before concrete is poured.

8. Reglet components are also susceptible to being inverted during installation.

9. Where possible, detail components either so that they are symmetrical and can be installed in either direction, or so that they are asymmetrical in a way that only permits them to be installed correctly. This curtain wall anchor tee cannot be installed upside down, because it is symmetrical: Either way will work. If the vertical spacing between bolt holes is different from the horizontal spacing, it will also be impossible to err by installing it sideways. ∎

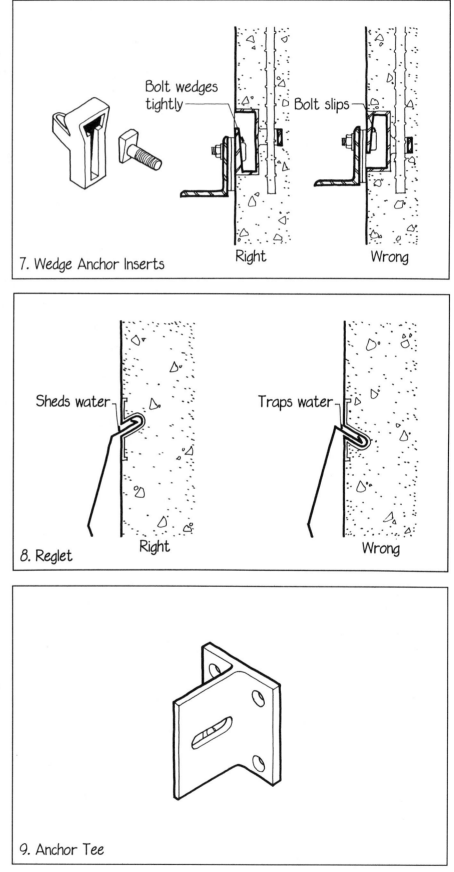

7. Wedge Anchor Inserts   Right   Wrong

Bolt wedges tightly   *Bolt slips*

8. Reglet   Right   Wrong

Sheds water   *Traps water*

9. Anchor Tee

REPETITIOUS ASSEMBLY

All other considerations being equal, details that construction workers repeat again and again are more economical and less error-prone than nonrepeating details.

1. Special conditions often lead to errors in construction. A steel floor frame in which all of the filler beams are the same size, with one exception, is likely to end up with the special beam in the wrong place, unless the connection details for that one beam are special enough to prevent a mix-up. For this reason, filler beams are usually engineered to be all the same size, even if this means a slight diseconomy in weight of steel. The same principle applies to reinforcing bar patterns in repetitive beams and slabs.

2. It is easiest and least error-prone for bricklayers to lay continuous facings of running bond, and this is all that most buildings require them to do. Unfortunately, running bond has little character, and bricklayers often enjoy a challenge to their craftsmanship more than the boredom of unrelieved repetition. When designing brickwork patterns that use corbeled, recessed, or different colored bricks, try to design patterns that are repetitious in their variety, so that the bricklayer can easily learn the pattern and keep track of what is going on. Highly intricate or irregular patterns require that the mason refer constantly to the drawings. This wastes time and can lead to errors that are difficult and expensive to correct.

3. Formwork construction accounts for a very large share of the cost of sitecast concrete structures. The easiest and least expensive forms to build are level, continuous, uninterrupted surfaces of plywood. This is why flat plate structures are usually the most economical system for light loads and short spans. It is also why joist bands, which use more concrete and steel but are extremely easy to form, often cost less

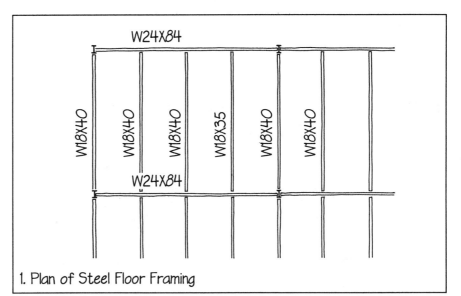

1. Plan of Steel Floor Framing

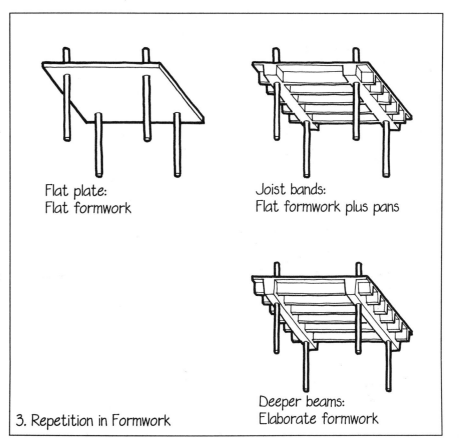

Flat plate:
Flat formwork

Joist bands:
Flat formwork plus pans

Deeper beams:
Elaborate formwork

3. Repetition in Formwork

overall than beams that are proportioned optimally for material economy but that require more complicated formwork. Where deeper beams are used in any concrete structure, it is usually more economical to make all the beams the same size so that their formwork will be repetitive, even if loads vary somewhat from beam to beam.

ACCESSIBLE CONNECTIONS

It is important to detail in such a way that workers can reach the work easily.

1. For maximum comfort and productivity, a worker should be standing on a level, secure surface, working between waist height and shoulder height, within a couple of feet of the front of the body. This ideal is readily achieved in a factory, but it is more difficult to achieve on a construction site. Overhead work is fatiguing, as is work that requires stooping or squatting. Excessive reaches are bad, because they put the worker dangerously off balance; they are also likely to result in less-than-perfect workmanship.

2. Cladding that is designed to be installed from inside the building saves money on scaffolding and generally results in high worker productivity and optimal workmanship.

3. Good scaffolding or staging with guardrails is the next best thing to standing on a level floor. A hydraulic bucket or a short stepladder would be nearly as safe and comfortable as scaffolding. A straight ladder or a very tall stepladder is more precarious than any of the foregoing means of support and also leads to lower productivity because of the difficulty of moving the ladder and the time it consumes. The least desirable means of worker support is a seat harness suspended on ropes—it is relatively dangerous, productivity is low, and good workmanship is hard to achieve. Detailing can sometimes take these differences into account by avoiding finicky work in awkward places, prefabricating assemblies that would be difficult to fabricate in place because of precarious access, and placing fasteners in locations that are easy to reach.

4. Avoid creating apparently logical details that cannot be assembled because of accessibility problems. This innocent-looking detail for attaching cladding panels to a masonry backup wall will not work, because there is no way for a worker to insert the screws into the lower edge of a panel.

5. Avoid connections that lie behind columns and spandrel beams, in sharp inside corners, or in re-entrant corners. These positions are difficult to reach, if they can be reached at all. In tight locations such as these, be sure not only that the worker can reach the connection but also that there is space for the hammer, wrench, or screwdriver that must be used to make the connection. It's also desirable that the worker be able to see the connection rather than have to work by "feel."

The best location for a cladding connection to the spandrel of a building is on top of the edge of a floor slab, where full access is easy. A connection in this location will have to be covered by interior finish surfaces, such as convector covers, but it is much easier to

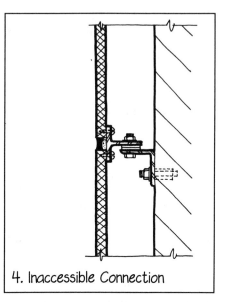

4. Inaccessible Connection

make than connections at the ceiling or in the cramped gap between the spandrel beam and the cladding. ∎

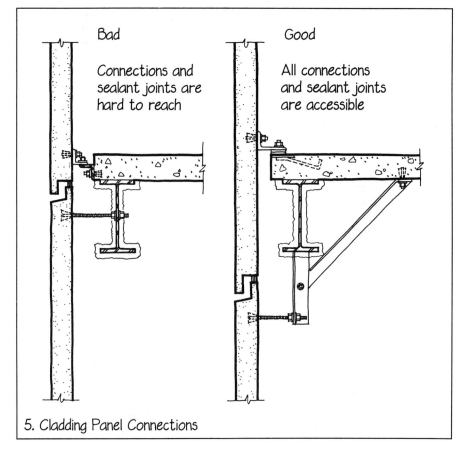

Bad

Connections and sealant joints are hard to reach

Good

All connections and sealant joints are accessible

5. Cladding Panel Connections

INSTALLATION CLEARANCE

Every component of a building needs a little extra space in addition to its own dimensions.

1. Any component that has to be installed between two other components needs a bit of additional room so that it can be maneuvered into place. A steel beam is always cut slightly shorter than the space between columns; if it were not, it would bind during insertion and would be almost impossible to install.

2. Similarly, a window or door unit is mounted in a rough opening that is slightly larger than the unit. This gives space to guide the unit into its final position, and it also allows adjustment for inaccuracies in both the wall and the window unit. The window unit is mounted in the rough opening with wedge-shaped shims that allow very precise adjustments for dimension and plumb. Follow the manufacturer's recommendations in sizing the rough opening for each window or door.

3. A bathtub or a kitchen base cabinet can be difficult to insert into the end of a room unless the room is slightly larger than the unit to provide a clearance for installation. The gaps at the ends of a cabinet are filled with filler strips that are provided by the cabinetmaker and cut to size on the construction site. The gaps around the tub are filled with wall finish materials (such as ceramic tile or a plastic tub surround) and a sealant. ■

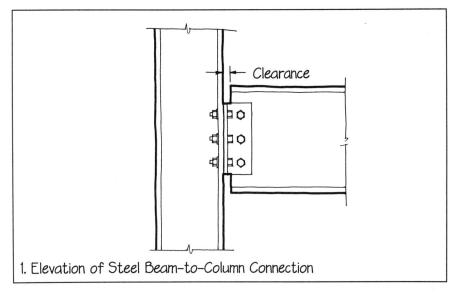

1. Elevation of Steel Beam-to-Column Connection

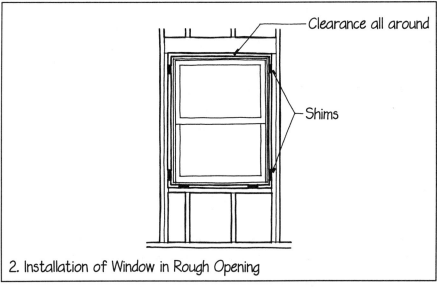

2. Installation of Window in Rough Opening

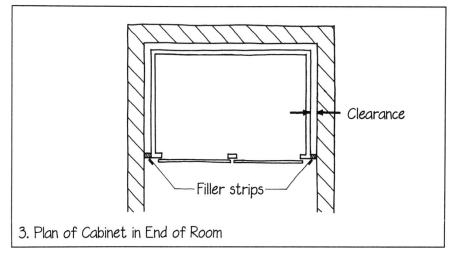

3. Plan of Cabinet in End of Room

NONCONFLICTING SYSTEMS

A building should be detailed so its various parts and systems mesh smoothly in three dimensions. This requires the detailer to create reserved zones for each of the systems.

1. In the usual project organization, in which the structural frame of a building is designed by one professional, the mechanical and electrical systems by others, and the enclosure and finishes by still others, coordination is necessary to avoid a situation in which a beam, a duct, a conduit, a sprinkler pipe, and a cladding attachment all are detailed to occupy the same space in the building. Separate zones need to be reserved throughout a building for vertical structure, horizontal structure, cladding, plumbing risers, and vertical and horizontal runs of the various mechanical, electrical, and communications services (see *Vertical Chase* and *Horizontal Plenum*, pages 98–103).

2. Suspended ceilings are so common because they avoid conflict by hanging in their own unobstructed zone beneath all the complex geometry of the building frame and building services. This makes them easy to install and consequently inexpensive.

3. Cladding that runs in its own zone outside the columns and spandrel

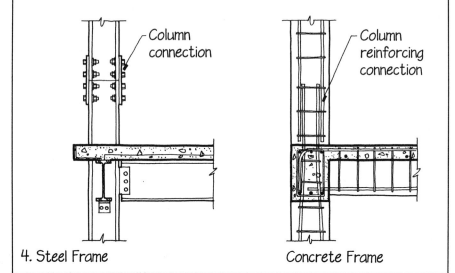

Column connection

Column reinforcing connection

4. Steel Frame   Concrete Frame

beams is much easier to detail and to install than cladding that is interrupted by framing members. (It has other advantages as well: The frame is protected from temperature extremes and moisture; thermal bridging of the frame is avoided; and there tend to be fewer problems with leaking and differential thermal movement.)

4. A section of steel column is connected to the next higher section at waist height rather than at the floor line. This is not only convenient for ironworkers to reach, but more importantly, it avoids conflict with the beam and girder connections that lie just below. The edge of the floor slab is usually cantilevered a short distance past the face of the columns and spandrel beams to avoid conflict between the framing and the cladding. Reinforcing steel in a concrete column is also spliced just above each floor level, rather than in the congested area just below where the steel from the slabs, beams, and girders intersects the steel in the column. ■

CONSTRUCTIBILITY:
FORGIVING DETAILS

T H E ability to create forgiving details is among the most rewarding skills of the detailer. A forgiving detail is one that always furnishes a way for a worker to deal easily with inaccuracies or mistakes. Most traditional details are very forgiving of inaccuracies and mistakes, because they evolved over a period of many years, gradually incorporating features that made them easier and more convenient for workers. When inventing new details, the designer should pay particular attention to avoiding features that will "trap" the worker if they are not done perfectly. The history of modern architecture includes many stories of architects who designed unforgiving details. The historical accounts generally depict the architect as struggling heroically to force factories, contractors, and workers to achieve new standards of precision and fit in their work, in order to make new kinds of details possible. Unfortunately, many of these stories ended badly, with the parties to the project estranged irreconcilably and construction costs and schedules out of control. A handful of patterns for designing forgiving details can help the designer avoid these mistakes. They are as follows:

DIMENSIONAL TOLERANCE

A dimensional tolerance is a maximum amount by which a dimension can be expected to vary from the intended measurement because of normal inaccuracies in manufacture and installation. There is a tolerance associated implicitly with every dimension on a set of drawings for a building. These tolerances have a direct effect on how details are designed.

1. Every trade and craft has its normal level of precision. Precision inside a door lock is very high; precision in pouring a concrete footing or driving a pile into the earth is very low. Good detailing takes into account the normal tolerances for dimensional inaccuracy in each phase of construction.

2. This base plate for a steel column is not attached directly to the top of a concrete footing or pile cap, because, although the footing cannot be very flat or very precisely located, the column location must be very precise indeed. Instead, the base plate is located and leveled on shims or leveling screws above the top of the footing, and the space between is filled with grout. This provides a tolerance for the expected imprecision of the footing and also a full bearing surface between the base plate and the footing.

Obviously, it is important that the top of the footing not be higher than the bottom of the base plate. At least 1″ of clearance must be provided for the insertion of grout. With regard to the bottom of the base plate, therefore, the top of the footing might be dimensioned to lie between 1″ and 2″ (25 and 50 mm) lower. Thus, there is a dimensional tolerance of 1″ within which the installers of the footing can work. This is reasonable for this type of work.

3. The accompanying table gives a small sampling of accepted industry standard tolerances for different materials and building systems. Every detail of a building should respect these tolerances. From this table, we

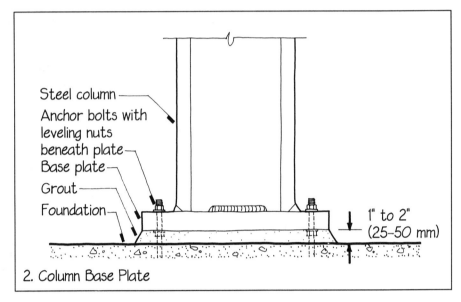

2. Column Base Plate

Steel column
Anchor bolts with leveling nuts beneath plate
Base plate
Grout
Foundation

1″ to 2″ (25–50 mm)

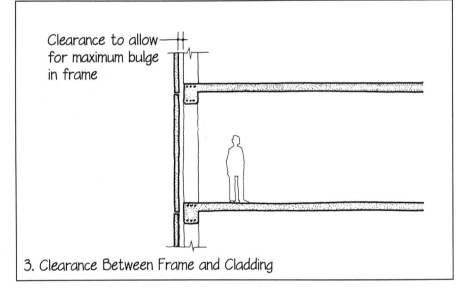

Clearance to allow for maximum bulge in frame

3. Clearance Between Frame and Cladding

see that it is considered normal for a concrete building frame to be out of plumb by as much as 1″ either way, and a steel frame may be even farther out of plumb. It is evident that we cannot design a cladding system to be attached tightly to the spandrel beams of a building. The cladding for a building with a concrete frame should be installed in a plane that lies at least 1″ outside the face of the spandrel beams, and a more generous distance than this would be wise, considering that

building frames are not always built to accepted tolerances. In actual practice, a cladding installer measures the faces of a building frame with great precision before beginning work and establishes planes for the cladding that will clear the largest bulges on each face. The cladding attachment details must provide for a range of dimensional adjustment, using such devices as shims and slotted fastener holes, that allow for these tolerance dimensions (see *Adjustable Fit*, page 146).

4. Deflections and creep in beams and slabs complicate the picture. It is unwise to detail prefabricated partition or cladding panels to fit closely under beams or slabs. Even a generous sealant joint between the two is often insufficient to accommodate normal deflections. It is better to locate cladding panels entirely outside the structure and to mount them in such a way that they are isolated as much as possible from deflections and creep in the frame. There must be good communication among the detailer, the structural engineer, and the cladding manufacturer to limit spandrel beam deflections and to provide sufficient horizontal movement joints in the cladding. Non-loadbearing partitions should be separated from the floor structure above by sealant beads or gaskets whose height is determined by the structural engineer (see *Structure/Enclosure Joint*, pp. 84, 85).

5. Where dimensional tolerances accumulate from a set of assembled components, each with its own individual tolerance, an overall tolerance can be calculated by taking the square root of the sum of the squares of the individual tolerances. If, for example, a bay of a building is clad with three precast concrete panels, each panel having a tolerance of $\pm\frac{1}{8}''$, and a window unit with a tolerance of $\pm 1/16''$, the overall dimensional tolerance for one bay is figured as follows:

Overall tolerance

$$= \pm \sqrt{(\frac{1}{8})^2 + (\frac{1}{8})^2 + (\frac{1}{8})^2 + (\frac{1}{16})^2}$$

$$= \pm 0.23''$$

■

A SAMPLING OF ACCEPTED DIMENSIONAL TOLERANCES IN U.S. CONSTRUCTION

Concrete

Dimension of footing	$-\frac{1}{2}''$, $+2''$
Squareness of residential foundation	$\frac{1}{2}''$ in 20'
Plumbness of wall	$\pm\frac{1}{4}''$ in 10'
Variation of wall from building line in plan	$\pm 1''$
Variation in wall thickness	$-\frac{1}{4}''$, $+\frac{1}{2}''$
Plumbness of column	$\frac{1}{4}''$ in 10', but not more than 1" in entire height
Variation in level of beam	$\pm\frac{1}{4}''$ in 10'; $\pm\frac{3}{8}''$ in any bay; $\pm\frac{3}{4}''$ for entire length
Variation in level of slab soffit	same as for beam

Structural Steel

Plumbness of column	1" toward or 2" away from building line in first 20 stories; 2" toward and 3" away for very tall buildings
Beam length	$\pm\frac{3}{8}''$ for depths of 24" and less; $\pm\frac{1}{2}''$ for greater depths

Marble, Limestone

Deviation from square in any one stone	$\pm 1/16''$

Masonry Bearing Wall

Deviation from plan location	$\pm\frac{1}{2}''$ in 20'

Wood Light Frame

Floor evenness	$\pm\frac{1}{4}''$ in 32"
Wall plumbness	$\pm\frac{1}{4}''$ in 32"

Interior Finishes

Plumbness of steel stud framing	$\pm\frac{1}{2}''$ in 10'
Flatness of suspended acoustical ceiling	$\pm\frac{1}{8}''$ in 10'

These values are excerpted from a number of standard industry sources. A full summary of construction industry tolerances would be a book in itself; consult publications of individual industry associations for tolerances for each material.

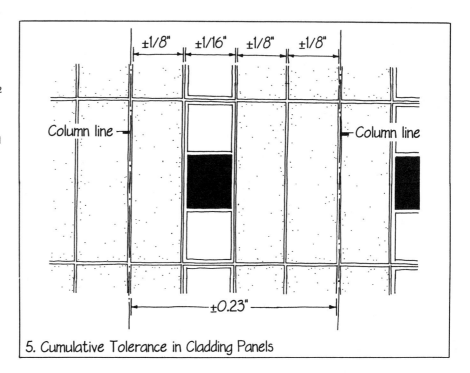

5. Cumulative Tolerance in Cladding Panels

SLIDING FIT

The easiest, most forgiving dimensional relationship between two components of a building is a sliding fit, in which one component overlaps another and can be positioned merely by sliding.

1. Overlapping shingles on a roof or a wall exemplify a sliding fit. Many wood trim details use a sliding fit to avoid difficult alignment problems. This wood eave soffit could be made from a single piece of wood, but this would be difficult, because two opposite edges of the same piece would have to be fitted at the same time. Because the dimension between the back of the fascia board and the siding tends to vary somewhat and because neither the fascia board nor the siding tends to be perfectly straight, it is much easier to install the soffit board to fit the fascia as tightly as possible while staying well clear of the siding. Then the gap at the siding is closed with a smaller trim piece or molding. To account for waviness of the fascia board, a small, flexible molding might be slid into the corner between the fascia and the soffit.

2. A wood baseboard is slid into place to cover the ragged gap between the wall and floor surfaces. A single-piece baseboard works well if the floor and wall surfaces are perfectly flat, but this is seldom the case. The baseboard is simply too stiff to bend into the low spots of the wall and floor. A traditional three-piece baseboard addresses this problem by adding two thin, flexible moldings: a cap to hug the contours of the wall and a shoe to mold itself to the floor. The cap and shoe combine a sliding fit against the baseboard with the flexibility to adjust to undulating contours.

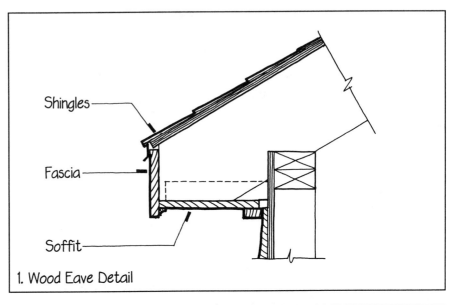

1. Wood Eave Detail

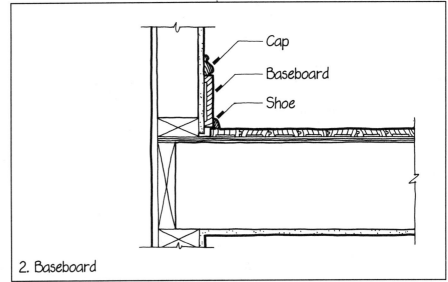

2. Baseboard

3. In general, a sliding fit involves aligning a component to two adjacent, perpendicular planes. The shingle is aligned to the surface plane of the next lower course of shingles and to a perpendicular plane that intersects the course line of the shingle. The soffit board is aligned to the horizontal plane of the level cuts on the rafter ends and to the vertical plane of the back of the fascia board. The baseboard aligns to the vertical plane of the wall and the horizontal plane of the floor. A kitchen base cabinet also aligns to the floor and wall planes. These are all easy fits.

When a third adjacent plane of alignment is added, the problem of fitting becomes more difficult. If the three planes are accurately perpendicular to one another and if the component to be fitted is perfectly square, the fit is easy. However if there is inaccuracy anywhere in the relationship, the component will have to be trimmed to fit.

If the third plane of alignment is opposite to one of the other planes rather than adjacent, the fitting problem is even more difficult.

When fourth and fifth planes of alignment are added, the fitting problem becomes acute. These situations should be avoided.   ▷

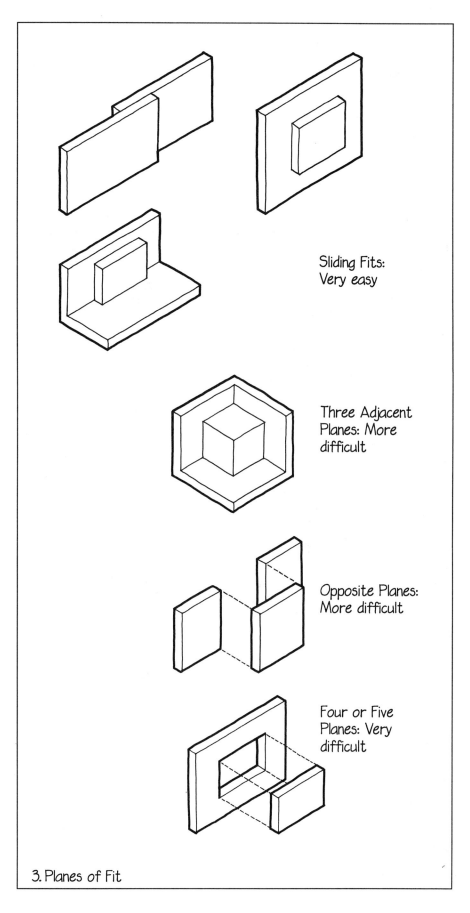

Sliding Fits: Very easy

Three Adjacent Planes: More difficult

Opposite Planes: More difficult

Four or Five Planes: Very difficult

3. Planes of Fit

4. Most prefabricated residential window units avoid five-plane fitting problems by specifying a rough opening in the wall that is considerably larger than the window unit. This generous clearance reduces the problem to fitting against the wall plane only. The flange on the window unit aligns to the plane of the wall sheathing, and the unit is leveled and plumbed as it "floats" in the rough opening, supported by pairs of wedges on all four edges that are adjusted easily and precisely to fill the gap between the framing and the window unit.

5. The more difficult part of window installation is fitting the interior casings. Because of normal tolerances in wall thickness caused by variations in framing lumber dimensions and plaster thickness, the frame depth of the window unit may not match exactly the thickness of the wall. The usual practice is to install wooden extension jambs that make up the difference between the depth of the window unit and the thickness of the wall. These extension jambs are a laborious fit, because they must align to two parallel planes: the inside face of the window unit and the face of the plaster. An easier fit is provided by a detail that returns the plaster onto the jambs of the wall. The plaster return must be shimmed out from the rough jamb to align with the jamb of the window unit. A small trim piece is usually required to cover the groove in the edge of the jamb of the window unit.

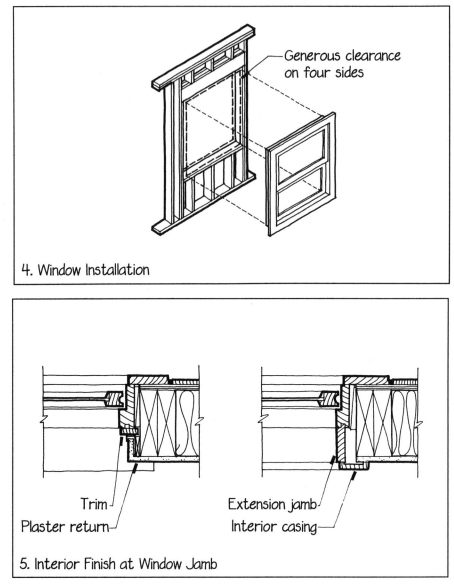

Generous clearance on four sides

4. Window Installation

Trim
Plaster return

Extension jamb
Interior casing

5. Interior Finish at Window Jamb

6. Butt-jointed cladding panels represent a potentially difficult five-plane fit. It is extremely important that the panels be manufactured to dimension, square, and flat within very narrow tolerances. This is generally feasible, because they are made in a factory using precision fixtures and machines.

In attaching the panels to the building, freedom of alignment in all three axes (X, Y, and Z) must be provided by the connectors (see ***Adjustable Fit***, immediately following). This allows the panels to be aligned easily to the same plane, to level, to plumb, and to horizontal and vertical dimension. The width of the joint that surrounds each panel and separates it from its neighbors must be sufficient to allow for any expected deviation in dimension and alignment (see ***Sealant Joints and Gaskets***, pages 31–36).

7. The common method of mounting large lights of glass makes them much easier to fit than cladding panels, because, in reality, they only align to one plane—the plane of the gaskets against which they are placed. The four edges of each light have a sliding fit into the mullions and against the gaskets, which allows for fairly large tolerances in dimension and squareness. ∎

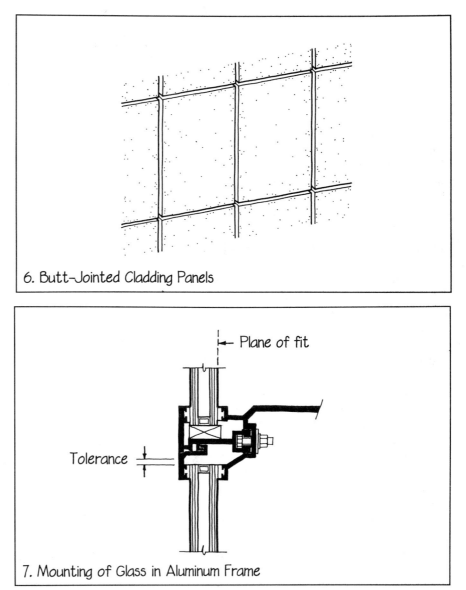

6. Butt-Jointed Cladding Panels

7. Mounting of Glass in Aluminum Frame

ADJUSTABLE FIT

Because of the impossibility of maintaining perfect dimensional accuracy in construction, every building component that must be positioned accurately should be detailed so that its alignment can be adjusted during and after assembly.

1. This manufactured bracket for a precut glass shelf must be aligned very precisely to a vertical line on the wall so that the shelf will mate snugly into the closed pocket in the bracket. To allow for a normal tolerance in measuring and drilling the screw holes in the wall, the matching holes in the bracket are slotted. Notice that the slots are horizontal so that the weight of the bracket will bear directly against the shank of the screw, regardless of where in the slot the screw is located. This detail does not provide for vertical adjustment of the bracket or for correction of any waviness in the plane of the wall; it provides for adjustment only in one axis.

Although crude shelf brackets such as the ones used to mount rough shelves in a basement or a garage might be nailed to the wall, a nail does not make any provision for precise adjustment or readjustment of the position of the bracket. Adjustable connections generally use threaded fasteners, either screws or bolts, to provide greater control during assembly and to allow for later readjustment, if necessary.

2. Anchor bolts in concrete are difficult to place with precision and are often out of alignment in two axes. This manufactured metal post base responds to the problem by providing a very large hole, together with an even larger washer in which the bolt hole is off center (eccentric). This allows for adjustment in two axes. If the height of the top of the concrete (the third axis) is inaccurate, steel shims or grout could be used beneath the post base. Usually, however, the post itself is cut a bit shorter or longer, as required.

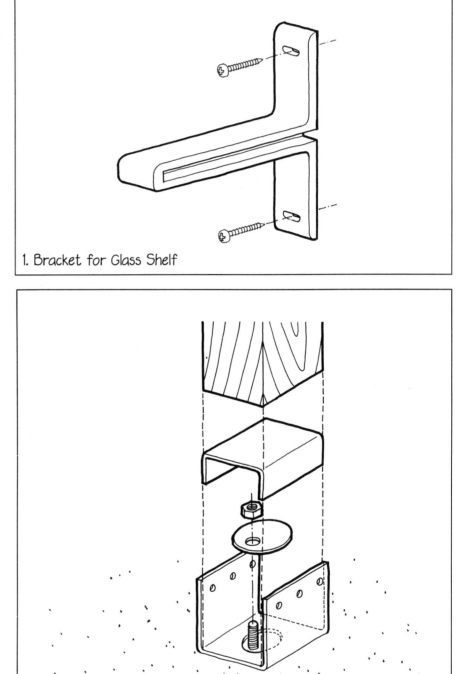

1. Bracket for Glass Shelf

2. Metal Post Base

3. This wedge insert and askew-head bolt allow for vertical adjustment of the location of a steel shelf angle used to support a masonry facing on a concrete building frame. The inner face of the outer wall of the insert and the head of the bolt comprise an opposing pair of wedges that lock securely together against a downward load in any vertical position.

In case the wedge insert does not align exactly in the horizontal plane with the prepunched hole in the shelf angle, the hole is punched as a horizontal slot. The horizontal orientation of the slot allows the shelf angle to transfer gravity loads directly to the bolt shank without slipping, regardless of the exact position of the bolt in the slot.

A third axis of adjustment is provided by the insertion of steel shims of various thicknesses between the shelf angle and the face of the concrete spandrel beam. The shims are horseshoe-shaped so that they will stay in place until the bolt is tightened.

By combining the wedge insert, the slotted hole, and the shims, a connection detail with triaxial adjustment has been created to reconcile the relatively large dimensional tolerances of a concrete frame with the close tolerances of building cladding systems. Similar connection details are used to attach shelf angles to steel framing.

4. This is a simple triaxial detail for fastening a stone or concrete cladding panel to the face of a building. Shims between the slab and the angle clip allow for vertical adjustment. In-and-out adjustment comes from the slotted hole in the base of the clip. Lateral adjustment in the plane of the cladding is provided by the horizontally slotted hole in the vertical leg of the clip. Notice again that the slots are

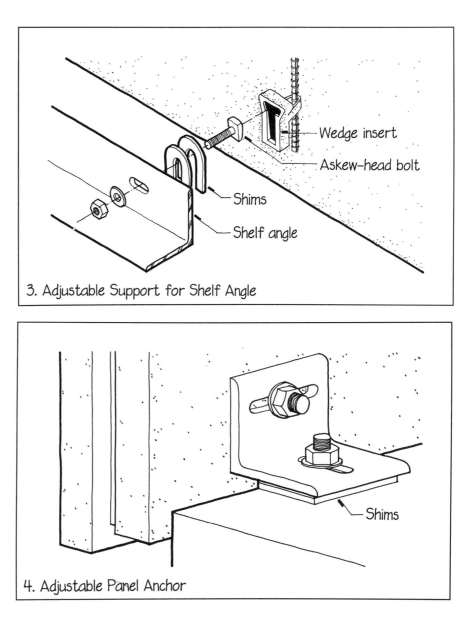

3. Adjustable Support for Shelf Angle

4. Adjustable Panel Anchor

oriented so that they do not compromise the load-carrying security of the connection: It would be a mistake to provide for vertical adjustment by using a vertically slotted hole in the vertical leg of the clip, because this might allow the bolt to slip under gravity loading. ▷

5. This steel angle frame for supporting a brick curtain wall over a long window opening needs to be adjusted very precisely so that the shelf angle is placed in exactly the right position. Pairs of slotted holes in opposing orientations make this easy but are not secure against slipping under load. This problem is avoided by welding all the connections once the proper alignment has been verified with surveying instruments. ∎

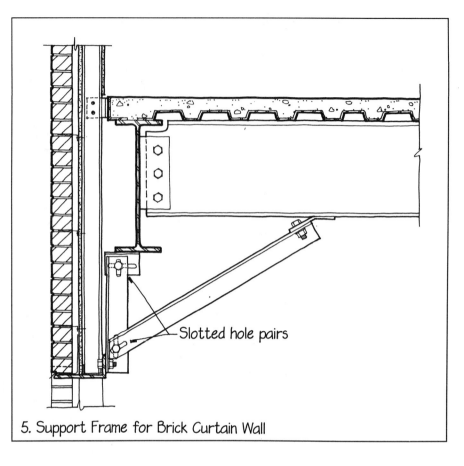

Slotted hole pairs

5. Support Frame for Brick Curtain Wall

REVEAL

A reveal is a recess or offset between two pieces of material where they come together. Its function can be to avoid having to make an exact alignment, to cast a shadow line for compositional purposes, or to cast a shadow line that hides minor defects in workmanship.

1. The finish carpenter works against heavy odds to create attractive, well-crafted trim: The surfaces being trimmed are often out of plumb, out of level, out of dimension, and wavy. The lumber with which he or she works is often slightly crooked or warped, even out of dimension, and will change dimension constantly during the life of the building in response to changes in humidity. These factors make it inadvisable to ask the finish carpenter to create a flush edge where two planes of trim come together at the jamb of a window or a door. If a small but significant reveal is included in the detail, slight misalignments, crooks, and moisture movements will never be noticed, because they will merely change the dimension of the reveal but not the presence of the reveal. If a flush detail is insisted upon, it will be more expensive to make, and it will be perfectly and reliably flush only at the instant that it is completed, before moisture expansion and contraction begin to take effect.

A reveal of this type also multiplies the parallel lines that surround the window or door—an effect that we often find pleasing.

2. A reveal of another type can be used to create a shadow line that conceals imperfections in a joint. The reveal itself becomes the apparent joint. ▷

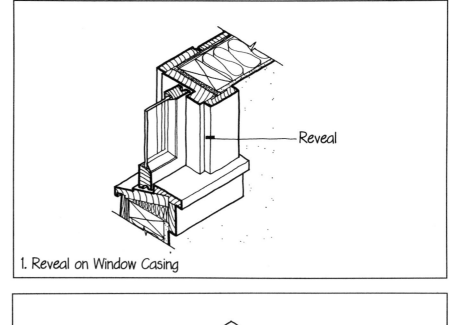

1. Reveal on Window Casing

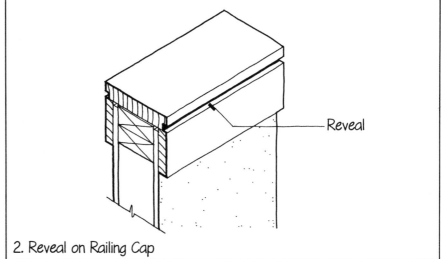

2. Reveal on Railing Cap

3. Reveals also work well at joints and exterior corners of stone and concrete facings, both to create shadow lines for compositional purposes and to disguise joinery that may be less than perfect. For another kind of reveal often used in this type of situation, see the quirk miter illustrated on page 153.

4. Rustication strips attached to concrete formwork create shadow lines that conceal irregularities that occur where one pour of concrete joins another or where one panel of formwork butts another. ■

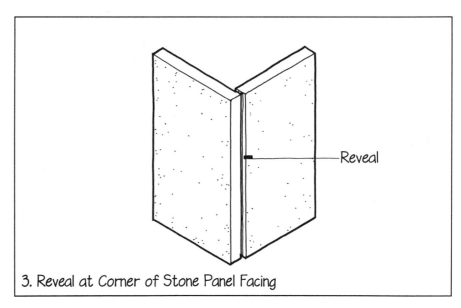

3. Reveal at Corner of Stone Panel Facing

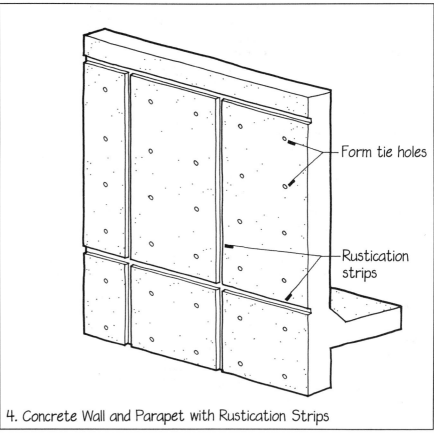

4. Concrete Wall and Parapet with Rustication Strips

BUTT JOINT

A butt joint is the simplest way of assembling two components. It is also the most desirable way of doing so under most circumstances.

1. Mitered corners are an attractive concept, but they present several problems. One is that they create a knife edge on each piece of material at the corner, and knife edges are both fragile and potentially dangerous. Another problem is that to realize its aesthetic potential, a miter must be fitted very closely and precisely. This is often difficult to do when the pieces being mitered are long, wide, or warped. A miter between pieces of wood presents a third problem: Because wood shrinks a great deal perpendicular to its grain and very little along its grain, a 45° cut across a board will no longer be 45° after the board has shrunk or expanded. Miters in wood tend to open up unattractively as the building is heated and the wood dries out. ▷

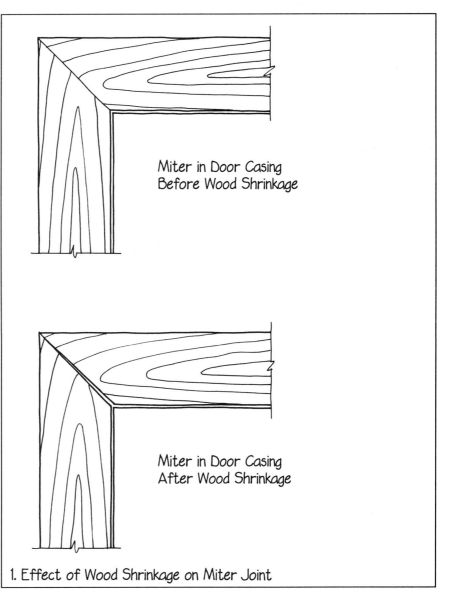

Miter in Door Casing
Before Wood Shrinkage

Miter in Door Casing
After Wood Shrinkage

1. Effect of Wood Shrinkage on Miter Joint

2. A simple butt joint avoids most of these problems. It has no knife edges. It is easy to fit. And if it does open slightly when the wood dries, it does so evenly. A butt joint is especially forgiving if it includes a reveal (see ***Reveal***, page 149). In this example the reveal is created by simply cutting the top piece of casing a bit longer than it needs to be.

3. Another satisfactory approach to this same connection is to use a corner block that is both thicker and wider than the casing pieces it joins, creating a total of four reveals and two butt joints.

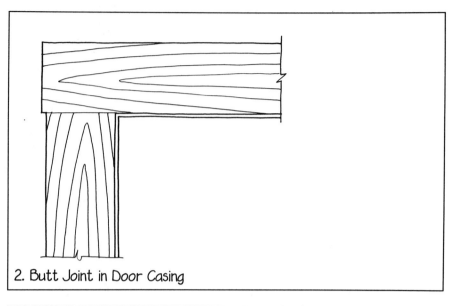

2. Butt Joint in Door Casing

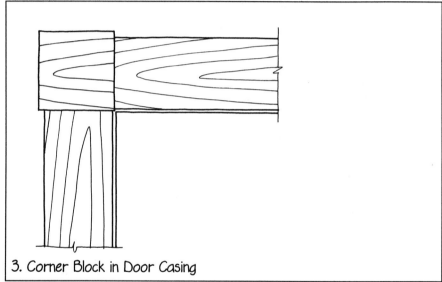

3. Corner Block in Door Casing

4. It is also possible to butt wood moldings at inside corners to avoid the unattractive opening up that might occur in a miter joint. This special type of butt joint is called a coped joint. It is produced in several steps. The first piece of molding is butted at right angles into the corner and nailed. The second piece of molding is mitered to establish the line of the cope. Finally, a coping saw is used to cut the second piece of molding at an angle of 90° or slightly less, following the edge of the miter as a guide. The coped end of the second piece butts tightly to the contoured side of the first piece. The coped connection looks exactly the same as a mitered connection but retains its tight fit even if the moldings shrink slightly.

5. Sometimes a good compromise for joining long edges is the quirk miter. It has no knife edges and is fairly forgiving of fitting problems because of its built-in reveal, but it retains the satisfying visual symmetry of a miter. ■

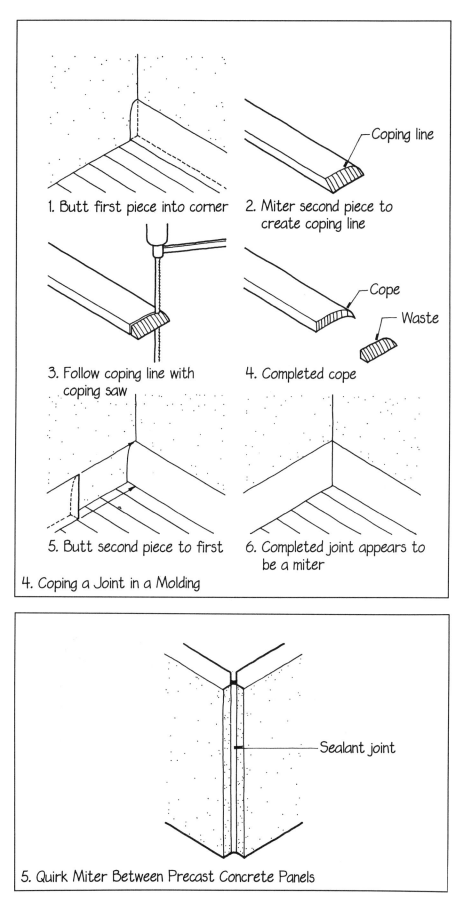

1. Butt first piece into corner

2. Miter second piece to create coping line — Coping line

3. Follow coping line with coping saw

4. Completed cope — Cope — Waste

5. Butt second piece to first

6. Completed joint appears to be a miter

4. Coping a Joint in a Molding

— Sealant joint

5. Quirk Miter Between Precast Concrete Panels

CLEAN EDGE

Where a material or a surface ends, it should do so neatly and decisively.

1. Two kinds of edges that are unforgiving are sharp edges and feather edges. Sharp edges are dangerous and are very susceptible to damage before, during, and after construction. If damaged, they are almost impossible to repair. Feather edges are created when we try to smooth one material into another, as in joining a plaster wall to a masonry wall that lies in the same plane by smoothing the edge of the wet plaster onto the face of the masonry. A feather edge looks terrible and is so fragile that it usually cracks apart in a short period of time. It is also impossible to make a smoothly feathered edge in anything but very fine-grained plaster or drywall finishing compound. It doesn't work, for example, to try to create a feathered wash with mortar on top of a masonry chimney: The sand in the mortar is too coarse to feather, and the thin, insubstantial wash will soon crack and detach itself from the masonry. Instead, a chimney should be terminated with a reinforced concrete cap that has a clean, thick edge and a wash on the top.

2. Avoid sharp edges on concrete. Sharp edges in formwork often do not fill properly with concrete during pouring and are likely to be damaged when the formwork is stripped—an operation that takes place while the concrete is still very brittle. Use chamfer or fillet inserts in the corners of formwork to eliminate sharp corners on concrete; even 90° corners are dangerous, unattractive, and difficult to do well if the designer tries to keep them sharp. Furthermore, they are much more susceptible to damage during construction and occupancy.

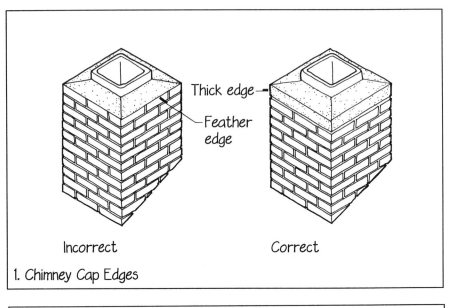

Incorrect   Correct

1. Chimney Cap Edges

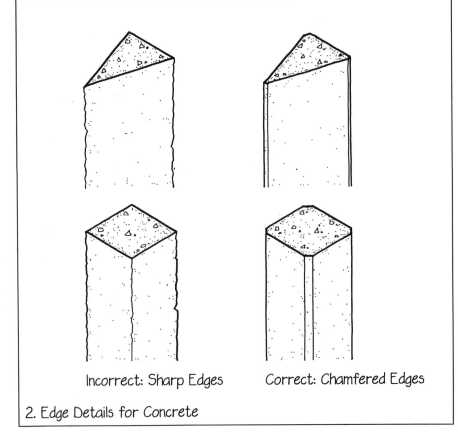

Incorrect: Sharp Edges   Correct: Chamfered Edges

2. Edge Details for Concrete

3. Sharp angles on stonework and masonry are also unforgiving of minor construction mishaps and are very difficult to repair. Chamfered edges, rounded edges, quirk miters, and reveals are clean, forgiving edge details for sharp masonry corners. To create these types of corners in brickwork, specify specially molded brick shapes. Acute-angle corners that are woven of square bricks have water-catching recesses that lead to premature deterioration. Bricks that are cut to an angle with a hammer or a saw have an unattractive finish on the cut surface.

4. Exposed edges of plaster, stucco, and gypsum board must always be bounded by the appropriate casing beads and corner beads. These help the plasterer to maintain a constant thickness of wall and to create clean edges that join neatly to surrounding materials. There are also many accessory strips manufactured in aluminum and plastic that the detailer can use to create crisp, cleanly finished reveals and joints in plaster surfaces. ■

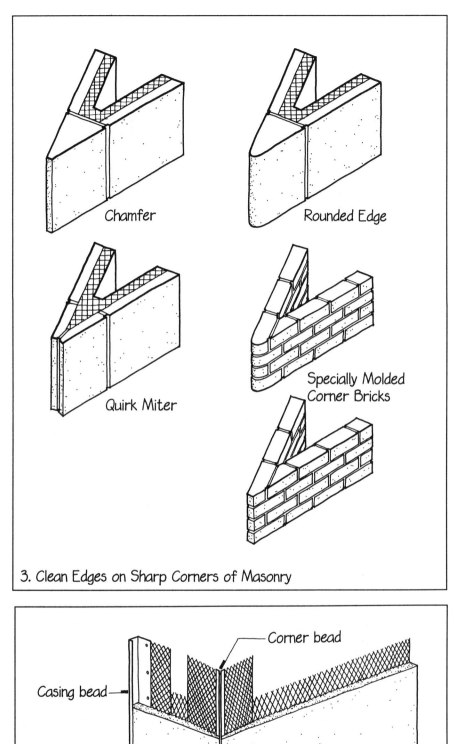

Chamfer

Rounded Edge

Quirk Miter

Specially Molded Corner Bricks

3. Clean Edges on Sharp Corners of Masonry

Corner bead

Casing bead

Casing bead

4. Clean Edges on Plaster and Stucco Surfaces

PROGRESSIVE FINISH

As a construction process progresses, each stage of work should be more finished than the stages that preceded it, and the installation of fine finishes should be delayed until as late in the construction process as possible.

1. Imagine two different ways of finishing the interior side of a wall of poured-in-place architectural concrete. One way is simply to form and pour the concrete very carefully and leave it exposed. The other is to form and pour the concrete somewhat less carefully, and then late in construction furr its interior surface and add a finish layer of gypsum wallboard and paint.

The exposed concrete surface would seem to be the more direct, simple, secure, and economical option to choose, because it involves less material, fewer steps, and fewer trades. It is, however, a very unforgiving finish. Any defects in the formwork and ties, any inconsistencies in vibrating the concrete, any "cold joints" or slight differences in color between batches of concrete, any staining or damage to the wall during subsequent stages of construction will be painfully obvious in the finished surface.

Using furring and gypsum wallboard, the concrete work can be done in a much less exacting way, and subsequent construction damage to the concrete surface is of no consequence. After most construction operations are done and the wall is completely sheltered from the weather, the furring strips are mounted to the concrete, shimming if necessary to produce a plumb, flat surface. The wallboard is mounted, taped, spackled, sanded, and painted. Its junction with the floor is concealed behind a baseboard. Any last-minute damage to the gypsum wall, even if someone puts a wrench or a foot through it, can be repaired quickly and invisibly with drywall compound and paint. The overall cost of the con-

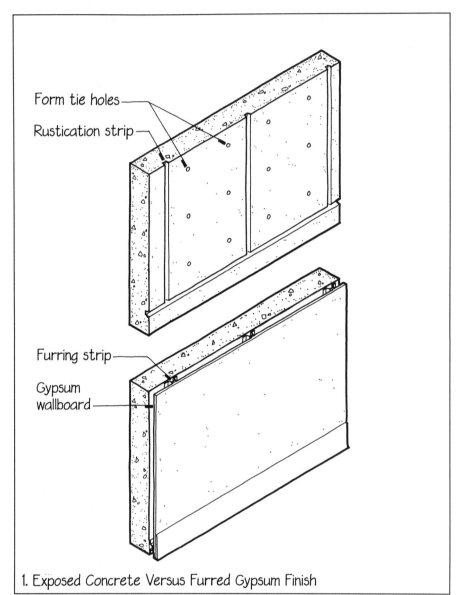

1. Exposed Concrete Versus Furred Gypsum Finish

crete wall plus painted gypsum finish may be less than the overall cost of simply exposing the concrete wall. This is because the wall with a painted gypsum finish has been finished progressively rather than in a single, irrevocable step. The progression is from rough, crude structural surfaces to finer gypsum surfaces to very fine surfaces of paint whose one rough edge is covered by a baseboard. Progressive finish involves successively bet-

ter approximations of the degree of finish ultimately desired, and it delays the finer degrees of finish until as late as possible in the construction process to avoid their being spoiled by rougher operations.

Of course, a painted gypsum surface does not have the satisfying solidity and character of a well-made concrete wall. The client and the designer may prefer the concrete, and they should have it, but they must recognize that it is an unforgiving finish, expensive and risky to produce, and difficult to repair, and they must detail, specify, supervise—and pay—accordingly.

2. Similarly, an exposed concrete slab is an unforgiving floor finish—one that should be used only if the designer is sure that the contractor will have experienced, reliable, highly skilled concrete masons to produce it. Even under these conditions, the slab is exposed to a considerable risk of damage or staining throughout the construction process. More forgiving and often less expensive overall is to cover the slab at the very end of the construction sequence with a material such as carpet, plastic tile, or ceramic tile.

3. Exposed ductwork, piping, and conduits can be attractive in their sculptural complexity, but they are not necessarily cheaper or easier overall than services concealed with a suspended ceiling. Additional expenses associated with exposed services include increased design time to lay out attractive arrangements of the lines, increased fabrication and erection time to allow for a higher standard of workmanship, durable covers for pipe and duct insulation, and painting. These extra expenses often add up to more than the total cost of a suspended ceiling. Fortunately, in many buildings, the extra money is available, and the blandness of the suspended ceiling can be avoided.

4. Light frame construction in wood or metal is based on the idea of progressive finish. The rough, unattractive structure is erected first; then the exterior is finished; and finally, the mechanical, electrical, and insulating work are done. The interior finishes come late in the process, covering the messiness of the frame and mechanical work and culminating in trim, flooring, paint, and wallpaper that cover all the preceding work in successive layers.

■

FORGIVING SURFACE

Some types of finish surfaces make things easier for construction workers because they conceal or camouflage small inaccuracies and blemishes.

1. Because of problems associated with working in the tiring, awkward overhead position, gypsum board workers and plasterers find it difficult to make a ceiling surface completely smooth and plane. There are almost always some slight flaws in the joints of gypsum board ceilings and minor blemishes in overhead plaster work. A textured finish on a ceiling can hide these imperfections beyond detection, making the prior operations easier and more economical. A smooth-surfaced ceiling, especially one with a gloss paint on it, accentuates every defect.

2. Avoid lighting a smooth plaster surface with a window or a light fixture that casts light across it at a very acute angle, because such light casts long shadows from otherwise insignificant flaws, making the surface look much worse than it really is. The same surface lit from an angle approaching 90° will appear to be of perfect workmanship. Alternatively, a very rough-textured surface can be attractive when lit at an acute angle.

3. Concrete that has been cast in formwork made of individual boards looks good even if there are many flaws in the boards or bubbles in the concrete, because such defects become lost in the overall texture. Concrete that has been cast against a smooth steel or plastic surface features any defects prominently, and an attempt to patch them will only make them more blatant. Almost any type of texture will work to hide defects in concrete: sand blasted, bush hammered, corrugated, ribbed.

4. In a wall constructed of very precisely made bricks, each brick must be laid with extreme care, because any slight dimensional misalignment of a brick will stand out from the rest of the pattern. Traditionally, bricks vary somewhat in size, color, and distortion. A wall made of such varied bricks is a richly textured tapestry in which minor misalignments only add to the visual interest.

5. A sheet of solid-color plastic laminate that has a small flaw in it may have to be discarded in the shop. A patterned laminate will camouflage many small scratches, spots, and dents. This is why solid-color laminates often cost more than patterns. ∎

CONSTRUCTIBILITY:
EFFICIENT USE OF CONSTRUCTION RESOURCES

E F F I C I E N T use of construction resources often follows directly from a building's details. A seemingly simple, straightforward detail, if not thoroughly considered from this point of view, can conceal endless problems of materials procurement, tool and machine utilization, construction scheduling, and even labor relations. The detail patterns associated with avoiding these problems include the following:

FACTORY AND SITE

In-factory work and on-site work each has its associated set of advantages and disadvantages. An important task of the detailer is to allocate the work of making a building judiciously between the two for optimum construction speed, quality, and cost.

1. In the factory, the weather is always dry and temperatures are always comfortable. Lighting is good, large machines and tools with impressive capabilities and extreme accuracy can be utilized, and workers can work in comfortable postures. Wage rates for factory workers are substantially lower than for on-site workers, and worker productivity (because of the factors mentioned earlier in this paragraph) is higher. But the sizes and weights of the components created by the factory are restricted by the dimensions and capacities of trucks.

On the jobsite, the weather and the light vary greatly in quality. Tooling is not as sophisticated. Access to the work is not always the best. Wage rates are high and productivity ranges from high to low, depending on weather, light, tooling, and access. But very large assemblies can be created and adjustments can be made to site conditions. Assemblies can be built to actual required size and shape, which is a particular advantage in renovation work.

2. At the scale of a custom-designed house, the optimum mix of factory and site operations is well established. Foundations, framing, roofing, siding, and insulating are done on the site, using simple factory-produced components, such as formwork panels, masonry blocks, dimension lumber, wood panel products, shingles, and insulation batts. Windows and doors, which require high precision and exacting finishes, are not made on site but are ordered as prefabricated units from factories. Electrical wiring, plumbing, and heating and cooling systems are installed on site, but such exacting components as fixtures, ductwork, furnaces, boilers, convectors, and registers are factory-made. Finish surfaces for ceilings, walls, and floors are installed on site, using factory-produced panel products in many cases. Interior doors and cabinetry are made as units in factories and simply nailed or screwed into the house. In general, the smaller, highly precise, highly finished components are made in the factory, while the larger elements of the building are created on site from simple, easily fitted pieces of factory-made materials.

3. In many larger buildings, the choices may not be so obvious. Should a concrete frame be precast or sitecast? Should a building be clad with brickwork or stonework that is assembled on the site, or should it be clad with factory-made panels? Should partitions be constructed on site, or should they be interchangeable prefabricated panels? These are complex choices that involve the entire building design team. ■

REHEARSING THE CONSTRUCTION SEQUENCE

The act of designing and drawing a detail should be based on a mental process of rehearsing the sequence in which the detail will be assembled on the building site.

1. In the mind of a construction manager or a construction worker, a detail drawing should create a vivid, dynamic picture of actual materials, fasteners, tools, and operations. From the detail drawing, the builder should easily be able to visualize a sensible, workable process for assembling that part of the building. A good habit for the detailer to develop is to design and draw each detail *in the order in which its pieces are assembled*, thinking simultaneously of the actual construction operations that are represented by each new element of the drawing and trying to see the detail not as an object, but *as a process*, which is how the builder will see it. This creates the opportunity for the detailer to rehearse mentally the construction sequence, searching for better ways of doing things, looking for "bugs" and for components that won't go together easily on the construction jobsite. For important details and elaborate assemblies, it can make sense for the detailer to sketch out for his or her own enlightenment and scrutiny a series of drawings that show the assembly sequence step by step. In cases where an entirely new and unfamiliar construction sequence is required, these sequential sketches should be cleaned up and used as part of the construction drawings.

To a beginning detailer, a detail drawing may appear almost as an abstraction that has little meaning in terms of actual materials, tools, and processes. Through office experience, reading, and jobsite visits, the beginner should acquire as quickly as possible a critical mass of knowledge of what details really mean to a builder.

▷

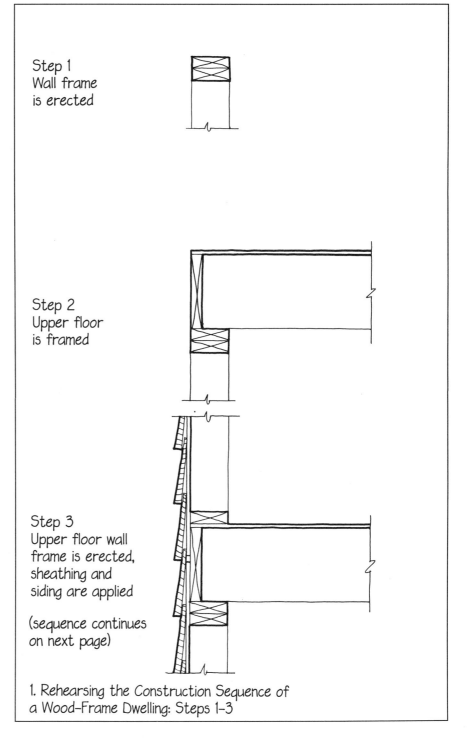

Step 1
Wall frame
is erected

Step 2
Upper floor
is framed

Step 3
Upper floor wall
frame is erected,
sheathing and
siding are applied

(sequence continues
on next page)

1. Rehearsing the Construction Sequence of
a Wood-Frame Dwelling: Steps 1-3

This knowledge is never complete and will grow throughout the detailer's career; the hardest part is to get a strong enough start in this learning process to become a fully effective designer of realistic details. Rehearsing the construction sequence mentally when drawing each detail can help materially in this education.

2. When rehearsing the construction sequence, look for such signs of inefficiency as excessive numbers of separate trades, repeated visits by the same trade, lack of temporary support for components, lack of alignment references, fitting problems (see *Sliding Fit*, page 142), and opportunities for spoiling of previously completed work by gouging, scratching, or staining (see *Progressive Finish*, page 156). Strive for a detail that requires a minimum number of trades, only one visit per trade, sliding fits only, little or no temporary support, no special tools, no ladders or scaffolding—in short, a detail that will go together like clockwork.

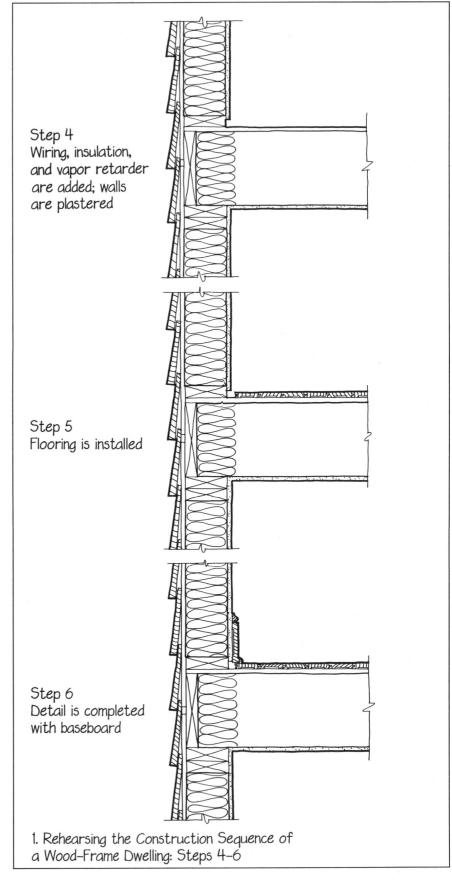

Step 4
Wiring, insulation, and vapor retarder are added; walls are plastered

Step 5
Flooring is installed

Step 6
Detail is completed with baseboard

1. Rehearsing the Construction Sequence of a Wood-Frame Dwelling: Steps 4-6

3. Rehearsal of a construction sequence can often turn up hidden problems with a detail that appears entirely satisfactory. Consider this detail for a recessed wood baseboard. It looks like a clean, contemporary detail that will be easy to build using standard components. But rehearse the construction sequence: Normally the gypsum wallboard and its casing bead will be installed first. Then the flooring will be laid, and lastly the baseboard will be installed. This means that the baseboard will have to be fitted precisely between two parallel planes, which is difficult (see *Sliding Fit*, page 142). If the surface of the hardwood floor is at all wavy (which is likely) or if the casing bead of the wallboard is not perfectly straight and level (which is also likely), fitting the baseboard between them will be a nightmare. Changing the construction sequence to install the flooring and baseboard before the wallboard risks water damage to the flooring and makes the floor sanding and varnishing more difficult. Precisely dimensioned wood blocks could be used as temporary gauges to locate the casing bead at the proper height above the subfloor, but this would not prevent difficulties arising from waviness of the subfloor or finish floor. This is fundamentally a bad detail—one that will be expensive and troublesome, and that may not even look very good when finished because of varying crack dimensions between the baseboard and the edge bead.

4. The recessed baseboard detail could be improved somewhat by adding a deep reveal to the upper edge of the baseboard in order to create a dark shadow that would conceal a variable crack width at that point, and a shoe molding to conform to the contours of the floor and allow a generous installation clearance for the baseboard. ■

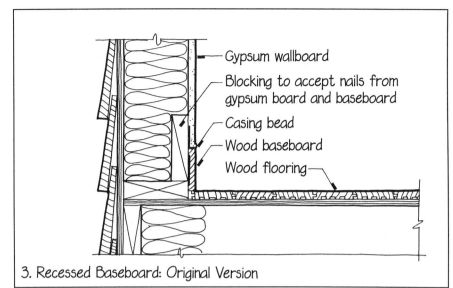

3. Recessed Baseboard: Original Version

- Gypsum wallboard
- Blocking to accept nails from gypsum board and baseboard
- Casing bead
- Wood baseboard
- Wood flooring

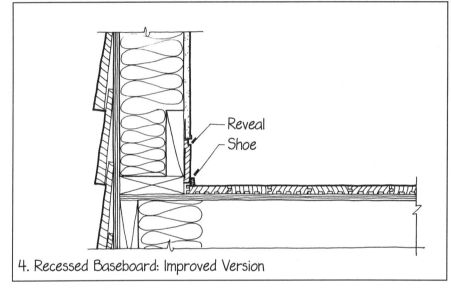

4. Recessed Baseboard: Improved Version

- Reveal
- Shoe

OFF-THE-SHELF PARTS

Materials and components that are readily available make everyone's lives easier during construction.

1. Certain building components are instantly available everywhere. The builder of a tract house can make a single telephone call to a materials supplier, and the next morning a truck will arrive at the construction site and leave behind every component needed to construct the frame and sheathe it: lumber, wood panels, nails, air barrier paper, and even shingles, siding, windows, and doors. Interior finish components for an ordinary house are equally available. But sometimes just one special component can cause the whole process to break down. Suppose your details and specifications call for a new, improved kind of air barrier paper that has just come on the market. Suppose further that you didn't check to see if it was locally available, and it isn't. The builder orders the paper from a distant supplier, and it takes several weeks to arrive. Meanwhile, the construction process has to stop, because the siding can't be applied because the air barrier paper isn't there. This causes delays and costs money.

The moral of this not-so-hypothetical story is simple: Don't use anything but standard, off-the-shelf products unless you have a strong reason to do otherwise. If the strong reason exists, then you should make a phone call or two to establish availability of the product. If necessary, work directly with the builder or contractor to be sure that the product is ordered well in advance of need, and be ready to specify an acceptable alternative product if supply problems persist and construction delays loom. Don't be afraid to use new products, but be aware of potential supply problems, and do your part to solve them before they occur. And don't try too many new products on the same project, or these problems will multiply. ∎

LOCAL SKILLS AND CUSTOMS

A building's details should reflect a knowledge of the labor force that will construct the building.

1. Know for what kind of contractors and work force you are detailing. A few years ago, an architect was asked to design a school campus in a remote forest in the Pacific Northwest in such a way that it could be framed with logs and heavy timbers by a crew of loggers using chainsaws and axes. The details were worked out from the beginning with this in mind, and the constructed buildings are not only handsome but also have a unique character that is created in large part by the unusual details. This may be an extreme example, but often you will find yourself detailing for do-it-yourself home-owners, volunteer laborers, or small contractors who have only rudimentary tools and equipment. Sometimes the jobsite will be remote from power lines, so the building's details should not require too many electrically driven tools that will overload a portable generator. Sometimes water will not be available on the jobsite until construction is well along, so the early stages of construction must be designed to require as little water as possible.

2. Even in more ordinary circumstances, know in advance what local labor practices are. Are the building trades unionized, and, if so, what are the union rules regarding jurisdictions and work practices? Does a particular mason's union, for example, specify the maximum weight of masonry unit that a mason can handle alone? Which union has jurisdiction over installing stone cladding panels on a steel truss backing: Is it the ironworkers or the masons? If the trades are not unionized, what are their usual ways of going about things? Try to detail in such a way that the labor force will have no trouble dividing the work among the trades and that it can follow its usual practices.

3. Builders in various regions have their own customary ways of doing things. In some areas of North America, most residential foundations are made of poured concrete, and, in other areas, they are made of concrete blocks. The predominant material in any one area is usually cheaper and is practiced by a larger group of competing subcontractors. Steel fabricators in some areas prefer to bolt even their shop-fabricated connections, while others like to weld them. Certain regions have excellent stucco contractors, whereas others do not. The same is true of tile roofing installers, wood shake installers, and several other trades. Don't necessarily be restricted by these customs, but exploit them whenever you can, and, when your design runs counter to the customs, be prepared to do the additional work necessary to help line up subcontractors and materials. ■

ALL-WEATHER CONSTRUCTION

Details should be designed with consideration of the weather sensitivities of the various construction operations and the time of year when those operations are likely to occur.

1. Certain construction operations are very weather sensitive. Low-slope membrane roofing can't be installed over a wet roof deck, but a low-slope structural standing seam metal roof can be. Exterior painting should not take place under rainy conditions, hot windy conditions, or cold conditions; this may indicate that prefinished exterior materials are preferable for certain projects. Concrete and masonry work can be problematic in very hot or very cold weather, which might lead the designer to select a precast concrete, steel, or heavy timber system instead if extreme temperatures are anticipated during construction. Stucco work can't be done in very low temperatures, but precast concrete panels can still be placed.

2. Select materials and components for each project with an eye to the time of year and the temperatures and precipitation that are expected when it will be built. Anticipate potential problems with weather sensitive operations, and eliminate the problems in advance through selecting appropriate systems and components if you can. In any case, be ready to propose alternative ways of doing things if weather problems develop. ∎

PRIDE OF CRAFTSMANSHIP

Rare is the construction worker who does not have a love of good work and a pride of craftsmanship that can be brought out by an inspired detail.

1. Most bricklayers spend months and years at a stretch laying nothing but running bond facings and are delighted (if sometimes tentative at first) to have an opportunity to create a more decorative pattern bond, a corbeled ornament, a curving wall, or an arch. Finish carpenters respond readily to the opportunity to work with fine hardwoods and delicate moldings. Certain plasterers still know how to do decorative texturing and even plaster ornament. Painters can easily be persuaded to do masking, striping, and stenciling to create colorful patterns. Most heavy timber framers already apply chamfers, quirks, and lamb's tongues to their beams and columns.

Proceed cautiously into these areas. Some of these traditional expressions of pride of craftsmanship can be exceedingly expensive if they are misused or overused, but it is often possible within even a modest construction budget to add a few small touches to the project that will lift it above the ordinary level of craftsmanship.

2. Even where you do not use these overt expressions of pride of craftsmanship, workers appreciate intelligent details that make the best possible use of their skills, and they dislike arbitrary, uninformed details that force them to do things that are awkward or difficult to do well. Learn what workers in each trade can do best and most economically, and detail accordingly. This will result in a lower contract price, and, just as importantly, it will get the workers on your side, helping to make the building the best that it can be. ∎

ACCEPTED STANDARDS

Details should conform to norms that are known, understood, and accepted throughout the construction industry. These norms are embodied in the published standards of a number of construction-related organizations. By conforming to these norms and referencing them in the written specifications for each project, the detailer eliminates many ambiguities and potential sources of misunderstanding from the construction documents.

1. Suppose, for example, that the detailer specifies a paving brick simply as "suitable for use as paving in the Chicago climate." This leaves considerable uncertainty as to what is "suitable." The masonry contractor may have had good experiences with a particular brick on previous jobs, but the bricks of the same type that are purchased for the current job may be defectively manufactured and may deteriorate rapidly in winter weather. The detailer could remedy this situation by specifying the maximum water absorption that the brick may have, but this leaves the contractor with the task of having to request absorption test results from the manufacturer. The entire dilemma could be avoided by merely specifying that the paving bricks must be Class SX pavers, as defined by ASTM C 902. ASTM C 902 is a standard specification for paving bricks that is promulgated by the American Society for Testing and Materials (ASTM), a major standards-setting organization in the construction industry. C 902 is known and understood throughout the masonry industry, and bricks that conform to it are so designated in manufacturers' literature. It includes standards for strength, water absorption, saturation, abrasion resistance, warpage, chippage, dimensional tolerances, efflorescence, and other criteria, as measured by standard laboratory tests. By citing ASTM C 902, the detailer not only avoids potential communication problems and misunderstandings but also adds to the construction contract a very powerful, well-considered set of requirements that avoid a number of potential disasters.

ASTM publishes standards for many construction materials; it is a major source of accepted standards in the industry. Many other organizations have also established standards for other materials and assemblies that have become widely accepted. The publications of some of the more prominent standards-setting organizations are included in the reference list at the end of the book. The detailer should become familiar with the accepted standards for all construction materials and assemblies, and use these standards as much as possible in specifying. ∎

AESTHETICS:
INTRODUCTION

A B U I L D I N G should please the eye. Its details play a large role in this important function. Every truly great building has great details—details that contribute to the aesthetic themes of the building, that harmonize with one another, and that create beauty out of the ordinary materials and necessities of construction. A building with a splendid thematic idea can fail as architecture if it has poor details—details that are badly matched to its primary aesthetic, that do not relate strongly to one another, and that fail to lift their materials above the ordinary.

The detail patterns that relate to aesthetics are few in number, but each is powerful, far-reaching, and requires greater effort and insight to implement than any of the patterns relating to function and constructibility. The foremost aesthetic requirement for detailing is that all of the details of a building should contribute to its formal and spatial theme. This requirement is developed in the detail pattern

Contributive Details (page 170)

Details may be elaborated to feature certain of their characteristics, or they may be decorated for purely visual effect:

Intensification and Ornamentation (page 172)

Lastly, details may be developed whose role is solely to unify the visual composition of building elements that otherwise might seem disjointed or unrelated. This role is introduced in the pattern

Formal Transitions (page 174)

These three patterns serve to focus the detailer's attention on some important aesthetic issues that arise in detailing. They constitute a small part of a much larger field of study, architectural composition, that will amply repay as much time as the detailer can devote to its study.

Although the emphasis in this section is on the visual qualities of a building and its details, the detailer should always look for opportunities to delight the other human senses. Tactile qualities of materials and details are important: the feel of a carpet or polished marble underfoot; the satiny smoothness of polished wood handles on a cabinet; deep, luxurious cushions on a bench; a nubby texture in a wall covering. Auditory qualities are also vital: Should a particular architectural space seem hushed and quiet? Should it be vast and echoey? Should one's footsteps resound throughout a room, or would it be more appropriate that one tread softly, as if floating noiselessly? Would it enhance the architectural experience if one heard the sounds of splashing water, of birdsongs, of wind in trees, of children chattering, of machines working productively? And consider the opportunities for olfactory delight in a building: the fragrance of cedarwood, the perfume of flowers, the freshness of grass growing, the moist breezes off a pond, the waxy smokiness of candles, the musky scent of leather. Once again, the designers of the greatest buildings have considered these possibilities and have often used them to their advantage.

CONTRIBUTIVE DETAILS

All of the details of a building should contribute to its formal and spatial theme.

1. Every detail has a style. The style may be incidental (the strictly utilitarian style of a steel framing connection) or intentional (the style of a Doric capital). A Doric temple is more than just a low gabled roof supported by closely spaced columns that encircle a walled rectangle. It is also a consistent set of intentional details, each one of which contributes to the overall appearance that we recognize instantly as Doric. The Gothic style was based on an obsession with tall, long spaces lit by generous windows. It encompassed a structural ideal of elaborate stone vaulting supported on slender piers, its thrusts absorbed by delicate buttressing, and a set of details very different from those of the Doric builders. Whereas the Doric details emphasized a thick, discontinuous, sticklike con-

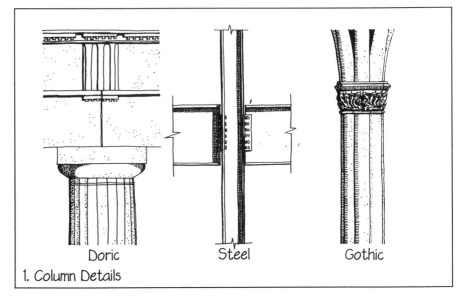

1. Column Details

structional aesthetic, the Gothic featured thin, flowing members that all contributed to an apparent continuity of space, form, and structural action.

2. In similar fashion we can analyze the details associated with each architectural style: Craftsman style with its celebration of wood joinery; Prairie style with its details that emphasize horizontality (sometimes even to the point of turning all exposed screws so their slots are horizontal); various Brutalist styles in which slabs and sticks of material seem to bang into one another without visible connectors; and High Tech style, in which the parts of a building are made to look like the pieces of a precision machine, joined with visible bolts and pins.

4. Try to imagine a building by Mies van der Rohe with Victorian Gothic details: If we could succeed in creating it, its composition would be so riven by internal conflict that it would fall apart compositionally before our eyes. The Minimalist space and form of a building by Mies are intended to be enhanced by Minimalist details; if they are not, it is not a Mies building. Try to imagine a Romanesque style building with High Tech details or a Baroque building with Brutalist details. It is impossible. A building's details are integral to its style.

5. Each designer of buildings works in his or her own style. The style may not have a name, but it has a personality. This personality stems from an approach to space, to form, to light, to color— and to details. The style of the details must be integral with the style of the building. As a designer's style evolves and changes over the years, so must the details. The details must contribute their proportional share to the style of the building.

6. A building's details should be all of a family. It won't do to copy one detail

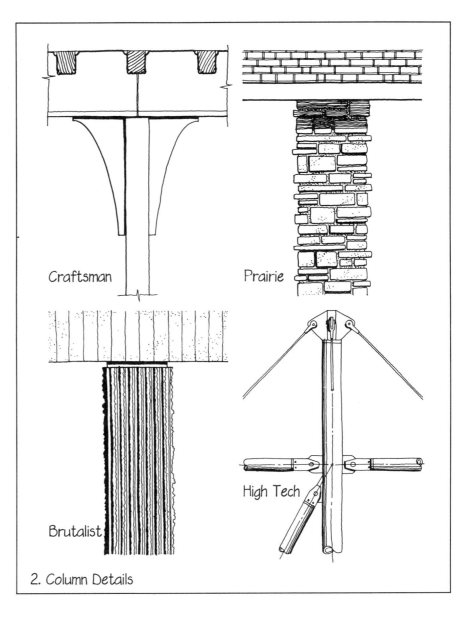

Craftsman

Prairie

Brutalist

High Tech

2. Column Details

from one source, another detail from another, and patch together a set of details that function well but bear no visible resemblance to one another. The designer should develop a matched set of a building's most important details as an ongoing part of the overall design process. This set of key details should then serve to guide the preparation of every other visible detail in the building. ∎

INTENSIFICATION AND ORNAMENTATION

Details can be embellished to add to the visual richness of a building.

1. Since the beginning of civilization, makers of things have evidenced love of their work by adding nonfunctional elements to their forms. Weavers have added textures, colors, and patterns. Tilemakers have added brightly decorated glazes. Carpenters have chamfered and carved their work. Shinglers have added scallops and sawtooth patterns. Masons have laid delightful patterns of headers, soldiers, rowlocks, and corbels in their walls. The results of these efforts are often very beautiful, sometimes because they bring out inherent beauties of material and craft, and sometimes because they are simply beautiful in the abstract.

Unadorned form   Intensification with striping   Ornamentation

2. Analysis of a Greek Vase

2. If we examine an ancient decorated Greek vase, we find two sets of patterns painted on it. One set is made up of circumferential stripes and bands that were created by holding a paintbrush against the clay vase as it spun on the potter's wheel. These stripes generally were applied at locations that were significant in relationship to the curvature of the vase—a change in the radius or direction of curvature. They might be termed *intensification*, because they are purposefully related to the process of making the vase and to its form, and thus intensify its aesthetic. The other set of patterns consists of scenes of animals, warriors, athletes, gods and goddesses—whatever suited the mood or mission of the potter. These bear little or no relationship to the manufacture or form of the vase, and might be termed *ornamentation*. Both intensification and ornamentation contribute to the beauty of the vase, but they sprang from different sources of inspiration.

3. Intensification and ornamentation have their places also in the work of the building trades. The carpenter's chamfers reduce the likelihood of splinters along the edges of a post or beam, and they make the member slower to catch fire, so they have functions to perform; however, they also bring the long, straight edges more prominently to our view, and their beveled facets add sculptural interest to the timbers. A chamfer could not continue into a joint between members without creating unsightly gaps, so carpenters developed stylish ways of terminating chamfers short of the end of the member, in devices such as sinuous lamb's tongues or various angular notches. In the joints themselves, most of the artistry of the carpenter was necessarily concealed in mortises, tenons, and laps, but pleasing patterns could be created of exposed pegs and brackets. All this might be considered as intensification, because it sprang from necessity but went beyond it to create a delight that enhances our understanding of the making of the building. If the carpenter went on to carve scenes or mottoes on the sides of the beams, this was ornamentation, because as attractive and contributive to the overall aesthetic of the building as it might be, it was not directly related to necessity.

4. The detailer should look first to intensification as a way of enhancing the aesthetic impact of details. The

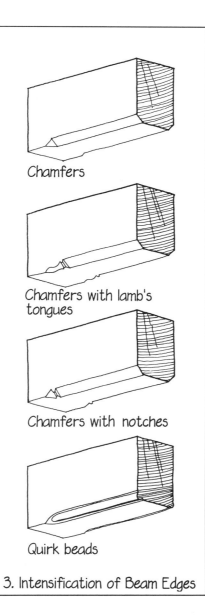

Chamfers

Chamfers with lamb's tongues

Chamfers with notches

Quirk beads

3. Intensification of Beam Edges

sources of inspiration are many: the need to put control joints into a stucco wall surface; the need to use form ties and rustication strips to create satisfactory surfaces of architectural concrete; the need to add brackets and bolts to connect members of steel or timber; the need to cover unsightly gaps where floors or soffits join walls; the need to install a lintel to support masonry over a window or a door opening; or the need to make closely spaced seams in a sheet metal roof. Each of these is an opportunity to intensify the form of a portion of the building by such strategies as adding lines or moldings to junctions between planes, creating rhythms and patterns of fasteners or seams, exaggerating sizes or numbers of things such as bolts or brackets, or adding contrasting colors. Each such effort is a celebration of the necessary, a virtuoso cadenza, a sharing of the joy of assembling a building with the viewer, who was not involved in its construction.

5. Ornamentation can be equally as effective as intensification, but it requires more dexterity and judgment, because it does not arise from a specific, tangible feature of the building but is created almost in a vacuum. Often intensification alone is sufficient to carry the building into the realm of the special, and applied ornament can look superficial, even awkward or tasteless if it is badly done.   ∎

FORMAL TRANSITIONS

Details can help to unify the visual composition of building elements that might otherwise seem disjointed or unrelated.

1. The masses and forms of a well-designed building generally merge pleasingly and require no further attention from the detailer, but occasionally a detail can help to correct the appearance of an awkward junction. A gable-roofed mass incorporated into a larger flat-roofed volume can appear weak and lifeless. Minor changes in detailing can create a strong pavilion that draws the attention of the eye.

2. An unarticulated transition from supporting piers to an arch appears indecisive. The addition of a string course and pier capitals gives a definite demarcation to the boundary between pier and arch.

3. Many Renaissance and Baroque churches used ornate, nonstructural buttresses to make a smooth transition from the main mass of the church to a superimposed dome or vault.

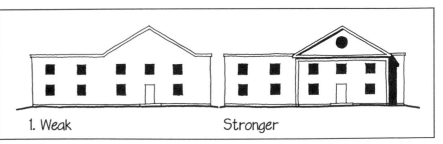

1. Weak   Stronger

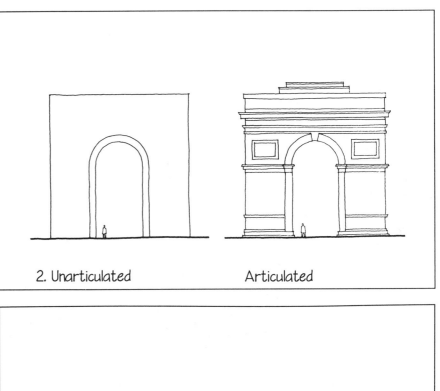

2. Unarticulated   Articulated

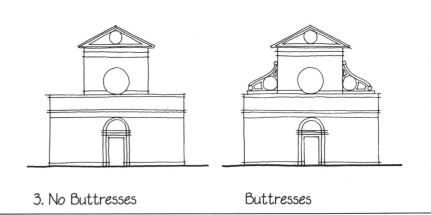

3. No Buttresses   Buttresses

4. On a smaller scale, a timber beam that simply emerges from the plaster of a supporting wall looks rather disjointed. An applied bracket and pilaster at this transition can establish a stronger visual connection between the two elements. Similarly, a structurally adequate connection between the beam and a column can appear weak and abrupt; brackets can ease this transition.

5. There are many details that require the graceful termination of a form: a finial on a newel post, a volute at the termination of a handrail, a pendant beneath an overhanging second story, a cheek detail at the end of an eave. In none of these examples is it visually satisfactory merely to chop off the member that is being terminated. ■

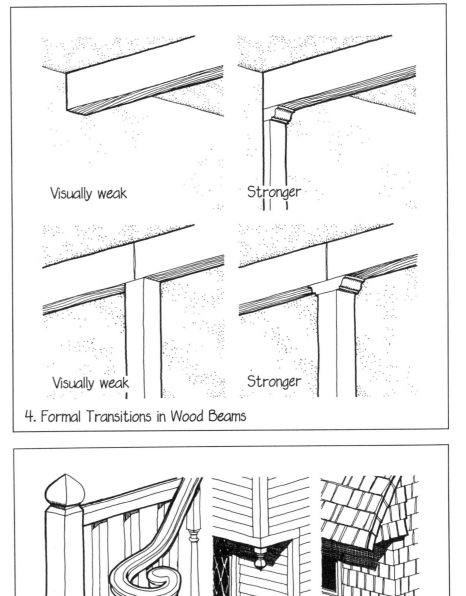

Visually weak

Stronger

Visually weak

Stronger

4. Formal Transitions in Wood Beams

5. Terminations

DETAIL DEVELOPMENT

APPLYING THE PATTERNS:

▽

DETAILING A BUILDING
IN WOOD LIGHT FRAMING

▽

DETAILING A BUILDING
IN ARCHITECTURAL CONCRETE

▽

DETAILING A BUILDING
IN BRICK VENEER CURTAIN WALL

APPLYING THE DETAIL PATTERNS

T H I S section of the book consists of three illustrated narratives. These describe the process of designing the key details of specific building projects in wood light framing, architectural concrete, and brick veneer on a midrise concrete frame. The intent is to show how one architect, the author, goes about designing the details of a building and to reveal something of his concerns, his mode of thought, and his way of working. Throughout these narratives, special emphasis is given to showing how the detail patterns are a natural part of the detailing process. Pattern names are given in bold italic so that they are readily identifiable.

Designing details is not a neat, linear, fully logical operation. Like any design process, it is engagingly messy and complex. It involves false starts, wrong turns, mental blocks, dead ends, backtracking, and moments of despair— as well as purposeful progress, intelligent decisions, creative synthesis, and gratifying moments of inspiration, insight, and triumph. These narratives, though they display many of these twists and turns, have been simplified a good deal to reduce their length and to make them easier for the reader to follow. The drawings, similarly, have been cleaned up and reduced in number from the innumerable freehand scribbles, countless tracing paper overlays, and smudged, densely overdrawn sections that are the usual interim products of the detailer. An attempt has been made to relate the drawing styles on these pages to the qualities of the actual drawings that the detailer produces along the way, starting with freehand pencil sketches and ending with precise, computer-drafted details.

It is readily apparent in these narratives that independently of a knowledge of the detail patterns and some conventions of drafting, detailing requires a ready familiarity with construction materials, tools, processes, and standards that must be acquired from sources other than this book. It is assumed that the reader has at least a beginning understanding of these areas and that it is being augmented constantly by reading the technical literature, consulting more experienced colleagues, and observing actual construction operations.

The three building designs presented here break no new stylistic ground. They aspire only to contribute to an initial understanding of mainstream detailing practice. As one acquires more experience, it is even more challenging and a good deal more fun to work on the detailing of an out-of-the-ordinary design.

There is a crucial theme that runs through these three examples: The design of the details of a building is a process that establishes with considerable precision both the technical means of its construction and its interior and exterior appearance. In each of the three examples, we begin the design of the details with only a crude idea of the form and texture of the building. By the time the mere handful of key details have been developed to a preliminary stage of completion, the building has come alive, not only because it has become patently constructible, but also because it has assumed a character and a personality of considerable depth. It follows that the design of the details of a building should begin while its form and space are still fluid. In this way, the materials selected, the processes by which they are assembled, and the developing character of the details can inform the form-making process for the building as a whole. There are few greater mistakes that a designer can make than to create a finished form for a building and only then begin to consider how to build it. Buildings designed in this way (and there are far too many of them) generally resemble flimsy, unsatisfying stage sets. Every truly great building, ancient or contemporary, incorporates its handling of materials and processes as an integral part of its aesthetic, showing that its designer expended as much love and expertise on its details as on its space and form.

DETAILING A BUILDING IN WOOD LIGHT FRAMING

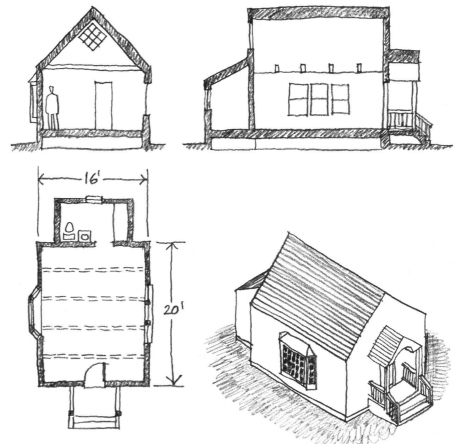

THE PROJECT

The project is a small sales office for a residential subdivision in coastal New England. The roof pitch is 12/12 (45°). Both the roof and the walls will be clad with red cedar shingles (*Surfaces That Age Gracefully*). The interior will be finished with gypsum board walls and ceiling and a varnished oak floor.

SETTING PERFORMANCE STANDARDS

We wish the building to convey the image of an uncomplicated cottage with a minimal, prismatic form. The details of the building should be as simple as possible in order to contribute to the minimalist, geometric architectural image, and they should relate closely to one another. The state building code requires *Thermal Insulation* values of R-19 for the walls and R-30 for the roof. The insulation must be done in a manner that allows the ceiling to follow the line of the rafters in order to create a tall interior space.

KEY DETAILS TO DEVELOP

The key details that will establish the constructional and visual character of the building are those circled on the section and plan diagrams below.

These must be developed as a consistent set of *Contributive Details* that work well with the building's architecture and with one another. They are the most general of the building's details. Details of special situations such as the

entry porch and the shed to the rear that houses the toilet room will be developed using these general details as a point of departure. ▷

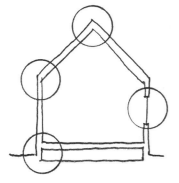

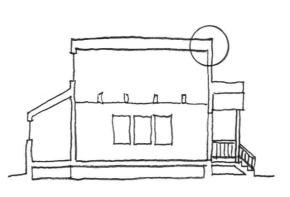

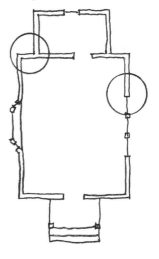

EARLY WORK ON FORM, MATERIALS, AND DETAILS

The prismatic form that we have envisioned presents an eave detailing problem: Under most circumstances the building code requires gutters and downspouts, which would disrupt the clean geometry of the building. Gutters could be built into the roof surface at the top of each wall, but we discard this idea because built-in gutters often prove to be troublesome in use. When they become clogged with leaves or ice, water is likely to back up under the shingles.

The building code offers an interesting alternative, however: If an eave overhang of at least 1′ is provided, no gutters are required because the overhang is an *Overhang and Drip* that protects the walls and windows. If we adopt this alternative, though, we will want to detail a drip trench filled with crushed stone in the ground beneath each eave, to prevent erosion and to minimize splashing of water and mud onto the siding at the base of the wall.

Roof overhangs complicate the form of the building and necessitate a change in our image of it. Perhaps we can use them to create a deeply sheltered feeling for the "cottage." And if the overhangs are deep enough, they can contribute to the overall simplicity of the form by eliminating the need for a separate roof over the bay window. The bay window is 12″ deep, so we adopt tentatively an 18″ overhang.

We sketch the building exterior with this overhang. It is an intriguing formal idea to pursue, but the vertical fascia board appears as a complicating, extraneous surface separating the roof and walls. Could we eliminate the fascia? This would result in a purer, simpler form for the building, one more in the spirit of the original idea.

Gutters and downspouts

With fascia

Without fascia

Structure and Thermal Insulation In addition to the R-30 roof insulation, the building code also requires a continuous 2″ ventilation space beneath the entire roof (*Cold Roof*) and a 36″ wide ice and water barrier sheet beneath the roof shingles at the eaves to minimize damage from ice dams. An R-30 roof can be difficult to achieve when there is no attic, because the roof structure must be deep enough to contain the thickness of the insulating material required to reach this level of thermal protection. Unfaced glass fiber batts with a separate vapor retarder sheet are generally the most economical way to insulate a small sloping roof. A check of insulation manufacturers' catalogs tells us the standard batt thicknesses and R-values, based on both normal- and high-density batting:

3.5″	batts	R-11 and R-15
5.5″	batts	R-21
6.25″	batts	R-19
6.5″	batts	R-22
8.5″	batts	R-30
10″	batts	R-30
12″	batts	R-38

If we decide to use plastic foam insulating materials, a further look at the manufacturers' catalogs reveals the following possibilities:

Extruded polystyrene	R-5.6 per inch
Isocyanurate foam	R-7.2 per inch
Phenolic foam	R-8.3 per inch

We also discover from *ASHRAE Fundamentals* that the R-value of a gypsum board ceiling and interior air film is only a bit over 1. The R-values of the ventilating airspace, sheathing, roofing, and exterior air film cannot be taken into account because the ventilating airspace is assumed to be at outdoor temperature. Therefore, we must find space for R-29 of insulating materials between the airspace and the gypsum board.

Structurally, the roof will consist of wood rafter pairs tied at intervals with horizontal wooden members. The building is 16′ wide, so each rafter must span about 8′, as measured in horizontal projection. We consult *Span Tables for Joists and Rafters* to find the necessary size for the rafters, reading from the table that gives values for members that carry a sloping gypsum board ceiling and a 30 psf snow load.

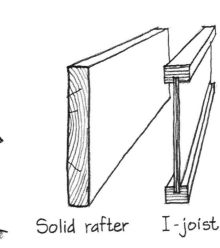

Solid rafter   I-joist

2×6 rafters at a 16″ spacing can span more than 9′, so they would be more than sufficient for this building. We recognize, however, that 2×6 rafters will probably not provide sufficient space for insulating materials, so we use the table to verify some other structural options to keep open:

2×8 rafters @ 24″ spacing

2×10 rafters @ 24″ spacing

2×12 rafters @ 24″ spacing

From a structural standpoint, rafters deeper than 2×8 could be spaced more than 24″ o.c., but we do not want to exceed this spacing for two reasons. One is ease of insulating: Standard insulating batts are made only for 16″ and 24″ spacings. The other is that the required thicknesses of plywood roof sheathing and gypsum board ceiling panels become excessive at rafter spacings greater than 24″.

As an alternative to solid wood rafters, we could use manufactured wood I-joists as rafters to create the depth we need. These come in standard depths of 9½″, 11⅞″, 14″, and 16″. The load-and-span tables in the manufacturers' literature tell us that I-joists in any of these depths could serve as rafters for this building at a 24″ spacing.

Now we return in our thinking to the thermal insulation problem: What are some insulation options that would achieve an overall rating of R-30 for the roof construction? We list a few possibilities:

1. 8.5″ batt (R = 30)

2. 6.25″ batt + 2″ of any foam plastic (R = 30.2 to 35.6)

3. 6.5″ batt + 1″ of isocyanurate or phenolic foam (R = 29.2 to 30.3)

4. 6.25″ batt + 3.5″ batt (R = 30 to 34)

5. 5.5″ of polystyrene foam (R = 30.8)

6. 4″ of phenolic foam (R = 33.2)

▷

Option 1, the 8.5″ batt, has the advantage of simplicity. If we add the required 2″ airspace below the roof sheathing, a rafter depth of 10.5″ would be required, which is ¾″ less than the actual depth of a 2 × 12. The disadvantage of this option is that long 2 × 12s are heavy and hard to handle at roof level during construction (*Parts That are Easy to Handle*). Manufactured wood I-joists 11⅞″ deep might be a good alternative because they are somewhat lighter, but they require a more elaborate, hard-to-make detail where they rest on the wall frame, so we decide to search for a solid-lumber solution if possible.

Looking at Options 2 through 4, we see that a 6.25″ or 6.5″ batt plus 2″ airspace would require a minimum rafter depth of 8.25″ to 8.5″. We round this up to the nearest standard lumber depth, 9.25″, for nominal 2 × 10 rafters. The foam panels could be nailed across the underside of the rafters, and the gypsum board could be attached with long screws that would pass through the foam and penetrate into the rafters about ¾″, the depth recommended by gypsum board manufacturers. For 2″ thick foam, a bit of arithmetic shows us that the screws would have to be about 3.25″ long to achieve a ¾″ penetration into the rafters. We find from the *Gypsum Construction Handbook* that the longest standard drywall screw is only 3″, so Option 2 is not feasible. Option 3 would work, however, because, with 1″ of foam insulation, a standard 2¼″ drywall screw would just achieve the necessary penetration. A side benefit of this construction would be that the foam panels would insulate the rafters as well as the spaces between them, acting as a *Thermal Break* for the more conductive wood.

Option 4 could be created by installing 2 × 4 furring on edge across the undersides of the rafters, as shown. This shares with Option 3 the advantage that thermal bridging through the wood of the rafters is minimized, and glass fiber insulation is generally cheaper per unit of thermal resistance than plastic foam. But this cost advantage would be negated by the additional expense of the 2 × 4s, and the toenailing of the 2 × 4s to the rafters would be somewhat difficult because of the awkward overhead position (*Accessible Connections*).

The options that involve using only foam plastic insulation (5 and 6) are problematic because it is difficult to fit the rigid foam panels tightly enough between rafters to eliminate thermal leakage. This problem could be eliminated by spraying polyurethane foam in place rather than using prefoamed panels. This involves another subcontractor, however, and would probably be rather expensive for so small a building.

Thus, we tentatively adopt Option 3, consisting of 6.5″ batts between nominal 10″ rafters spaced 24″ o.c., with a 1″ thick layer of isocyanurate or phenolic foam panels attached across the bottom of the rafters. We will proceed with the detail on this basis and see if everything works out satisfactorily.

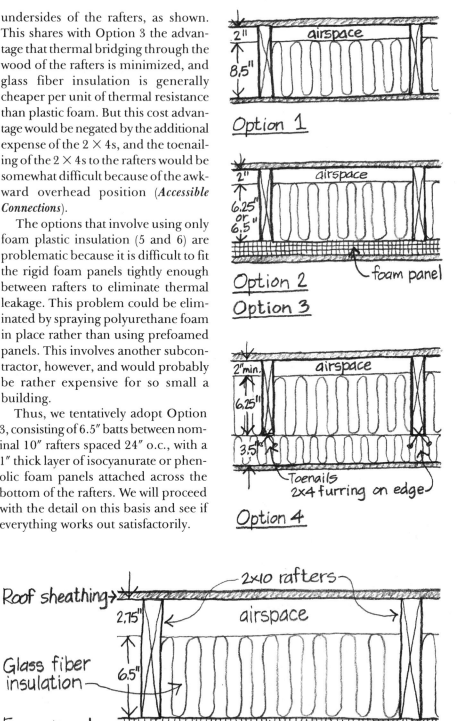

DETAILING THE EAVE

We will begin our detailing of the building with the eave, because this one detail does the most to establish the appearance of the building and also seems to present the most problems. We adopt the customary scale of 1½″ = 1′, which allows us to show all but the most intricate of features. In developing this detail, we follow step by step the process that the carpenters will use to construct it, *Rehearsing the Construction Sequence*. We draw first the studs, top plate, and sheathing of the wall that supports the rafters, and add to it the rafters with their triangular birdsmouth cut that allows them to bear on the top plate and sheathing.

Detailing the Exterior Features To create the fascialess eave that we sketched earlier, we will ask the carpenters to make a level cut on the bottom end of the rafters. For the moment, we draw this with a full 18″ overhang on the rafter itself; later we may adjust this dimension if the finished overhang dimension is too large or too small.

Next, we add roof sheathing panels. Plywood or oriented strand board (OSB) panels for 24″ rafter spacing can be as thin as 7/16″, but experience with other buildings has shown us that a ⅝″ thickness produces a roof plane that is less prone to show sagging between rafters.

The lower edges of the sheathing panels will need to be supported at the eave to prevent an unattractive waviness from showing along the edge of the roof. The soffit can provide this support if it is stiff enough (*Small Structures*). It could be made from ¾″ plywood and/or nominal 1″ boards. (Again, experience comes into play here. Engineering analysis might show that a thinner plywood soffit would be strong enough and stiff enough, but hands-on experience and field observation tell us that thinner plywood will be too flimsy.) We could make the soffit from a single strip of plywood, but we would have to cut into it for ventilation openings, and the wide pieces of plywood would be heavy and hard to fit accu-

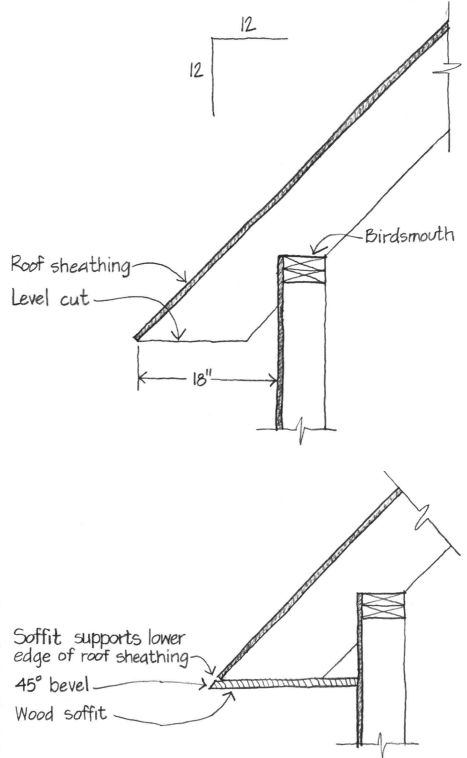

rately into place (*Parts That are Easy to Handle*). Furthermore, the 45° (12/12) bevel on the outer edge would be hard to cut in a perfectly straight line with a hand circular saw, and its knife edge would be fragile because of the layered construction of the plywood (*Clean Edge*). If we adopted a square edge rather than a 45° edge, the exposed edges of the laminations in the plywood would not be very attractive, especially because there tend to be voids in the interior layers.   ▷

A square-edged piece of solid lumber could make an excellent outer edge for the soffit. Soft pine would be adequate, but we know from experience that vertical-grain Douglas fir tends to be very straight and is much stiffer than pine, and could give good structural support to the lower edge of the roof sheathing. It could also support one edge of a formed aluminum continuous louver strip in the soffit to ventilate the roof cavities.

The building code requires that we install an *Air Barrier Surface* of 15 pound asphalt-saturated felt (tarpaper weighing 15 pounds per 100 square feet) over the roof sheathing. This helps keep the wind from blowing water through the shingles and the joints in the roof sheathing (*Rainscreen Assembly*). It also serves as a backup layer of waterproof material in case there should be a leak in the shingles. The ice and water barrier sheet is installed in place of the lowest strip of felt and should drain out over the edge of the soffit board. It is a very soft, flexible material that cannot support itself, however, so we add a narrow strip of aluminum flashing beneath it to carry any water drainage free of the soffit (*Small Structures*).

The wood shingles of the roof are applied at the industry-recommended exposure of 5½″, which gives so-called triple coverage, in which no portion of the roof is protected by fewer than two layers of shingle, giving considerable security against water leakage, even if a shingle should crack. The undercourse and first course of shingles should overhang the soffit board by the 1½″ dimension (measured horizontally) that is recommended by the Red Cedar industry to allow water to drip free and not run back under the soffit (*Overhang and Drip*). It will be important to show this overhang dimension on the finished drawing, because carpenters need to be alerted to its importance or they will often provide a smaller overhang.

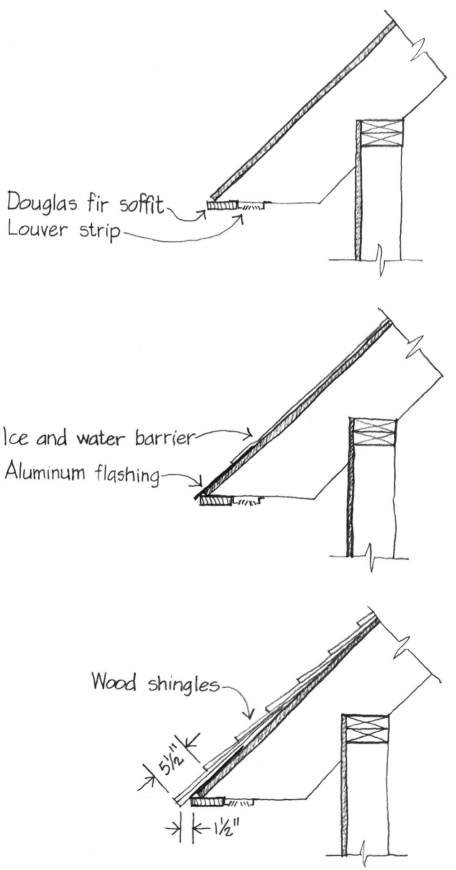

Douglas fir soffit
Louver strip

Ice and water barrier
Aluminum flashing

Wood shingles

5½″

1½″

This takes care of the roof edge in a way that is simple, attractive, and functionally satisfactory. Now we must finish off the soffit area. To support the innermost portion of the soffit, we must provide horizontal framing all the way back to the wall sheathing (*Small Structures*). We do this with a header strip nailed to the wall and short lookouts face-nailed to the side of each rafter tail, butting to the header. Working to scale, we see that the 2×4 stock normally used for such framing will not fit but that 2×3 stock will. The span of the lookouts is extremely short —only a few inches—so 2×3s will be sufficiently stiff to nail against. ▷

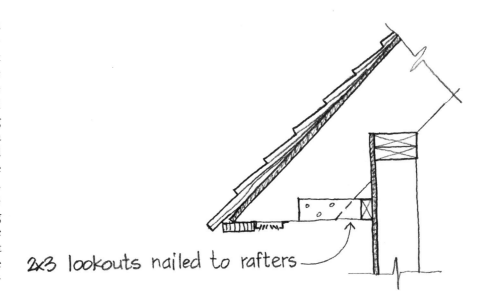

2x3 lookouts nailed to rafters

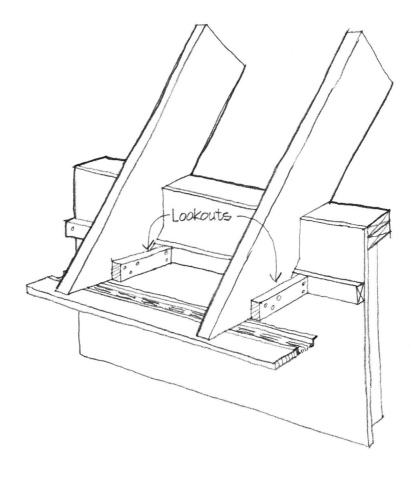

Lookouts

We could close the soffit with fir or pine boards. These would look very handsome but would require finicky blind nailing in very tight quarters in a difficult overhead position (**Accessible Connections**). A strip of A-face plywood with one edge planed perfectly straight could work well here: The planed edge would fit against the aluminum strip vent, which would conceal most of the raw edges of exposed plies. The other edge, with its slightly wavy cut that is characteristic of hand circular saw work, can be held short of the siding by a comfortable margin (¼″ or so) to allow for inaccuracies (**Dimensional Tolerance**); this gap will be covered by a trim strip that will be nailed in place after the siding has been installed.

We add the 15 lb. felt **Air Barrier Surface** and wood shingles over the wall sheathing. We select a 7½″ exposure for the wall shingles. The literature from the Red cedar shingle industry allows an exposure of 8½″ on walls, which should give the necessary double coverage, but our experience on prior projects has been that many shingles are far shorter than their nominal 18″ length, leading to the exposure of small areas of building paper at the tops of the joints unless the exposure is reduced somewhat. The top courses of shingles will have to be cut off where they meet the soffit board, leaving an exposed line of nail heads and a rough upper edge of shingles. We conceal the irregular edges of both the shingles and the soffit board with a Red cedar 1 × 2 trim piece that forms an easy **Sliding Fit** to close the soffit detail tightly and attractively.

Thinking About Fasteners and Finishes
The soffit boards will be exposed to view. It is tempting to try to attach them with finish nails, but we must keep in mind that the Douglas fir 1 × 4 is semistructural, lending stiffness to the edge of the roof sheathing. Ladder pressure during construction might dislodge the 1 × 4 if it were finish nailed, pulling the lumber off over the headless nails. In service, under heavy snow loadings, the same thing might occur. We need headed nails, but com-

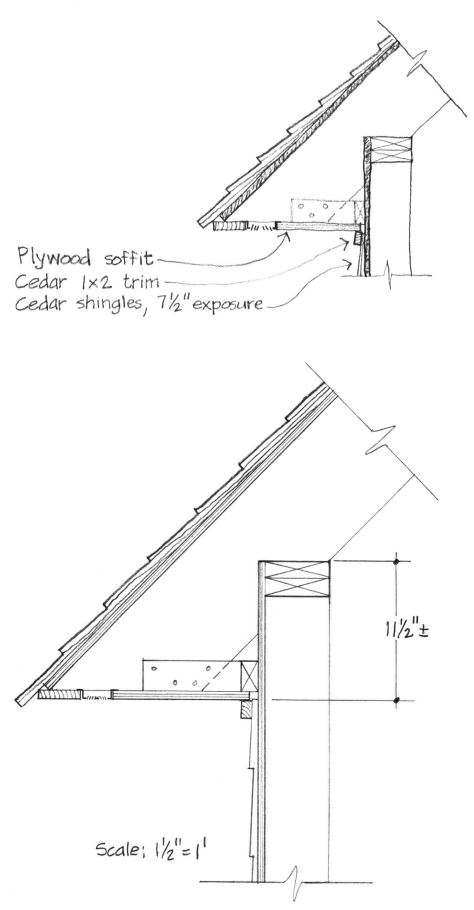

Plywood soffit
Cedar 1×2 trim
Cedar shingles, 7½″ exposure

11½″±

Scale: 1½″=1′

mon nails with their large heads would look rather crude. Siding nails, which have smaller heads, are one good choice for fastening the soffit boards to the framing. Another good choice would be finish drywall screws, which have very small heads and which would draw the boards up tightly to the framing. In either case, the fasteners should be stainless steel, aluminum, or hot-dip galvanized to minimize corrosion staining, because even a protected soffit attracts some condensation that wets the surface and corrodes metal fasteners. There probably won't be space on the drawings to indicate the fasteners, so we make a note to be sure that this information is in the written specifications for the project.

At this point, we need to be thinking also about how the soffit will be coated. If it will be painted, the heads of the nails or screws can be recessed and their holes filled and sanded before painting. Painting is generally a three-coat process—a primer plus two coats of latex paint—with sanding between coats to assure a smooth finish. Staining, either with transparent or heavy-bodied stain, requires only two coats and no sanding, so it is more economical. We adopt a heavy-bodied stain finish and make a note to include this in the written specifications.

Checking the Spatial Implications of the Eave Detail   It is apparent that the steep roof pitch and the broad overhang place the soffit some distance below the top of the wall. Will this push the window heads too low? We construct the detail to scale and measure that the soffit lies almost 12″ below the top of the wall plate. If the wall is framed at a standard 8′ height, this will place the window heads at about 7′, which is more than sufficient for a structure at this small scale.

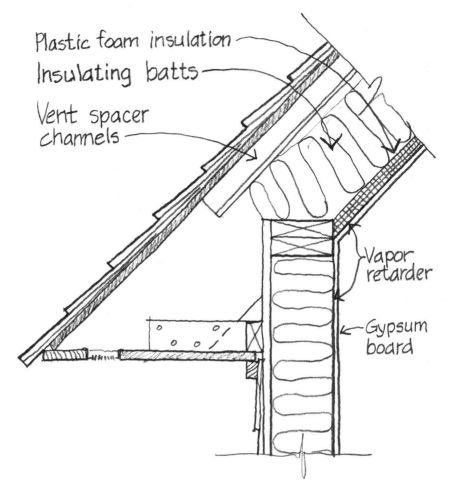

Detailing Insulation, Ventilation, and Interior Finishes   We now add to our eave detail the plastic foam insulating panels, gypsum board interior finish layer, and glass fiber insulating batts that we selected earlier. Where the insulating batts tend to push up into the ventilating airspace over the exterior walls, we provide short lengths of foam plastic vent spacer channels to maintain a free flow of air. We note on our drawing the continuous vapor retarder that is installed on the interior side of the insulation in the walls and ceiling (*Warm Side Vapor Retarder*). We scribble a reminder to list this in the written specifications for the building as a 4 mil (0.004″) polyethylene sheet. This is twice the thickness that insulation subcontractors typically install, but we prefer it, because its resistance to vapor flow is greater, it is more resistant to damage during construction, and its additional cost is very small.   ▷

DETAILING THE RAKE

The eave detail that we have designed looks good to us, but it represents only one edge of each roof plane. The opposite edge of each roof plane is the ridge, and the two adjacent, sloping edges are the rakes. Until the ridge, rakes, and wall corners are designed and their details coordinated with the eave, we will not assume that the eave detail we have just developed is final. By "coordinated" we mean that the details should be consistent with one another aesthetically, that they should be a consistent set of *Contributive Details*, and that they should meet gracefully and comfortably at the corners where they come together. With this in mind, we design the rakes next, with special reference to how the rakes join the eave.

Rake board

Rake shingles

Exterior Features of the Rake The building that we are designing does not have a rake overhang. Our task therefore is simply to design a detail

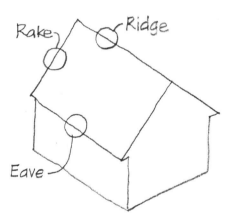

that will keep out rain and snow at the sloping edges of the roof while covering the rough edges of materials where the wall siding and roof shingles joint.

We have already selected cedar shingles for both the roofing and the siding. We could finish the rake with a rake board; if we did this we might want to use an unfinished cedar board to match the shingles, or, if it were pine, we might coat it with a heavy-bodied stain to match the soffits. We could also finish the rake with a sloping trim course of shingles. In comparison to the stained trim board, this would minimize the prominence of the rake lines and would in turn contribute to the minimalist aesthetic that we have in mind. We decide to use shingles for the rake trim.

The sloping course of rake trim shingles could be applied directly over the top edge of the sidewall shingles, but this top edge is very irregular in thickness because of the sawtooth profile of the shingled wall. To provide a flat surface to which to nail the trim shingles, we attach over the top edge of the wall sheathing a concealed nailing strip, a narrow board whose thickness, ¾″, is about the same as the maximum total depth of the sidewall shingles. To protect and conceal the cut shingle

edges and nail heads along the very top edge of the sidewall shingles, we make this nailing strip about an inch narrower than the trim shingles, thus allowing the trim shingles to overlap the sidewall shingles by a generous amount. We must specify a width for the rake trim shingles; 3″ is perhaps the minimum that will allow for proper nailing to the nailing strip beneath. We select the actual width by studying the appearance of rake trim courses of various widths on the end elevation of the building. We select 3½″, which results in a nailing strip 2½″ wide (a 1 × 3, a conveniently standard size: *Uncut Units*). Wood shingles are customarily furnished by the manufacturer in assorted random widths ranging from about 3″ to 12″, so the builder will use a table saw to cut constant-width shingles for the rake from wider shingles.

The wood shingles on the roof must overhang the rake trim shingles by 1″ or so to prevent water from running under the rake edges. If we install a ¾″ thick nailing strip and the rake shingles are about ¾″ thick at their maximum, the roof shingles must be laid with a total rake overhang of 2½″ beyond the sheathing of the gable wall. It is wise to note this dimension on the final detail drawing, because the roof is usually shingled before the walls and rakes. The builder must have the foresight to provide a sufficient overhang or else face a difficult and expensive reshingling of the roof edges. The detailer should go out of his or her way to avoid this catastrophe.

The lower corner of each rake must terminate gracefully at the triangular cheek area on each corner of the building. Probably the simplest way to finish the cheek is to extend the sheathing and sidewall shingles onto it. The spacing of the rake trim shingles can be matched to the spacing of the roof shingles for a neat appearance. The last rake trim shingle at the bottom can be left square, as shown, or cut off level, as dictated by appearance considerations. At the ridge of the roof, the two rake trim courses can intersect with a miter. The two mitered shingles will be the only ones on the facade that will have exposed nail heads, unless a mastic construction adhesive is used to glue these two shingles in place.

There is one other aspect of the rake detail that requires our attention, and that is the framing of the triangular wall of the gable. Carpenters are accustomed to building houses with attics, but our building has none. In houses with attics, the wall studs in the gable ends are normally interrupted at ceiling level by a double top plate, and short studs on top of this plate are used to frame the triangular gable. The top plate is supported laterally by the attic floor. In our building, which has no attic floor, this type of framing would not be strong enough against wind loads. The gable wall studs in our building must be single pieces that stretch from floor to rafter. We scale an elevation drawing to find that the longest stud will be about 15′ tall. We are using 2 × 6 studs 24″ apart. Are these strong and stiff enough for such a tall wall? We check a table in the building code and find that they are. We know from experience that carpenters will not frame the end walls with fullheight studs unless we tell them to do so, so we make a note to call this out on the elevations and sections of the construction drawings.   ▷

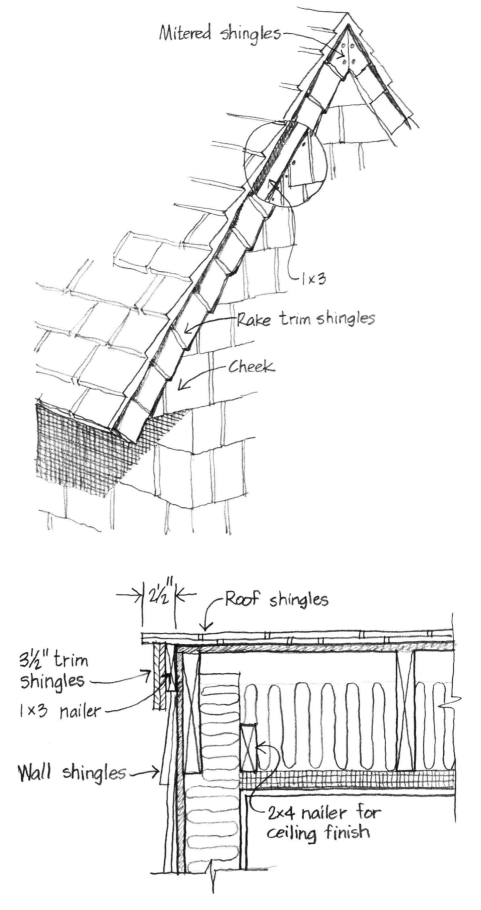

Developing the Soffit Termination Looking up from beneath, the eave soffit must terminate neatly against the inside surface of the cheek shingles, which should hang down to form a drip 1″ or so below the soffit. If the soffit boards and continuous vent strip were simply butted to the cheek, a somewhat rough appearance would result. The most finished appearance would result from mitering the 1 × 4 outer soffit piece to form a return at the end of the soffit. This will work if the 1 × 4 is made of well-seasoned lumber, such as the kiln-dried Douglas fir that we have already chosen. If there is any uncertainty about the moisture content of the soffit lumber, it is better to use a butt joint to avoid the opening of the miter joint that will occur if the wood shrinks (***Butt Joint***). Notice that the location of the butt joint is chosen to conceal the end grain of the wood against the vertical surface of the cheek shingles, rather than expose it under the sloping roof shingles.

Our design for the rake detail is now complete, pending a later check for consistency with the other details of the building.

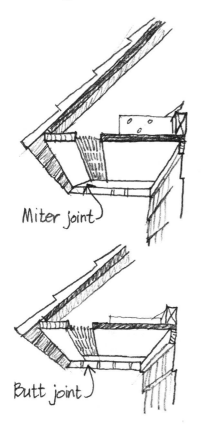

Miter joint

Butt joint

DETAILING THE RIDGE

We must design a detail for the ridge that is consistent with the eave and rake details. We begin by drawing the structural elements of the ridge: the rafters from each side and a ridge board between their plumb cuts. The building code requires only a nominal 1″ ridge board, but we know that most builders prefer to use a nominal 2″ ridge board because it usually leads to a straighter ridge (***Local Skills and Customs***). Before we settle on the height of the ridge board, however, we must work out the ventilation opening at the top.

The functional requirements for the ridge detail are that it divert water to the roof surfaces on either side and that it provide screened, water-protected openings for ventilation of the airspaces between the rafters. An easy way to satisfy both of these requirements is to use a manufactured aluminum ridge vent strip that is simply nailed over the top course of shingles on each side. The strip is designed with screened ventilation openings that are protected from gravity-driven water by overhangs and from wind-driven water by aerodynamic baffles. For our building, the disadvantage of the aluminum ridge vent is that we don't feel its appearance is up to that of a roof finished with a high-quality material such as wood shingles. We would prefer to finish the ridge either with a pair of cedar or redwood boards, or with a traditional "Boston ridge," composed of the same wood shingles that are used for the roofing. This leaves us with the problem of providing ventilation openings that are protected from water penetration and insects.

Some catalog research turns up several proprietary designs for protected ridge ventilation strips that can be covered with shingles or boards. We select one that we know is available locally (***Off-the-Shelf Parts***) and trace its catalog detail onto our developing ridge detail. We draw the plywood sheathing and hold the top edge of each slope back from the ridge line by the 2″

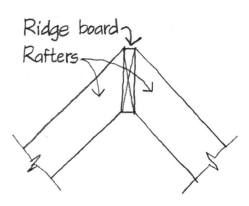

Ridge board
Rafters

dimension recommended by the vent strip manufacturer. We draw the courses of wood shingles leading up to the ridge, and we cut them off at the upper edge of the plywood. We add the vent strip with its flexible center portion that adjusts to any roof pitch. We look again at the size of the ridge board and decide that, in order to keep the ventilation passages free, it can be only a 2 × 10.

How will we finish over the vent strip? The catalog shows that there is only a narrow zone available for nailing on each side of the vent strip. This is not sufficient for shingles, which would require two lines of nails on either side of the ridge, so we decide to use ridge boards. We will specify that these be made of unfinished Red cedar, to match the shingles. In drawing the ridge boards, we note that because of the taper of the shingles, the boards do not meet at right angles. On the final detail drawing we will add a note to the carpenter to measure the angle and plane the edges of the boards to match it. Because of the difficulty of doing exacting cutting and fitting while standing on roof scaffolding, we will recommend in the written specifications that the ridge board pairs be assembled on sawhorses on the ground and then carried up and attached. To prevent cupping of the boards as far as possible, we show a ***Relieved Back*** on each board, and we specify brass screws for all of the fastenings (nails often pull out under cupping stress; screws cannot).

Moving to the interior of the ridge detail, we add the insulating batts. We

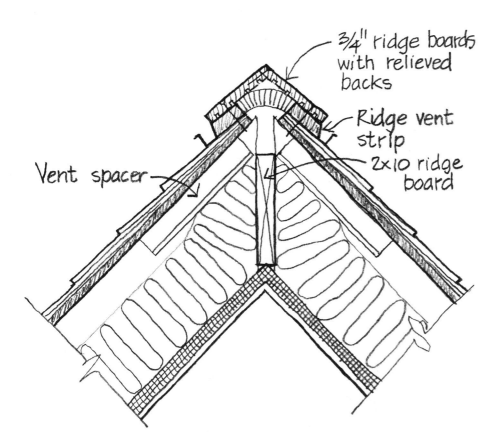

see that the ends of the batts might push up against the ridge board and block the air passages, so we add foam plastic vent spacers. We complete the ridge detail by adding 1″ of plastic foam insulation, the vapor retarder, and the gypsum board ceiling planes. To simplify installation of the foam, we adjust the vertical position of the ridge board to allow the panels to butt beneath it (*Butt Joint*).

How will we terminate the ridge detail? If the detail that we have drawn simply runs to the ends of the building, there will be a raw end of vent strip to cover over and the raised profile of our ridge detail will not be consistent with the minimal geometry that we are creating. After some sketching of alternatives, we decide to stop the vented ridge detail 1′ short of each end wall, closing the vent strip with standard end caps. This should still provide plenty of ventilation for the last rafter space at each end, and the last foot of ridge boards can be applied directly to the shingled slopes.

We must be sure that we have provided enough roof ventilation to meet the building code requirement of 1 square foot of ventilation per 300 square feet of floor area. Our building has a floor area of about 320 square feet, so we need about 1.1 square feet total of free ventilation openings. The code requires that this be divided equally between the eaves and the ridge. Multiplying the catalog values for the free ventilation areas per foot of the soffit vent and ridge vent strips by

the linear footages of each strip, we find that we have provided several times the legal requirement, so even the end rafter spaces will be adequately ventilated.

With the finishing of the designs for the eave, rake, and ridge details, we can now visualize completely how the roof will look. We make a freehand perspective to be sure that we like the way our details work with one another and with our design intentions for the form of the building (*Contributive Details*). We note with satisfaction that our details are beginning to create a soft, pleasing personality for the building.　▷

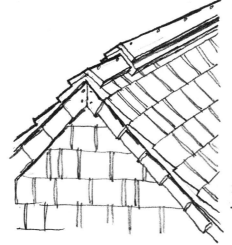

DETAILING THE GRADE CONDITION

There are three choices for the floor and foundation system: (1) a concrete slab on grade, (2) a basement with a wood floor structure above, or (3) a crawl space with a wood floor structure. In the New England climate, a slab on grade, even if properly insulated, tends to feel cold in winter unless it is heated with hot water coils or electric resistance wires. In the humid days of summer, a slab will often be cool enough to condense moisture from the air, unless the room is continually air-conditioned or dehumidified (**Warm Interior Surfaces**). We reject the slab option. We also decide against the basement option, because our client has no use for a basement in this particular building. We will detail a crawl space foundation.

We check the code requirements for a crawl space. It must be at least 18″ high, with an access door at least 18″ × 24″. It must be insulated around the perimeter to at least R-11. It must be cross-ventilated with screened openings. If a moisture barrier is applied over the soil in the crawl space, this ventilation must total at least 1 square foot of free area for every 1,500 square feet of crawl space area. This calculates to be only about one-quarter of a square foot of ventilation area for our small building.

Structuring the Floor Before we can draw the grade detail we must also know the size of the floor joists. We consult the floor joist design table in *Span Tables for Joists and Rafters*, keeping in mind that the framing lumber most commonly available in New England lumberyards is Spruce-Pine-Fir, a mix of several species that are rated at a

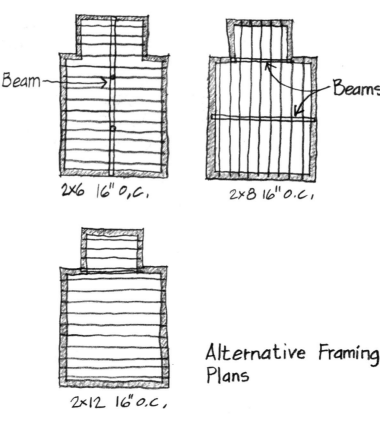

Alternative Framing Plans

modulus of elasticity (E) of 1,300,000 psi. From experience we know that joists designed to this E tend to feel a bit bouncy underfoot, so we customarily design joists as if their E were only 1,000,000 psi. Following down this column in the floor joist table for a 40 psf live load, and assuming a 16″ spacing of joists, we find that a 2 × 6 can span 8′4″; a 2 × 8, 11′0″; a 2 × 10, 14′0″, and a 2 × 12, 17′0″. We overlay some tracing paper framing diagrams on the floor plan: We could span the floor with 2 × 6s across the 16′ dimension with a beam in the middle; we could span it with 2 × 8s across the 20′ dimension with a beam in the middle. 2 × 10s offer no new solutions, but 2 × 12s would allow us to span the width of the building without using a

center beam. Without doing a detailed check of the comparative costs, we know that eliminating the beam would eliminate having to form beam pockets in the foundation, would eliminate the cost of the beam itself, and would eliminate a line of joist connections across the middle of the building. In other words, the 2 × 12s would greatly simplify the framing of the floor. There are two reasons for not wanting to use such deep members: They raise the floor another few inches above grade, and they are heavy and harder to handle. But the higher floor is of no consequence in this particular building, and the heavier framing members are not too hard to handle at ground level. We decide to use 2 × 12 floor framing.

Developing the Basic Detail As we develop the grade detail, we are *Rehearsing the Construction Sequence* step by step. We draw a customary 16″ × 8″ concrete footing, whose bottom surface lies the code-mandated 4′ below grade (*Foundation Below Frost Line*). Knowing that sitecast concrete foundations are the norm in this area (*Local Skills and Customs*), we show an 8″ concrete foundation wall on the footing. To reduce cracking of the wall, we insert pairs of #5 reinforcing bars top and bottom. (The size and number of bars is not based on rigorous engineering analysis in this case but on conventional practice.) To tie the frame down to the foundation, we show an embedded anchor bolt every 4′ around the perimeter of the building (*Small Structures*). The code permits a single 2 × 6 sill, but we prefer to double the 2 × 6 for greater stiffness and better nailing. We note that the lower sill piece should be made of preservative-treated wood to avoid decay from soil moisture rising by capillary action (*Dry Wood*).

Now we draw the framing and sheathing in order of construction: The 2 × 12 joists and header, the ⅝″ plywood subfloor, the 2 × 6 stud wall, and the ½″ wall sheathing. We have dimensioned the floor plan of the building so that the subfloor will consist entirely of full and half sheets of plywood (*Uncut Units*). The exterior wall finish is drawn on the detail: an *Air Barrier Surface* of asphalt-saturated felt and a weathering layer of cedar shingles. We show the undercourse and bottom course of shingles projecting 1″ below the top of the foundation to form an *Overhang and Drip* that will help keep the sill dry.   ▷

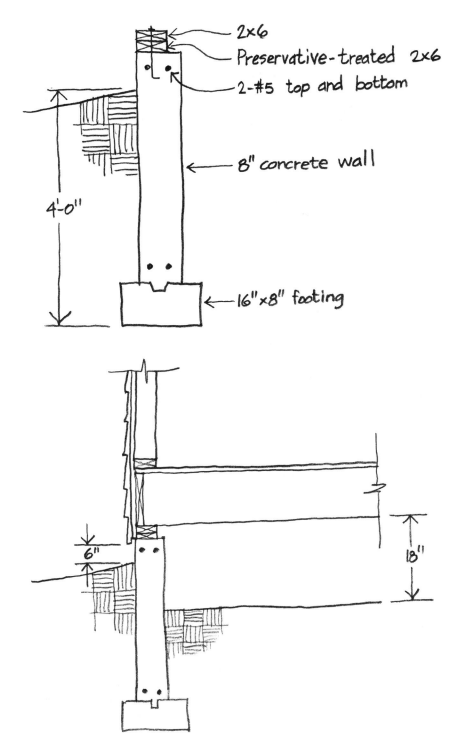

Insulation in the walls will be the normal glass fiber batts with an inside vapor retarder of polyethylene. Short batts will be inserted between the ends of the joists in the crawl space. This leaves us with the problem of how to insulate the floor against heat losses and gains. We could insulate between the floor joists, above the crawl space. This would be simple and comfortable, but it would leave the crawl space cold in winter, which would lead to excessive heat losses from the ductwork and frozen water pipes below the toilet room. We must insulate *around* the crawl space so that it will remain relatively warm. A bit of library research tells us that the earth floor of the crawl space does not need to be insulated if we insulate its perimeter properly, because the protected earth within the crawl space will remain at a fairly high temperature throughout the winter. There are two ways of insulating the perimeter. One is to install a couple of inches of foam polystyrene board on the outside of the foundation. The other is to nail glass fiber batts to the inside of the sill and drape them down the inside of the foundation wall and several feet onto the floor of the crawl space. We try these options on tracing paper overlays: The outside insulation would require moving the foundation wall inward a couple of inches from the edge of the floor frame and cantilevering the sill by this dimension to create space for the boards of foam plastic. This is acceptable structurally, because most of the wall and roof load is transmitted to the sill through the joists anyway, and these would still have a firm bearing through the sill to the concrete wall. The insulation would also have to be coated above grade to protect it from sunlight and mechanical damage. This coating would be some sort of stucco or synthetic stucco, perhaps with a reinforcing mesh. The inside insulation, on the other hand, although it would be installed under somewhat cramped conditions (**Accessible Connections**), would require no special coating and would probably end up being a little easier for the builder, and therefore less expensive. We draw the insulation

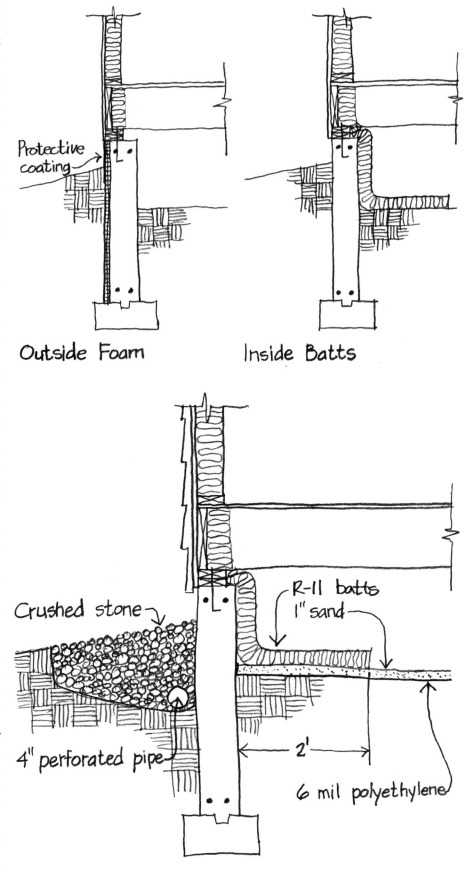

Outside Foam   Inside Batts

Protective coating

Crushed stone

4" perforated pipe

R-11 batts

1" sand

2'

6 mil polyethylene

on our sketch, and finish the crawl space floor with a heavy 6 mil (0.006″) polyethylene moisture barrier on top of the soil, and 1″ of dry sand to hold down the moisture barrier and protect it from damage.

Outside the foundation, we keep the bottom of the siding at least 6″ above grade level (*Dry Wood*). We slope the grade away from the building for good drainage (*Wash*). Under the drip line of the eaves, we provide a broad, shallow trench filled with coarse crushed stone. This will prevent soil erosion (*Building Armor*) and also keep dripping water from splashing mud up onto the siding (*Dry Wood*). We note that the floor of the crawl space lies a few inches below the outside grade. This could lead to flooding of the crawl space if there is a crack in the concrete wall. We add an asphaltic damp-proofing layer to the outside of the wall below grade, but this will not bridge cracks that may form in the wall. We decide to play it safe and add a perforated drainage pipe around the foundation, below the level of the crawl space floor, laid in crushed stone (*Foundation Drainage*). On our drawing the crushed stone of the drip trench encroaches on the crushed stone in which we want to lay the pipe, so we simply combine the two into a single trench filled with stone. We examine the contours on the site plan and discover that we can slope the discharge pipe from this trench to drain by gravity into a nearby swale, avoiding the need for a pump.

Detailing the Interior Finishes   The interior finishes are straightforward: a gypsum board wall, hardwood flooring, and a baseboard (*Building Armor*). We notice that the standard patterns of flooring and baseboards all have *Relieved Backs* to reduce cupping problems. We decide that this small showpiece building deserves the luxury of a three-piece baseboard, in which the shoe and cap moldings are slender, flexible strips that mold themselves to the irregularities of the wall and floor with a *Sliding Fit*. The *Reveal*

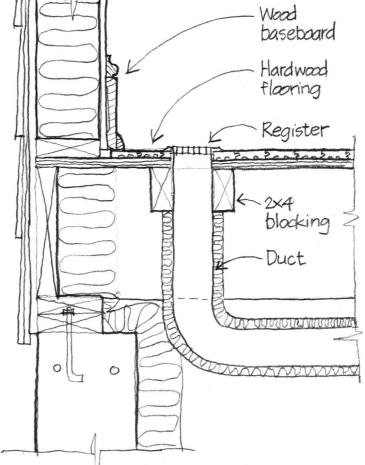

at the junction of the cap and baseboard allows this to occur without creating unsightly misalignments of the two pieces.

We plan to heat and cool the building with an electric heat pump and forced air. The floor registers for this system will be fed from insulated ductwork in the crawl space (*Horizontal Plenum*). We add a typical floor register to our detail, showing structural blocking on either side to support the subfloor and flooring around the register (*Small Structures*).

We have now solved the crawl space detailing, except for the required *Vapor Ventilation* and *Maintenance Access*. The standard vent louvers used in crawl space walls are not especially attractive, so we decide to locate one of them under the front stoop, which will be an open, wood-framed structure, and the other of them directly opposite, in the

back wall of the toilet room. After a search of various catalogs we make a note to specify a particular vent that can be inserted into the top of the concrete formwork before pouring, and that has a mechanical thermostat that closes it in cold weather so the crawl space remains warm. For access, we decide to avoid exterior complications by providing a trapdoor in the floor of the toilet room.

DETAILING THE CORNER

Working in plan view at the same scale as the other details (1½″ = 1′), we construct details of typical outside and inside corners. As usual, we do this in order of construction as a way of *Rehearsing the Construction Sequence*. One complete wall of the building will be framed to the full length of the building on the floor platform and tilted up into position. The other wall will be framed short of the corner by the depth of a stud so that it mates to the first wall with a simple *Butt Joint*, and so on, around the building. As we draw this condition at the inside corner (the corner where the toilet room joins the main mass of the building), we provide a flat-framed 2 × 6 stud for attachment of the wall of the toilet room. We notice that the edge of the sheathing to the left of this flat stud has nothing to be fastened to. We add a 2 × 4 stud as a nailer; the 2 × 4 is less expensive than a 2 × 6, and it avoids thermal bridging. Although the wall between the main room and the toilet room would ordinarily be framed with 2 × 4s, in our building it must be framed with full-height 2 × 6s, as previously noted, because it becomes an exterior gable wall above.

We must decide how we want the corner to look on the outside. We glance back at our early design sketches for the building and our three-dimensional sketches of the eave and rake details, looking for clues as to what we should do with the wall corners to create a consistent set of *Contributive Details*. We are weighing two basic choices for the outside corner: to use vertical corner boards to which the wall shingles are butted or to "weave" the shingles directly together at the corners. We have a slight preference for the first choice. Corner boards are the dominant corner finish on older buildings in the area, and they are simpler and quicker for the carpenter

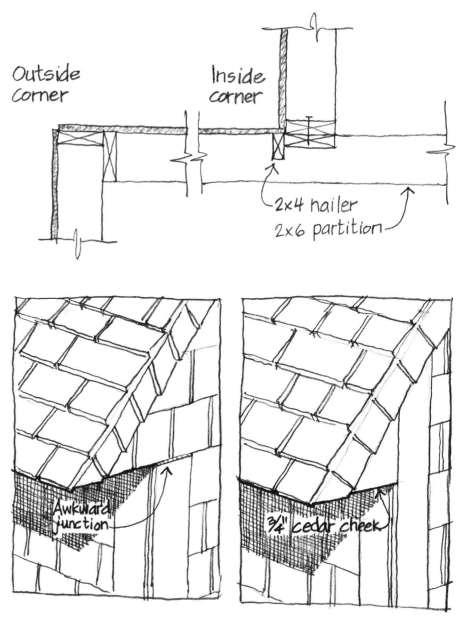

because of the simple *Butt Joint*. A woven corner requires more labor, because the two corner shingles in each course must be planed to join one another tightly and neatly.

Our sketches of the area where the corner, rake, and eave join together show that there would be an awkward connection where the corner boards join the shingled triangular cheek area that we had envisioned earlier, because

the end grain of the corner board is exposed and is very vulnerable to water penetration. We could avoid this by running the corner board on the gable end of the building all the way up to join the 1 × 3 spacer beneath the rake trim shingles. Then we would want to finish the cheek with a piece of ¾″ cedar rather than shingles. We decide to do this.

The traditional corner boards in the neighborhood are rather wide, usually around 7″ to 8″. We will use a cedar 1 × 8 on one wall and have the carpenter trim about 1″ off the 1 × 8 that butts inside it, so the apparent widths of the two boards will be the same. We show a ¼″ ***Reveal*** at the butt joint so that the carpenter can avoid some of the more finicky fitting that otherwise would be required. We also show shallow saw cuts in the back of each board, a ***Relieved Back*** detail that can be created with a table saw on the building site to reduce cupping of the wide boards. Eight-penny galvanized finish nails will be used to attach the boards, and the shingle courses will be butted tightly to them on either side. We will not paint the corner boards: they, like the cedar shingles and trim, will be left to weather naturally (***Surfaces That Age Gracefully***).

Detailing the inside corner, we follow the standard practice of using a full 1″ × 1″ stick of cedar in the corner, butting both planes of shingles tightly against it.

Inside the building, the insulating batts will be installed between the studs and the vapor retarder across them. Then the gypsum board will be applied. We see that the gypsum board on two walls has no stud to which it can be nailed. There are several ways to provide such a stud at the outside corner; we choose to show a 2 × 4 that allows access for insulation to be stuffed behind it to the corner, eliminating a potential thermal bridge. A similar stud is required at the inside corner.

▷

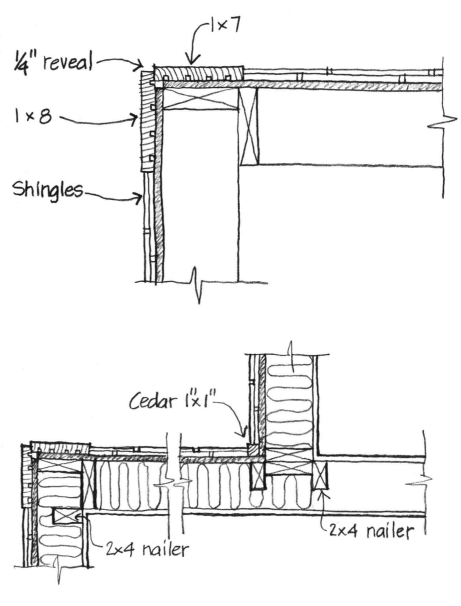

DETAILING THE WINDOWS

Selecting a Window Again taking a cue from nearby historic houses, we decide to use double-hung wood windows in our building. We plunge into the catalogs of several reputable manufacturers in order to choose the windows that we will use. We look for low maintenance and good appearance, and we decide to use a wood window that is clad with white vinyl on the exterior (*Surfaces That Age Gracefully*). We look for good thermal performance and find that all of the manufacturers whom we are considering provide *Multiple Glazing* with selective coatings to achieve excellent insulating values. We look for *Rainscreen Assembly* details and find that, although all of the manufacturers use certain features of rainscreen detailing, none markets a true rainscreen design. We examine their details further and find that one manufacturer's details make more consistent use of *Overhang and Drip* features to protect the window and the surrounding wall. The tested performances of this window are impressive, too: The overall thermal resistance of the window unit, including the frame, is R-3.2. Because of a clever *Weatherstripped Crack* detail, the air infiltration is only 0.08 cfm per foot of crack—about one-third of the quantity permitted in a Grade 40 wood window. We also know that this manufacturer has a good network of dealers in the area and a solid reputation for on-time delivery (*Off-the-Shelf Parts*). We photocopy the catalog details and slide them under a sheet of tracing paper to begin designing our window details. (If we were developing our details using computer-aided drafting (CAD), we could read the details directly onto our drawing from a diskette furnished free of charge by the manufacturer.)

There is only one significant difference between the details that the window manufacturer furnishes and the details that we want to draw: We are using studs that are 2″ deeper. We will

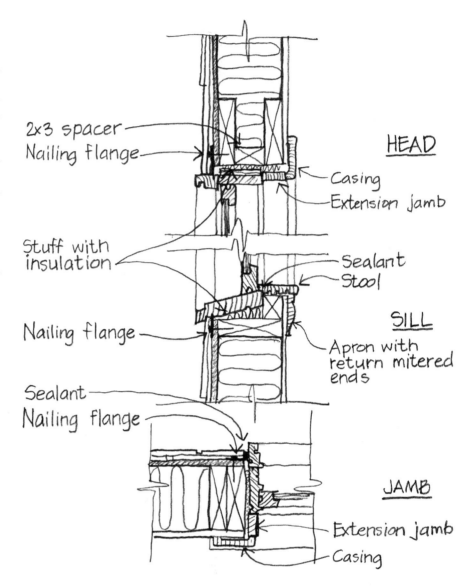

2x3 spacer
Nailing flange

Stuff with insulation

Nailing flange

Sealant
Nailing flange

HEAD

Casing
Extension jamb

Sealant
Stool

SILL

Apron with return mitered ends

JAMB

Extension jamb
Casing

develop our details in order of construction and see how this affects our design.

Developing the Basic Detail We draw the studs, header, and wall sheathing of the rough opening in the standard head, sill, and jamb details. We space the two header pieces with a 2 × 3 to bring them out to full frame thickness, and we show insulation inside the header (*Thermal Break*). The window unit is tilted up into the rough opening from the outside and pushed inward until the plastic nailing flanges lie flat against the air barrier and sheathing. (There is a generous *Installation Clear-*

ance and *Dimensional Tolerance* between the manufacturer-recommended rough opening dimension and the outside dimensions of the window unit that makes this potentially difficult five-plane fit into an easy *Sliding Fit*). The window unit is held by hand while the sill is centered in the rough opening and leveled; then the sill flange is nailed to the sheathing and framing, using galvanized shingle nails, whose broad heads offer a more secure bearing against the relatively fragile plastic. One jamb of the window unit is then plumbed up, and its flange is nailed to the frame. The window is checked to make sure that it operates freely and that the cracks around the sashes are of constant width. Then the remainder of the flanges are nailed.

The exterior shingling presents no problems. There is a convenient notch in the underside of the sill to provide an *Overlap* with the shingles and create a *Clean Edge* where the two intersect. At the jambs, the shingles are held ¼″ away from the unit to leave space for sealant. These are "nonworking" sealant joints, in which very little movement is anticipated, so no backer rod is used. The plastic flange at the window head doubles as a flashing. The manufacturer's detail shows sealant between the shingles and the head of the window, but this makes no sense, because the sealant would restrict the free drainage of water from the cracks between the shingles. We detail the head without sealant.

Moving indoors, the spaces between the window unit and the rough framing are stuffed with glass fiber insulation. This is done primarily to provide an *Air Barrier Surface* that will reduce the leakage of air. The stuffing must be done gently to avoid distorting the window frame and causing the sashes to bind.

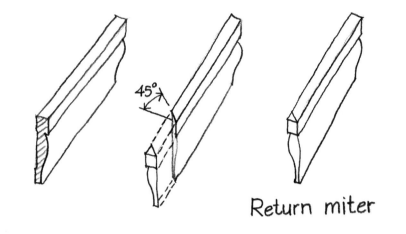

Return miter

Detailing the Interior Finishes The first interior finishing operation around each window will be to install the stool, extending it past the opening on both sides so that the jamb casings can butt to it neatly. We show a strip of wood blocking to support the stool and the upper edge of the gypsum board. We rabbet the stool over the windowsill and install a thin bead of sealant between them to provide a small *Upstand* against the penetration of wind-driven rain. We detail a *Relieved Back* to reduce cupping distortions and a rounded *Safe Edge* on the inside. We make a note to specify back priming for all the interior window trim pieces. To cover the gap between the gypsum board and the stool, we install a wood apron. We decide to use very simple, flat casings and a simply molded apron to trim the window. At the two ends of the apron, the *Relieved Back* will show unless we ask the carpenter to do a return miter. This is easily done using a power miter saw.

▷

The greater depth of the framing of our building must be dealt with at the jambs and head of the window. This is done with simple square-edged extension jambs that are nailed and glued to the window frame. Some plane work is usually required to adjust the exact depth of the extension jambs to match the level of the gypsum board all around. Then the jamb and head casings are applied, leaving a small *Reveal* where they meet the extension jambs so as to simplify fitting. At the two upper corners, we have a choice between miter joints and butt joints. We select *Butt Joints* to avoid any chance that miters could open up in an unattractive way because of wood shrinkage, although this is a small risk with kiln-dried millwork of this relatively narrow width. The butt joints do require that return miters be created at the two exposed ends to conceal the relieved back.

There is always the danger with window details that we may design a feature that does not carry around the corner to the next detail in a satisfactory way. We avoid this in part by always showing with light lines the elevation of features that lie behind the plane through which the section is cut. Additionally, we prepare a couple of three-dimensional sketches to see how the corners look.

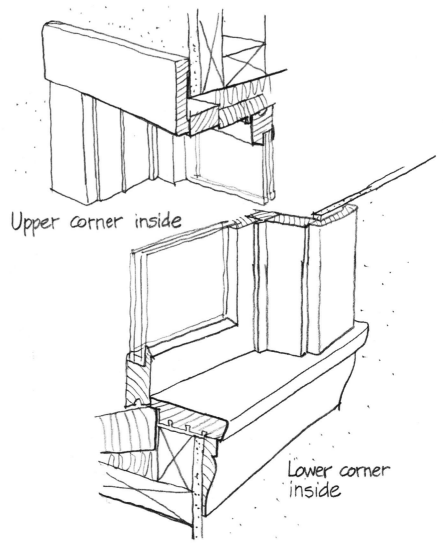

Upper corner inside

Lower corner inside

DESIGNING THE RAFTER TIES

Because this structure has neither an attic nor a ridge beam, exposed horizontal ties must be installed at intervals to keep the bottoms of the rafters from spreading. Some experimentation in plan and perspective leads us to decide tentatively on a spacing of 4′ between ties. A simple mathematical analysis shows that, at this spacing, the tension in each tie will be 720 lb under a full snow load. This is a very small force: A 1 × 3 could carry it safely. But there are reasons to use a larger piece of wood than this: Occupants of the building over the years are likely to hang things from the ties. Workers may lay planks across them to facilitate work on the ceiling. There would be difficulty making a 720 lb connection at the ends of a 1 × 3: A quick calculation shows that nine tenpenny nails are needed or else a bolt; neither of these options would work with a member as small as a 1 × 3. We recognize that the nails will be much cheaper to install than the bolt, because the required fasteners and installation tool will already be in the carpenter's belt (*Off-the-Shelf Parts*). Perhaps the most compelling reason to use a larger tie is that a 1 × 3 would simply look too slender and weak. We decide to try a pair of 2 × 8s with a 1½″ space between. The 2 × 8s will be strong enough to support scaffolding planks and large enough to accept the required nails at the end. The space between allows the twin ties to sandwich the end of a rafter, creating an easy connection. We make a note to dimension the rafter locations carefully on the roof framing plan so that the ties will occur at precisely the desired locations.   ▷

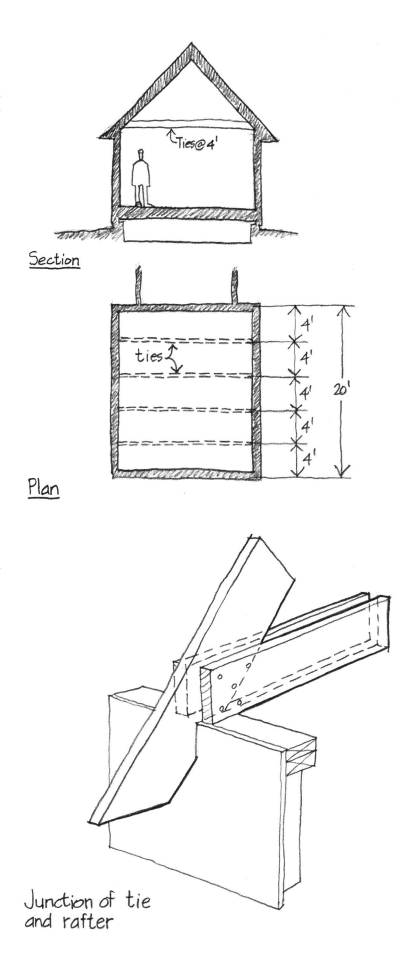

Section

Plan

Junction of tie and rafter

We draw the 2 × 8 ties accurately on a ¼″ scale cross section of the building. They look heavy and overbearing, their horizontality seemingly negating much of the soaring quality of the roof space. They even appear to sag a bit, an optical illusion caused perhaps by their contrast with the upward-angling ceiling planes. After a series of experiments on tracing paper overlays, we decide to taper the ties from full thickness at the walls to a reduced thickness in the middle, making all the taper on the undersides of the members so as to create a slightly arched room space below. We also add a vertical member connecting the center of the ties to the ridge. The vertical member has little structural function, but, together with the tapering, it seems to overcome the stodgy horizontality of the ties, relating well to the full height of the room. The tapers on all of the members express the structural tension in them, much as the taper in a strand of pulled taffy expresses its stretching (**Intensification**).

The vertical member will sandwich neatly between the twin ties but will have to butt to the underside of the rafters at the ridge—a difficult connection to make. We decide to make the vertical member of a pair of ¾″ thick pieces that will spread and flex slightly as they rise from the ties so that they can be nailed to either side of the rafters at the ridge. The center of each of these pieces will have to be notched to go around the ridge board.

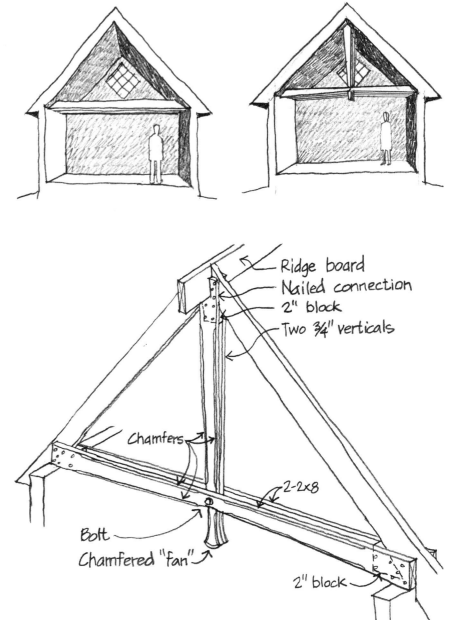

We will connect the vertical members to the horizontal ones at the center of the ties with a single exposed bolt. All the nailed connections will be buried in the roof and wall construction, making them invisible. In each of the three locations where paired members pass through the interior finish layer, we add a short block to close the gap between the members. We note that casing beads should be detailed around each of these penetrations to make a **Clean Edge** on the gypsum board finish.

To dress up the ties a bit, we decide to chamfer the edges, except in the zones near the ends and the center connection. This is a form of **Intensification** that will further bring out the tensile role of the members by making them appear thinner and more rounded in profile.

The lower end of the vertical member seems arbitrary and abrupt if it is merely cut off horizontally. We try many sketches of pendant designs before settling on a chamfered fan as a suitable termination (**Ornamentation**).

In our notes for the written specifications we record that ordinary framing lumber can be used for these members but that the builder should select the pieces carefully so as to use wood of good visual quality. The grade

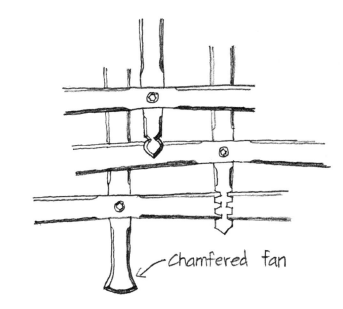

—*Chamfered fan*

markings and any other stray marks or scuffs should be sanded off. Depending on our final decisions regarding interior finishes, we will either stain the wood members, or sand, prime, and paint them. The wood will probably not be of such a quality that we would want to varnish it.

Next Steps We have now finished the preliminary design of the key details for the sales office. We draft precisely scaled, finished-looking versions of all these details for review. There are still a few important details to design: the bay window, the porch, and the intersection of the roof and wall where the main mass of the building joins the toilet room. When these have been completed, we will check all of the details simultaneously to be sure that they are consistent in style, and to see that the thermal insulation and vapor retarder are complete and continuous all around the building.   ▷

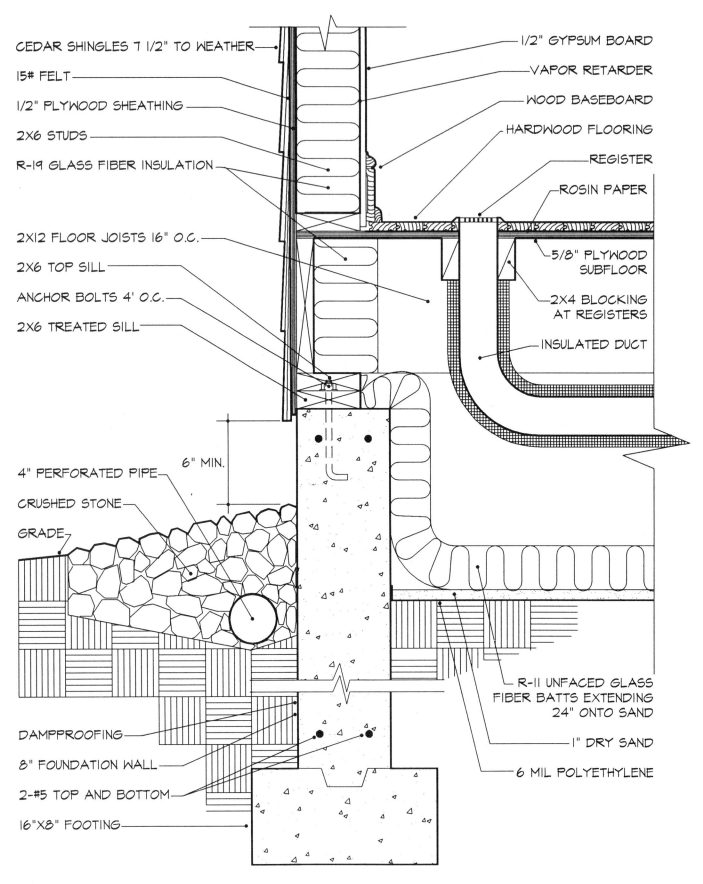

CEDAR SHINGLES 7 1/2" TO WEATHER

15# FELT

1/2" PLYWOOD SHEATHING

2X6 STUDS

R-19 GLASS FIBER INSULATION

2X12 FLOOR JOISTS 16" O.C.

2X6 TOP SILL

ANCHOR BOLTS 4' O.C.

2X6 TREATED SILL

1/2" GYPSUM BOARD

VAPOR RETARDER

WOOD BASEBOARD

HARDWOOD FLOORING

REGISTER

ROSIN PAPER

5/8" PLYWOOD SUBFLOOR

2X4 BLOCKING AT REGISTERS

INSULATED DUCT

6" MIN.

4" PERFORATED PIPE

CRUSHED STONE

GRADE

R-11 UNFACED GLASS FIBER BATTS EXTENDING 24" ONTO SAND

1" DRY SAND

6 MIL POLYETHYLENE

DAMPPROOFING

8" FOUNDATION WALL

2-#5 TOP AND BOTTOM

16"X8" FOOTING

FOUNDATION DETAIL
Scale 1 1/2"=1'

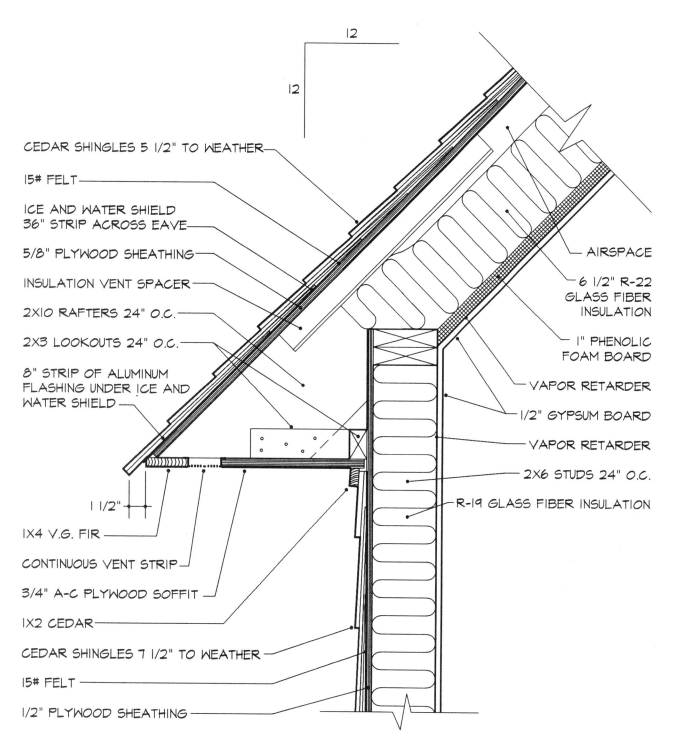

CEDAR SHINGLES 5 1/2" TO WEATHER

15# FELT

ICE AND WATER SHIELD
36" STRIP ACROSS EAVE

5/8" PLYWOOD SHEATHING

INSULATION VENT SPACER

2X10 RAFTERS 24" O.C.

2X3 LOOKOUTS 24" O.C.

8" STRIP OF ALUMINUM
FLASHING UNDER ICE AND
WATER SHIELD

1 1/2"

1X4 V.G. FIR

CONTINUOUS VENT STRIP

3/4" A-C PLYWOOD SOFFIT

1X2 CEDAR

CEDAR SHINGLES 7 1/2" TO WEATHER

15# FELT

1/2" PLYWOOD SHEATHING

12

12

AIRSPACE

6 1/2" R-22
GLASS FIBER
INSULATION

1" PHENOLIC
FOAM BOARD

VAPOR RETARDER

1/2" GYPSUM BOARD

VAPOR RETARDER

2X6 STUDS 24" O.C.

R-19 GLASS FIBER INSULATION

EAVE DETAIL
Scale 1 1/2"=1'

#10 BRASS SCREWS 16" O.C.

HOLD BACK PLYWOOD 2"
EACH SIDE OF RIDGE

RIDGE VENT STRIP

2X10 RIDGE BOARD

VENT SPACER

3/4" RIDGE BOARDS W/
RELIEVED BACKS

NOTE: RIDGE BOARDS DO
NOT MEET AT RIGHT ANGLE.
MEASURE ACTUAL ANGLE AND
BUTT BOARDS TO FIT.

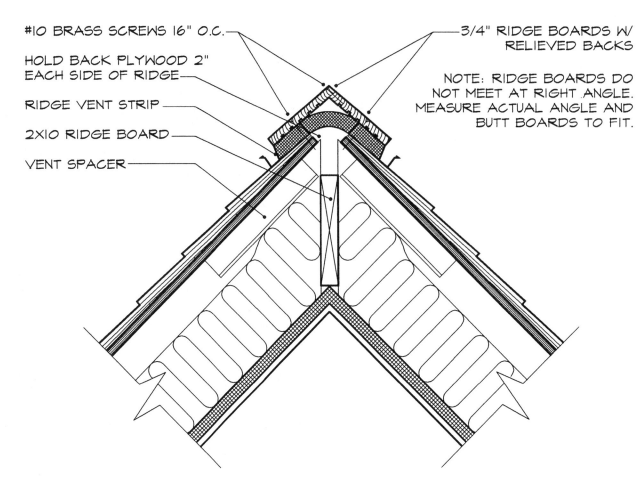

RIDGE DETAIL
Scale 1 1/2"=1'

CEDAR SHINGLES

15# FELT

2 1/2"

3 1/2" WIDE RAKE
TRIM SHINGLES

1X3 NAILER

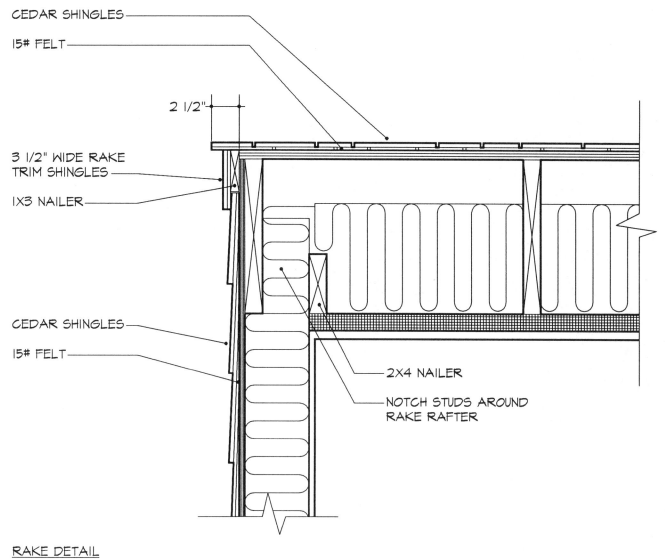

CEDAR SHINGLES

15# FELT

2X4 NAILER

NOTCH STUDS AROUND
RAKE RAFTER

RAKE DETAIL
Scale 1 1/2"=1'

CEDAR 1"X1"

CEDAR 1X7 WITH
RELIEVED BACK

1/4" REVEAL

CEDAR 1X8 WITH
RELIEVED BACK

CEDAR SHINGLES

15# FELT

1/2" PLYWOOD SHEATHING

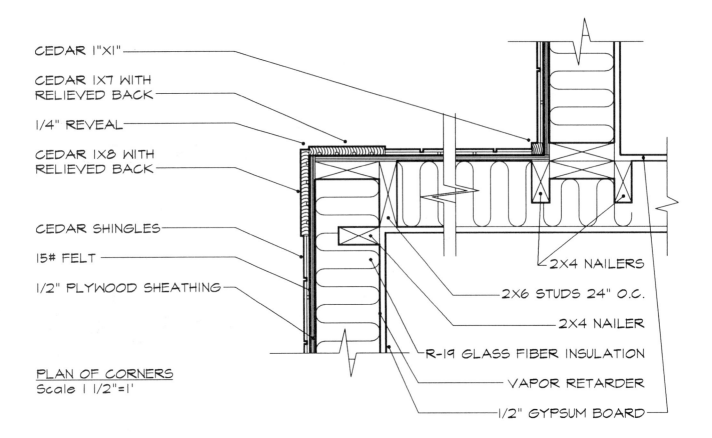

2X4 NAILERS

2X6 STUDS 24" O.C.

2X4 NAILER

R-19 GLASS FIBER INSULATION

VAPOR RETARDER

1/2" GYPSUM BOARD

PLAN OF CORNERS
Scale 1 1/2"=1'

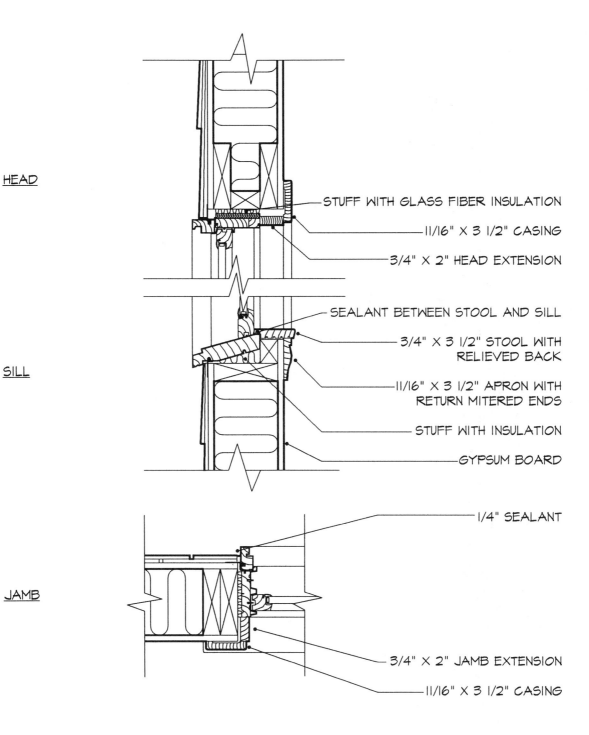

HEAD

STUFF WITH GLASS FIBER INSULATION

11/16" X 3 1/2" CASING

3/4" X 2" HEAD EXTENSION

SILL

SEALANT BETWEEN STOOL AND SILL

3/4" X 3 1/2" STOOL WITH RELIEVED BACK

11/16" X 3 1/2" APRON WITH RETURN MITERED ENDS

STUFF WITH INSULATION

GYPSUM BOARD

1/4" SEALANT

JAMB

3/4" X 2" JAMB EXTENSION

11/16" X 3 1/2" CASING

WINDOW DETAILS
Scale: 1 1/2"=1'

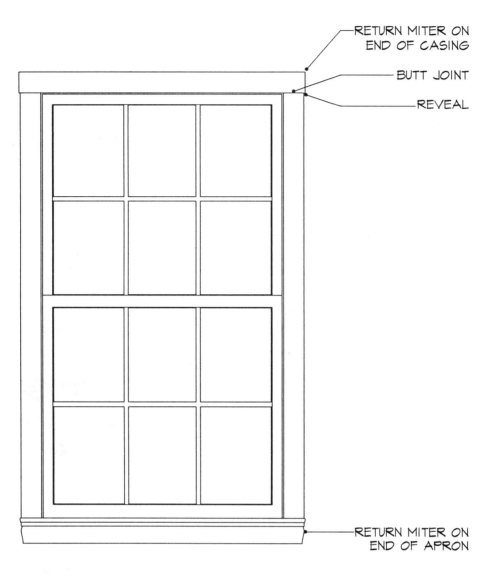

RETURN MITER ON
END OF CASING

BUTT JOINT

REVEAL

RETURN MITER ON
END OF APRON

INTERIOR ELEVATION OF WINDOW FINISH
Scale: 3/4"=1'

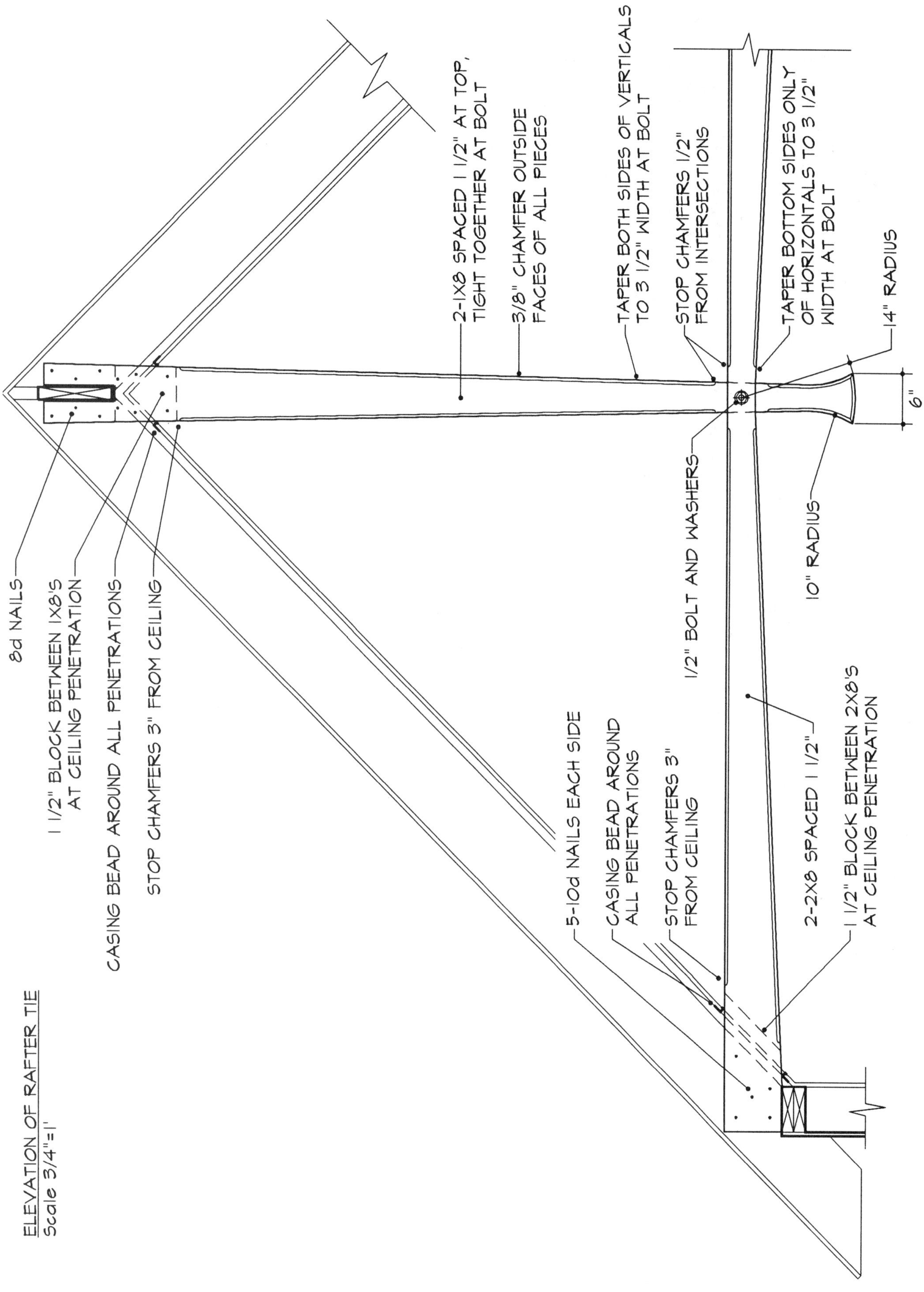

ELEVATION OF RAFTER TIE
Scale 3/4"=1'

8d NAILS

1 1/2" BLOCK BETWEEN 1X8'S AT CEILING PENETRATION

CASING BEAD AROUND ALL PENETRATIONS

STOP CHAMFERS 3" FROM CEILING

2-1X8 SPACED 1 1/2" AT TOP, TIGHT TOGETHER AT BOLT

3/8" CHAMFER OUTSIDE FACES OF ALL PIECES

TAPER BOTH SIDES OF VERTICALS TO 3 1/2" WIDTH AT BOLT

STOP CHAMFERS 1/2" FROM INTERSECTIONS

TAPER BOTTOM SIDES ONLY OF HORIZONTALS TO 3 1/2" WIDTH AT BOLT

14" RADIUS

6"

10" RADIUS

1/2" BOLT AND WASHERS

5-10d NAILS EACH SIDE

CASING BEAD AROUND ALL PENETRATIONS

STOP CHAMFERS 3" FROM CEILING

2-2X8 SPACED 1 1/2"

1 1/2" BLOCK BETWEEN 2X8'S AT CEILING PENETRATION

There has been an important aesthetic component to our work: The architectural character of the building has emerged in a very exciting way as we have developed these key details. Unsympathetic detailing can destroy the aesthetic of an otherwise well-designed building, while thoughtful detailing can make it even better, a point that is lost on many architects who fancy themselves to be designers but who are unwilling to work on the detailing of their buildings.

As we prepare to draft the final drawings of all the details for this building, we gather and organize the notes that we made to help us remember key aspects of these details in other phases of the project work. We make a list that reminds us to include in the specifications such special items as the ridge vent strip, the soffit vent strip, the soffit boards, the ice and water shield, the insulation vent spacer channels, the flashing metal, the foam insulating boards, the thicker vapor retarder sheet, the longer screws for the gypsum board ceiling finish, and the hot-dip galvanized fasteners for the soffit boards, as well as the more usual components, such as shingles, sheathing, air barrier sheet, insulating batts, and gypsum board.

We also make some notes on things to keep in mind as we visit the site again and again during the construction process. It would be good to call to the builder's attention in advance the need to frame the gable walls with full-height studs and the need to overhang the shingles at the rakes and eaves by the required amounts, thus avoiding some very costly potential errors. The ridge detail is complex enough so that we should discuss it in detail with the builder before it is constructed. The crawl space moisture barrier, sand, and insulation could also benefit from an advance conference. The exposed roof ties will require extra attention from both architect and contractor. Other than this, these details are largely based on common practice and probably need no special mention on the jobsite.

KEY REFERENCES

The following are important reference materials that were used in developing this set of details. Full bibliographic information on these publications is given in the reference list at the back of the book.

1. The local building code.

2. Various manufacturers' catalogs.

3. American Plywood Association, *Structural Design Data for Plywood*.

4. National Forest Products Association, *National Design Specification for Wood Construction*.

5. National Forest Products Association, *Span Tables for Joists and Rafters*.

6. Rob Thallon, *Graphic Guide to Frame Construction: Details for Builders and Designers*. ■

DETAILING A BUILDING IN ARCHITECTURAL CONCRETE

THE PROJECT

The project is a college classroom building in southern Ohio.

SETTING PERFORMANCE STANDARDS

Most of the existing campus is made up of nineteenth-century buildings handcrafted in gray granite. College officials would like a solid, well-crafted building, but they feel that they cannot afford granite. A building with an exposed concrete exterior has been agreed upon. The building code specifies R-19 walls and an R-30 roof.

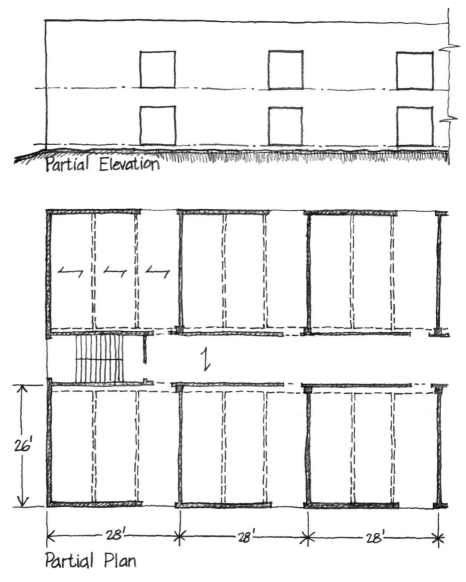

Partial Elevation

Partial Plan

KEY DETAILS TO DEVELOP

We will begin the detailing process by designing the details indicated on the section and plan diagrams to the right. These are the most general details and will serve as a base from which to design more special details, such as those of the main entrance. We want to develop these key details as a consistent set of **Contributive Details** that work well with one another.

EARLY DECISIONS CONCERNING MATERIAL, STRUCTURE, AND FORM

Each two-story wing of the building has evolved as two rows of classrooms flanking a double-loaded corridor. Working with the structural engineer, we have developed a one-way concrete slab and beam system for the upper floor and roof. Each structural bay of the building is 28′ × 26′ to match the desired size of the classrooms. The floor and roof slabs will be 6″ thick and will span across concrete beams spaced 9′4″ apart. The outer end of each beam will rest on a concrete loadbearing wall that is 10″ thick. The inner end will be supported by a concrete girder that spans between columns 28′ apart. The floor-to-floor height has been tentatively fixed at 12′ and the window head height at 8′.

The classrooms will be heated and ventilated by a variable air volume sys-

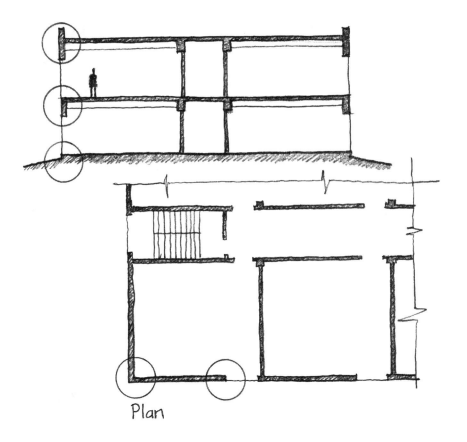

Plan

tem whose main ducts will run in a **Horizontal Plenum** above the central corridor, with branches to diffusers in the classrooms. There will be no suspended ceiling, except in the corridors.

The tentative fenestration scheme for the building is based on a single, large window opening into a corner of each classroom. This results in a very simple, quiet elevation.

EARLY WORK ON MATERIALS AND DETAILS

Working on a typical elevation of a classroom wing, we develop a mullion pattern for the window opening that will provide two opening sashes and a safety rail at waist height. The asymmetry of the arrangement is intended to harmonize on the interior with the asymmetrical location of the window in each room. We check the building code and find that tempered glass will be required in the lower lights of the window, because they exceed the area permitted for ordinary annealed glass so close to the floor (**Safe Glazing**). We make a note to inform the specifications writer.

It will be necessary to construct the concrete wall in a number of separate pours, starting from the ground and working upward. The seams between pours will be visible no matter what we do, so we will follow the standard practice of using recessed rustication strips at the pour lines to create a pattern of **Reveals** that will mask the seams with a regular grid of shadow lines. We must also anticipate the cracking that will occur in the wall as the concrete shrinks by designing a pattern of **Control Joints** to channel this cracking in an acceptable manner. Additionally, the formwork for the wall will need form ties at close intervals; these will leave visible holes in the concrete that we will make as clean as possible (**Clean Edge**) by using plastic cones to form neat recesses at the ends of the ties. From the pour lines, the control joints, and the form tie holes, we will create a visual composition for the face of the building (**Intensification and Ornamentation**).

The concrete pours resolve themselves naturally into horizontal layers, one for each floor slab and spandrel, and one for each story height of wall. Each wall pour will be 8′ high, requiring a form a few inches taller than 8′.

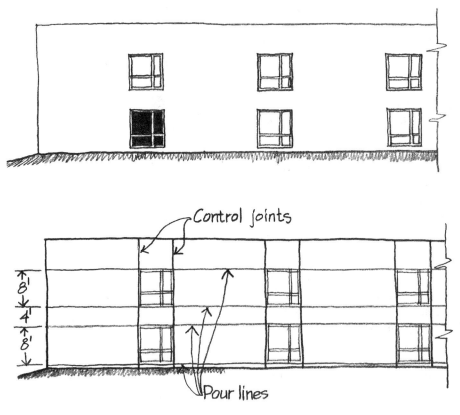

The extra dimension is necessary to allow for overlap of the previously poured wall layer below and to prevent concrete from overspilling the form at the top. A check of some manufacturers' catalogs shows that formwork plywood up to 10′ long is readily available, and the structural engineer says that an 8′ pour height will not require unusually strong formwork to resist the pressure of the wet concrete. We will dimension the building repetitiously so that the sections of formwork can be used again and again as construction progresses (**Repetitious Assembly**).

Control joints should be located to control cracking at points of weakness in the wall. Such points occur at each of the window openings. The American Concrete Institute (ACI) recommends a maximum joint spacing of 20′, so we decide to place a control joint at each side of each window opening. We make a note to specify water-reducing admixtures to minimize the shrinkage of the concrete; these will reduce the potential for cracking and will also help eliminate unattractive voids in the exterior surface of the concrete by making the concrete flow more easily into the forms.

We look up the standard **Dimensional Tolerances** for poured concrete structures in ACI publication 117, *Standard Tolerances for Concrete Construction and Materials*. These indicate that the overall dimensions of the constructed building may vary by as much as 1″ either way and that wall thicknesses may vary by as much as ⅜″. Individual wall length dimensions may vary by up to ½″. We will detail accordingly. ▷

Having made these tentative decisions, we construct an elevation drawing to see what the building face will look like with the rustication strips and control joints in place. After studying this drawing, we move the vertical control joints a few inches outside the window jambs to give the lintel area of the spandrel an apparent bearing on the walls below.

We now consider how to integrate the pattern of form tie holes with the tentative pattern of rustication strips and control joints. The structural engineer tells us that form ties are normally spaced at about 2′ intervals, both vertically and horizontally. Looking at a piece of wall that runs from one window to the next, we see that it will require five sheets of plywood, each 4′ × 9′, with the long dimension vertical. Consulting a book on formwork construction, we find that the plywood needs to be braced by studs running across the width of the sheet, which will be horizontal in this case. The studs are supported by walers running perpendicular to the studs, and the walers are supported by the metal ties that run through the formwork to the walers on the other side. If we space the form ties 1′ away from each edge of each sheet of plywood, this produces a regular pattern of holes that works well with the plywood joints and gives a 2′ spacing horizontally. Vertically, if we divide each sheet into three spaces between holes that are placed 1′ from the top and bottom, the tie spacing comes out to be 2′. The structural engineer does a preliminary check on the stiffness of the walers. He says that the 2′ dimension will be fine and notes the importance of specifying stiff formwork to avoid unattractive bulges in the surface of the finished wall (*Small Structures*). Formwork is ordinarily engineered by the contractor, not the architect or engineer, but we can specify maximum allowable deflections for the plywood, studs, and walers.

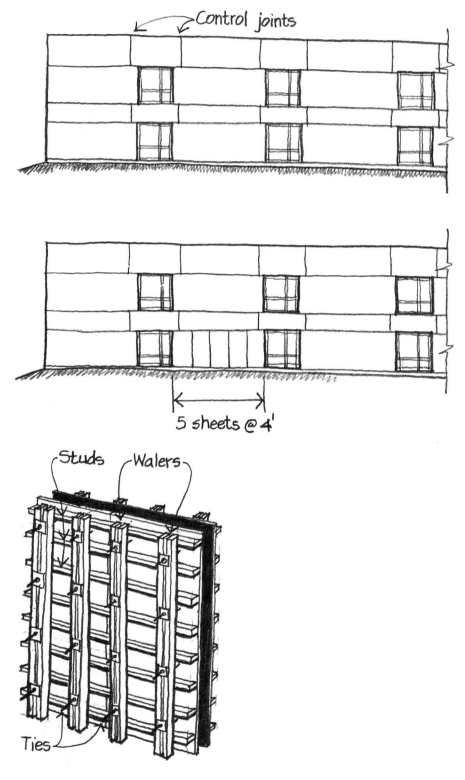

With form tie holes added to the drawing, we examine the pattern and proportions of the elevation: The pattern is orderly and well proportioned, but somewhat bland. The discussion turns to surface textures for the concrete. A texture might combat the blandness of the facade and would also help conceal small defects in the concrete work (*Forgiving Surface*). After considerable experimentation on tracing paper overlays, a decision is made to use a vertical board texture on the walls and to sandblast the spandrels lightly to create a matte surface that should contrast nicely with the boards. The board texture will also obscure the marks of the vertical joints between panels of formwork, and the sandblasted texture will soften them considerably.   ▷

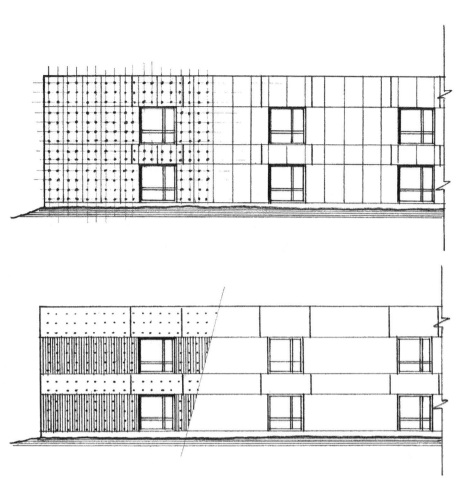

FORMULATING AN APPROACH TO THE IMPORTANT WALL FUNCTIONS

Water Leakage   Architectural concrete, because of its simple, massive geometry, does not adapt readily to a rain-screen approach to watertightness. Instead we must detail it to eliminate as best we can the openings through which water can penetrate the wall. We will start by specifying a strong, dense concrete and by insisting on careful vibration of the concrete into the forms to eliminate voids. We will control cracking by designing a concrete mix that uses minimal water, by providing sufficient steel reinforcing for the wall, by insisting on long and careful wet curing, and by providing sealed control joints at appropriate intervals.

Thermal Insulation and Water Vapor
Concrete is a poor thermal insulator. We review some options for installing **Thermal Insulation**: We could place it on the outside of the wall, using an exterior insulation and finish system (EIFS). This would give the building the advantage of an **Outside-insulated Thermal Mass**, and it would allow the concrete work to be done to a much less expensive level of workmanship (**Progressive Finish**). We reject this option, however, because its external appearance would be that of a fuzzily defined stucco building, not a crisply delineated concrete one, and because we feel that EIFS is not sufficiently resistant to physical damage for use on a college campus.

A second option would be to install plastic foam insulation within the formwork and to pour the concrete either

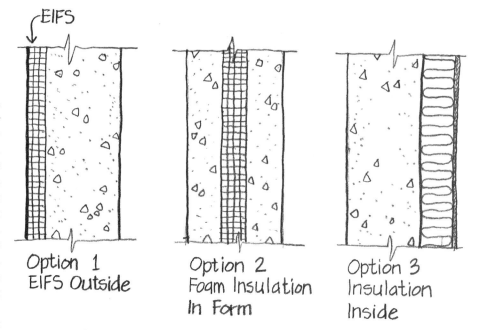

Option 1
EIFS Outside

Option 2
Foam Insulation
In Form

Option 3
Insulation
Inside

around or against it. After some discussion among members of the project team, we discard this idea, because the foam is fragile, tends to float, and would therefore create many potential complications during the forming and pouring operations.

As a third option, we consider installing the thermal insulation on the interior side of the concrete wall in a separate operation carried out later in the construction process. Metal furring strips would be required to support an interior finish layer (probably gypsum wallboard or veneer plaster) over the insulation. The mechanical engineer does a few scribbles and announces that either 2″ of phenolic foam insulation or 3½″ of high-efficiency glass fiber insulation would be sufficient to meet building code requirements for energy efficiency, provided a 1″ airspace is also incorporated into the detail. The plastic foam alternative would create a bit more usable floor space but would be more costly and would not integrate as well with electrical work. The glass fiber alternative would provide ample space for electrical wiring; we decide tentatively to adopt this approach. We note with regret that the exterior walls cannot be a very useful part of the thermal mass of the building with the insulation on the inside, but considerable **Outside-insulated Thermal Mass** still remains in the floor and roof structures. And although we are losing the exposed concrete finish on the interior surfaces of the walls, the painted gypsum wall finish will contrast handsomely with the exposed concrete ceilings, and the concrete workers can concentrate their attention on creating a perfect finish on just one side of the wall—the exterior.

We now take up the problem of the thermal bridges that exist where the slabs and beams join the exterior bearing wall. The structural engineer decides that there is no reason that the one-way slabs must join the walls directly, and a ***Thermal Break*** detail is sketched out that involves simply inserting a strip of plastic foam insulation into the formwork at the edges of the slabs prior to pouring. This leaves only the beam intersections as thermal bridges, and the mechanical engineer estimates that the effect of these is negligible in the overall heat loss of the building. Furthermore, the potential for moisture condensation on the interior surfaces of a beam near the outside wall proves to be minimal, because calculations show that the insulating value of the 15″ of concrete through which heat must travel to escape along a beam is sufficient to assure a ***Warm Interior Surface***—not warm to the touch, but about as warm as the interior surface of a double-glazed window, which is good enough to avoid condensation under most conditions. There is a more serious thermal bridge at the end walls of the building, where the slab is supported continuously by the wall. After much discussion with the engineer, we decide to support the slab edge on another beam in this location and to separate the beam from the wall by a foam ***Thermal Break*** similar to the one used on the side wall. We will have to provide reinforced concrete connec-

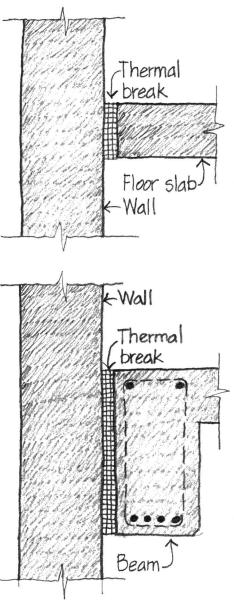

tions between the beam and the wall at intervals, however, to give lateral support to the wall, and these will have to remain as thermal bridges.

The thermal breaks do raise a problem of code compliance. Given the use, height, and floor area of the building, the building code requires that the floors have a two-hour fire resistance rating. The plastic foam thermal breaks have no fire resistance. To solve this, we will specify that the foam thermal breaks be removed after the concrete has cured and replaced with mineral fiber safing suspended on sheet metal clips. The safing is a high-melting-point batt that is almost as good a thermal insulator as the plastic foam. The foam may be removed most easily by burning it out with a propane torch. The combustion products of polystyrene foam are similar chemically to those of wood smoke, but we will have to check to see if local air quality regulations will permit this means of removing the foam.

A particular make and model of aluminum window is adopted by the design team based on its aesthetic, functional, and economic success in several previous buildings that the office has designed. The design of this window incorporates many detailing patterns, the most important of which are ***Multiple Glazing*** and ***Thermal Break***.

▷

DETAILING THE WALL SECTIONS

These tentative decisions having been made, we're ready to begin designing the construction of the key details for a typical wall, working at a scale of 1½" = 1" (1:8) so that we can visualize the details rather completely. We pencil lightly the outlines of the slabs and walls for a spandrel detail and a parapet detail. The safing and an approximate pattern of steel reinforcing (obtained from the engineer) are added to the concrete work on the wall section. Given the required thickness of thermal insulation, we decide to add a full 3⅝" steel stud wall inside the concrete wall instead of ordinary furring strips. Rather than place the studs directly against the concrete wall surface, we leave a 1" space between them. This will provide the airspace requested for insulating purposes by the mechanical engineer, and it will also give a considerable *Dimensional Tolerance* to avoid conflict with occasional bulges or inaccuracies in the concrete surface. Where the stud wall joins the ceiling, a *Structure/Enclosure Joint* is created by cutting the studs somewhat short of the inside of the metal runner track; this allows for the ¼" potential differential of combined slab deflection and creep from one floor to the next that the structural engineer has estimated. The insulation will be installed between the studs. The studs also provide a form of *Horizontal Plenum* for the electrical wiring. Between the insulation and the gypsum wall finish, we place a *Warm-Side Vapor Retarder* of polyethylene film.

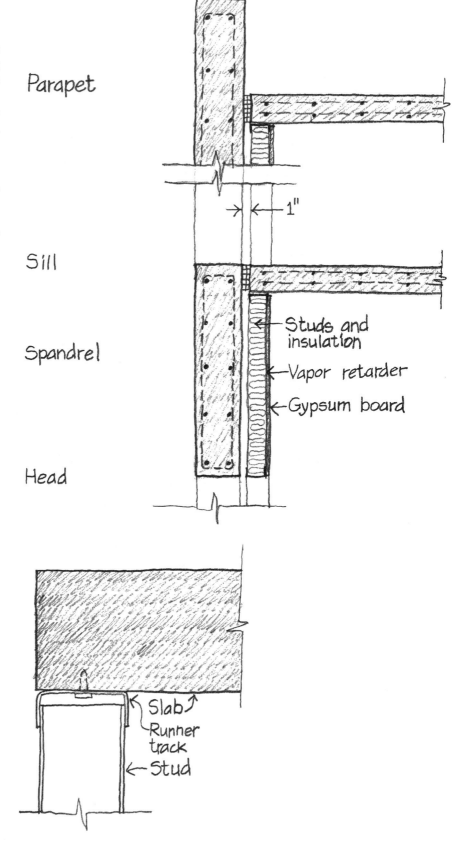

Parapet

Sill

Spandrel

Head

1"

Studs and insulation

Vapor retarder

Gypsum board

Slab

Runner track

Stud

Detailing the Window Openings After considerable trial and error on tracing paper overlays, the window head and sill are added to the developing section. These details will have to be refined further after consultation with the window manufacturer. Working from the window catalog "typical detail" that shows rough jambs of wood, we are proposing tentatively that the head and jambs of the window unit be screwed to strips of plywood that are mounted to the concrete with screws and expansion anchors. The plywood should be treated with a preservative so that it will not decay if it is exposed to water leakage or condensation (*Dry Wood*). A manufacturer-specified *Installation Clearance* between the plywood and the window frame will be taken up by shims. The nominal size of this gap, ⅞″, will take into account the maximum expected inaccuracy in the concrete work (±½″) plus the space necessary to allow the aluminum window unit to slide easily into position (⅜″). Each plywood strip will extend into the building to stabilize the steel stud wall, to which it will be fastened with self-drilling, self-tapping screws. The gypsum wall finish will return around the plywood with a corner bead to finish against the window frame with a *Clean Edge* created by a metal casing bead. On the outdoor side, the thickness of the plywood will provide for installation of a generously sized *Sealant Joint* and backer rod. Except for the sealant joints, the windows will be installed from inside the building (*Accessible Connections*).

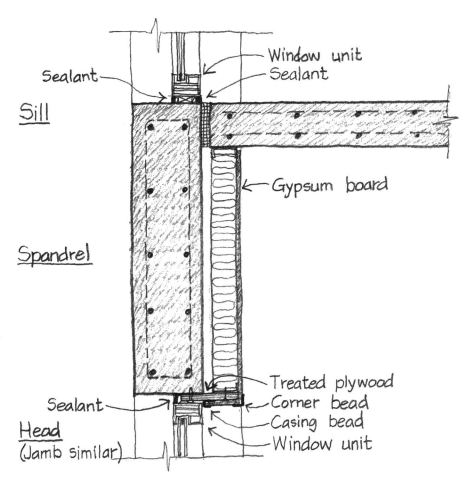

The joint at the head of the window is well protected from water by the drip groove and overhang of the spandrel above, so a defect in the sealant is unlikely to create a water leak. The sealant joints at the jamb and sill are likely to be wetted during rainstorms, however, and could leak if they are defective. We decide to treat the exterior sealant joint as a deterrent seal and to provide a second sealant joint along the interior edge of the window unit as an air seal. If the exterior sealant is flawed, the interior seal and the space around the window unit will create a *Rainscreen Assembly*.

We recognize that the head and jamb details of our design are virtually identical, so for now we will develop the head detail only. ▷

Detailing the Interior Finishes The interior details are finished with a standard vinyl casing bead that has compressible "wipers" to provide for ceiling slab deflection along the top edge of the gypsum board, a standard vinyl base as *Building Armor* at the foot of the wall, and an aluminum box extrusion with a *Sliding Fit* at the windowsill to cover the foam plastic thermal break. The box extrusion will be screwed to the floor only, not to the window, forming a *Structure/Enclosure Joint* that allows the floor slab to deflect without stressing the window. To cushion the box section against the hard, slightly irregular concrete slab, we bed it in sealant. This is a nonworking sealant joint (meaning that the slab and the aluminum box will have little or no movement between them), so we don't provide a backer rod or worry about the exact thickness of the sealant. The sealant will simply be applied to the underside of the aluminum piece just before it is screwed down, and the excess sealant that squeezes out of the joint as the screws are tightened will be wiped off. To create a soft, quiet joint between the window frame and the box extrusion, we show a synthetic rubber gasket (*Quiet Attachments*). We make a note to consult with the window manufacturer about furnishing these extrusions in a finish to match the window frame. We draw an interior perspective sketch of a typical window opening to see how our details will look and to check how the pieces will meet at the corners.

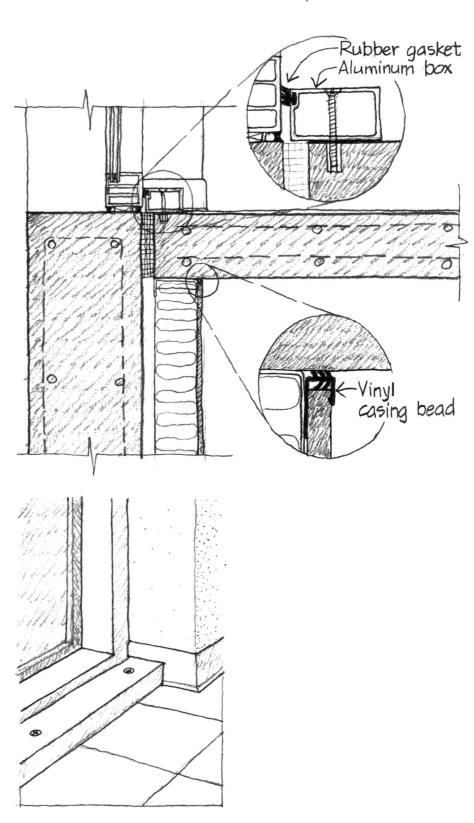

Detailing the Exterior Outdoors, much of the wall detail remains to be designed. We begin by creating an *Overhang and Drip* with a groove at the head of the window. This will be made with a simple strip nailed into the formwork. At the sill we make a sloping *Wash* to conduct water away from the window. The termination of the wash at the jambs will have to be studied later in an elevation sketch.

Checking the building code, we find that a parapet is not required on this building because of the wide spacing between buildings on the campus, but we will construct one anyway, because we want to create a greater apparent thickness for the roof. We put a *Wash* on the top of the parapet to shed water toward the roof. This will help prevent unattractive water staining of the concrete facade. For the roofing system we adopt an inverted roof assembly, with polystyrene foam insulation in a thickness specified by the mechanical engineer installed above the roof membrane (*Warm-Side Vapor Retarder*). A heavy layer of stone ballast anchors the insulation boards in place and protects them from degradation by sunlight.

A reglet insert in the formwork of the parapet provides an *Overlap* between the concrete wall and the metal counterflashing. The bend in the counterflashing allows it to clamp tightly against the upturned edge of the roof membrane by spring action, and the underlying airspace that this creates acts as a *Capillary Break*. The bottom of the counterflashing turns outward to form an *Overhang and Drip*.

We add the rustication strips to the section, tapering the edges of each strip at least 15°, as recommended by the ACI, so that they can be removed easily and without damage from the concrete. A wall pour will terminate at the top of the rustication strip beneath the spandrel. The spandrel formwork will be placed after the wall formwork

has been removed and will contain an indentical rustication strip that will mate with the profile of the concrete at this location to help align the formwork for the higher pour. (Notice that here, as in many other parts of this detail development process, we are *Rehearsing the Construction Sequence* as a way of understanding the basis for our design decisions.) ▷

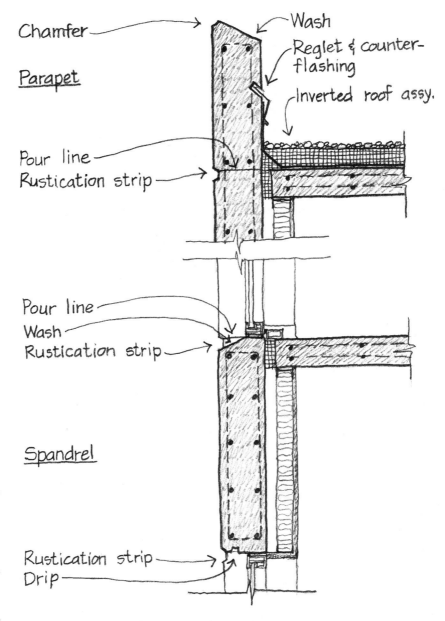

DETAILING THE GRADE CONDITION

We develop the grade detail rather quickly on a tracing paper overlay of the spandrel detail. The ground floor will be a concrete slab on grade, which the structural engineer figures should be 6″ thick and reinforced with bars in both directions. We will place a 6 mil polyethylene moisture barrier beneath the slab to prevent ground water from rising into the building. After soil testing has been completed, the geotechnical engineer will assist in working out a detailed specification for compacted backfill and a layer of crushed stone beneath the slab. Between the slab edge and the concrete wall, we insert a 2″ thick layer of polystyrene foam extending downward to 4′ below grade to retard the passage of heat through the slab and soil to the outdoors. We choose to run the slab down the wall rather than fold it back under the slab, as is sometimes done, because we do not want the soil under the slab to freeze and heave.

DETAILING THE CORNER OF THE BUILDING

Working in plan view, we detail an exterior corner of the building. We chamfer the concrete corner to avoid breakage (**Clean Edge**). We create vertical **Control Joints** 4′ from the corner on either wall. These will absorb the concrete shrinkage stresses that are likely to accumulate at the corner by inducing controlled cracking in the concrete. As recommended by ACI, we discontinue half the horizontal reinforcing bars at each control joint to help create a plane of weakness. ACI also recommends that a control joint have grooves on both sides of the wall to a total depth of one-quarter the thickness of the wall, which is 2½″ in our building. We decide to use a standard ¾″ deep rustication strip on the inside face and a 1¾″ deep strip on the outside. This deeper strip must be

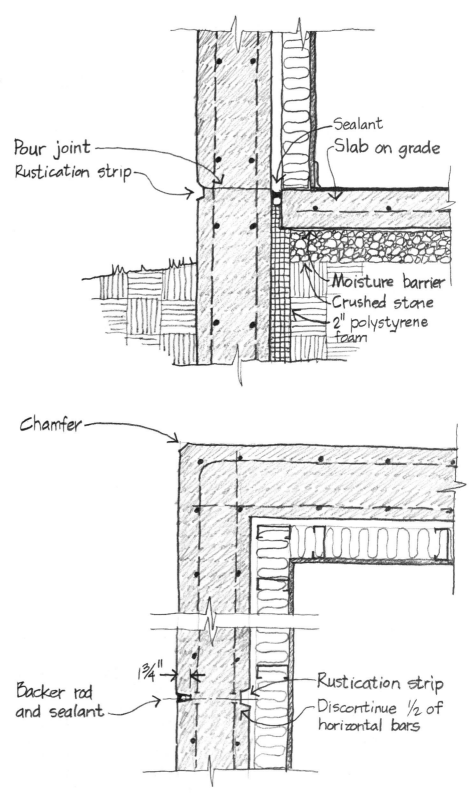

narrower to accept a backer rod and sealant; the sealant will keep water and air from penetrating the expected crack in the concrete.

The studs, gypsum board, and insulation are detailed in the standard way, holding the studs away from the corner several inches in the manner recommended by the manufacturers of the studs and boards. We contemplate placing a control joint in the gypsum board in the same plane as the control joint in the concrete wall, but we realize that the gypsum board is supported on the floor slab, which has no joint at this location and is not connected in any way to the concrete wall. We do not need a control joint in the gypsum.

ELEVATION STUDIES

We need to study at larger scale the relationships of the rustication strips, the terminations of the various pours, the window openings, and the control joints. For this purpose we construct a larger-scale elevation view showing the form tie holes, rustication strips, control joints, and sill wash. After some tracing paper studies of alternatives, we decide to terminate the wash with a sloping end plane. The pattern of the recessed strips and form tie holes strikes us as being neatly organized and satisfying.

The control joint around each window lintel, like the control joints at the corner, needs to extend at least one-quarter of the way through the wall, or 2½″. Again, half the reinforcing bars should be discontinued at this plane (we make a note to coordinate with the structural engineer to see that this is detailed properly on the structural drawings). But the detailing of the exterior slot of the control joint gives us some difficulty because of the way it is tied in with the horizontal rustication strips and the sloping sill. Ideally, we'd like to make the control joint slot as wide as the rustication strip for visual simplicity, but this would result

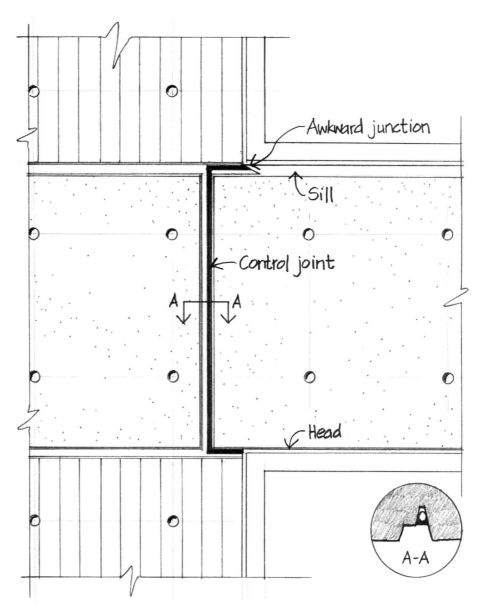

in an excessively wide joint that would waste sealant. Forming a narrower, deeper slot at the bottom of the recessed strip seems a bit fussy and difficult. We also realize that the line of the control joint as we have drawn it in elevation is not really satisfactory, because any shrinkage in the concrete is likely to cause ugly diagonal cracks at the corners of the lintels rather than cracks that follow obediently along the difficult path we have laid out. Furthermore, the top end of the control joint joins the sloping sill in a very awkward way that will be hard to make (**Clean Edge**). We must try again.   ▷

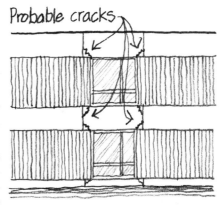

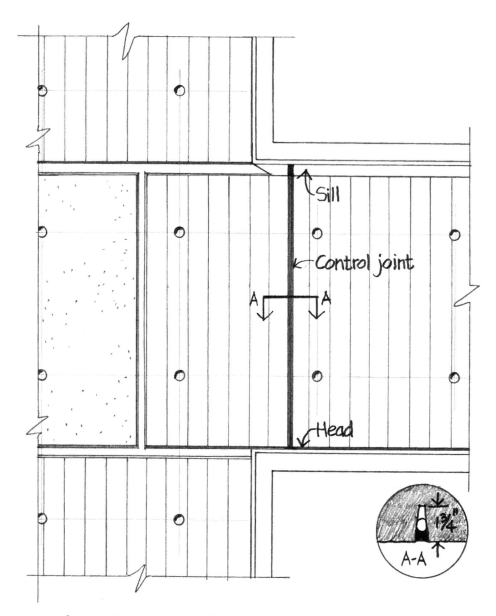

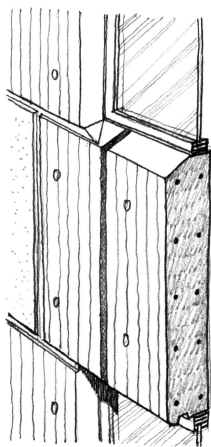

After much exploration of alternatives on tracing paper overlays, we arrive at a solution that we like much better. We move the control joints several inches out onto the lintel and give them the narrower width they require, creating a simple, straight-line path along which cracking can occur.

The control joint with its sealant will have to continue up over the sloping sill until it joins the sealant beneath the aluminum window frame. To retain the visual identity of the lintel, we set it off from the rest of the spandrel with a vertical rustication strip at each end. To reinforce the visual integrity of the lintel further and to minimize the appearance of the control joints, we give the lintel a board texture, while retaining the sandblasted texture on the rest of the spandrel. This creates a strong pattern on the facade, puts the control joints where they will do the most good, and is easy to construct.

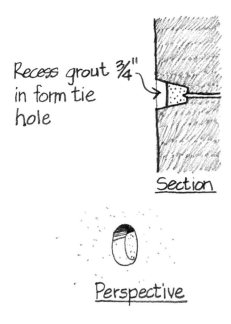

Recess grout ¾"
in form tie
hole

<u>Section</u>

<u>Perspective</u>

The holes left by the form tie cones must be sealed in some way to prevent the broken ends of the metal ties from rusting and staining the facade. This could be done with sealant, with a plastic or rubber plug, or with stiff grout compacted into the hole. We avoid trying to fill the holes flush with grout, because the grout would smear onto the wall surface in a messy way and would inevitably contrast in color and texture with the poured concrete around it. After weighing the options, we elect to use the grout and to recess it well into the conical hole using a large wood dowel and mallet to compact the surface. The recess constitutes a shadow-casting *Reveal* that will conceal any messiness in the grout work.

As our preliminary details near completion, we run an eye counter-clockwise around the perimeter of the heated and cooled space of the building on our details, starting in the middle of the roof, looking for thermal bridges. If the cant strip were made of plastic foam, the insulating layer of the building would wrap neatly around the roof–wall junction without a thermal bridge, except for the intermittent concrete beams that we have already

considered and decided to accept as inevitable. We make a note to specify a foam plastic cant strip. The floor edges are well broken thermally, and the window openings will offer no thermal bridges if we add a strip of glass fiber batting to the inch-thick gap behind the steel stud furring at the jambs.

NEXT STEPS

We have amassed a long list of items to communicate to the specifications writer: notes on the exact qualities of the materials to be used for the formwork; the need for air entrainment in the concrete to minimize weathering damage; the need to select a nonstaining form release agent for the walls and to specify the same agent also for use in the slab and beam forms, because, if two different release agents are in use, there might be confusion that would lead to the wrong release agent being used on the exterior surfaces; the need to specify noncorroding or plastic-tipped spacers and chairs for the reinforcing bars to avoid rust stains. Also, the cement color must be chosen carefully. We want the specifications to require that all the cement be from the same kiln batch and that all the aggregates come from the same part of the same quarry, to avoid color variations. Pouring, vibrating, curing, and sandblasting procedures must be standardized. We must specify measures to protect finished concrete surfaces from gouging and staining during subsequent construction operations, using tarpaulins, mats, and wooden corner guards. A certain amount of repairing of exposed concrete surfaces will undoubtedly be required; we must specify the materials and procedures very carefully to avoid garish patches.

We will specify that a full-scale sample wall be erected on the site in advance by the contractor, using a representative sample of the workers

who will build the building, not an elite team of the best workers. This will allow the owner, the contractor, the contractor's foremen, and all the design professionals to work out the last problems with materials and details. We will require that the specified patching procedures be tried out and refined on this sample wall. We will also specify a preconstruction conference of all parties during which materials and procedures can be discussed in detail; this will help avoid false starts and inconsistent workmanship.

Architectural concrete work is not very forgiving of errors or sloppiness. Though we have made it somewhat more forgiving in our building by a judicious use of rustication strips and textures, it would still court disaster to use an inexperienced contractor on the project. We will work with the owner to assemble a list of qualified contractors who have built architectural concrete buildings successfully before. Unqualified contractors will not be allowed to bid.

At this point in the process of designing the details we can prepare a clean, accurate set of drawings that summarize clearly all the design decisions we have made. These details are still only semifinished; they cannot be completed until some of the loose ends that we have already identified have been cleaned up, until they have undergone more extensive review by other members of the project team, and until the rest of the working drawings and specifications for the project have been brought to a similar stage so that inconsistencies can be identified and corrected. A logical next step will be to develop other important details of the building, including special conditions such as entrances and stairwells, to discover if the aesthetic established in this set of details can be applied consistently to the entire building (*Contributive Details*). It is reasonable to expect that some adjustments will be required.

▷

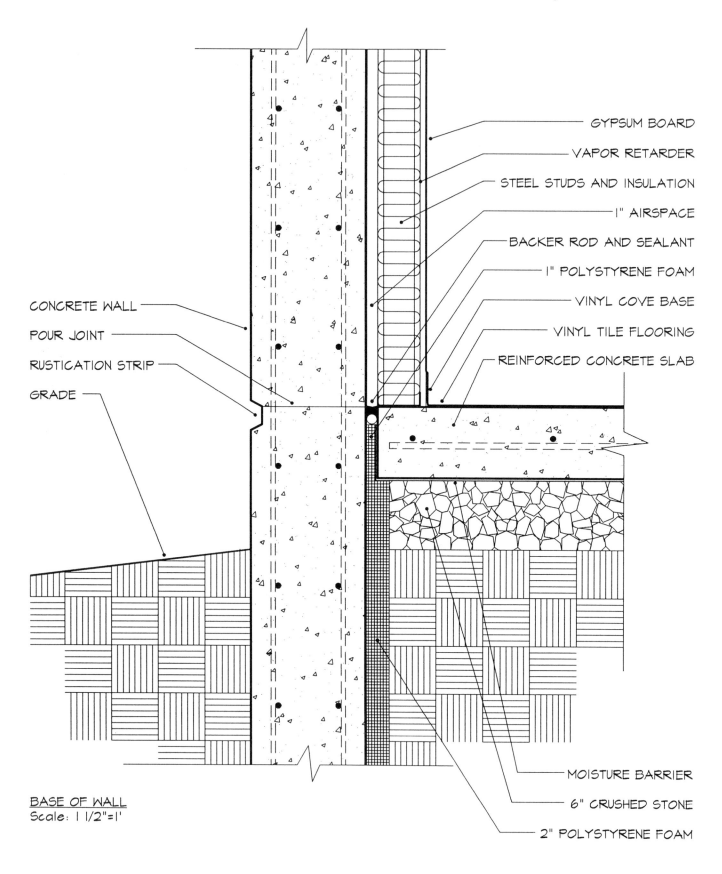

GYPSUM BOARD

VAPOR RETARDER

STEEL STUDS AND INSULATION

1" AIRSPACE

BACKER ROD AND SEALANT

1" POLYSTYRENE FOAM

VINYL COVE BASE

VINYL TILE FLOORING

REINFORCED CONCRETE SLAB

CONCRETE WALL

POUR JOINT

RUSTICATION STRIP

GRADE

MOISTURE BARRIER

6" CRUSHED STONE

2" POLYSTYRENE FOAM

BASE OF WALL
Scale: 1 1/2"=1'

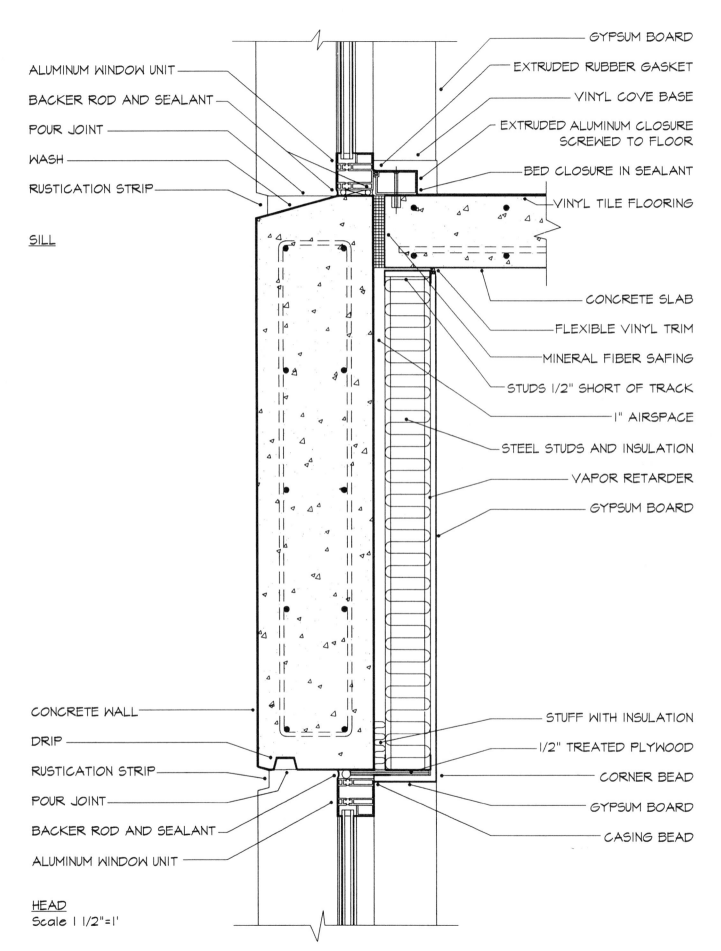

ALUMINUM WINDOW UNIT

BACKER ROD AND SEALANT

POUR JOINT

WASH

RUSTICATION STRIP

SILL

GYPSUM BOARD

EXTRUDED RUBBER GASKET

VINYL COVE BASE

EXTRUDED ALUMINUM CLOSURE SCREWED TO FLOOR

BED CLOSURE IN SEALANT

VINYL TILE FLOORING

CONCRETE SLAB

FLEXIBLE VINYL TRIM

MINERAL FIBER SAFING

STUDS 1/2" SHORT OF TRACK

1" AIRSPACE

STEEL STUDS AND INSULATION

VAPOR RETARDER

GYPSUM BOARD

CONCRETE WALL

DRIP

RUSTICATION STRIP

POUR JOINT

BACKER ROD AND SEALANT

ALUMINUM WINDOW UNIT

STUFF WITH INSULATION

1/2" TREATED PLYWOOD

CORNER BEAD

GYPSUM BOARD

CASING BEAD

HEAD
Scale 1 1/2"=1'

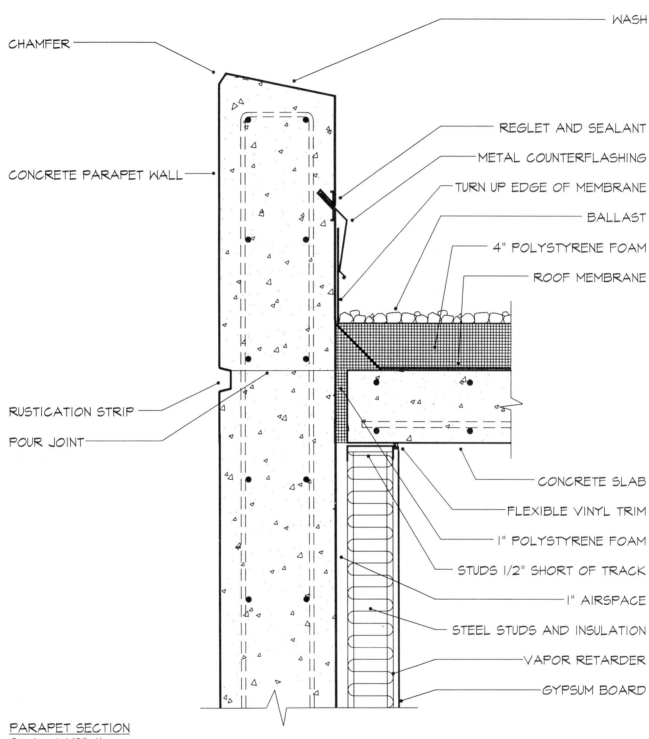

CHAMFER

WASH

CONCRETE PARAPET WALL

REGLET AND SEALANT

METAL COUNTERFLASHING

TURN UP EDGE OF MEMBRANE

BALLAST

4" POLYSTYRENE FOAM

ROOF MEMBRANE

RUSTICATION STRIP

POUR JOINT

CONCRETE SLAB

FLEXIBLE VINYL TRIM

1" POLYSTYRENE FOAM

STUDS 1/2" SHORT OF TRACK

1" AIRSPACE

STEEL STUDS AND INSULATION

VAPOR RETARDER

GYPSUM BOARD

PARAPET SECTION
Scale: 1 1/2"=1'

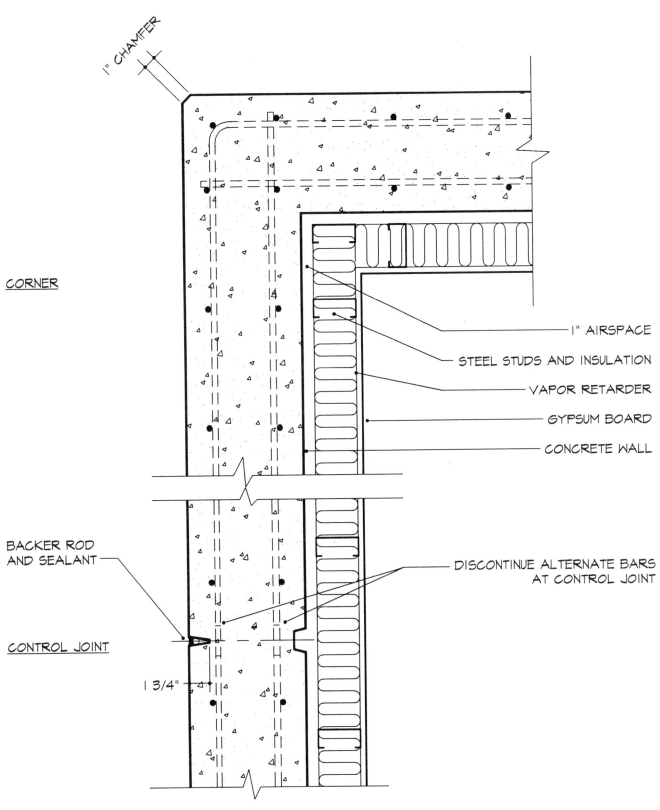

1" CHAMFER

CORNER

1" AIRSPACE

STEEL STUDS AND INSULATION

VAPOR RETARDER

GYPSUM BOARD

CONCRETE WALL

BACKER ROD
AND SEALANT

DISCONTINUE ALTERNATE BARS
AT CONTROL JOINT

CONTROL JOINT

1 3/4"

PLAN OF CORNER AND CONTROL JOINT
Scale: 1 1/2"=1'

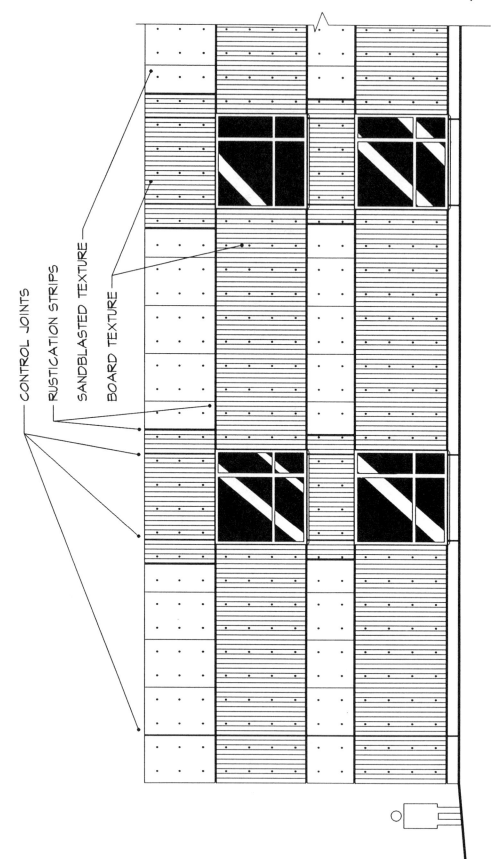

CONTROL JOINTS

RUSTICATION STRIPS

SANDBLASTED TEXTURE

BOARD TEXTURE

TYPICAL ELEVATION

Scale 1/8"=1'

KEY REFERENCES

The following are important reference materials that were used in developing this set of details. Full bibliographic information on these publications is given in the reference list at the back of this book.

American Concrete Institute Committee 303, *Guide to Cast-in-Place Architectural Concrete*.

American Concrete Institute 117, *Standard Tolerances for Concrete Construction and Materials*.

Hurd, M. K. *Formwork for Concrete* (5th ed.).

United States Gypsum Company. *Gypsum Construction Handbook*. ■

DETAILING A BRICK FACING ON A CONCRETE FRAME

THE PROJECT

The project is 17-story luxury apartment building in a mountainous area of the Pacific Northwest, seismic zone 3.

SETTING PERFORMANCE STANDARDS

The owner desires a well-finished, durable building. The applicable code specifies R-19 walls, an R-30 roof, and double-glazed windows. Seismic requirements of the Uniform Building Code (UBC) apply to the design of the structure and cladding. Each dwelling must have a high degree of acoustical privacy.

KEY DETAILS TO DEVELOP

The key details that will establish the visual character and mode of construction of the building are those circled on the section and plan diagrams to the right. These must be developed as a consistent set of *Contributive Details* that work well with the building's architecture and with one another. They are the most general of the building's details. Details of special situations, such as the entrance, the lobby, and junctions between towers of differing heights, will use these general details as a point of departure. Of these key details, the spandrel is the detail from which the other key details will be derived, so it is where we will begin our work.

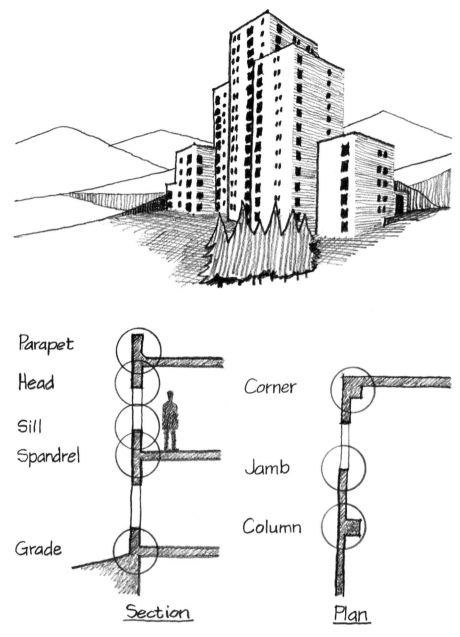

EARLY DECISIONS CONCERNING MATERIAL, STRUCTURE, AND FORM

Working together with the structural engineer, we have made a preliminary choice for the structure of the building. It is a two-way flat plate concrete system supported by concrete columns that are generally spaced on 24′ centers. Floor-to-floor height is approximately 9′. The floor slabs will be 10″ thick. Column size will vary—large at the bottom of the building and small at the top. There will be perimeter beams around the edges of all the floors; the role of these beams will be partly to strengthen the edge of each floor plate, partly to stiffen the frame against lateral loads, and partly to support the weight of the cladding system.

The apartments will be heated and cooled by fan-coil units at the exterior walls. The pipe risers that feed these units with heated and chilled water from the basement mechanical room will have to be housed in **Vertical Chases** at various locations. Each fan-coil unit will require an exterior louver for air intake and exhaust.

We wish to face the building with brick masonry. A brick exterior is attractive to the eye and gives an impression of quality and permanence—the more so because it is a **Surface That Ages**

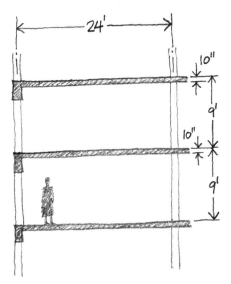

Gracefully, improving with age. Windows will be casement and fixed units constructed of wood with a vinyl cladding on the exterior. These will occur in varying sizes and in somewhat random locations that suit the interior arrangements of the apartments.

Inside, floors will be carpeted except for ceramic tile floors in kitchens, baths, and laundries. (The carpeting has been selected partly becuse it is a desirable material and partly because it will contribute to acoustic privacy through the **Cushioned Floor** pattern). Walls will be of veneer plaster mounted on steel studs. Ceilings will be the painted undersides of the slabs.

EARLY WORK ON MATERIALS AND DETAILS

We find from page 141 that the standard **Dimensional Tolerance** for a concrete frame is ±1″ from a vertical plane; our details will have to take this into account.

There are three different ways in which we might go about applying a brick exterior to this building. One is to shop-fabricate the brickwork in large reinforced panels that can be trucked to the site, lifted, and attached to the building with relatively little on-site work. This is an attractive option, but we discard it for this project, because there are a number of excellent masonry contractors in the area who will be able to construct the cladding in place at an economical price (**Local Skills and Customs**). Another option is to construct the cladding in place as a brick facing over a concrete masonry backup wall. We must weigh this against a third option, which is to construct the cladding in place but to use a steel stud backup wall rather than concrete masonry, probably at a significant saving in cost. We have studied this question in some detail, partly by observing constructed buildings of both types and partly by reading many current articles in technical journals. We conclude that there are unanswered questions concerning

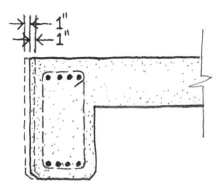

the long-term durability and safety of brickwork attached to steel stud walls. These stem from the relative flexibility of the studs, which may allow cracking of the brick facing, and from the potential for corrosion and disintegration of the steel and gypsum components of the system. For this building, in which durability is a major design criterion, we choose to design an all-masonry wall that will be constructed in place.

The backup wall will be made of nominal 8″ hollow, lightweight concrete blocks, reinforced horizontally with steel wire joint reinforcement and vertically with reinforcing bars in grouted cores. We have decided to use modular bricks, which measure 2¼″ × 3⅝″ × 7⅝″, because their dimensions will coordinate well with the dimensions of the building and the backup masonry, thereby avoiding most cutting of masonry units (**Uncut Units**). We will use standard ⅜″ mortar joints. Given the high wind loads on the walls of this building, we will use very stiff metal ties to give lateral support to the brick facing. The UBC requires that the ties be spaced so that each supports no more than 2 square feet of wall area. It also requires that the ties connect to joint reinforcing of 9-gauge wires in the brick facing. To prevent deflection and cracking of the facing, we propose to avoid adjustable masonry ties, which tend to have excessive dimensional "play." Instead, we will use joint reinforcing that includes the ties and the reinforcing wires for both brick and block in a single welded assembly.

FORMULATING AN APPROACH TO THE IMPORTANT WALL FUNCTIONS

Thermal Insulation and Water Vapor
For maximum security against water leakage, we will detail the exterior wall as a cavity wall. We sketch it freehand in section, working from outside to inside: It will consist of a brick facing, a cavity, a concrete masonry backup wall, and a furred interior wall facing of veneer plaster. It will probably need some additional thermal insulation to achieve the required R-19 value. We propose tentatively to accomplish some of this by using "blueboard" (veneer plaster base) with a bright foil backing. When applied to the furring strips, this will create a *Reflective Surface and Airspace*, as well as furnishing a *Warm-Side Vapor Retarder*. Using values from *ASHRAE Fundamentals*, we determine the thermal resistance of the wall components:

Thermal Resistance of Wall Components

Outside air film	0.17
3.5″ of brick @ R = 0.20	0.70
2″ cavity	0.90
8″ lightweight CMUs	1.72
1″ furring space, bright foil on one side	3.55
½″ plaster	0.45
Inside air film	0.68
Total thermal resistance	8.17

We must add at least R-10.8 of *Thermal Insulation* to the wall to meet the code requirement of R-19. Consulting again the list of R-values in *ASHRAE Fundamentals*, we see that we can do this with either 3½″ batts of glass fiber or 2″ of extruded polystyrene foam. We make freehand sketches of both options: The glass fiber, in order to remain dry, would have to be on the interior side of the concrete masonry wall, which would require very deep furring strips and would reduce the available floor space in the apartments. It would also leave the edges of the floor slabs uninsulated. The poly-styrene foam, which is resistant to moisture, could be installed by the masons in the wall cavity. This would wrap the concrete structure and the concrete masonry walls in a virtually unbroken blanket of insulation, avoiding thermal bridges and creating an *Outside-Insulated Thermal Mass* that would make the building easier to heat and cool, and *Warm Interior Surfaces* that would not condense moisture in cold winter weather. It would have the added advantage of sheltering the structure of the building from outdoor temperature extremes. We decide to try the foam insulation in the cavity.

The vinyl-clad wood windows that we have selected for the building easily meet the energy requirements of the code. With the relatively low conductivity of the wood frame there is no need for a *Thermal Break*, and the *Multiple Glazing* of the window achieves the necessary R-value and a sufficiently *Warm Interior Surface* to avoid condensation. ▷

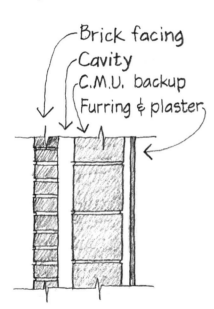

Brick facing
Cavity
C.M.U. backup
Furring & plaster

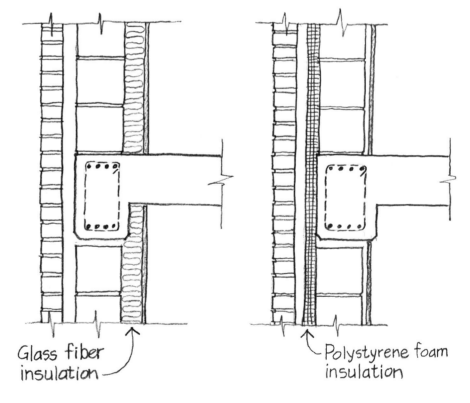

Glass fiber insulation

Polystyrene foam insulation

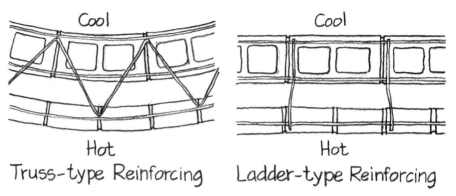

Truss-type Reinforcing   Ladder-type Reinforcing

Water Leakage The cavity wall will operate as a **Rainscreen Assembly** if we detail it with a proper rainscreen, air barrier, and pressure equalization chamber. The brick facing will be a satisfactory rainscreen. The cavity will serve as the pressure equalization chamber, and we will **Drain and Weep** the cavity with weep holes and flashings. The air barrier will consist of the concrete masonry wall and the portions of the perimeter beams and columns that are exposed to the cavity. To maintain the integrity of the air barrier, we will apply a **Sealant Joint** where the concrete masonry joins the frame, but some air will diffuse through the concrete blocks themselves, so we need to apply an airtight membrane or coating to the blocks to create an **Air Barrier Surface** that will both contribute to thermal comfort and prevent water leakage through rainscreen action. It is probable that the air barrier material will also be relatively impermeable to water vapor, but the mechanical engineer assures us that, because it will be on the inside surface of the insulating foam boards, its temperature will always remain above the dew point. It will act as a **Warm-Side Vapor Retarder** and will not trap any condensate.

Acoustic Privacy Acoustic privacy and the reduction of noise transmission between apartment units are extremely important issues in multiple dwellings, especially in the luxury market, where tenants demand quiet apartments. The design team has hired an acoustical consultant. She suggests that the padded carpeting over the heavy concrete slabs will provide a **Sound-Absorbing Surface** and will go a long way toward solving the problem of noise transmission through the floors (**Cushioned Floor**). She will propose ways in which to cushion floors beneath the ceramic tile areas, which would otherwise generate and transmit too much impact noise. She recommends that the walls between units be framed with double rows of studs with acoustic batts and extra layers of gypsum board (**Airtight, Heavy, Limp Partition**). Walls within units, she says, can be made of a single row of steel studs with double layers of gypsum panels; she will make more precise proposals for these as the details develop. She applauds the choice of fan-coil units for heating and cooling, because these avoid the ductwork that might furnish a flanking path for sound between apartments, but she notes that penetrations of the piping through floors and walls will have to be sealed very securely. She will work with the mechanical engineer to select fan-coil assemblies that are inherently quiet and have **Quiet Attachments** to the structure of the building.

Movement The accommodation of movement will be an extremely important function of the details we are drawing. The concrete masonry backup walls will shrink and must have **Control Joints**; but, because the backup walls are interrupted at approximately 22' intervals by the concrete columns, this function can be served by the perimeter sealant joints we are already thinking to provide as part of our air barrier strategy. The brick masonry facing will expand slightly after installation. It will also expand when it is heated by the sun and air and contract when cooled, while the frame of the building, insulated with the polystyrene foam, will remain constant in dimension.

We note also that the thermal expansion and contraction of the brickwork wythe will occur while the outside-insulated concrete masonry wythe to which it is tied remains constant in dimension. If we divide the brick facing into fairly small panels with movement joints, the relative motions between the two wythes will be small and can be taken up by small amounts of flexing in the metal ties. It is important, however, that we use ladder-type joint reinforcing and ties rather than truss-type, because the truss-type, with its diagonals crossing the cavity could cause the two wythes to act as a single structural unit, bending when exposed to temperature extremes, much like the bimetallic spring in a thermostat. This phenomenon is shown in much exaggerated form in the accompanying plan views.

The columns and beams of the building frame will deflect under gravity loads. Because the frame is made of concrete, there will also be creep, a small but significant, irreversible, long-term shortening of the columns and sagging of the beams. Wind loads and seismic loads will cause the concrete building frame to flex and drift. All these structural movements will apply loads to exterior and interior walls unless the walls are separated from the frame by **Structure/Enclosure Joints**. The most important of these will be the so-called soft joints that must be provided under the shelf angles that support the brick facing.

Locating and Sizing Movement Joints
We look at possible patterns for dividing the brick facing into panels. The facing will be supported on a steel shelf angle at each floor, so we will provide a horizontal movement joint beneath each angle. In the vertical direction, we recognize that vertical cracking might tend to occur at the corners of the window openings, where the facing is weakest. However, it is difficult to organize vertical joints at the window openings in a visually satisfactory way, and the end bearing details of the steel window lintels in the brick facing create certain technical uncertainties in this approach. It would be much simpler to install a movement joint at the center line of each column, thus dividing the facade into story-height panels 24' long—a dimension so short that it will minimize potential cracking forces at the windows. We try this pattern as an overlay sketch on the building elevation and decide that it is acceptable visually.

We size the vertical joints by following the procedure outlined on page 35:

$$W = \frac{100}{X}(\varepsilon L \Delta T + M_0) + t$$

Assuming a silicone joint sealant with a movement capability of ±50% (an assumption that we will later communicate to the specifications writer),

$$W = \frac{100}{50}[(0.0000036 \text{ in/in/}°\text{F})(288")(180°) + 0.06"] + 0.125"$$

$$W = 0.62"$$

Use a ⅝" sealant joint at each column line.

In this calculation, 0.0000036 in/in/°F is the coefficient of thermal expansion of brickwork, taken from page 36. 288" is the same as 24', the distance between joints. 180° is the maximum range of temperature that the

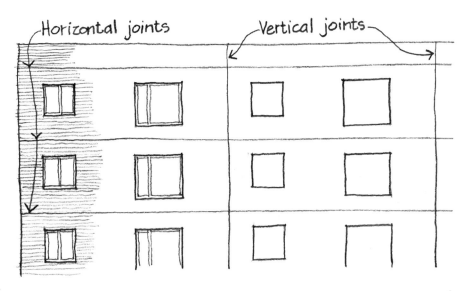

brick facing will experience. This may seem large, but research has shown that dark-colored masonry in summer sunlight can easily reach 140°F, and winter nighttime temperatures in this region can go well below zero. The 0.06" is a calculated value for moisture expansion (page 77). 0.125" is a ***Dimensional Tolerance*** for the brickwork, a relatively small amount, because we know the masons can easily make small dimensional adjustments in the head joints of mortar to maintain a constant width of expansion joint.

We apply the same formula to sizing the horizontal joint, the soft joint that must be provided below every shelf angle. The structural engineer wants to allow a full ½" for deflection and creep in the concrete structure, and we include the same ⅛" tolerance:

$$W = \frac{100}{50}[(0.0000036 \text{ in/in/}°\text{F})(107")(180°) + 0.5"] + 0.125"$$

$$W = 1.26"$$

Use a 1¼" soft joint beneath the shelf angle.

The engineer also tells us that the shelf angle will have to be ⅜" thick, so the overall height of the horizontal joint at each story will be 1⅝". ▷

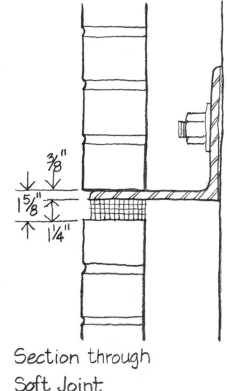

Section through
Soft Joint

DETAILING THE SPANDREL

We begin our detail development with the spandrel. Once the spandrel has been worked out, the remainder of the key details can be developed with comparative rapidity on tracing paper overlays over the spandrel section.

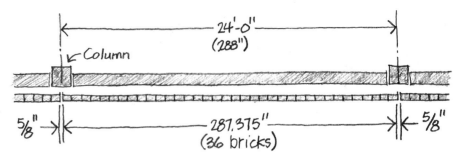

Horizontal Brickwork Dimensioning
As we begin laying out a preliminary spandrel section, we confer with the structural engineer on several important points. First of all, we would like for the variation in column size to occur entirely within the building so that the face of the framing will lie in a single flat plane. He readily agrees. Second, we would like to coordinate the dimensions of the frame with the dimensions of the masonry work so as to avoid as much cutting of masonry units as possible (**Uncut Units**). This will result in as much of a **Repetitious Assembly** process as possible.

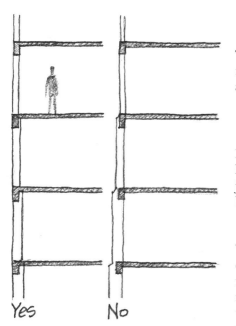

Yes   No

We do some calculations of masonry dimensions: In the horizontal direction, the center-to-center column spacing has been set at 24'-0", and we have already determined that there will be a ⅝" sealant joint at each column. Thus, the space available for brickwork in each bay will be

$$(24 \text{ ft})(12 \text{ in/ft}) - 0.625'' = 287.375''$$

Each brick is 7⅝" long and 3⅝" wide, and mortar joints are ⅜" thick. There will be one fewer mortar joints than bricks in each course. The number of bricks needed to occupy this space can be approximated as

$$N = \frac{287.375''}{7.625'' + 0.375''} \approx 36 \text{ bricks}$$

Thirty-six modular bricks with their mortar joints would ordinarily occupy an exact length of

$$36(7.625'' + 0.375'') - 0.375''$$
$$= 287.625''$$

Because we have only 287.375" of length available between expansion joints, the course of bricks will have to be squeezed by a dimension of

$$287.625'' - 287.375'' = 0.25''$$

We will suggest on our construction drawings that the masons make the first two head joints at each end 1/16" narrower to accomplish this, lining up the rest of the head joints accurately with those of the backup wall so that openings will be easy to create.

Vertical Brickwork Dimensioning The brick coursing must be coordinated vertically with the floor-to-floor height. If the floor-to-floor height is 108" and the total height of the soft joint plus

shelf angle thickness is 1⅝", the space to be filled with brickwork is

$$108'' - 1.625'' = 106.375''$$

Each course of brickwork, with its mortar joint, is 2⅔" high. This works out well with the block coursing in the backup wall, because 3 courses of brickwork are the same height as 1 course of blockwork. In calculating the height of the brick courses, we must take into account that the bricks will not have a mortar joint on the shelf angle, nor will they have one under the soft joint. Thus, there will be one fewer mortar joints than courses, and we must add a nonexistent mortar joint to our story height to be able to calculate the number of courses:

Number of courses

$$= \frac{106.375'' + 0.375''}{8/3'' \text{ per course}}$$

$$= 40.03 \text{ courses}$$

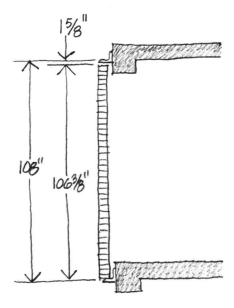

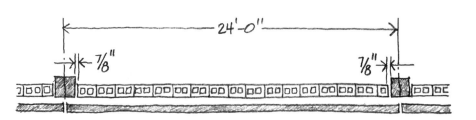

We can't ask the masons to build 0.03 courses, so we calculate the height of an even 40 courses, remembering to deduct the height of one mortar joint:

$$\text{Height} =$$
$$(40 \text{ courses})(8/3 \text{ inches/course}) - \tfrac{3}{8}''$$
$$= 106.29''$$

This is slightly less than the 106.375″ we were shooting for. Suppose we try to make up the difference in the soft joint:

Height of joint beneath shelf angle
$$= 108'' - 106.29'' - 0.375''$$
$$= 1.34''$$

(The 0.375″ in this calculation is the thickness of the shelf angle.) We wanted a joint that is 1.25″ high, so the 1.34″ dimension is only about 1/10″ more.

Concrete Masonry Dimensioning The concrete masonry backup wall has to fit between columns in each bay, and it would speed the masonry work (and reduce its cost) if no blocks had to be cut. With uncut blocks, masons can produce wall lengths in any multiple of 8″, less ⅜″ to account for the fact that a wall contains one fewer mortar joints than blocks. The center-to-center column spacing is 24′, which is an even multiple of 8″. Therefore, any column size that is a multiple of 8″ would avoid cutting of blocks. We ask the structural engineer if the columns could be standardized in width at either 16″ or 24″, letting the depth vary as needed. He looks at his preliminary figures and says that he will probably need 24″ width on the lower floors but could make a transition to 16″ on the higher floors. Meanwhile, however, we have noted the need to provide a movement joint at each end of each segment of the backup wall to allow for block shrinkage and seismic motion of the frame. If the columns were a full 16″ or 24″ in dimension, this would allow only ⅜″, the dimension of a standard mortar joint, for sealant at each end. If we squeezed the columns to 15″ or 23″, this would permit a generous ⅞″ joint

at each end. The engineer agrees that this is acceptable.

In the vertical direction, the backup wall of concrete masonry units will have to fit between the top of the floor slab and the underside of the perimeter beam. The floor-to-floor height is 9′. The engineer would like the depth of the perimeter beam to be about 18″ (measured downward from the top of the slab), but he says that he can be somewhat flexible on this, because he can change the width of the beam and add or subtract reinforcing if necessary to achieve the same strength and stiffness. We will install a soft joint between the top of the concrete masonry wall and the bottom of the beam to allow for deflection and creep. Working from the calculated dimension of the exterior soft joint and subtracting the portion attributable to temperature movement, we decide to make this joint ¾″ high. Thus, the height available to be filled with concrete masonry is

$$(9 \text{ ft})(12 \text{ in/ft}) - 18'' - \tfrac{3}{4}'' = 89.25''$$

Because each course of standard concrete blocks, including mortar, is 8″ high, we see that it would take about 11 courses to fill this space. We calculate the beam depth that would be required to end up with an even 11 courses of blockwork:

Beam depth + (11 courses)(8 in/course) + 0.75″ joint = 108″
Beam depth + (11 courses)

The structural engineer says that this would be fine, but it is wise to round off the dimension to 19″ for ease of formwork fabrication. This would give a soft joint of a full inch, which is acceptable. We also need to check the head-

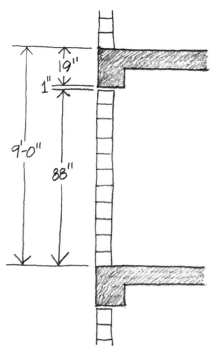

room under the perimeter beam; the building code does not permit a soffit height of less than 7′, and we must allow an extra 1½″ for finish beneath the beam.

Headroom = 108″ − 19″ − 1.5″ = 87.5″
$$= 7'{-}4'' \text{ (OK)}$$

The preliminary dimensioning of the bricks and the concrete masonry units is now complete.   ▷

Starting the Spandrel Detail   Now we can proceed with the construction of our preliminary spandrel detail for the building, working at a scale of 1½″ = 1′ (1:8), which is large enough so that we can see all the important features, including thicknesses of mortar joints and positions of flashings. We pencil in the slab and the perimeter beam. We show chamfers on the two lower edges of the beam to prevent breakage of the edges when the forms are removed (**Clean Edge**). We draw the concrete masonry units and their soft joint beneath the beam. We add a vertical layer 2″ thick against the outside of the backup wall and perimeter beam to indicate the polystyrene foam insulation in the cavity. We add another 2″ for the open portion of the cavity, which is the minimum width that masons can keep clean of mortar droppings, which otherwise would clog the weep holes at the bottom and form a water bridge between the wythes. Outside the cavity we lay out the 3⅝″ thickness of the brick facing wythe.

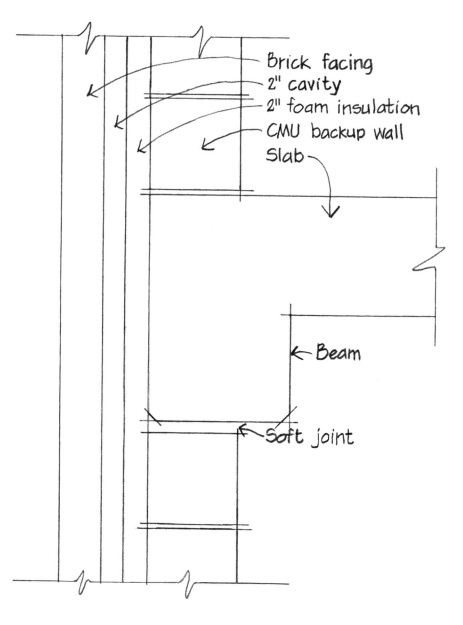

Brick facing
2″ cavity
2″ foam insulation
CMU backup wall
Slab

Beam

Soft joint

We have to choose an exact vertical position for the shelf angle. Obviously, it must be positioned immediately beneath a course of bricks. The brick coursing must match the concrete block coursing in order for the ties to connect, so we begin by working downward from the horizontal mortar joint where the blockwork rests on the floor slab. We would like to keep the shelf angle high on the concrete beam. This will minimize the amount of flashing material required and eliminate the need for masonry ties to penetrate the flashing—a situation that would have the potential for both water leaks and galvanic corrosion. A high shelf angle position will also minimize interference between the shelf angle and the flashings that will occur over window heads, as we shall see later. To achieve the code-mandated density of masonry ties, we must place ties 16″ apart both horizontally and vertically. This means that there will be ties in every second horizontal mortar joint in the backup wall. It is unwise to place ties and a flashing in the same mortar joint: There isn't space for both, and galvanic corrosion could result from contact of the dissimilar metals. Thus, a convenient location for the top surface of the shelf angle will be not lower than one block height below floor level, so the first row of ties can be placed on top of the first course of blocks, one course above the flashing. After trying this to scale on the drawing, we decide to place the shelf angle 3 brick courses, the same as 1 block course, below the top of the floor slab. ▷

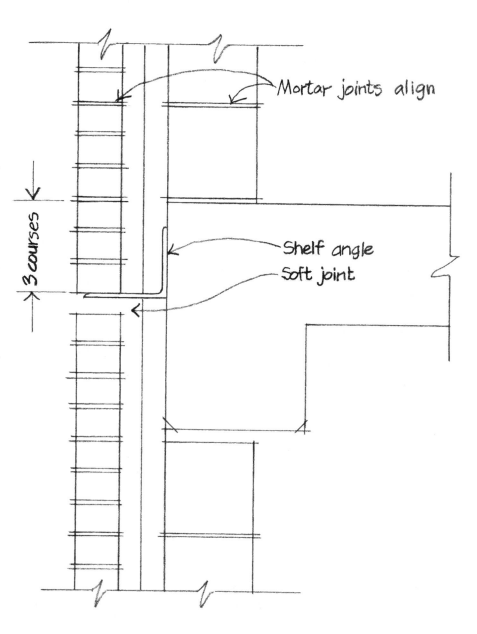

Mortar joints align

Shelf angle
Soft joint

3 courses

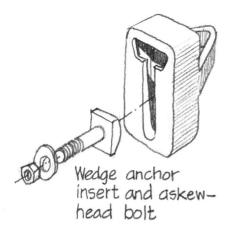

Wedge anchor insert and askew-head bolt

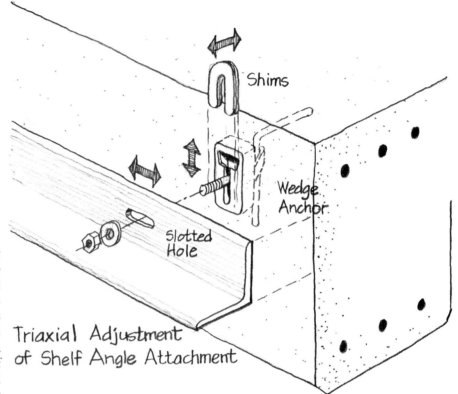

Triaxial Adjustment of Shelf Angle Attachment

We now turn our attention to the problem of fastening the shelf angle to the concrete structure. The structural engineer has proposed to do this with malleable iron wedge anchor inserts cast into the face of the concrete beam at 6′ intervals. In addition to having a high loadbearing capacity, this type of anchor allows for vertical dimensional adjustment by means of a sliding bolt with an askew (sloping) head that locks securely against the wedge-shaped front of the insert at any height. The shelf angle and its fasteners constitute a very important *Small Structure* designed by the engineer to be strong and stiff enough to support the facing safely. The angle itself is a 7″ × 6″ × ⅜″ steel shape that falls about ⅝″ short of the outer face of the brickwork, leaving space for sealant.

The wedge anchors provide ample *vertical* adjustment for inaccuracies, but what about the ±1″ tolerance in the *horizontal* location of the beam? If the beam falls a bit short of its correct location, we can make up the difference with steel shims inserted between the angle and the face of the concrete. If it falls far short, we can use an angle with an 8″ leg rather than a 7″ leg to avoid having to use a thick stack of shims. If the beam lies outside its correct location, an angle with a shorter leg may be required. The structural engineer will determine whether the longer and shorter angles need to have different thicknesses than the normal angle so that their stiffnesses will match. The shelf angles should be located

accurately by surveyors as the formwork is stripped from each floor, giving time to special order angles if necessary. The angles will be punched or drilled for the bolts at the fabricating plant, and we detail the holes to be horizontal slots that will allow considerable leeway for wedge inserts that were not accurately placed. Thus, we have provided a fully triaxial *Adjustable Fit* that will compensate for expected levels of inaccuracy in the making of the concrete frame: vertical adjustment with the wedge anchors, in-and-out adjustment with shims and different sizes of angles, and lateral adjustment with horizontally slotted bolt holes in the shelf angles. We make a note, nevertheless, to have the construction inspector see that formwork and wedge anchor locations are checked before the concrete is poured. The inspector should also be sure that all the wedge anchors are installed right side up, because a wedge anchor is only secure against loading in a direction that drives the askew head of the bolt more tightly against the wedge.

Tie in Dovetail Slot

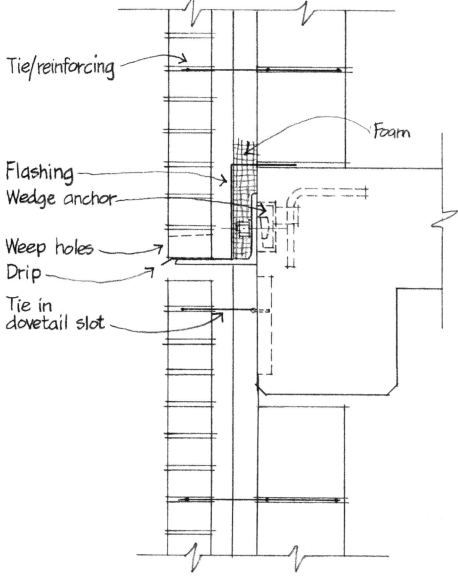

Tie/reinforcing

Flashing
Wedge anchor

Foam

Weep holes
Drip
Tie in dovetail slot

Ties and Flashings Returning to our drawing, we add the masonry courses and ties. We notice that there need to be ties that connect the brick facing to the spandrel beam above the top of the concrete masonry backup wall. We provide for these by installing vertical dovetail slots 16″ apart on the face of the concrete beam so that the masons can insert dovetail ties to the brick facing. The slots are small metal channels filled with low-density plastic foam. They are nailed to the inside of the formwork before the concrete is poured. The foam keeps the concrete from filling the slot but is easily removed by the masons as they install the ties.

We add to our drawing the continuous sheet of flashing that comes from beneath the backup wall, over the shelf angle. This catches any water that may enter the cavity and drains it through weep holes to the outdoors. There are several details of importance here: The flashing should go over the foam insulation rather than under, so that the foam cannot work loose and block the weep holes. This arrangement has the side benefit that the foam can serve to protect the flashing from being punctured by the bolt ends on the shelf angle. Notice that the flashing forms an *Upstand* about 8″ high to prevent the wind from driving water up into the backup wall. From page 29 we see that this 8″ dimension is sufficient to prevent leakage at a wind velocity of about 125 mph, far higher than occurs in this region. The flashing should project well beyond the toe of

the angle at a downward slope of 45° to form an *Overhang and Drip* that will shed water free of the wall instead of allowing it to seep back in. This means that the flashing should be of a material that is sufficiently stiff to form the drip and that is unaffected by sunlight. This rules out most plastic and synthetic rubber flashings. Copper sheet would be the best material, but in order to prevent galvanic corrosion it needs to be protected from contact with the zinc coating on the shelf angle (*Similar Metals*). We make a note to research and specify a flashing material that laminates copper between layers of inert materials for this purpose.

There are many ways to form weep holes: plastic or metal tubes laid in the mortar joints, cotton wicks, and so on. Believing in the virtues of simplicity and generosity, we choose to create large weep openings 2′ apart by simply omitting the mortar from every third head joint of the brick course immediately above the flashing. These tall, vertical openings allow for some accidental accumulation of mortar droppings at the base of the cavity, and they are easy for masons to make. ▷

Detailing the Soft Joint We need to look more closely at the construction of the shelf angle, soft joint, and flashing. For this we find that we need a larger scale of drawing, so we prepare a detail at one-half full size. The soft joint that we propose is unusually thick (⅜″, which is grossly inadequate for a concrete frame building, is a traditional standard). We have made the joint this thick because we are being extremely careful to allow for the creep and deflection that we expect in the concrete frame. We make a note to check the availability of sponge rubber compressible filler strips in the thickness we need. These should have an adhesive coating on one side so that the masons can adhere them to the undersides of the shelf angles.

The sealant joint at the toe of the angle also presents a couple of problems: There is not really enough space for a backer rod, and such a tall sealant joint may be difficult to make without the wet sealant sagging out before it cures. Perhaps we could use an adhesive bond breaker tape rather than a backer rod. As an alternative to a liquid sealant material, we find in the catalog file a precompressed sponge sealant strip that is inserted into the joint and expands to fill the gap. The sponge is saturated with a liquid sealant material that cures on exposure to the air.

Many architects try to hide the soft joint by minimizing its thickness, recessing the outer lip of the flashing into the mortar joint, and using L-shaped bricks to conceal its additional thickness. These are all dangerous expedients. A soft joint that is too thin will not be able to absorb all the movement that occurs, and the brick facing may be put under a structural load that will cause it to crack and buckle. A recessed flashing leads to a wet shelf angle that can corrode. The lips of L-shaped bricks are fragile and subject to freeze–thaw spalling.

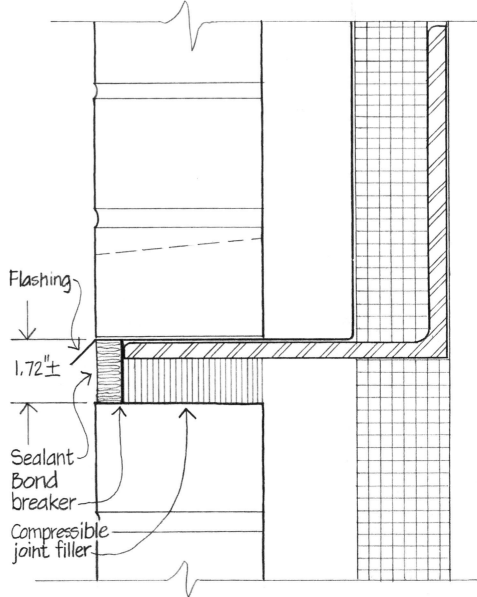

Flashing

1.72″±

Sealant

Bond breaker

Compressible joint filler

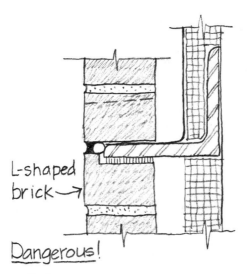

L-shaped brick →

Dangerous!

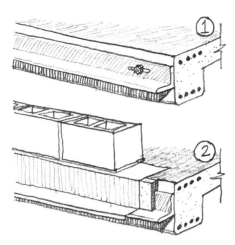

Detailing the Air Barrier Returning to the original section drawing, we *Rehearse the Construction Sequence* to see if it makes sense. First, ironworkers will install the shelf angles, setting them to accurate alignment marks that surveyors have left on the perimeter beams (1). Next the masons will begin their work by installing the foam strips and flashings over the shelf angles, lapping and sealing the flashings at end and corner junctions. Then they will lay the first course of concrete blocks in the backup wall, which brings them to the height at which the first strip of metal joint reinforcing and ties must be placed (2). This strip, once in place, will obstruct any further work in the cavity, so we realize that the air barrier, insulation, sealant at the column faces, and brick facing must be completed up to this level before the strip is installed. This forces us to think more deeply about these components of the wall.

A bit of catalog research reveals that there are two general types of air barrier materials available for cavity walls: flexible sheet materials that are cemented or fastened mechanically to the backup wall and asphaltic mastics that are troweled onto the wall. We note that some of the sheet materials are available in widths that are designed to match the every-second-block-course spacing of ties that we are using. This is handy, but we also notice that the sheet materials must be cut to fit around the ties, and a mastic must then be used to seal these penetrations. We also see

that for the cemented systems the blockwork must be primed with a coating that takes at least an hour to cure before the sheet material can be adhered. These all seem like severe disadvantages, especially the curing time, which might delay the progress of the work. Asphaltic mastics have none of these disadvantages. Compared to the sheet materials, they would simplify the masons' work greatly. However, if some mastic should slop onto the top surface of the concrete masonry, it would destroy the adhesive bond of the mortar to the blocks and weaken the wall. We decide to adopt a mastic air barrier, but we make a note to specify that it be held back 1″ from the upper edge of the blocks until the next two courses have been laid. We also note that the sealant joint where the backup wall meets each column must be completed before the mastic is spread, to avoid mastic contamination of the surfaces to which the sealant must adhere.

To rehearse again the masons' work thus far, they must install the first strip of foam insulation over the shelf angle, place the flashing, lay the first course of concrete blocks in the backup wall, install backer rod and sealant on the outside face where this course meets the columns at either end (the inside sealant joints can be done later), and trowel on the air barrier mastic. Then they must install the next strip of foam insulation, only 8″ high, pressing it into the wet mastic. This raises a problem: We were going to specify that the mastic coating be held 1″ below the top of the concrete masonry, to be continued from that level after the next block courses have been laid. But once the foam insulation is installed, it will be impossible to get behind its top edge with a trowel to continue the mastic work as an unbroken air barrier membrane. We must rethink the sequence.

Suppose that we have the masons do everything as we have already planned but leave out the foam for the moment, constructing the first six courses of brickwork instead. Then they could place the strip of foam insu-

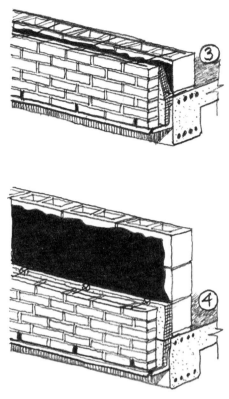

lation loosely in the cavity, install the joint reinforcing and tie strip above the insulation (3), and lay the next two courses of backup blocks. At this point the backup wall would be 16″ higher than the brick facing. The masons could then apply the sealant at the junction between the columns and the backup wall, and trowel on the next strip of mastic, spreading it carefully to seal around the ties and over the top edge of the previous strip of mastic. Next they could reach through the ties into the cavity to push the 8″ strip of insulating board into position, locking it in place with standard plastic clips that snap over the ties (4). This would seem to work smoothly, presenting no problems of worker access. Each clip is designed to hold the top of one sheet and the bottom of the next. The strip of foam just above the flashing would have no bottom restraint, but we could get around this by asking the masons to daub some spots of mastic onto the back of the foam with the tip of the trowel just before pushing it into place and installing the clips.   ▷

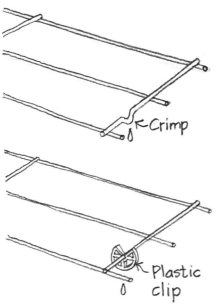

←Crimp

←Plastic
clip

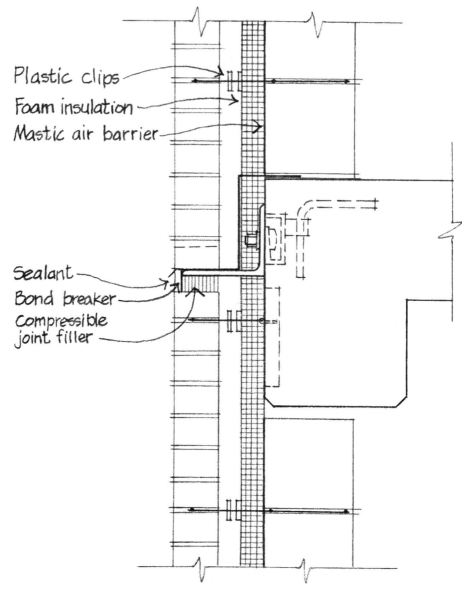

Plastic clips
Foam insulation
Mastic air barrier

Sealant
Bond breaker
Compressible
joint filler

Many types of masonry ties have a V-shaped crimp located at the midpoint of the cavity. Its function is to act as a *Drip* to keep adhering drops of water from working their way across the tie from the outer wythe to the inner wythe. The crimp reduces the structural stiffness of the tie, so our structural engineer proposes that we not include it in the ties we are using. We note in the tie manufacturer's catalog, however, that the clip we are using to retain the insulation boards may also be used to create a drip on each tie. This will require a second clip on each tie, because the clip that is pushed up tightly against the insulation cannot drip free into the cavity.

The combination joint reinforcing and tie strips that we have selected neatly solve the problems of reinforcing the backup wall in a horizontal direction, providing ties between the backup and face wythes of masonry, reinforcing the face wythe, and creating the code-mandated mechanical connection between the face wythe reinforcing and the ties. These strips are welded from steel wire and then galvanized (zinc coated) to retard rust. But galvanizing is not a permanent cure for rust; if the outer wythe leaks water into the cavity or if the mortar joints allow moisture to reach the embedded wires, both of which are

likely to occur during the life of the building, then the zinc coating will gradually disintegrate and the wires will ultimately rust. Given the owner's insistence on durability and our own desire to construct a building that will not start to fall apart a few decades from now, we will specify stainless steel wire rather than galvanized carbon steel. The additional expense expressed as a percentage of the overall cost of the building will be very small. We will specify a very heavy zinc coating for the shelf angles, which are sheltered by the overhanging flashing and sealant joint and are less likely to be exposed to water.

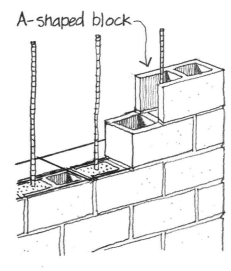

A-shaped block

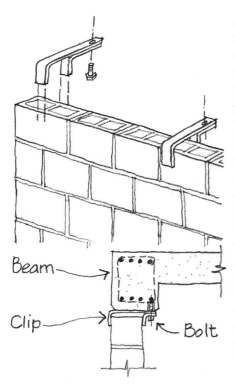

Beam

Clip

Bolt

Detailing the Backup Wall The backup wall must be engineered very carefully, because it supports the air barrier mastic and the brick facing against wind and seismic loads (*Small Structures*). The structural engineer has chosen the type of concrete masonry units, the thickness of the wall, the size and frequency of the horizontal joint reinforcement and ties, and the size and frequency of the vertical reinforcing bars in this wall on the basis of wind and seismic load calculations. He has determined that the friction between the base of the backup wall and the floor slab is sufficient to transmit the lateral loads between them. At the top, where the wall joins the perimeter beam, a mechanical connection must be made to transmit lateral loads from the wall to the beam. The engineer furnishes a sketch of a clip that he is designing for this purpose. There will be several such clips in each bay. Each will be bent from steel plate, drilled, galvanized, and attached with a machine screw and expansion sleeve into a hole drilled into the underside of the perimeter beam. The clip joins the beam in a *Sliding Fit* that easily accommodates any inaccuracies. The engineer will furnish exact numbers and dimensions of the clips later, as the details develop.

Rehearsing the next portion of the construction sequence, we visualize the masons laying the first few courses of concrete blocks, inserting joint reinforcement as they go, and bringing up the air barrier coating and brick facing as previously described. Then they will insert the vertical reinforcing bars into the cores of the blocks as directed by the structural drawings and grout the cores that have bars in them. These bars will project upward and extend almost to the bottom of the perimeter beam, making it impossible to thread succeeding courses of blocks over them. From this point up they will have to use A-shaped blocks that can be installed easily around the reinforcing; these are a standard shape that is readily available. After the backup wall has been erected in each bay, the lateral load clips will be installed. Then the soft joint will be created between the top of the wall and the underside of the perimeter beam, using a compressible joint filler strip in the center of the wall, and a backer rod and sealant on each face.

▷

Detailing the Interior Finishes We now turn our attention to adding the interior finishes to our detail of the spandrel. Vertical, galvanized steel, hat-shaped furring strips (a stock item) will be fastened to the wall 16″ apart with powder-actuated fasteners, and foil-backed veneer plaster base will be screwed to the furring strips. (Veneer plaster base is commonly called "blueboard." It is a gypsum board that is designed to serve as a base for a thin coating of veneer plaster.) Electrical wiring for wall receptacles will be run in a metal conduit; we note that a gap should be left in the furring strips for this purpose (**Horizontal Plenum**). A standard 1½″ deep electrical box will just fit in the thickness provided by the furring and plaster.

The clips that restrain the top of the backup wall must be covered with a finish layer, so we furr and plaster the beam as well as the wall. Because of the potential for movement in the soft joint between the perimeter beam and the backup wall, we use a resilient vinyl trim bead, a stock item from the gypsum supplier's catalog, to provide a movement joint between the plaster wall and the plaster soffit under the beam.

At the base of the wall, we install a wood baseboard (**Building Armor**) using finish screws that, like finish nails, are almost headless, to attach it through the plaster to the metal furring strips. To keep the plaster flat and firm behind the baseboard, we show a horizontal furring strip at the base of the wall. After the baseboard is in place, the pad and carpet can be installed, using a tackless strip to form a neat edge against the baseboard. A call to our acoustic consultant brings bad news, however: A floor detail that consists of a carpet and thick pad over a 10″ concrete slab has an Impact Insulation Class of about 70, which is excellent, but its Sound Transmission Class (STC) is only about 53, which is below stan-

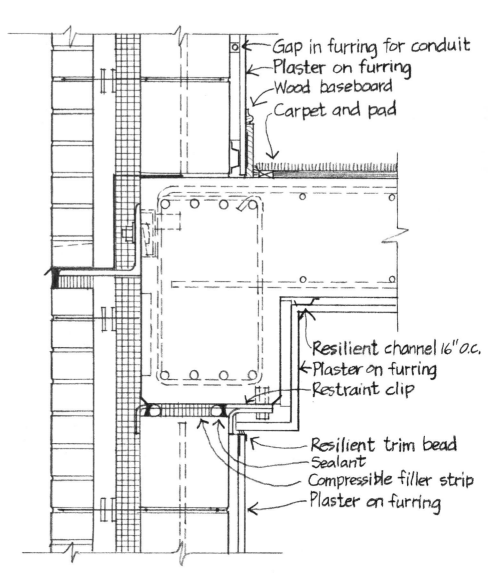

Gap in furring for conduit
Plaster on furring
Wood baseboard
Carpet and pad

Resilient channel 16″ o.c.
Plaster on furring
Restraint clip

Resilient trim bead
Sealant
Compressible filler strip
Plaster on furring

dard for a building of this quality. She would like us to install suspended plaster ceilings with acoustic batts on top. We would like to avoid doing this, because it is extremely expensive, not only because of the cost of the ceiling itself, but also because it would add a few inches of height to each story of the building, adding column height and exterior wall area as well as requiring a more heavily braced structure for the taller building. After a few telephone calls back and forth, we settle on a compromise: Rather than just paint the underside of the slab, we will install

a ⅝″ veneer plaster ceiling, screwing it to resilient metal channels that are fastened directly to the underside of the slab. This will raise the STC to approximately 60, which she considers acceptable. Because the channels are only ½″ deep, we can accommodate the entire ceiling assembly in the story height we have already established.

We have now completed the design of the spandrel detail. A fully annotated, accurately drawn version of this detail is shown at the end of this section of the book.

DETAILING THE WINDOW OPENINGS

Our basic spandrel section is now complete and becomes the base drawing from which we can prepare the other detail sections. On the first of these, we will work out the installation of windows. For this we rely heavily on the window manufacturer's suggested details, which are conveniently presented in its catalog at the same scale that we are using: 1½″ = 1′. We photocopy these catalog details so that we can slide them under our drawing paper and trace them.

The window selection process began early in the building design process, based on the client's expressed preference for casement windows and a satisfactory set of building elevations that uses a combination of casements and fixed sash. We selected the manufacturer as one who is reputable, makes a good product, and has good technical representatives to help with design, ordering, and installation problems. Also important is the manufacturer's willingness to make custom sizes of windows, because it is virtually impossible to fit stock sizes of windows into brickwork without cutting bricks or using exposed filler strips around the window units. We will work out masonry opening dimensions for windows that fit the brick and block coursing, and the windows will be manufactured to fit these openings. Using the standards of the National Wood Window and Door Association (*Accepted Standards*), we choose a Grade 60 window as being

Precast concrete lintel

appropriate to the weather exposure in the area where we are building.

Before beginning our window details, we think about the process of installation. We could have the masons build the window units into the walls as they go, but this has serious disadvantages. The masons are already working with a number of different materials and components—blocks of several sizes and types, bricks, mortar, flashings, two different kinds of ties, insulation boards and clips, air barrier mastic, backer rod, sealant, compressible filler strips, lintels—and we would like not to complicate their task any further (*Minimum Number of Parts*). The inevitable mortar droppings from

masonry work above could damage the glass and frames. And undoubtedly the masons will find it very convenient to use the unobstructed window openings as access and supply points. So we will detail in such a way that the windows can be installed after the masons have finished their work.

The head of the window falls one block course below the perimeter beam. We could support this line of blocks across the window opening on a steel lintel, but this would seem to be laborious and expensive. Instead, we could show a precast concrete lintel that is the same in cross-sectional dimensions as the course of concrete masonry and 16″ longer than the width of the masonry opening for the window. This extra length gives a good bearing on the wall at each end and exactly replaces a half-block on each end. The masons could lay the lintel into the wall as if it were simply a long concrete block. There is a catch, however: We calculate that a typical lintel weighs about 300 pounds, which will require at least four masons to lift, unless a small, hand-operated hoist can be used from inside the building. The precast lintel is definitely not a *Part That is Easy to Handle*. Perhaps the masonry contractor would prefer to use a steel lintel after all or to make a reinforced block lintel using temporary centering, U-shaped blocks, rebars, and grout, all of which are easy to handle. We will offer these as alternatives and let the contractor choose.

▷

To express the window openings more prominently on the exterior of the building, we want to place a soldier course of bricks over each lintel. We use a steel angle lintel to support the brick facing across the window opening. As with any horizontal interruption of the cavity, we must flash and weep over the window unit and lintels to catch and drain any water that may leak through the brick facing. This necessitates a reglet (*Overlap*) in the face of the beam. We see that the dovetail slots will have to be shortened above the windows to make this possible. We decide to use a cut limestone sill to avoid the leakage and deterioration of rowlock brick sills that are likely in this severe climate. We install another flashing beneath the sill to deal with leakage between the sill and the window unit, or through any defects in the sill. Both the head and sill flashings must be continued longitudinally past the jambs of the window and terminated with an end dam; we will show this with a pictorial view in the final working drawings and will mention it in the specifications, because, if it is omitted, spillage of water off the end of the flashing can cause severe leakage. Both flashings must also terminate at the outdoor side in an *Overhang and Drip*, and we must provide weep holes over both flashings. The weeps over the sill flashing are

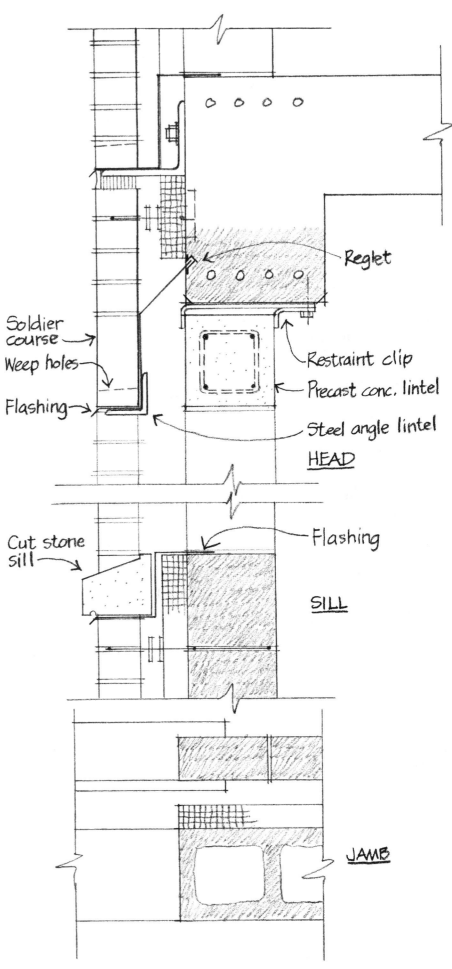

Reglet

Soldier course →

Weep holes →

Flashing →

Restraint clip

Precast conc. lintel

Steel angle lintel

HEAD

Flashing

Cut stone sill →

SILL

JAMB

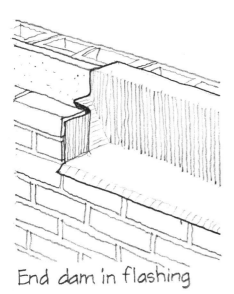

End dam in flashing

created by laying pieces of clothesline rope into the mortar under the stone sill and then pulling them out after the mortar has hardened a bit.

The easiest installation process for wood windows is one that mimics the installation of windows in a wood frame dwelling. After leveling and shimming the window unit, nails are simply driven through an exterior flange, or through the window frame itself, into the wood framing to attach the unit. We must modify this procedure in a couple of respects for our brick cavity wall, fastening through the frame rather than a flange and using screws rather than nails to avoid the impact of hammering, which might crack or dislodge masonry units from the wall. We will mimic the wood frame of the house by installing a rough frame of preservative-treated wood in the cavity. Then the window unit can be slid into the frame from inside the building, leveled and shimmed, and attached with finish screws.

We decide to fasten the rough frame to the backup wythe only, to avoid a rigid connection between two wythes that need to be able to move independently. Also, the backup wythe is the one that is designed to bear the wind load, including the wind load from the window itself. We design the rough wood frame for easy installation. A piece will be installed in each of the

jambs first, attached to the backup wall with powder-driven studs through sheet metal plates. Then the sill piece can be lowered into the cavity by holding onto two metal clips, and attached to the jamb pieces with screws driven through perforated sheet metal angles at the corners. The metal clips, besides offering convenient installation handles, also join the sill to the backup blocks. Glass fiber insulation is stuffed lightly beneath the head flashing. The head piece goes in last and is fastened to the jamb pieces in the same manner as the sill.

Once the rough frame is complete, the window installation becomes easy. Two carpenters slide the window unit into the opening, center it carefully between the jambs (the masonry and the rough frame have a generous *Installation Clearance* all around), align and level the sill (shimming as necessary with wedges of wood shingle, *Adjustable Fit*), and screw down the sill to the rough frame. Then they square the frame of the window unit and check to see that each jamb is shimmed plumb before fastening the jambs and head. The last task is to insert backer rods and sealant around all four sides of the window unit, outside and in, to create air and water seals. If a water leak should occur in or around the window unit, the water will be caught and drained by the sill flashing.   ▷

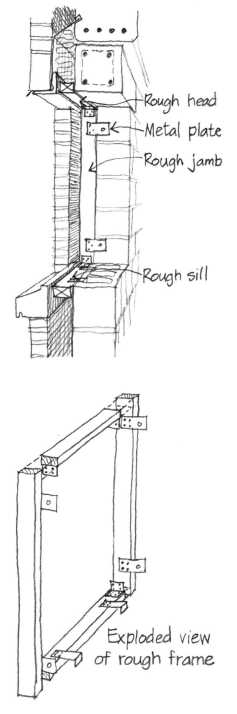

Rough head
Metal plate
Rough jamb

Rough sill

Exploded view of rough frame

We construct an outside elevation of a typical window at the same scale as the section, to see how our details look from another vantage point. We see that in order to lock the stone sill into the wall it will have to project a half-brick length into the wall at either end. This will also place its flashing end dams sufficiently outside the jamb of the window to catch any leakage from the vertical sealant joints. It will necessitate a sill design with level lugs that project above the sloping *Wash* of the sill to support the brickwork at the jambs.

We lay out all the bricks carefully on the elevation and notice that only masonry openings that are multiples of a full brick length will be symmetrical, something we make a note to consider when we are choosing window dimensions. We also see that the lintel looks best if the course just below it terminates with full bricks at the window opening, thus eliminating a weak-looking vertical alignment of head joints. We will work backward from this to specify how the first brick course will be laid out on the shelf angle. We experiment with the idea of using specially molded bricks, such as quarter-rounds, for the jambs: They add a good deal of character at relatively little cost, but their use necessitates more expensively shaped lugs on the sill. We will think it over as the overall design progresses.

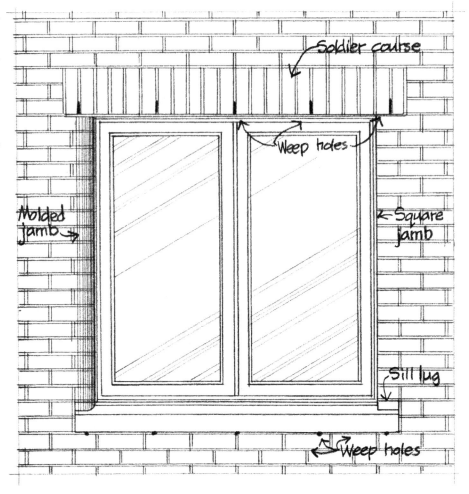

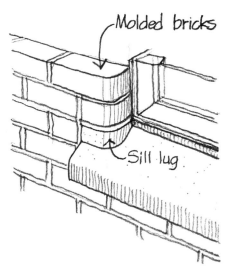

We return to our window sections. Inside, we continue the plaster at the window head to meet the frame of the window—a simple, elegant, and inexpensive detail. We do the same with the jambs. At the sill, we decide to install a marble stool, because a wood stool so wide would be likely to cup. A wood apron molding finishes the gap between the stool and the plaster. We make a perspective sketch to be sure that the interior finish details of the window will give the desired appearance. The preliminary version of the window details is now complete. We check carefully to be sure each element lies in the same plane in head, jamb, and sill details. ▷

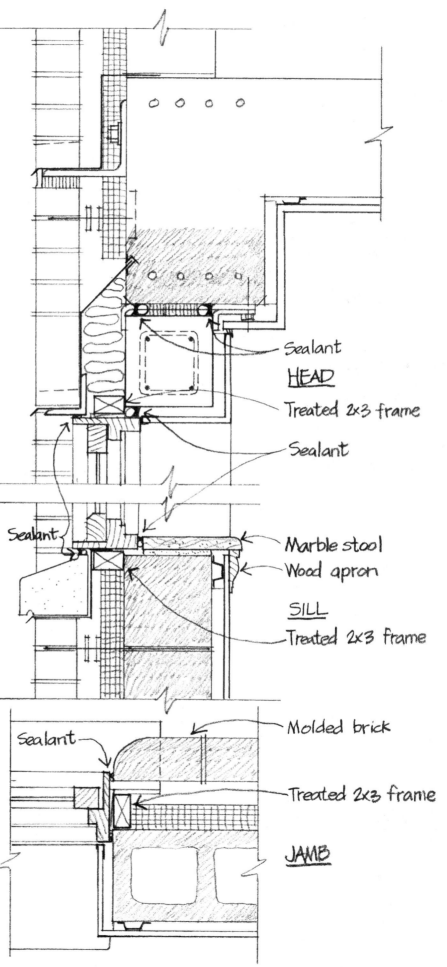

Sealant

HEAD

Treated 2x3 frame

Sealant

Sealant

Marble stool

Wood apron

SILL

Treated 2x3 frame

Sealant

Molded brick

Treated 2x3 frame

JAMB

DETAILING THE CORNERS AND COLUMNS

Now we develop a detail of the wall at the same scale, but in horizontal section (plan view), examining what happens at the columns and at the corners of the building. The basic arrangement of the components follows almost automatically from the spandrel detail developed earlier. We add dovetail slots and anchors to tie the ends of the brick wall segments to the columns. In accordance with the joint pattern worked out earlier in elevation view, we show the *Expansion Joint* in the brick facing at the centers of the columns. At the outside corner of the building, we must add an expansion joint to allow plenty of dimension for differential expansion and contraction of the adjacent wall planes as the sun moves around the building. We try first to do this with a single joint a half-brick length from the corner, but this seems weak both physically and visually. Instead we settle on two joints at each corner, centered on the adjacent faces of the column. We add to the detail the *Structure/Enclosure Joints* where the backup wall meets the columns. We don't bother to insert movement joints in the foam plastic insulation boards, because the foam is so weak and pliable that it simply compresses or expands very slightly as movement occurs.

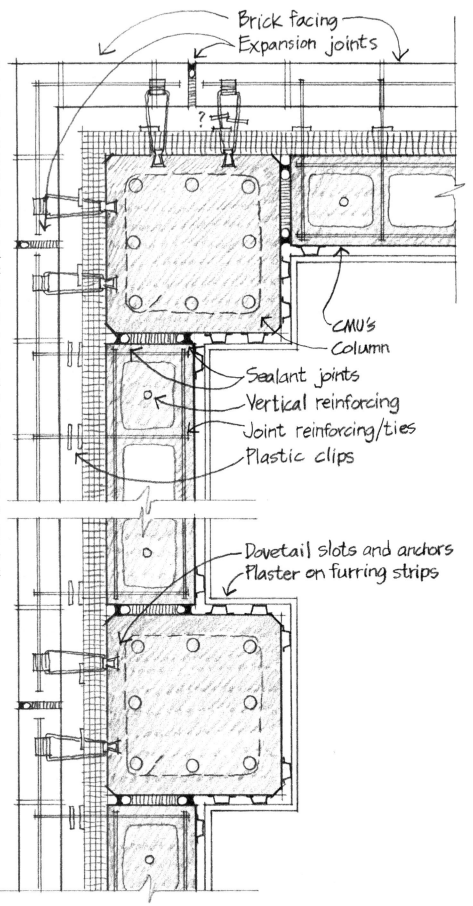

Brick facing
Expansion joints

CMU's
Column

Sealant joints
Vertical reinforcing
Joint reinforcing/ties
Plastic clips

Dovetail slots and anchors
Plaster on furring strips

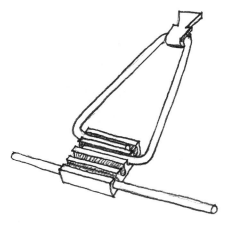

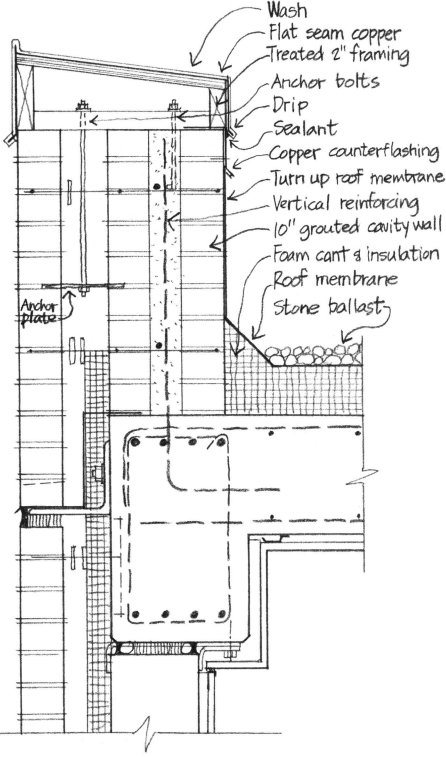

Wash
Flat seam copper
Treated 2" framing
Anchor bolts
Drip
Sealant
Copper counterflashing
Turn up roof membrane
Vertical reinforcing
10" grouted cavity wall
Foam cant & insulation
Roof membrane
Stone ballast

Anchor plate

We recognize in this drawing that the dovetail anchors do not satisfy the building code requirement of tying mechanically to reinforcing in the joints of the brickwork. We find in the catalogs a tie manufacturer who can furnish plastic clips that lie in the mortar joint and accomplish this purpose. It is unclear whether it will be feasible to install two drip clips on each dovetail tie, because of the close spacing of the two wires. We will have to obtain samples and try them out.

DETAILING THE PARAPET

Masonry parapets should be avoided whenever possible. Because they are exposed to the weather on both sides they tend to leak, and they experience more thermal expansion and contraction than the walls below, which often leads to severe cracking between the parapet and the walls of the top story. On this project, however, we are required by local code to have a parapet. Working on a tracing paper overlay over the basic wall section, we make a horizontal mark 30″ above the roof slab, the legally required minimum height for a parapet. We use the standard shelf angle support and extend the brick facing up to near this mark. We also extend the backup wall, but to avoid problems of differential expansion and contraction we will build it entirely of brickwork rather than concrete masonry. To keep the parapet in place against wind and seismic loads we build the backup wall as a reinforced brick wall: Dowels of reinforcing bar that emerge from the roof slab are grouted into the cavity. Horizontal reinforcing for the wall is provided by the same wire joint reinforcement and tie combination that is used in the walls below. Both the facing and the backup wall are cut completely by sealed expansion joints at the column lines.   ▷

A standard coping detail for this parapet would feature cut stone or precast concrete coping sections placed on top of a continuous flashing at the top of the wall, held in place by dowels that project through the flashing. This detail does not satisfy us, because we are afraid that mountain storm winds or earthquakes could dislodge the stones. There are proprietary aluminum coping systems available, but we don't think they would look good on this building. We invent, instead, a coping that is built in place of preservative-treated wood and plywood, and sheathed in copper; we will have to compare its cost with the heavier alternatives. It features a *Wash* that directs water back toward the roof to prevent staining of the facade, an *Overhang and Drip* on each side, and anchor bolts that fasten the whole coping assembly securely to the masonry. One bolt is simply embedded in the grouted core of the backup wall; the other reaches deep into the open cavity, through a galvanized steel anchor plate, to engage enough weight of brickwork to avoid being pulled off by high winds. The copper sheets that cap the parapet are applied with ordinary flat-seam roofing technology. The copper counterflashing beneath the coping overlaps the turned-up edge of the roof membrane to protect the back of the parapet completely from water.

It is impossible to eliminate the thermal bridge that occurs where the parapet joins the roof slab. To minimize the thermal transfer, we run the foam in the cavity well up into the parapet, creating a rather long path that heat must travel through concrete and masonry in order to move in or out of the building.

DETAILING THE GRADE CONDITION

Having developed details for the floor edges, windows, corners, columns, and parapet, we now address the matter of how the building meets the ground. We would like to get the brickwork close to the ground in order to avoid showing large expanses of the foundation walls. The foundation walls must have *Thermal Insulation*, preferably located on the outside for *Outside-Insulated Thermal Mass*. We have a rough detail from the structural engineer that shows the structural slab of the ground floor supported on the top of the concrete foundation wall and doweled to it with reinforcing bars. We begin the design of this intersection by sketching a freehand detail on tracing paper laid alternately over the typical spandrel detail and the structural engineer's detail, trying to bring the two together. We rest the backup wall on the structural slab and the brick facing on the top of the wall, but we must increase the engineer's 12″ wall to a 16″ thickness to make this work. We bring 2″ of polystyrene foam insulation up the outside of the foundation wall and find that it meets the flashing at the bottom of the brick facing in an awkward way. There is also a large thermal bridge

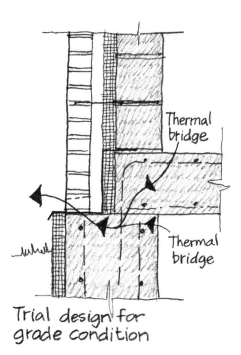

Trial design for grade condition

through the edge of the slab and the top of the foundation wall.

Looking for a better alternative, we abandon this sketch for the moment and try another, this time using the same shelf angle detail as in the rest of the wall. Suddenly the particulars of the detail all fall into place: The concrete wall drops back to the desired 12″ thickness. The insulation that emerges from the ground can be turned back under the shelf angle to form a *Thermal Break*. We adopt this detail and finish it: The basement wall must be dampproofed before the insulating boards are applied. Where the insulation is exposed above ground level, we can protect and finish it with galvanized stucco lath and the same polymer-modified stucco materials used in EIFS cladding. We leave a space between the foam and the angle, protect it with an ***Overhang and Drip*** on the flashing, and seal it with a backer rod and sealant. We make a note to be sure that grade never approaches closer than 6″ to this joint, to protect the angle from corrosion and to keep the weep holes clear at the base of the brick facing. We assure good ***Foundation Drainage*** by sloping the ground away from the buildings (***Wash***) and by installing a porous drainage panel on the outside of the insulation that will conduct groundwater to a system of drainage pipes around the footings.

Checking for Thermal Bridges We examine the perimeters of the conditioned spaces on all the exterior details, looking for thermal bridges. The polystyrene foam insulation does a remarkably good job of wrapping the building. The only serious breach in this insulating layer, as we noted earlier, is where the backup wall emerges through it at the parapet. The masonry ties and shelf angles throughout the wall are also thermal bridges but constitute such small cross sections of metal that they conduct very little heat.

▷

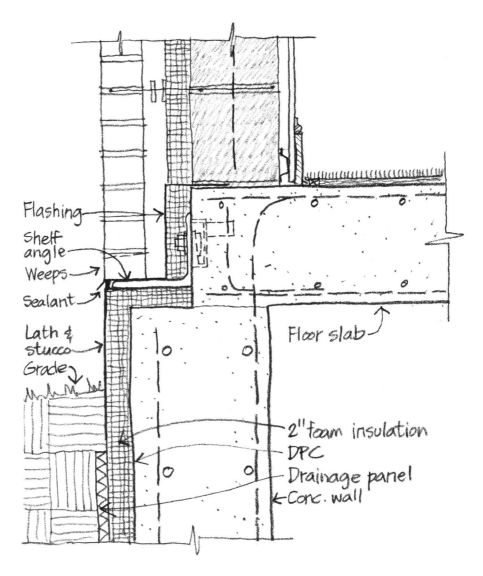

Elevation Studies   In designing these preliminary details, we have made many decisions that affect the appearance of the building both inside and out. We have laid a grid of movement joints onto the facades, have designed a parapet coping and window surrounds, and have detailed the way in which the building meets the ground. Now we visualize the cumulative effect of these decisions by overlaying a tracing paper sketch on one of the original design elevations. When we first drew the design elevation, before the design of the details began, we had only a vague idea of how the building would be put together. Now we are working with a tangible, buildable reality, and we find ourselves in the powerful position of knowing how the building is put together and how to change it to make it exactly what we want it to be. We summarize our work on the design of the details in a set of accurately constructed drawings.

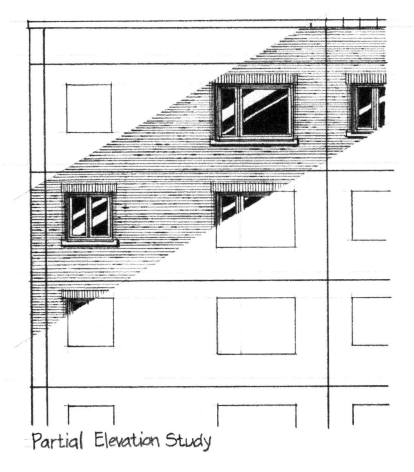

Partial Elevation Study

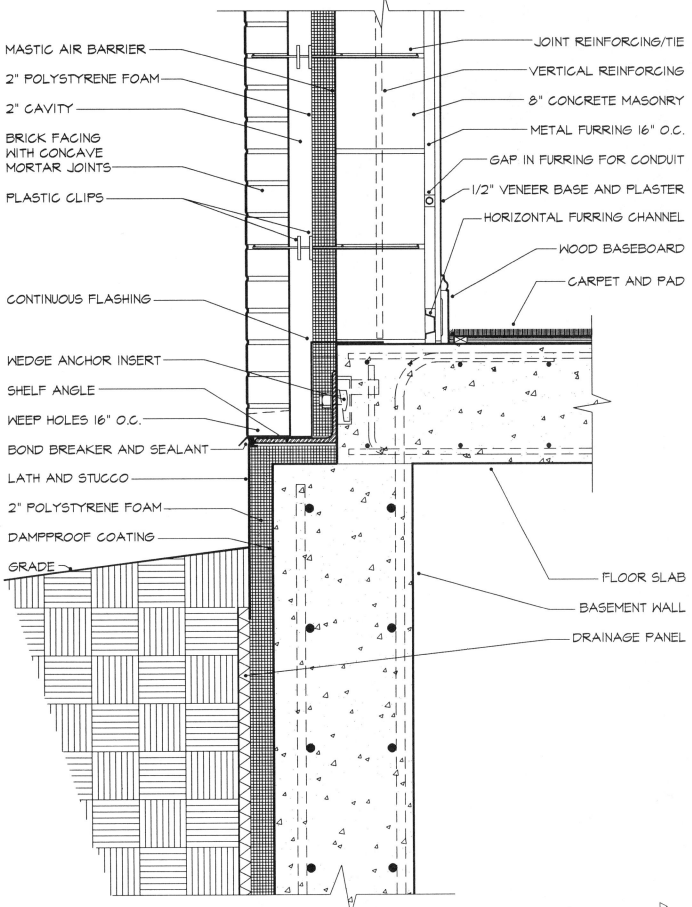

MASTIC AIR BARRIER

2" POLYSTYRENE FOAM

2" CAVITY

BRICK FACING
WITH CONCAVE
MORTAR JOINTS

PLASTIC CLIPS

CONTINUOUS FLASHING

WEDGE ANCHOR INSERT

SHELF ANGLE

WEEP HOLES 16" O.C.

BOND BREAKER AND SEALANT

LATH AND STUCCO

2" POLYSTYRENE FOAM

DAMPPROOF COATING

GRADE

JOINT REINFORCING/TIE

VERTICAL REINFORCING

8" CONCRETE MASONRY

METAL FURRING 16" O.C.

GAP IN FURRING FOR CONDUIT

1/2" VENEER BASE AND PLASTER

HORIZONTAL FURRING CHANNEL

WOOD BASEBOARD

CARPET AND PAD

FLOOR SLAB

BASEMENT WALL

DRAINAGE PANEL

SECTION AT GRADE
Scale 1 1/2"=1'

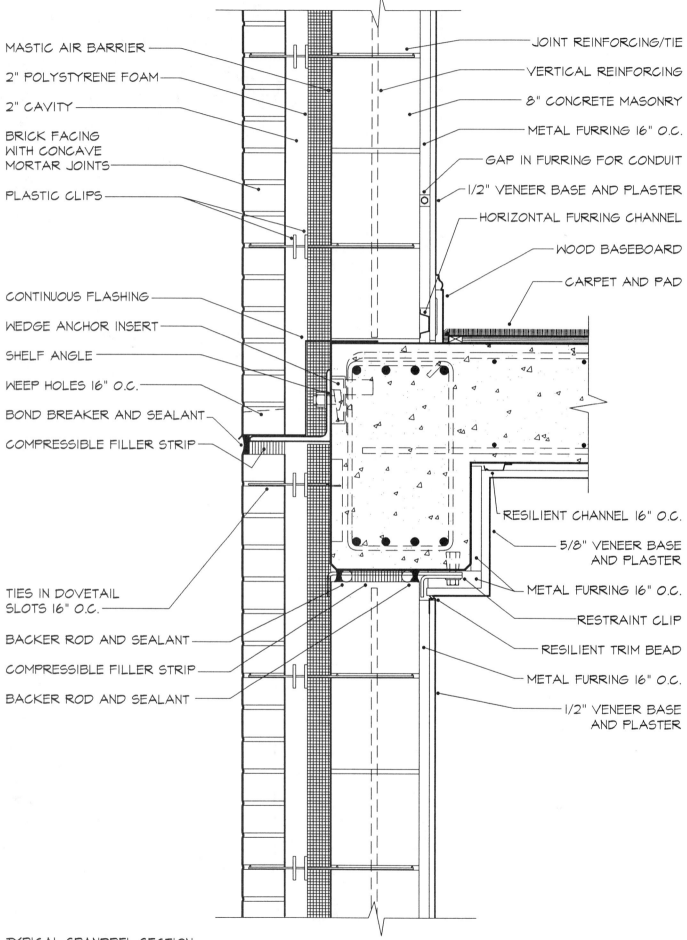

MASTIC AIR BARRIER

2" POLYSTYRENE FOAM

2" CAVITY

BRICK FACING
WITH CONCAVE
MORTAR JOINTS

PLASTIC CLIPS

CONTINUOUS FLASHING

WEDGE ANCHOR INSERT

SHELF ANGLE

WEEP HOLES 16" O.C.

BOND BREAKER AND SEALANT

COMPRESSIBLE FILLER STRIP

TIES IN DOVETAIL
SLOTS 16" O.C.

BACKER ROD AND SEALANT

COMPRESSIBLE FILLER STRIP

BACKER ROD AND SEALANT

JOINT REINFORCING/TIE

VERTICAL REINFORCING

8" CONCRETE MASONRY

METAL FURRING 16" O.C.

GAP IN FURRING FOR CONDUIT

1/2" VENEER BASE AND PLASTER

HORIZONTAL FURRING CHANNEL

WOOD BASEBOARD

CARPET AND PAD

RESILIENT CHANNEL 16" O.C.

5/8" VENEER BASE
AND PLASTER

METAL FURRING 16" O.C.

RESTRAINT CLIP

RESILIENT TRIM BEAD

METAL FURRING 16" O.C.

1/2" VENEER BASE
AND PLASTER

TYPICAL SPANDREL SECTION
Scale: 1 1/2"=1'

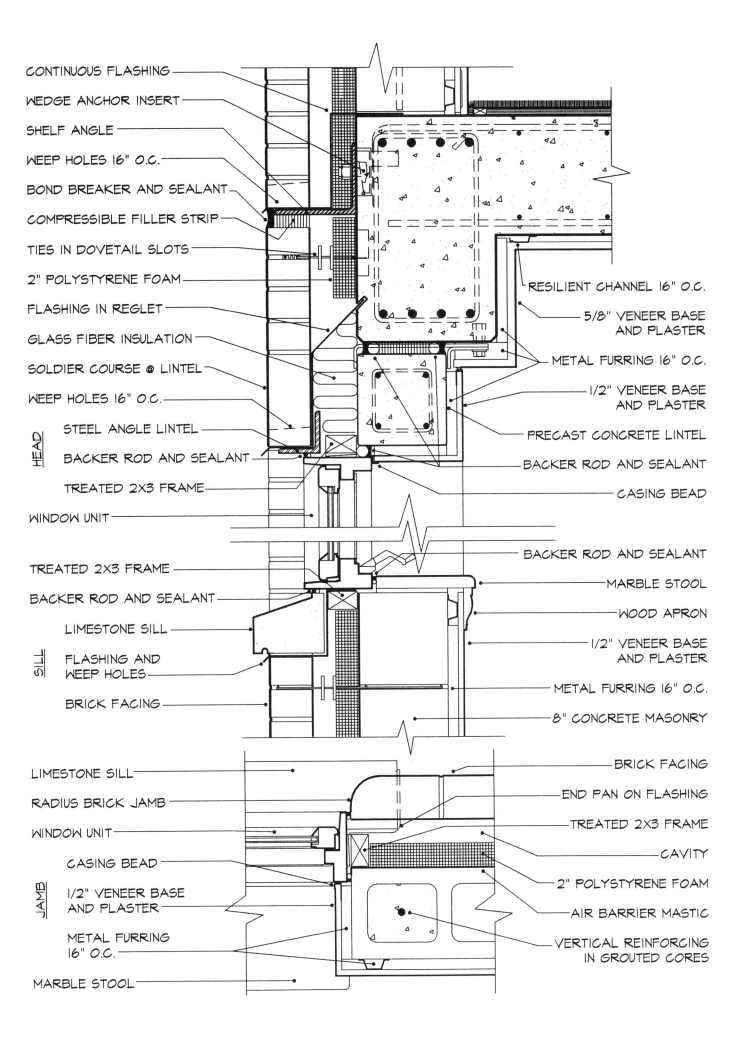

CONTINUOUS FLASHING

WEDGE ANCHOR INSERT

SHELF ANGLE

WEEP HOLES 16" O.C.

BOND BREAKER AND SEALANT

COMPRESSIBLE FILLER STRIP

TIES IN DOVETAIL SLOTS

2" POLYSTYRENE FOAM

FLASHING IN REGLET

GLASS FIBER INSULATION

SOLDIER COURSE @ LINTEL

WEEP HOLES 16" O.C.

STEEL ANGLE LINTEL

BACKER ROD AND SEALANT

TREATED 2X3 FRAME

WINDOW UNIT

HEAD

RESILIENT CHANNEL 16" O.C.

5/8" VENEER BASE AND PLASTER

METAL FURRING 16" O.C.

1/2" VENEER BASE AND PLASTER

PRECAST CONCRETE LINTEL

BACKER ROD AND SEALANT

CASING BEAD

TREATED 2X3 FRAME

BACKER ROD AND SEALANT

LIMESTONE SILL

FLASHING AND WEEP HOLES

BRICK FACING

SILL

BACKER ROD AND SEALANT

MARBLE STOOL

WOOD APRON

1/2" VENEER BASE AND PLASTER

METAL FURRING 16" O.C.

8" CONCRETE MASONRY

LIMESTONE SILL

RADIUS BRICK JAMB

WINDOW UNIT

CASING BEAD

1/2" VENEER BASE AND PLASTER

METAL FURRING 16" O.C.

MARBLE STOOL

JAMB

BRICK FACING

END PAN ON FLASHING

TREATED 2X3 FRAME

CAVITY

2" POLYSTYRENE FOAM

AIR BARRIER MASTIC

VERTICAL REINFORCING IN GROUTED CORES

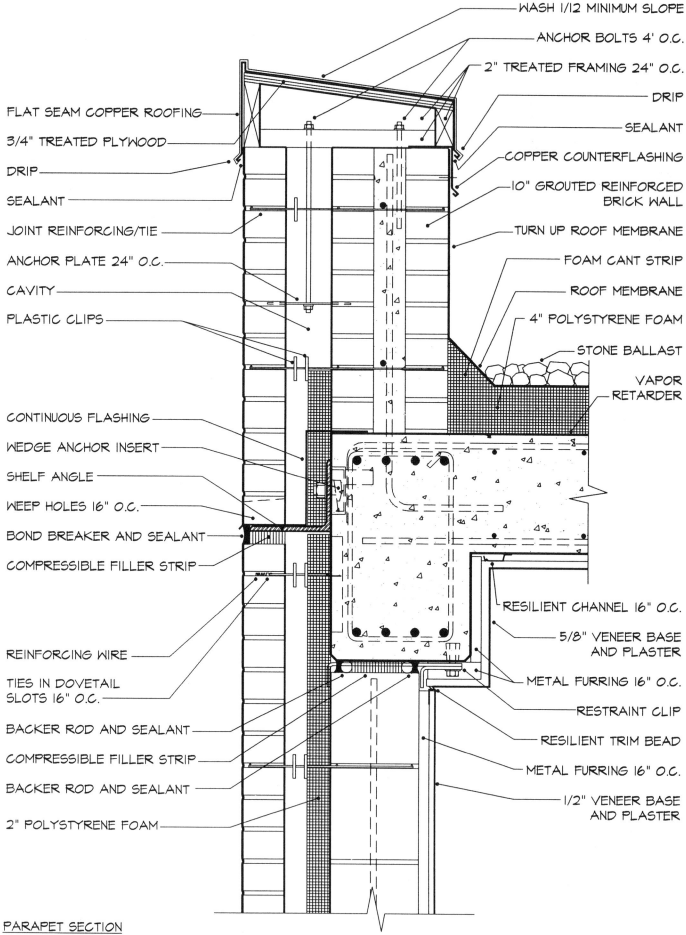

WASH 1/12 MINIMUM SLOPE

ANCHOR BOLTS 4' O.C.

2" TREATED FRAMING 24" O.C.

DRIP

SEALANT

COPPER COUNTERFLASHING

10" GROUTED REINFORCED BRICK WALL

TURN UP ROOF MEMBRANE

FOAM CANT STRIP

ROOF MEMBRANE

4" POLYSTYRENE FOAM

STONE BALLAST

VAPOR RETARDER

RESILIENT CHANNEL 16" O.C.

5/8" VENEER BASE AND PLASTER

METAL FURRING 16" O.C.

RESTRAINT CLIP

RESILIENT TRIM BEAD

METAL FURRING 16" O.C.

1/2" VENEER BASE AND PLASTER

FLAT SEAM COPPER ROOFING

3/4" TREATED PLYWOOD

DRIP

SEALANT

JOINT REINFORCING/TIE

ANCHOR PLATE 24" O.C.

CAVITY

PLASTIC CLIPS

CONTINUOUS FLASHING

WEDGE ANCHOR INSERT

SHELF ANGLE

WEEP HOLES 16" O.C.

BOND BREAKER AND SEALANT

COMPRESSIBLE FILLER STRIP

REINFORCING WIRE

TIES IN DOVETAIL SLOTS 16" O.C.

BACKER ROD AND SEALANT

COMPRESSIBLE FILLER STRIP

BACKER ROD AND SEALANT

2" POLYSTYRENE FOAM

PARAPET SECTION
Scale 1 1/2"=1'

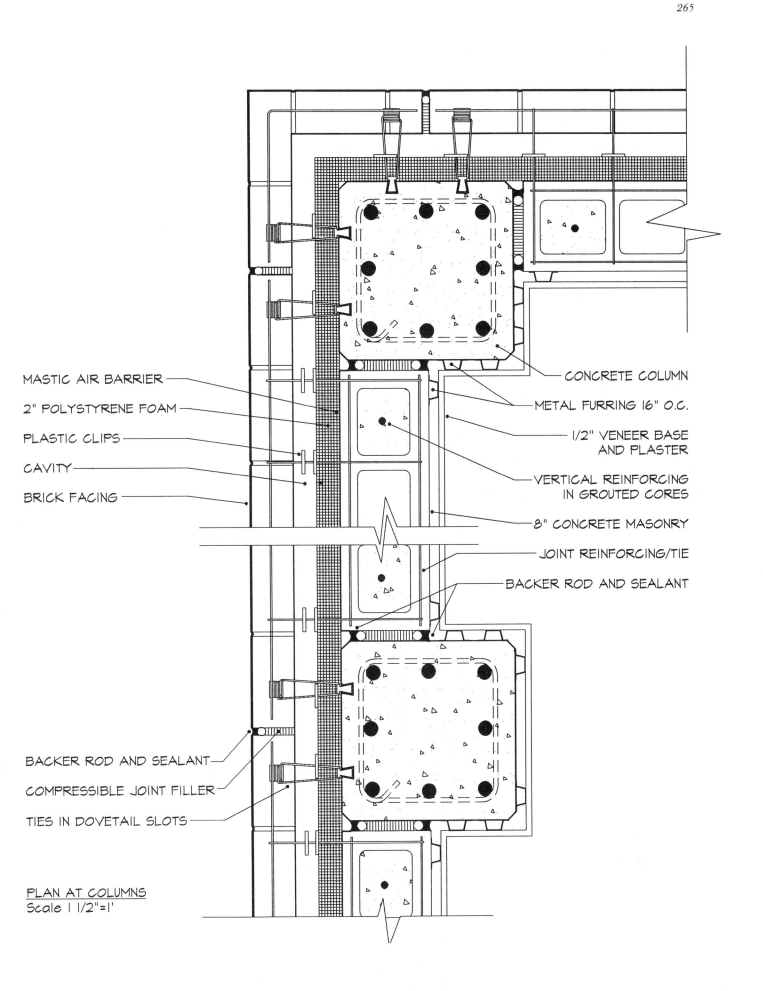

MASTIC AIR BARRIER

2" POLYSTYRENE FOAM

PLASTIC CLIPS

CAVITY

BRICK FACING

CONCRETE COLUMN

METAL FURRING 16" O.C.

1/2" VENEER BASE
AND PLASTER

VERTICAL REINFORCING
IN GROUTED CORES

8" CONCRETE MASONRY

JOINT REINFORCING/TIE

BACKER ROD AND SEALANT

BACKER ROD AND SEALANT

COMPRESSIBLE JOINT FILLER

TIES IN DOVETAIL SLOTS

PLAN AT COLUMNS
Scale 1 1/2"=1'

ELEVATION OF TYPICAL WINDOW
Scale 3/4"=1'

NEXT STEPS

Though we are well along in the process of detailing the building, much remains to be done. We have not yet tackled such special details as the main entrance, the lobby, the corridors and elevators, fire exit stairways and doors, and the service areas of the building. Working with the acoustical consultant, we must develop details for a set of interior finishes, including walls between dwelling units, corridor walls, stairway and elevator enclosures, interior partitions of dwellings, and flooring details. The two major functional criteria to which we will be working will be acoustical privacy and fire safety. Working with the mechanical engineer, we will design details of *Vertical Chases* in which to run the pipe risers for the heating and cooling systems, coordinating these with the locations of the fan coil units in each apartment. At the same time, we will determine the size and proportions of the external air louvers for the fan-coil units, will develop a detail for installing the louvers, and will experiment with various arrangements of louvers on the elevation drawings. We still have unfinished business with the structural engineer concerning such matters as sizes of beams and columns and details of the grouted reinforcing in the backup wall and parapet. We must still examine the overall size and massing of the building to see if it needs one or more *Building Separation Joints*. We will do further investigations of the feasibility of our copper parapet coping detail. We will use various three-dimensional sketches and drawings to visualize the effects of alternative ways of detailing both the exterior elevations and the interior spaces of the building, working to achieve a consistent architectural expression. And we will do a more thorough research into the provisions of the Uniform Building Code that relate to our details, being sure that we are in complete conformance, especially with regard to *Firesafe Materials, Fire-Resistant Assemblies*, and seismic provisions. We must take care to provide at least the mandated number of apartment units that are of *Barrier-Free Design*. This code research will lead eventually to a meeting with the local building inspector to discuss the code conformance of the design and to iron out any problems before construction begins.

Soon we will meet with the specifications writer, taking with us the voluminous notes we have made concerning items that are a bit out of the ordinary that need to be mentioned in the specifications, such as the thick joint filler strip, the precompressed sponge sealant, and the stainless steel joint reinforcing. Much of our meeting will center on the task of selecting *Accepted Standards* by which to specify the bricks, concrete masonry units, mortar, masonry ties and reinforcing, grout, sealants, galvanizing, flashing, roofing, and so on. We also want to be sure we specify *Nontoxic Materials*, paying particular attention to carpets, carpet adhesives, particle board interior components that may give off formaldehyde, and paints and varnishes. This is not just a matter of altruism; many prospective tenants will not rent apartments that have strong odors of organic chemicals.

We also begin to organize our notes that we will pass on eventually to the construction supervisor concerning things that need to be checked especially closely during the construction process such as the dimensional accuracy of the formwork; the accuracy with which wedge inserts, dovetail slots, and reglets are placed in the formwork; whether the wedge inserts and reglets are installed right side up; lap joints and end dams on flashings; the cleanliness of the cavity behind the brick facing; the integrity of the air barrier coating of mastic; the spacing of the masonry ties; and the construction of the horizontal soft joints. Recognizing the intricacy of the wall we have designed and the extent to which its functional success hinges on such matters as these, we decide to hold an extensive preconstruction conference with the successful bidder in order to go over these concerns one by one. We also decide that it would be wise to specify that the successful bidder construct a small, full-scale mock-up of the wall on the construction site, using actual materials. This will give everyone involved in the construction, ourselves included, an advance opportunity to work out any problems in the construction sequence we have designed, to get used to its complexities, and to see how the wall will look. We can also use the mock-up to experiment with alternative brick and mortar colors, sealant colors, joint toolings, and special brick work details around the openings, and the contractor can use it to teach masons exactly how the work must be done.

KEY REFERENCES

The following are important reference materials that were used in developing this set of details. Full bibliographic information on these publications is given in the reference list at the back of the book.

Beall, Christine. *Masonry Design and Detailing for Architects, Engineers, and Builders.*

Brick Institute of America. *BIA Technical Notes on Brick Construction.*

National Concrete Masonry Association. *Architectural and Engineering Concrete Masonry Details for Building Construction.*

National Concrete Masonry Association. *A Manual of Facts on Concrete Masonry.*

Sheet Metal and Air Conditioning Contractors National Association, Inc. *Architectural Sheet Metal Manual.*

Uniform Building Code.

United States Gypsum Company. *Gypsum Construction Handbook.* ∎

THE DETAILER'S
REFERENCE SHELF

▽

FORMULATING EXERCISES FOR
SELF-STUDY OR CLASSROOM USE

▽

INDEX

THE DETAILER'S REFERENCE SHELF

E V E R Y detailer will have his or her favorite selection of essential references. These are mine. The list is selective rather than exhaustive.

It would be unwise and expensive to try to assemble this entire shelf of references at one time. It is better to acquire references one or several at a time as they are needed, and the collection will gradually fill itself out. If you are determined to acquire a minimum shelf of detailing references immediately, start with the publications indicated by an asterisk(*). Ordering information is given for all references, except books by recognized publishers. There is a charge for most of these publications; the main exceptions are manufacturers' catalogs, most of which are free.

1. CODES

Contact the building department of the city or town in which a building will be built to determine the relevant codes. The major model building codes from which most local and state codes are derived are the following:

The BOCA National Building Code. Building Officials & Code Administrators International, Inc., 4051 West Flossmoor Road, Country Club Hills, IL 60477-5795. (This code predominates in the Midwest and the East.)

The Standard Building Code. Southern Building Code Congress International, 900 Montclair Road, Birmingham, AL 35213-1206. (This is the model code for most of the Deep South and the Southeast.)

Uniform Building Code. International Conference of Building Officials, 5360 South Workman Mill Road, Whittier, CA 90601. (This code has been adopted throughout most of the West.)

National Building Code of Canada. Associate Committee on the National Building Code, National Research Council, Ottawa, Ontario, Canada, K1A OR6.

*Lathrop, James K. (ed.). *Life Safety Code Handbook*. National Fire Protection Association, Batterymarch Park, Quincy, MA 02269. (This book, updated frequently, sets forth and illustrates the life safety and egress provisions that are common to all the building codes.)

2. STANDARDS

American National standard for Buildings and Facilities—Providing Accessibility and Usability for Physically Handicapped People. ANSI A117.1. American National Standards Institute, Inc., 1430 Broadway, New York, NY 10018. (The title is self-explanatory.)

ASTM Standards in Building Codes. Philadelphia, American Society for Testing and Materials. (This four-volume work, updated frequently, covers all the ASTM standards under which building materials and assemblies are specified and detailed.) Address for ordering: ASTM, 1916 Race Street, Philadelphia, PA 19103-1187, (215) 299-5585.

3. GENERAL REFERENCES ON DETAILING

The AIA Service Corporation. *Masterspec*. Washington, D.C. (Updated continually, this is an encyclopedic reference on selecting and specifying materials and components for buildings. It is available in both printed form and on diskettes.) Address for ordering: The AIA Service Corporation, 1735 New York Avenue, N.W., Washington, D.C. 20006, (800) 424-5080.

*Allen, Edward. *Fundamentals of Building Construction: Materials and Methods* (2nd ed.). New York, John Wiley & Sons, 1990. (This is a solid, general reference on how buildings are put together, and gives a basic set of details for each type of construction.)

Construction Specifications Institute. *Manual of Practice with Masterformat*. Alexandria, VA. (Updated frequently, this is the standard by which nearly all construction specifications are written.) Address for ordering: Construction Specifications Institute, 601 Madison Street, Alexandria, VA 22314-1791, (703) 684-0300.

*Construction Specifications Institute. *Standard Reference Symbols*. Alexandria, VA, 1989. (This is a booklet that establishes standard symbols for use on construction drawings and details.) Address for ordering: See above.

*Hornbostel, Caleb. *Construction Materials: Types, Uses, and Applications*. New York, John Wiley & Sons, 1978. (This is a large handbook that offers comprehensive information on every conceivable material used in building, including many standard details.)

*Ramsey, Charles, and Harold Sleeper. *Architectural Graphic Standards*. New York, John Wiley & Sons. (This large handbook, which is updated frequently, is the standard reference for architectural detailing.)

Sweet's Catalog File. (This is a weighty collection of bound volumes of manufacturers' catalogs, covering every area of architectural construction. It is issued yearly by the McGraw-Hill Book Company to architectural and engineering firms that design a sufficient volume of buildings to meet McGraw-Hill's qualification criteria. The only way for individuals and small firms to obtain this file is to solicit year-old copies from larger firms.)

Timesaver Standards. New York, McGraw-Hill Book Company. (This is a competitor to *Architectural Graphic Standards*, and it is also updated frequently.)

Underwriters Laboratories. *Fire Resistance Directory*. Northbrook, IL, Underwriters Laboratories, Inc. (Updated annually, this directory lists and illustrates all the building assemblies that UL has tested, and gives their fire resistance ratings.) Address for ordering: Underwriters Laboratory, Inc., Publications Stock, 333 Pfingston Road, Northbrook, IL 60062.

4. COLLECTIONS OF ARCHITECTURAL DETAILS

*Ballast, David Kent. *Architect's Handbook of Construction Detailing*. Englewood Cliffs, NJ, Prentice-Hall, 1990. (Reliable collections of details are rare; this book is based on reliable sources and is referenced to MASTERFORMAT section numbers for convenient specifying.)

*Ford, Edward R. *The Details of Modern Architecture*. Cambridge, MA, MIT Press, 1990. (Much more than just a collection of details, this volume analyzes dozens of details of acknowledged masterworks from the years 1890–1932.)

5. DETAILING WOOD

*American Institute of Timber Construction. *Glued Laminated Timbers for Industrial, Commercial and Institutional Buildings*. (This is a good general reference on the topic, including section properties, span tables, and typical details. It is updated frequently.) Address for ordering: AITC, 11818 S.E. Mill Plain Blvd., Suite 415, Vancouver, WA 98684-5092, (206) 254-9132.

American Institute of Timber Construction. *Typical Construction Details*. (This pamphlet contains dozens of examples of how to detail heavy timber frames.) Address for ordering: See above.

*American Plywood Association. *Structural Design Data for Plywood*. (This is a thick ring binder filled with the authoritative data needed to select and to detail plywood and other wood panel products.) Address for ordering: American Plywood Association, P.O. Box 11700, Tacoma, WA 98411, (206) 565-6600.

Dietz, Albert G. H. *Dwelling House Construction* (5th ed.). Cambridge, MA, MIT Press, 1990. (This is a text with hundreds of lucid illustrations of how to put a wood frame house together, including interior and exterior finish components.)

National Forest Products Association. *National Design Specification for Wood Construction*. (This is the basic reference from which wood structures are engineered, and it is updated frequently. It is especially useful to the detailer for working out structural connections between wood members.) Address for ordering: See below.

National Forest Products Association. *Span Tables for Joists and Rafters*. (Using this booklet of tables, you can easily design structures for residential floors, ceilings, and roofs.) Address for ordering: National Forest Products Association, 1250 Connecticut Avenue, N.W., Washington, D.C. 20036.

*Simpson Strong-Tie Company, Inc. *Connectors for Wood Construction*. (This annual catalog is the best single reference on metal framing connectors for wood light framing and heavy timber framing.) Address for ordering: Simpson Strong-Tie Company, Inc., 1450 Doolittle Drive, P.O. Box 1568, San Leandro, CA 94577, (415) 562-7946.

*Thallon, Rob. *Graphic Guide to Frame Construction: Details for Builders and Designers*. Newtown, CT, The Taunton Press, 1991. (This is a complete, exhaustive collection of reliable details for almost every conceivable situation in a wood frame house.)

*Western Wood Products Association. *Wood Frame Design*. Portland, OR, 1985. (This is an extraordinarily useful booklet of details and code references for wood light frame construction.) Address for ordering: Western Wood Products Association, 1500 Yeon Building, Portland, OR 97204, (503) 224-3930.

*Western Wood Products Association. *Dimensional Stability of Western Lumber Products* (2nd ed.). Portland, OR, 1990. (The charts in this booklet are extremely useful in estimating moisture movement in wood.) Address for ordering: See above.

6. DETAILING MASONRY

*Beall, Christine. *Masonry Design and Detailing for Architects, Engineers, and Builders* (2nd ed.). New York, McGraw-Hill, 1987. (This is the best general detailing reference for masonry of all types.)

*Brick Institute of America. *BIA Technical Notes on Brick Construction*. (Updated frequently, this is a large ring binder that contains the latest information on every conceivable topic needed to detail brickwork.) Address for ordering: Brick Institute of America, 11490 Commerce Park Drive, Reston, VA 22091, (703) 620-0010.

Indiana Limestone Institute of America, Inc. *Indiana Limestone Institute of America, Inc., Handbook*. (Updated frequently, this manual gives complete information for detailing limestone.) Address for ordering: Indiana Limestone Institute of America, Inc., Suite 400, Stone City Bank Building, Bedford, IN 47421, (812) 275-4426.

Marble Institute of America. *Dimensional Stone*. (This large looseleaf binder, updated frequently, emphasizes the detailing of marble, but it is applicable also to granite.) Address for ordering: Marble Institute of America, 33505 State Street, Farmington, MI 48024, (313) 476-5558.

*National Concrete Masonry Association. *Architectural and Engineering Concrete Masonry Details for Building Construction*. McLean, VA, 1976. (A treasury of typical concrete masonry details.) Address for ordering: National Concrete Masonry Association, P.O. Box 781, Herndon, VA 22070-0781, (703) 435-4900.

*National Concrete Masonry Association. *A Manual of Facts on Concrete Masonry*. (A large, continually updated ring binder with everything a detailer needs to know about concrete masonry.) Address for ordering: See above.

Randall, Frank A., and William C. Panarese. *Concrete Masonry Handbook for Architects, Engineers, and Builders*. Skokie, IL, Portland Cement Association, 1988. (This is an excellent, well-illustrated reference on detailing concrete masonry.) Address for ordering: Portland Cement Association, 5420 Old Orchard Road, Skokie, IL 60076, (708) 966-9559.

7. DETAILING STEEL AND STRUCTURAL METALS

The Aluminum Association. *Aluminum Standards and Data*. (Updated every two years, this is a basic reference on aluminum alloys and product forms.) Address for ordering: The Aluminum Association, Suite 300, 900 Nineteenth St., N.W., Washington, D.C. 20006.

The Aluminum Association. *Structural Design with Aluminum*, 1987. (A short introduction to aluminum structures.) Address for ordering: See above.

*American Institute of Steel Construction. *Manual of Steel Construction* (9th ed.). Chicago, 1989. (This contains basic information on available steel shapes, their properties, and steel connections.) Address for ordering: AISC, One East Wacker Drive, Suite 3100, Chicago, IL 60601-2001, (312) 670-5435.

American Institute of Steel Construction. *Detailing for Steel Construction*. Chicago, 1983. (This is a textbook for beginning detailers of structural steel.) Address for ordering: See above.

8. DETAILING SITECAST CONCRETE

*American Concrete Institute Committee 303. *Guide to Cast-In-Place Architectural Concrete*. (This is an excellent guide to detailing and specifying exposed concrete surfaces.) Address for ordering: ACI, Box 19150, Detroit, MI 48219-0150.

*American Concrete Institute 117, *Standard Tolerances for Concrete Construction and Materials*. (Dimensional tolerances for concrete work are spelled out in detail.) Address for ordering: See above.

**Concrete Buildings: New Formwork Perspectives*. (This is a very useful and beautifully illustrated booklet on selecting, laying out, and detailing concrete work for maximum economy.) Address for ordering: Ceco Industries, Inc., 1400 Kensington Road, Oak Brook, IL 60522, (800) 368-4842.

**Greenstreak Form Liners for Architectural Concrete*. (This small catalog illustrates standard form liner textures, rustication strips, and chamfer strips.) Address for ordering: Greenstreak, Box 7139, St. Louis, MO 63177, (800) 325-9504.

*Hurd, M. K. *Formwork for Concrete* (5th ed.). Detroit, MI, American Concrete Institute, 1989. (This is an excellent and comprehensive general reference on the detailing of concrete.) Address for ordering: See above.

Richmond Screw Anchor Company, Inc., Catalog. (Richmond produces a complete line of standard and proprietary products for forming concrete and anchoring to concrete.) Address for ordering: Richmond Screw Anchor Company, Inc., 7214 Burns Street, Richland Hills, Fort Worth, TX 76118, (817) 284-4981.

Symons Architectural Form Liners and Concrete Forming Systems. (This small catalog illustrates standard form liner textures and rustication strips for exposed architectural concrete.) Address for ordering: Symons Corporation, 200 East Touhy Avenue, Des Plaines, IL 60018, (312) 298-3200.

9. DETAILING PRECAST CONCRETE FRAMING

Prestressed Concrete Institute. *Design and Typical Details of Connections for Precast and Prestressed Concrete*. Chicago, 1988. (This manual contains a large collection of drawings of standard connection details.) Address for ordering: PCI, 175 West Jackson Boulevard, Chicago, IL 60604, (312) 786-0300.

10. DETAILING ROOFING

*National Roofing Contractors Association. *NRCA Construction Details* (3rd ed.). Rosemont, IL, 1986. (This volume contains seventy-five drawing plates of details for low-slope roofs.) Address for ordering: NRCA, One O'Hare Center, Rosemont, IL 60018, (312) 318-NRCA.

*National Roofing Contractors Association. *NRCA Steep Roofing Manual* (3rd ed.). Rosemont, IL. (This book contains details for steep roofs in asphalt shingles, wood shakes and shingles, clay and concrete tiles, and slate.) Address for ordering: See above.

Revere Copper Products, Inc. *Copper and Common Sense* (7th ed.). New York, 1982. (This is an excellent manual of sheet copper design principles and construction techniques.) Address for ordering: Revere Copper Products, Inc., P.O. Box 300, Rome, NY 13440.

*Sheet Metal and Air Conditioning Contractors National Association, Inc. *Architectural Sheet Metal Manual* (4th ed.). Vienna, VA, 1987. (This is the standard reference for details of metal roofing systems and also for flashings, copings, fascias, gravel stops, and other sheet metal roofing details.) Address for ordering: Sheet Metal and Air Conditioning Contractors National Association, Inc., P.O. Box 70, Merrifield, VA 22116, (703) 790-9890.

11. DETAILING CLADDING

*American Architectural Manufacturers Association. *Aluminum Curtain Wall Design Guide Manual*, Chicago, 1979. (This is the best general reference on detailing cladding systems that are based on aluminum extrusions.) Address for ordering: American Architectural Manufacturers Association, 1540 East Dundee Road, Suite 310, Palatine, IL 60067, (708) 699-7310.

*Anderson, J. M., and J. R. Gill. *Rainscreen Cladding: A Guide to Design Principles and Practices*. London, Butterworths, 1988. (This small book presents very simply and clearly the theory behind watertight cladding design.)

FGMA Glazing Manual. Topeka, KS, Flat Glass Marketing Association. (This booklet, which is frequently updated, shows standard methods of supporting and sealing glass in windows and cladding systems.) Address for ordering: FGMA, 3310 Harrison, Topeka, KS 66611-2279.

*National Research Council Canada. *Construction Details for Airtightness*. Ottawa, Canada, 1980, NRCC #18291. (Description below)

*National Research Council Canada. *Cracks, Movements, and Joints in Buildings*. Ottawa, Canada, 1976, NRCC #15477. (Description below)

*National Research Council Canada. *Walls, Windows, and Roofs for the Canadian Climate*. Ottawa, Canada, 1973, NRCC #13487. (These three books are invaluable references on how to detail a weathertight enclosure. The third book has revolutionized the design of building cladding.) Address for ordering: Institute for Research in Construction, Ottawa, Ontario K1A OR6, Canada.

*PPG Industries, Inc. *The Right Glass*. (Updated annually, this is PPG's glass catalog, which includes valuable information on specifying and detailing glazing.) Address for ordering: PPG Industries, Inc., One PPG Place, Pittsburgh, PA 15272.

Precast/Prestressed Concrete Institute. *Architectural Precast Concrete* (2nd ed.). Chicago, 1989. (This is a complete, lavishly illustrated guide to detailing precast concrete cladding.) Address for ordering: Precast/Prestressed Concrete Institute, 175 West Jackson Boulevard, Chicago, IL 60604, (312) 786-0300.

Precast/Prestressed Concrete Institute. *Recommended Practice for Glass Fiber Reinforced Concrete Panels*. Chicago, 1987. (This is a complete guide to designing GFRC cladding.) Address for ordering: See above.

*Zero International, Inc. *Sealing Systems for Doors and Windows.* (This is Zero's annual catalog of weatherstripping and other ingenious devices for sealing around doors and windows.) Address for ordering: Zero International, Inc., 415 Concord Avenue, Bronx, NY 10455-4898, (800) 635-5335.

See also the references on brick masonry, concrete masonry, and stone masonry listed in section 6 of this bibliography, which contain all the necessary information on detailing curtain wall assemblies in these materials.

12.   DETAILING INTERIOR CONSTRUCTION

*Architectural Woodwork Institute. *Architectural Casework Details.* Arlington, VA. (This is a source book of conventional details for casework.) Address for ordering: Architectural Woodwork Institute, 2310 South Walter Reed Drive, Arlington, VA 22206 (703) 671-9100.

Armstrong Architectural Building Products. *Armstrong Ceilings.* (This is Armstrong Architectural Building Products' catalog of a wide range of acoustic ceiling systems.) Address for ordering: Armstrong Architectural Building Products, Park 80 West, Plaza One, Saddle Brook, NJ 07662, (201) 843-0300.

*Gypsum Association. *Fire Resistance Design Manual.* (Updated frequently, this booklet gives fire resistance ratings and sound transmission classes for a large number of wall and ceiling assemblies using both plaster and gypsum board.) Address for ordering: Gypsum Association, 1603 Orrington Avenue, Evanston, IL 60201.

*National Association of Architectural Metal Manufacturers. *Hollow Metal Technical and Design Manual.* Chicago, 1977. (This is a complete guide to hollow metal interior doors and frames, includ-

ing fire-rated doors.) Address for ordering: NAAMM, 600 S. Federal Street, Suite 400, Chicago, IL 60605. (NAAMM also publishes *Metal Stairs Manual, Pipe Railing Manual, Metal Finishes Manual, Metal Bar Grating Manual,* and *Lightweight Steel Framing Systems Manual.* The entire set of publications is available at a single price.)

The National Terrazzo & Mosaic Association, Inc. *Terrazzo Design/ Technical Data Book.* Des Plaines, IL. (This booklet is updated frequently. The standard methods of installing and detailing terrazzo floors, bases, and stairs are covered.) Address for ordering: The National Terrazzo & Mosaic Association, Inc., 3166 Des Plaines Avenue, Suite 15, Des Plaines, IL 60018.

Stagg, William D., and Brian F. Pegg. *Plastering: A Craftsman's Encyclopedia.* New York, Crown Publishers, 1985. (This is a complete guide to all the intricacies of ornamental plastering. It is especially useful in restoration work.)

*Tile Council of America, Inc. *Handbook for Ceramic Tile Installation.* Princeton, NJ. (Updated frequently, this book contains all the standard details for ceramic tile and quarry tile installation in every type of construction.) Address for ordering: Tile Council of America, Inc., P.O. Box 326, Princeton, NJ 08540.

*United States Gypsum Company. *Gypsum Construction Handbook.* Chicago, 1992. (This is a superb reference, packing into 500 well-illustrated pages everything one needs to know to specify and detail plaster and gypsum board walls and ceilings.) Address for ordering: U.S. Gypsum Company, 101 South Wacker Drive, Chicago, IL 60606.

In addition to these print sources, there is a growing number of sources of CAD details on diskette. Many manufacturers distribute their proprietary details in this format, and several companies market collections of general details.

FORMULATING EXERCISES FOR SELF-STUDY OR CLASSROOM USE

I T I S impossible to become good at detailing without repeated practice. Such practice is most effective when the resulting details are used to construct actual buildings, because then it is possible to experience the results of one's decisions and to see what has turned out well and what could be done better in the next building. However, this actual experience may not be fully available to students and interns, and one may wish to become more expert before attempting details that will actually be built. In these cases, it is easy to formulate several types of exercises that will help develop detailing skills.

1. ANALYZE AND MODIFY EXISTING DETAILS

A good way to begin the study of architectural detailing is to analyze existing building details from available sources, such as actual working drawings, books of details, details in architectural journals, details in manufacturers' catalogs, and details in this book.

Identify Detail Patterns Photocopy or make a print of a detail, reducing it if necessary to allow plenty of white space around it on the sheet. Add notes and arrows in the white space to identify all the detail patterns that are embodied in the drawing. Consider whether there are patterns that should have been considered that are missing.

Modify Existing Details Use the pattern analysis of a detail to help identify deficiencies in its design. Then lay tracing paper over the detail and modify it to correct the deficiencies. Make a list of the patterns employed in your redesign.

2. DESIGN VARIATIONS ON EXISTING DETAILS

A logical next step in this progression of exercises is to start with a photocopy or a print of an existing detail and then arbitrarily to change one important parameter and redesign the detail accordingly. An easy example would be to start with a detail of a carpeted floor intersecting a gypsum plaster wall in a wood frame house and then to change the flooring material to oak and the wall material to cherry paneling. A bit more difficult exercise relating to the same building would be to change a flat ceiling with an attic overhead to a sloping ceiling beneath a heavy timber roof.

Other exercises on the same set of details might be to change the floor from a wood platform over a basement to a concrete slab on grade and then to change the wall construction from wood framing to concrete masonry. A variant of this exercise is to design an additional detail that is not present in the given set of details, such as a balcony railing or a porch roof that will harmonize with the rest of the design.

Exercises of this type can be as difficult as you wish. A really tough one is to take a spandrel detail for brick veneer cladding over a reinforced concrete building frame (such as the one on page 262 of this book), assume a steel frame instead, and redesign the detail accordingly. Less demanding would be to change the window type in a masonry wall, to design an alternative roof edge detail to achieve a different appearance, to develop a grade-level detail from an upper-floor spandrel detail, and so on.

3. DESIGN NEW DETAILS FROM SCRATCH

Difficult, but the most realistic, are those exercises that involve developing details for a new building design. Three examples of this process are illustrated in the *Detail Development* section of this book.

Starting from a basic concept of the space and form of a building, a good plan of action would be the following:

1. Create a list of appropriate materials.

2. Select the key details to be developed.

3. Check the applicable building code for provisions relevant to the detailing process, and keep the code book close by for ready reference.

4. Obtain the necessary information on the building's structural and mechanical systems. This might be done by using consultants in an office, by using other technical teachers in a school, or by consulting *The Architect's Studio Companion: Technical Guidelines for Preliminary Design* by Edward Allen and Joseph Iano (New York, John Wiley & Sons, Inc., 1989).

5. Develop the details in stages, aided by studio-style critiques at frequent intervals from a teacher or a senior colleague.

This exercise is most effective if the original building design can be modified as the details are developed. This teaches the positive effect that detailing can have on the form and space of a building—a lesson that will be lost if the original building design is considered to be complete and inviolable.

4. USE THE PATTERNS TO DO BUILDING DIAGNOSTIC WORK

Once the patterns have been learned and understood, they can become a powerful basis for figuring out the causes of various building failures. Problems in real buildings make the most effective vehicles for these exercises. As practice exercises and problems for classroom discussion, you can invent such situations as the following:

1. Narrow, parallel bands of dampness occur at 2′ (600 mm) spacings on the ceiling of a single-story industrial steel frame building in the winter. What is the likely cause? Can you draw a detail that represents the probable existing condition that causes the problem? Can you modify this detail to eliminate the problem?

2. A brick facing is buckling on a six-story classroom building. . . .

3. A stucco wall is cracking badly. . . .

4. People in the waiting room can hear conversations between a psychiatrist and her patients. . . .

5. The plaster immediately beneath a window stool becomes damp after a prolonged wind-driven rainstorm. . . .

6. During renovation work, carpenters discover that the insulation in a ten-year-old wood frame wall is saturated with moisture and the framing is beginning to decay. . . .

7. Ice dams are occuring on a roof. . . .

8. An outdoor deck floored with pine 6 × 2s traps puddles of water during rainstorms. . . .

9. The flashings in a masonry chimney are corroding. . . .

10. A brick paving is spalling badly. . . .

5. TRY SOME FREESTYLE DETAILING EXERCISES

It can be refreshing and instructive to step outside the world of building now and then to attempt to detail other kinds of useful objects. Imagine designing and detailing an end table, a child's wagon, a garden trellis, an improved nail hammer, a refrigerator container system, a shelving system, or an automobile trash container. Materials can be mixed and matched as desired: Within a class, for example, everyone might attack the same design problem, but students could be assigned different materials to work with. Comparisons of design solutions and details then become all the more meaningful.

INDEX

Detail patterns are in *bold italics*.